"*Reach for the Rainbow* is probably the most human, straight-forward and conclusive book on the subject today." Review—*Book Dealers W̶o̶r̶l̶d̶*, ~~~~er 1990

"An outstanding new book for abuse ~~~~~~~~~~~~~~~~ them, presenting survivor concerns and se ~~~~~~~~~~~~~~~ ficient manner...a new step forward in the lit ~~~~~~~~~~~~~~~ *ews & Notes*, Apr-May 1990

"Best of its kind!" James Fadiman, Ph.D., psychologist and author of *Unlimit Your Life*, Palo Alto, CA

"Inspiring and illuminating - a wonderful book - bringing relief to me and my clients. *Reach for the Rainbow* provides a comprehensive knowledge base for understanding abuse." Barbara Belnap, M.S.W., Survivor, Sexual and Substance Counselor, Salt Lake City, UT

"Human, sincere, easy to read and practical...a useful guide for therapists and survivors which makes a painful subject easier to face." Claire Massecar, Community Worker, Tracom Mental Health Crisis Center, Montreal, Quebec

"Must reading for any survivor of child abuse. I especially like the easygoing, clear style and the personal approach of the question and answer format. I felt like she was speaking to me." Phil E. Quinn, D.Min., Survivor, National Educator and Counselor in the field of child abuse; award-winning author of *Cry Out! Inside the Terrifying World of the Abused Child*, Hermitage, TN

"Lynne has arrived at a place in her journey where the light and warmth of awareness allow her to reach out with love and compassion, encouraging and guiding others to find their own way to healing." Carolynn R. Hamilton, M.Ed., Drug and Alcohol Counselor and Youth Corrrections Educator, Anchorage, AK

"Essential reading for survivors and those who would support them. Full of compassion, understanding and hope." G. Hugh Allred, Ed.D, Professor of Marriage and Family Therapy, Brigham Young University

Reach for the Rainbow empowers readers to nurture and reparent themselves. It increased my insights into sexual abuse." Stephen J. Bavolek, Ph.D, President of Family Development Resources, Inc.; author of *The Nurturing Programs*. Pinebrook, UT

"I've recommended *Reach for the Rainbow* to many of my patients. It gives them hope as well as concrete suggestions for healing." E. Alan Jeppsen, M.D., Psychiatrist, Western Institute of Neuropsychiatry

"I just had to write to thank you for writing *Reach for the Rainbow*. It's the best, most helpful book I've ever read on the subject." D.R., Survivor, Pittsburgh, PA

Reach for the Rainbow

Advanced Healing for Survivors of Sexual Abuse

by

Lynne D. Finney, J.D., M.S.W.
Survivor and Therapist

Changes Publishing
Park City • Malibu

Cover design by Judy Taylor
Computer typography by Kenneth S. Hulme

First printing, March, 1990
Second printing, June, 1990
Third Printing

Library of Congress Catalog Card Number 89-63619

ISBN 0-9625883-0-X

Changes Publishing
P.O. Box 681539
Park City, UT 84068-1539

Reach for the Rainbow

Song by Robin Frederick

I have walked through the darkest of canyons,
Lost sight of the last piece of sky.
With no moon and no stars to guide me
Somehow I got by.

Now I'll build a home in the sunshine.
Let go piece by piece of the past.
The storms that clouded my life
Have thundered their last.

"Now" is the time I must live in,
Each day that dawns is my own.

> *I will reach for the rainbow,*
> *Reach through the rain.*
> *I will reach for the rainbow,*
> *Reach past the pain.*
> *I can be happy, I can be free—*
> *I know there's a piece of the rainbow for me.*

I have lived with ancient, angry voices.
There were times when they tore me apart.
But I heal myself with words of loving kindness
And mend my wounded heart.

I'm a survivor. I can make it.
And I believe that I am not alone.

> *I will reach for the rainbow,*
> *Reach through the rain.*
> *I will reach for the rainbow,*
> *Reach past the pain.*
> *I can make my life what I want it to be—*
> *I know there's a piece of the rainbow for me.*

This book is dedicated

to Jim who supported me through discovery of my painful past and therapy and who made me believe that "I don't live there anymore;"

to all of the kids at ARTEC, the Adolescent Residential Treatment and Education Center in Salt Lake City, whose courage and resilience impelled me to write this book; and

to all of the survivors—the hurt children in the world who have survived the agony of physical and sexual abuse.

Acknowledgments

This book covers the major events of my life, as well as much of what I learned during my healing, and thus these acknowledgments are for many of the significant people in my life. Some of these people may seem to have nothing to do with this book. But I might not have survived to write the book were it not for their help, support and love.

I am infinitely grateful to my brother who was my only source of love and comfort during my childhood, and for whom I have the greatest love and admiration. My adolescence was made lighter by my friend, Suzanne Reynolds, who brought laughter into my life and was the sister I wished I had. I am thankful for her love, for the fun we had, and for teaching me the nature of real friendship. And I send love and immense gratitude to Ron and Rosemary Murray who became my substitute parents and friends through their acts of caring and who showed me that parents could be loving and gentle.

I want to acknowledge Howard Friedman, Robert Holtzman, Alden Pearce, Al Rothman and especially Al Smith, in my Los Angeles law firm, for always treating me as a professional and equal. You taught me not only to be a good lawyer, but that I was worthy of respect, and that men and women could work together and be friends. Another professional relationship that sustained me through a difficult time in Washington, D.C., was my friendship with Jim Schmidt. Your constant encouragement and praise gave me the courage to continue to follow my conscience. And my appreciation to Jack Buckley who steered me through the rapids of Washington politics and was always ready with encouragement and good advice.

I send love to my friends who cared enough to help me survive:

To Bob and Veda Charrow, the most amazing and patient of friends who nurtured and sustained me through many years of pain. I would not have written this book nor would I be here at all if it were not for your love and friendship. And to Robin Frederick who has always been a white light in my life. Your friendship, honesty and common sense have pulled me through difficult times. Your comments on my book were invaluable and your song is one of the loveliest gifts I have ever received.

And to Camille Chamberlain and Marcia Frederick, two exceptional friends who have remained constant and caring throughout the years. I always knew I could count on you and it helped me feel safe. And my thanks to Lee Wright for teaching me the forgiveness affirmation.

I send special love to Jacqueline Nelson who radiates joy and has an empathy beyond her years. Thank you, Jackie, for helping heal the child in me by being my pal for always. And my thanks to all the Nelsons for making me part of your warm, accepting family.

I will always be indebted to Dr. Nancy Foster, the most compassionate, sensitive and creative therapist I have met. Thank you for saving my life and my sanity and for being there when I needed you. And my gratitude to Dr. Alan Jeppson whose therapeutic talent greatly facilitated my healing. I thank you for encouraging me to direct my therapy and for caring enough to learn innovative techniques to speed the process and make it less painful.

I am devoted to Dr. Betty Vos for her patience and thoroughness in acting as my faculty advisor and editing the original manuscript. Your guidance helped me keep perspective and I am grateful for your suggestions. I am also grateful to Dr. Amanda Barusch, Dr. Jerry Braza, Dr. Au-Deane Cowley, Dean Kay Dea, Dr. Mark Frazer, Assistant Dean Garth Meacham, Dr. Peter Pecora and John Seaman, the bright spots in my social work graduate program, who encouraged me to do the work I wanted to do. I appreciate your support in my efforts to write this book. And my thanks to the Park City Library for supplying information and research.

Especially warm thanks to Stephen and Ondrea Levine for their generosity in sharing the "Opening the Heart of the Womb Meditation" with readers of this book and for helping me love myself and treat myself and others with mercy.

My love and admiration to Elaine Jarvik, a true friend, whose editing of the final version made this book more readable and whose moral support kept the author going.

Table of Contents

I LIVING WELL
IS THE BEST REVENGE

Congratulations! If you have been sexually or physically abused and you are reading this book, you are a survivor. You have survived one of life's most painful and difficult experiences. You have endured rape and perhaps violence; you may have been beaten and humiliated; you have felt overwhelming fear, rage, hatred, guilt, sadness, worthlessness and betrayal; and your sanity has been tested.

Most of you survived your horrors as children, when you had far fewer resources than you have now. What is more, most of you suffered these horrors totally alone because no one rescued you or helped you. There was no one to rely on but yourself and *you* got yourself through.

The fact that you are alive now and reading this book means you are incredibly strong, courageous and intelligent. You protected yourself. You have already proven that you can help yourself and take care of yourself; all you need now is a little help to make it easier.

What about all of the problems you are having now? They are only the aftermath, the unresolved feelings from your experience and the fallout from decisions you made in a time of pain which may not be helpful to you anymore. These problems are far less painful and damaging than what you have already survived.

I am not trying to minimize the pain you are still experiencing. Having gone through that pain and confusion for about forty years of my own life and having worked with other survivors of sexual abuse, I am certainly not going to discount the confusion, pain, fear, anger, depression, shame and dysfunctional behavior which abuse causes. I only ask you to take a minute and compare what you have already survived with what you are going through now. I think you will discover that you have already survived the worst.

As you read this book, you may sometimes find what I say overly optimistic. I certainly was not optimistic when I first began to remember my abuse; I was almost pathologically pessimistic and depressed. Like some of you, I was in such pain that I did not believe I could ever be happy. I really did not know what happiness was. But in just over two years of therapy and with a lot of self help, my life has changed so dramatically that I hardly recognize myself.

I do not think that I am unique because I know other survivors who have experienced similar transformations. And I do not think *you* are so unique that you cannot change your life in the same way. My purpose in writing this book is to let you know the facts about your problem and to assure you that, as bad as it seems at this moment, you will get better and you will find happiness, and there are many ways to do it.

This book provides active therapy as you read it. I have included many of the same reprogramming techniques I would use in therapy to help correct common misconceptions you may have about yourself and your abuse. This book also contains a number of self-help techniques that have been tested and proven effective in helping abuse victims and they are designed to help you overcome some of the problems you now face. If you work at these techniques and obtain the help of an experienced therapist, you will be able to change your life and obtain the happiness you deserve.

The most important thing to recognize is that *you* are now in control of your life. The problems you have now are problems over which you have control, control you did not have before when your abuse was taking place. (If your abuse is still going on and you are old enough to be able to read this book, then you also have the ability to control what is happening to you and you can stop it now. Please turn to Question 34, *I am still being abused.*)

Most of us have a tremendous sense of shame because of what has been done to us. But we have it backwards. The real blame should be on the people who abused us; we are not at fault. I hope that this book will help you understand that you are not to blame for what others did to you, no matter what they did or how long they did it. You did not have control at that time, but you have it now. You now have the power to make your life the way you want it to be.

I hope this book will help you recognize your strengths, answer your questions, relieve your pain, and gain control of your life. I decided to write this book because I wanted to make some good come out of my own pain.

Sometimes the points I make may seem too easy. But remember, I have taken almost three years to reach this place. I did not get here all at once, nor was it easy. I only hope that my experience and the knowledge I have gained will help you make it faster and more easily.

If this book does not meet your needs, there are hundreds of other helpful books. Go to your local bookstore to the psychology, self-help, and religion sections and pick the books that appeal to you. The ones you are drawn to are probably the ones you need.

It is time for you to make it easy on yourself. Choose people to help you that you feel comfortable with. Help yourself at your own pace. You have been through enough hard times; it is time for you to be gentle with yourself. Most of all, it is time for you to realize that you deserve to be happy.

You can blame your abusers for the rest of your life, or you can get on with your life secure in the knowledge that *living well is the best revenge.*

Reach for the Rainbow

II REACH FOR THE RAINBOW

Like you, I am a survivor of sexual abuse. My story, like yours, is unique but we have shared similar pain.

* * *

I stood alone on a dusty road, with emptiness surrounding me. My long red pigtails and black patent mary janes shone in the hot sun. A faint fear enveloped me, increasing as I gazed into the distance. I knew it was coming and I could not escape.

Suddenly from far off, I saw a cloud of dust rising up from the brown dirt of the road. As I watched, the cloud grew larger and I began to quiver with fear. It came closer and I could hear the beat of a thousand thundering hoofs coming towards me, coming for me.

I was paralyzed with terror. I knew there was nowhere to run; they would get me. And then the dust cloud was close enough that I could see the long, pointed tusks and sharp hoofs of a thousand wild boars charging towards me. I could not breathe and I could not scream.

The first wave hit me and I fell. They were on me, over me, tearing me with their tusks, pounding me with their hoofs. They kept coming, they were tearing me to shreds. And I knew I was dying. I could see the boars running over me, and then I was dead. I heard myself saying, "I'm dead. I'm dead. I'm dead."

And I knew that I was dead even though I could still see and hear the boars ripping me apart.

* * *

I awoke shaking with terror from this nightmare until I was almost thirty years old. I could not figure out what it meant.

I didn't even know when the nightmare began because I had no memories about my childhood until I was eleven years old. I thought my childhood was ideal and that we were a happy family—we all said we were.

My father was a well-known screenwriter and had published a couple of novels. Some of his movies are shown occasionally on television: *Call Northside 777* with James Stewart and the classic *Laura* starring Gene Tierney and Dana Andrews for which my father was nominated for an Academy Award. My mother was petite and pretty with flaming red hair and blue eyes. She was an accomplished painter and had sold some of her portraits before my father became successful. From then on she did little painting and became a more traditional wife, mother and clubwoman, although she always had maids to help her.

When I was about three, we moved from a small house in Beverly Glen Canyon in Los Angeles to a larger house in Westwood Village where my brother was born when I was four years old. The newspaper featured our beautiful house and our ideal family in its Sunday supplement. Ideal, unless you notice my vacant, shellshocked eyes in one photograph and my vain attempt to get as far away from my father as possible in the other.

I went to a private progressive grammar school where I excelled academically. We moved to a home among the movie stars in Brentwood when I was eight. My memories begin a couple of years after moving into this house.

I remembered nothing of my childhood before the age of eleven. After that my memories are of always being scared, angry, insecure and alone. I had few friends in grammar school because I was unkempt, my hair often unwashed, and I was very defensive. An artist drew a sketch of me at about twelve in which he portrayed me as furiously angry, shouting and shaking a finger. He told me that was the way I always seemed to be.

Although I continued to do well in school, I did not do well socially. In high school, my insecurity increased. I was so unhappy that I asked my parents to send me to a psychiatrist, but they talked me out of it, saying I did not need one.

When I went away to college, I began to feel somewhat happier. "Somewhat happier" does not mean I stopped considering suicide, but I began to learn to laugh and have fun. After I graduated, I spent the better part of two years in Paris, working as a glorified secretary and writer's assistant for a friend of my father.

When I returned to Los Angeles, a judge talked me into entering law school. I agreed because I thought it would help me protect myself, although I did not really understand this motivation. During law school, I met a man who had just graduated from law school and we were married eight months later.

When I became an attorney, I joined a large Los Angeles law firm to become a trial lawyer. I was the only woman and the men in that firm were wonderful to me; it was the first time that anyone appreciated my work. Their respect and approval made me realize the tremendous effect positive reinforcement can have on people. The support of these men was in sharp contrast to my father's constant criticism.

My father and I had terrible fights as far back as I can remember. He was a demanding, perfectionistic, unreasonable man with a terrible temper. But then much of the same could have been said about me; I seemed to mimic him. We were best friends and worst enemies. We were able to talk about anything but would often erupt in rage because both of us were so sensitive. Sometimes his rage would take the form of blows, and he would beat me with his fists, sometimes breaking down the locked door to my bedroom where I retreated. He was jealous and possessive of me—but he could also be very gentle and understanding. He had a wonderful wit and an insatiable desire to learn everything in the world. He read the dictionary and the encyclopedia for amusement and taught himself Spanish by speaking to Mexicans on his ham radio.

Although he had successes, my father's career did not prosper, as much because of his refusal to compromise and his uncontrollable temper as the demise of the movie industry. Our enormous house was always on the brink of foreclosure but my father would not sell it, despite the drain on our finances, because it was a symbol of his success. Without it, he felt he was nothing.

When I was a teenager, he would come to me, desperately unhappy, saying he had been a terrible father and done terrible things to me, and that he wanted to commit suicide because we would be better off if he were dead. I tried to console him but I was upset by these confessions, and I asked my mother about them. She said that he was just worried about the decline of his career. Although her explanation never quite rang true, I could find no alternative.

Later while I was practicing corporate law and representing the motion picture companies my father had worked for, my father's declining finances finally forced the sale of our house. My parents decided to move to Mexico where my father had friends and living costs would be cheaper. I had been helping my parents conduct a sale of much of their furniture, books and art objects when my father and I had our last

7

dreadful fight. He said I was a terrible daughter who did not care about him, and I screamed back that I hated him and that he was a terrible father. I said I would never see him again. And I never did. He died in Mexico City three weeks later of a massive heart attack.

I told the psychiatrist I had been seeing for several years that I would never forgive myself if my father died. And I didn't, not for a long time. My psychiatrist had been trying to make me see my father's faults because I had idealized him to such an unrealistic extent. I clung to the family myth that we were so lucky to be a happy family who loved each other. But things grew worse for me after my father's death.

My marriage deteriorated. My husband and I assumed that our problems were due to working too hard and living in a congested, polluted city. So we moved to the Santa Cruz mountains in northern California where we lived among the giant redwoods. Our relationship seemed to improve for the first year but quickly started downhill again. I was living in one of the most beautiful places I have ever seen, with a husband I thought I loved, teaching at the University of Santa Clara Law School which I enjoyed—and I was miserable.

When my marriage broke up, I decided to move to Washington, D.C. I consulted a psychiatrist in San Jose before I left. He brutally told me that until I dealt with my problems, I would be unhappy wherever I went, so it didn't matter whether I stayed or left. I left ostensibly to take a job as a Congressional investigator, but I really fled from my unhappiness. I knew the Government paid 80 percent of the cost for therapy and I was determined to get well, whatever I had to do.

For almost eight years, I went to two of the most highly recommended psychiatrists in Washington, D.C., but neither of them ever suspected the real cause of my problems. These men did not think it was significant that I could not remember the first eleven years of my life. Even when I was hospitalized for a couple of weeks and begged the second psychiatrist to find a hypnotherapist for me, he refused, saying that I didn't need it because I was doing so well professionally.

Yes, my career was flourishing. I was driven to overachieve in order to subdue my massive insecurity. I had gone from Congressional investigations to become a U.S. senator's chief counsel and from there to a banking law firm. My first case for that firm involved representing two savings and loan associations against a federal agency in a federal court trial, and I won. The Court of Appeals upheld the decision which generated quite a bit of publicity, at least in the banking industry.

Just after the Supreme Court upheld the lower court's decision, Jimmy Carter was elected president. He was looking for women to fill executive positions, so I was appointed to the agency I had beaten. I was also named to a White House Task Force on Women because for several years I chaired a professional women's network that I had created. I traveled all over the country making speeches on economics and banking issues and setting up women's networks.

Outwardly, and according to the press, I was a success. But inwardly, I was a failure. Only my best friends were aware that I sometimes sobbed in the ladies' room before making a speech. My persistent inner fear had not abated, my personal life was a mess, and I had not found happiness. In the eight years I had been in Washington, despite all my therapy, I had not been able to establish a stable relationship with a man. Somehow that was my measure of success. My other personal relationships were also less than successful. Many people found me threatening, perhaps because of the anger always seething inside me that exploded at inopportune times.

I took a year off to decide what I wanted to do. I thought that if I found a job that was more meaningful to me, I might be happy. I was reading every self-help book I could get my hands on and trying all of the techniques recommended. My main goal still was to find inner peace and contentment.

I finally decided to become an attorney-advisor to the Agency for International Development at the State Department where I could help people in underdeveloped countries. I loved the work overseas; it helped me feel useful, especially my appointment as policy advisor on United Nations issues in the development agencies. The high point of my career was debating the Soviet delegate—a well-known KGB agent—at a U.N. Development Programme conference in Geneva and persuading the nonaligned countries to vote with the United States. But the thrill of my accomplishments was always shortlived. Since I had no inner sense of self-worth, I always sank back into insecurity and depression.

It was shortly after my return from Geneva that my memories started to emerge—although I didn't understand at the time what they were. My first experience was terrifying. I had some very strange thoughts, so I checked myself into a hospital. I did not know that my memories were coming back, and neither did the psychiatrists at the hospital because they never tried to talk to me. I was terrified because no one seemed to know what was happening to me, but they all seemed to think it was serious.

When I returned to work, I decided I needed a vacation. I had been trying to be nice to myself by doing things I liked and skiing was one I liked best. So I went to ski at my favorite place, Park City, Utah, and my ski instructor arranged a date for me with a lawyer in town. Jim and I were married a couple of months later.

I moved to Park City and the first couple of months were like a dream. But it didn't last. It quickly became apparent that I had married back into the same pattern I had tried so hard to avoid. Although he did not hit me, my husband's temper reminded me of my father. We fought constantly. The ecstasy of the first few months changed to the familiar despair.

About that time I went to a gynecologist. I had been having problems with my menstrual periods for years. Two operations had not revealed the cause of the excessive pain and bleeding. The new gynecologist in Utah was also unable to explain my symptoms and suggested that since I had used self-hypnosis for a couple of years, I might be able to use it to control the pain and bleeding. He sent me to an hypnotherapist.

During the first session the therapist told me that my symptoms usually indicated some kind of trauma in childhood. He asked if I would be willing to explore that possibility under hypnosis. I said I would and mentioned my inability to recall the first eleven years of my life. His eyebrows went up, and we began hypnotherapy.

It immediately became apparent from my terror that something dreadful had happened in the Westwood Village house. Over the next few months I learned that I had been raped, beaten and tortured by my father from the time I was almost four years old until I was almost eight.

At first I would not believe it. I fell apart. I could not accept that such a thing could happen in *my* family. All of the carefully constructed myths collapsed. But at the same time I finally had explanations for so many inexplicable things in my life.

The memories were not really clear until I switched from my first hypnotherapist in Utah, a male, to a woman hypnotherapist who was caring and supportive and the most creative therapist I have met. She rescued me when all of the memories began spilling out. We were both horrified at the brutality of what my father had done. Aside from the sexual abuse, he had stuck a fire poker, part of a doll, a chisel, a letter opener, and a few other things up me. He also walked on my chest and killed my kitten in front of me.

As the memories emerged, the meaning of my recurrent dream about the wild boars was finally revealed. I remembered one night when my father came into my bedroom and I tried to get away. My running and screaming inflamed him into a fury, and he caught me and began to pound me with his fists. The blows continued and continued. They only stopped when he violently raped me and then he started to beat me again. At some point I went numb, which was the "death" in my dream. But in the dream and in reality, the horror continued and the pain did not stop.

The memories came out in a variety of ways, as I describe in several sections of this book, and I learned to do much of my own hypnotherapy by myself at home. I did not have a classic case of multiple personality disorder, as I later learned my father did, but I was certainly close.

Unable to cope with the violent emotions of terror, helplessness, grief, anger, hate and pain engendered by my abuse, my mind split the emotions and memories into separate pockets, which are called ego states, and stored them away, out of my consciousness. I had ego states for hate, pain, anger, sadness and others which held individual memories of hideous events. Most of the latter were based on my experiences at a particular age so that I had my two-year-old ego state, my four-year-old, my five-year-old and so on. It seemed almost like filling a computer floppy disk; once a portion of my mind was saturated with pain, it created a new disk. When one of my child ego states spoke through me under hypnosis, each spoke and thought like a child at that age. It was as if parts of me had been frozen in time and had never grown up.

We had to release the memories and reeducate these child-like parts of my mind so that they could grow up and be integrated back into my mind. Although these ego states did not come out and take over as in multiple personality disorder, the emotions trapped in each state had magnified the emotions I had felt throughout my life and exaggerated my reactions out of all proportion.

Once the memories and emotions were released, my reactions became more controlled and realistic, and my anger and anxiety decreased.

Memories started to emerge that convinced me that my mother knew what was happening. She had even walked in when my father was raping me. She was terribly distraught and tried to rescue me on the couple of occasions when she saw what my father was doing, but she did not stop what was happening. When I begged her to send me away, she hit me and said that it was all my fault and that she could not do anything about it. From then on, she ignored the blood and my bruises. She escaped by sleeping so soundly that to this day she will not wake up even when you scream in her ears. She protected her sanity with a childlike pollyanna attitude which denied the existence of anything unpleasant and by a myth that labeled me unstable, and even crazy, so that I am not to be believed. She denies to this day that anything happened. Her story is presented in more detail in Question 12, *Why didn't my mother protect me?*

Because I could not understand how my memories could be so different from my family's myth, my therapist and I began to explore my parents' backgrounds. Since my father was a writer and had always conceded that his books were autobiographical, we began with his novels. Most of his books, written in the first person, left glaring clues about his past and his personality. My therapist quickly concluded that my father had multiple personality disorder. One of his "I" protagonists states clearly in a novel that he has an evil personality named "Spud" inside him which comes out, takes over and makes him do destructive things. And this book was written long before *The Three Faces of Eve.*

Multiple personality disorder would explain the brutality of his attacks, as well as the fact that he virtually ignored my mother's screams the first time she entered my bedroom while he was raping me. It would explain the fact that during these brutal attacks, he never called me by my name. Multiple personality disorder would also explain his blinding headaches which are a symptom of personality change. The amnesia of multiple personality disorder also explains how he could be so gentle and loving at other times and explains his horror when he finally realized what he was doing to me. The realization came when I picked up a chisel he had been using on me and stabbed him with it. He was apparently shocked back into reality and he ran screaming out of the house and into a clinic. The sexual abuse and torture stopped in 1948.

At the time my abuse stopped, virtually nothing was known about multiple personality disorder. But my father was fortunate enough to have a psychiatrist who was a hypnotherapist and evidently could deal with the problem. My mother recalls that the psychiatrist also hypnotized *her*, but she cannot remember *why* she was hypnotized.

But how did my father acquire multiple personality disorder? Therapists now agree that this disorder only results from severe physical or sexual abuse over a prolonged period of time. I remembered my father telling me about his terrible childhood. My mother confirmed these recollections. His mother was Viennese, a dreadful woman, tough without softness, selfish and cold. Her husband left her in New York when my father was six-months-old, and she survived by taking in sewing and knitting which she later turned into a profitable business. She left my father with her five sisters and a grandmother who was especially cruel. My father used to refer to them as "the six harpies," and he said that all of them used to beat him. Perhaps they did other things as well.

My father's life got worse when his mother remarried. His stepfather was a crude, uneducated man who had no love for my father who was only four at the time. Both parents showered all of their love on the new baby sister, who learned to torment my father by falsely screaming that he was hurting her. They beat him severely, never believing the truth.

I also know that my father had a violent fear and hatred of the Nazis, not just because he was Jewish but because of his personal experiences. His Viennese mother sent him from New York to school in pre-Nazi Austria. Although the Nazis had not yet taken over Austria when my father was there, there was a virulent anti-Jewish sentiment in the country. He told us he hated that Viennese school but he never elaborated.

My father's hatred of the Nazis was also based on other events which are described in one of his novels. In his youth, he had a couple of friends in school, including his boy scout leader Hans whom he worshipped. Hans' real name is used in the book. After the Nazi invasion, my father's friends, who opposed the Nazis, were trapped in Austria and in danger of being sent to the concentration camps. My father went back to Austria and fronted a bicycle trip of "American" students from Vienna into Switzerland so that his friends could escape. But Hans decided he had to help his friends still trapped in Austria and he returned. Hans was captured and died in a Nazi concentration camp. My father never got over his death or those of so many of his relatives and childhood friends.

My father's reaction to his fear of the Nazis was bizarre. He dyed his hair white blond, not only on his head but all over his body. A professional photograph on the jacket of one of his books is chillingly like the stereotypes of Nazi S.S. officers in the movies. The eyes are cold, the mouth tight and cruel, and the white-blond, crewcut is strikingly Aryan. Some of the things my father did to me are reminiscent of the Nazi atrocities and experiments he used to describe to me in later years because, he said, "I had to know about what the Nazis did."

I could not understand how he could have turned into what he hated most until my therapist explained how victims can often become victimizers to overcome the helplessness they felt when they were abused. I do know that when my father got help and the abuse stopped, he let his hair grow back to its natural dark color. His "Nazi" had died.

I am not going to tell you that giving up the family myth and assimilating this nightmare into my history was easy. It wasn't. But, it explained so many things that had caused me problems throughout my life, and those explanations gave me a chance to change my behavior. I was relieved to learn that I was not crazy and that I had never been crazy. Knowing that I had survived such brutality gave me a great deal of confidence. I realized that if I could survive what my father did when I was only four and had no one to help me, I could get through anything now.

My therapy helped me release my violent, long-repressed feelings about my parents and others who failed to respond to my pleas for help.

This resulted in my finding an inner peace I did not know existed. I used to think it was normal to hurt inside all the time, but now I know it is not. My relationships have improved dramatically because I no longer explode in anger over trifles. I am beginning to learn to trust people and not to expect betrayal.

But I think the most profound change is that I have learned to love myself, and because of that life is no longer a struggle. Everything is so much easier! I walked through the pain and I reached for the rainbow. I hope you will reach for the rainbow too.

> *The mind is its own place, and in itself*
> *Can make a Heav'n of Hell, a Hell of Heav'n.*
> John Milton, *Paradise Lost*

III SURVIVORS' QUESTIONS

1. I feel like I am crazy because I've been abused. Can I ever lead a happy life?

Yes, there is life after abuse. And it can be a happy and fulfilling life, although I know that you won't believe this at first. Sometimes it may feel as though you are going crazy. Whether you were sexually or physically abused or both, what you suffered is going to stir up powerful emotions. You will feel overwhelmed by rage and hate at your abusers and also at the people who should have protected and helped you but did not. You may try to suppress these feelings because you are afraid to admit you hate people to whom you are related, but your anger will explode in other situations and may even turn to violence. You will feel almost unbearable pain at your betrayal by people you trusted. If your mother or father was your abuser, you will be torn by the love that you want to feel for a parent and the betrayal and hate you feel for what happened to you.

You may feel shame and guilt because you fear that you were responsible for what happened. You may experience waves of terror in everyday situations without knowing why. And you will feel depressed coupled with the belief that you are bad and worthless. That depression can sometimes make you feel like taking your own life.

Your present fears of going crazy may also be heightened by what you felt during your actual abuse. Many victims felt as if they were pushed to the brink of insanity while they were being abused. As a child, the rush of violent feelings was overpowering. In order to preserve your sanity, you probably suppressed your feelings until you were old enough

15

to deal with them. Now as an adult, you have to deal *both* with the emotions you felt at the time of your abuse and the emotions you feel today. So part of your present fear may be based on your past emotions, and your present feelings may be greatly exaggerated.

The fact is that you did not go insane despite the horror of what you suffered; you protected yourself. Even if you have been hospitalized because of your reaction to the abuse, you cannot be insane now or you would not be able to read this book. Insanity is losing contact with reality. You are all too aware of what happened to you and are facing the pain of reality, so you cannot be insane.

With all of these emotions whirling like a tornado inside you, it may be difficult to believe that you could ever experience peace, let alone joy. My main purpose in writing this book is to let you know that there will be an end to the pain and that you have the ability to find the peace and happiness you long for. I cannot promise you eternal bliss, but I can promise that it will get better. The pain you feel will diminish as you work through your turbulent emotions. And it will also diminish just through the passage of time.

A few years ago when I first discovered that I had been abused as a child, I was a basket case. Nightmares at night and uncovering hideous memories during the day made my life unbearable. I could hardly function; some days I stayed home from work and sobbed in my bed. I knew I was crazy. I thought that no one could go through what I had been through and not be crazy. I even told my therapist that I should be hospitalized. Luckily, she laughed. It was a turning point for me.

By the time another year had passed, I was having fun. I could forget about what happened to me for most of the day, sometimes for days at a time. I enjoyed skiing and hiking and started to think about a new career. Now, three years later, I've become a writer and a therapist instead of a lawyer, have treated myself to my first puppy—a fluffy white samoyed, have written this book and am actually enjoying life.

I believe that survivors of abuse can be better for the experience. Wait! Please don't put this book down until you really consider what I have to say. The victims I know are truly survivors; they are stronger than other people because they have survived greater ordeals. Many of them are professional people, lawyers, doctors, therapists, managers, police officers, artists, etc. But regardless of what they do for a living, they have had to be strong. Many abused children die, but we did not. We survived the worst part. We can certainly get through the aftermath since we are no longer being abused.

Survivors of abuse tend to be exceptionally compassionate. They know what it is like to suffer and when they conquer their own pain, they

16

go to great lengths to avoid inflicting pain on others. Survivors often tend to be in the helping professions where they can alleviate the suffering of others.

You will also obtain some lifelong benefits from going through therapy. In therapy you not only deal with the issues of your abuse, but you learn skills for solving other problems that may arise in your life. Confronting your fears not only produces inner strength but prepares you for dealing with future trials. Facing your pain teaches you to understand the nature of pain and its impermanence.

Therapy also makes you sensitive to your thoughts and actions so you can make rational decisions and take control of your life. This awareness puts you way ahead of most people who live their lives in the dark, slaves of their childhood injuries and of their parents' critical voices echoing forever in their minds. When you face your demons and deal with your pain, you are free. You are free to make your own decisions and to live your life as you choose.

Your situation is far from hopeless. We know that survivors of even the most severe physical and sexual abuse can be healed. There is only one necessary requisite: you must *want to be healed*. Even if you want to die (a feeling based in part on what you felt when you were being abused), therapists today are able to help restore your will to live and your desire to find happiness. However much despair and hopelessness you feel, by picking up this book you have already demonstrated that inside you is some kernel of hope and the wish to be healed. These can provide the basis for your journey toward health.

You have the ability to make yourself happy. You have complete control over your life from now on. No one controls you anymore. You can get help to work through your problems or you can live with them. You can continue to think you are worthless, or you can review your strengths and learn to love yourself. You can decide never to trust anyone again, or you can refuse to let a few rotten apples spoil your barrel of humanity for the rest of your life. All of the choices are up to you now. And it's all downhill from here, if you let it be.

> *If you can get through life,*
> *you can get through anything.*
> Unknown

2. What is abuse?

Abuse is a sickness that is sapping our country's strength. It is growing by exponential proportions as it is passed from generation to generation. Abused children who are not treated become parents who are likely to abuse their children who, if not treated, will abuse their children, and so on, in a chain of abuse which multiplies as each abused child forms a new family.

The shameful fact is that we have the power to break this chain today. Abuse is a learned behavior and is curable. We have the knowledge to wipe out this disease, to heal the children and adults who have suffered so much, but we refuse to spend the money required to adequately staff our child protection agencies and to pay for trained therapists to treat the victims of abuse and their families. And so more and more children endure the anguish and horror of abuse each year.

It is estimated that one out of every two or three Americans is a victim of some form of childhood abuse.

For practical purposes, there are four basic types of child abuse: sexual abuse, physical abuse, neglect and emotional abuse. Although this book focuses on sexual abuse, the emotions evoked and the low self-esteem caused by sexual abuse are similar to those experienced by victims of the other types of abuse; thus the principles and self-help techniques in this book will also be helpful to survivors of the other three. Also, abused children usually experience more than one type of abuse, so it is difficult to talk about one type without talking about the others.

Sexual abuse

The clearest definition I have heard of *sexual abuse* is *any unwanted touching.*[1] Although the examples I discuss involve more severe acts of sexual abuse, children can develop low self-esteem, feel helplessness and experience the other violent emotions of abuse solely by being touched in ways to which they object. When a child cannot prevent or control an objectionable touching or fondling of his or her body, the child is victimized and that is abuse. Sexual abuse also includes rape, statutory rape, sodomy, incest or inducing a child to pose for pornography or to engage in prostitution. While we would like to believe that such conduct is rare, the sad fact is that tens of thousands of American children are victims of these acts every year.

Researchers quibble over whether sexual abuse includes noncontact abuse, such as verbal propositions and exhibitionism, and whether nonadult peers are perpetrators. There is also some controversy over the criteria for determining which relationships are abusive based on a difference in age between victim and perpetrator. No one disputes that abuse exists where there are sexual acts between a young child and an adult, even in the absence of coercion, but what about acts between two teenagers? These disputes have so far prevented an official definition of sexual abuse.[2]

Incest

Incest is a type of sexual abuse defined as *sexual activity between two people who are closely related.* The most common form of incest is between natural fathers and daughters and between stepfathers and stepdaughters. But incest is also common between fathers and sons, brothers and sisters, grandfathers and grandchildren, and uncles and their nieces and nephews. Female members of a family occasionally commit incest against their children or grandchildren.[3] Eighty percent of sexual abuse is committed by a family member and is thus incest.

The sexual abuse commonly involves intercourse and may include oral sex, anal sex and mutual masturbation. Incest can begin in infancy; a number of children become victims before their first birthday. The "average age" when abuse starts is variously estimated to be 6, 8 and 11. In most instances, the sexual abuse, sometimes coupled with physical abuse, takes place for an average of two years and may continue for a longer period of time. It usually stops in adolescence when the victim obtains outside help or threatens to expose the abuser.

Incest is perhaps the most difficult kind of abuse for children to endure because the feelings it generates are so overwhelming, confusing and conflicting. Children instinctively love their parents and other family members and cannot reconcile this love with what is being done to them. They are torn between love and hate, and tormented because of the betrayal by those they trusted. They are overwhelmed by helplessness because they cannot escape; they have nowhere to go. The very people to whom they should run for protection are their abusers. And they believe that if they tell, they will destroy their families and their source of survival. They are trapped and helpless. And they are tortured by the conviction that they are bad or evil and that they are somehow to blame.

Physical abuse

Another type of child abuse is physical abuse. The legal definition of *physical abuse* is *injury caused by acts or omissions of a parent or a person responsible for the child which cause pain and are a threat to the child's safety*. Any intentional infliction of pain is abuse because it destroys the child's self-esteem and trust. The variety of physical abuse defies imagination and ranges from beatings with a strap or club to biting and burning with cigarettes and metal branding irons. The ultimate physical abuse results in death and many children die of abuse every year.

Neglect

Neglect is another common type of physical and emotional abuse and is defined as *the chronic absence of a parent or person responsible for the child, without providing for a substitute caretaker, and / or failure to provide the physical or emotional necessities of life for the child*. This category includes failing to feed a child or change its diapers as well as the extreme neglect of a boy whose parents locked him in a closet for two years. He was never allowed out; the closet was his dining room, his bedroom and his toilet. When he was released, he could not walk, but after intensive physical and psychological treatment, he is now walking. He asks why his mommy and daddy didn't love him.

Emotional abuse

Emotional abuse is the most insidious type of abuse because it is so hard to pinpoint, yet it can be the most devastating. The most painful emotional abuse can be a parent's failure to provide love and affection or a parent's constant criticism. A parent's refusal to give praise or to say "I love you" can destroy a child's self-esteem and ability to give and receive love. The legal definition of *emotional abuse* is *a psychological condition which renders the child chronically and severely anxious, agitated, depressed, socially withdrawn, psychotic, or in fear of his / her life or safety*. Some definitions also include mental conditions which interfere with a child's education or ability to develop normally.

I believe the emotional abuse I received from my parents was worse than the sexual abuse and torture. I have had to work harder to erase the psychological effects of being told that I was evil and a child of the devil than to overcome the violent feelings caused by the abuse of my body.

It is difficult to separate emotional abuse from other abuse. The boy who was locked in a closet clearly suffered emotional abuse from his neglect. And the emotional impact of physical and sexual abuse is also devastating. Because emotional abuse is almost always intertwined with another type of abuse, it is rarely the sole basis for protective action, but it is usually a factor in determining the degree of abuse.

The prevalence of child abuse in our country is overwhelming. The National Study on Child Neglect and Abuse Reporting collects reports of abuse filed with protective service agencies throughout the country. A study filed in 1986 documents 2,086,000 reports of abused and neglected children in the United States and its territories. This is an eight percent increase over 1985 and a 212 percent increase since 1976.

The dramatic increase in reported cases is due both to increased instances of abuse and partly to increased public awareness of the problem.

Of the 2,086,000 cases reported, 737,000 were "substantiated" by child protective agencies or the courts. The study is quick to point out that this does not mean the other cases were false. It reflects the unfortunate fact that overloaded child protective agencies did not have the resources to follow up on many reports, that families had moved by the time a caseworker could find time to work on the case, or that the agency could not assemble sufficient proof to take action. It means that our system failed to help more than one million children, and that their abuse continues.

The National Study reports that 132,000 accounts of sexual abuse were "substantiated" out of over 300,000 reports during 1986. Again, no one investigated many of the "unsubstantiated" incidents of sexual abuse. And many cases of sexual abuse are not reported at all. Some researchers estimate that at least one in four adult women were sexually abused as children.

Other studies on the prevalence of sexual abuse in North America vary considerably. These studies attempt to estimate the proportion of a population that was sexually abused during childhood. Rates range from six percent to 62 percent for females and from three percent to 31 percent for males.[4] Most people who work in the field of sexual abuse concur that approximately 33 percent of the total population has been sexually abused and that the numbers are increasing.

The effects of sexual abuse are devastating. Sexual abuse can cause both physical and mental pain that does not fade and that can only be released by working through the memories and emotions of the abuse, usually in therapy. Sexual abuse evokes intense anxiety, fear, rage, shame and depression that can lead to suicide. Victims are trapped in destructive patterns that hurt their relationships and their lives; their abuse may even impel them to repeat the pattern of their abuse with their own children.

But the effects of sexual abuse can be healed. The pain can be released and the destructive patterns reversed, and survivors of abuse can lead *normal*, whatever that is, healthy and productive lives. Once a survivor recognizes that she or he has a problem due to past abuse and starts to work on it, the healing process has begun. By picking up this book, those of you who have been abused have taken the first step out of your pain toward health and happiness. The following chapters should answer some of your questions, diminish some of your fears and provide ways for you to obtain help and help yourself.

> *Nothing in life is to be feared.*
> *It is only to be understood.*
> Madam Curie

3. Do I need therapy if I have been abused?

Yes. I believe it would be helpful under most circumstances. However, there are many paths to healing the wounds of sexual abuse. Some involve therapy, while others involve your own innate ability to heal and still others depend on your own commitment and the efforts you make to get well. The most effective combination usually involves commitment, enthusiasm, therapy, your own healing power and a variety of self-help measures you can do on your own.

Neither the therapy nor the work you do on your own will solve all of your problems by themselves. Showing up at your therapist's office once a week will not magically cure you. And working from self-help books without the guidance of a competent therapist may also fail to address many key issues of your abuse. A well-thought out balance of therapy and your own efforts has been proven by experience to bring the quickest, most comprehensive and lasting results.

However, the strength of your commitment to getting well and the importance you place on that goal is probably the single most important factor in your progress. How much do you hurt, how badly do you want to get well, and how long do you want to take? The answer to those questions will determine how hard you are willing to work, how much courage you will have to face the hard issues, and how much time, money and effort you are willing to devote to achieve your goal.

Even without doing anything consciously, you will improve on your own. Human beings have an incredible, built-in ability to heal themselves, not just physically but also mentally. We are all aware of our bodies' mechanism for growing new skin over wounds and producing cells to fight infection. Our minds also heal automatically without our having to do anything consciously. Even while we sleep, our minds heal us through our dreams which gently show us our past traumas, often cloaked in symbols, thereby enabling us to release our past pain.

We also use our minds to heal when we experience new situations that cause us to revise our old opinions. For example, each time someone treats us kindly, that small act begins to erode away a bit of our childhood conclusion that people cannot be trusted because it forces our minds to consider the possibility that our childhood stereotype of people was distorted. And of course we can use our conscious minds to learn more about our abuse and how to help ourselves by reading self-help books, like the one you are reading now, by watching television shows and movies, and talking to other people about our problems.

If we are willing to listen and our friends are willing to be candid, good friends can often help us gain new perspectives and change our behavior. In fact, the perceptions good friends have about us may be even more helpful than those of a therapist because our friends know us better. But remember that you can quickly wear your friends out by too frequently deluging them with the problems you have coping with your abuse. Friends have problems of their own and even the best of friends can become exhausted if they have to deal with someone else's problems on a regular basis. Friends may become frustrated because they are overwhelmed by the magnitude of your situation and feel inadequate to help you.

If your friends become overly burdened because your talks are repetitive and nothing seems to change, this may be an indication that therapy would be useful. A therapist can listen patiently to your traumatic experiences and, if he or she is trained in sexual abuse cases, will know how to help you work out your problems with the least amount of distress.

Another way of changing our opinion of ourselves is by experiencing success. Every success increases our mental health and has an especially beneficial effect on victims, since even a small success becomes a major building block for future accomplishments. Each small success, in school, jobs and relationships, chips away at our childhood image of ourselves as victims and failures and forms the basis for a new image of autonomy and success. We also learn from the example of others and just by living. But by far the most powerful remedy for mental injuries is love, kindness and approval. Acts of kindness and caring can often change childhood patterns and restore a victim's faith in humanity.

So why do you need therapy if you might simply heal on your own? The main reason is that it's faster. You can rely on your innate healing power to work out the pain of your abuse, but it may take you most of the rest of your life. In the meantime, you may continue to suffer from the tempest of your emotions and to be enslaved by the dysfunctional patterns of behavior that are a product of the way you were treated in your childhood and how you reacted. Although you have the ability to overcome the effects of your abuse, you need a therapist to help you use that ability properly so that you can put the pain behind you and begin to enjoy life as quickly as possible.

I was in too much pain not to grab any shortcut I could find. I went to therapists, did therapy on myself at home, read every self-help book I could get my hands on and formed a telephone network of abused women so I would have someone to talk to when I felt down. Notwithstanding my many self-help efforts, I do not think I could have made it without my therapists. In fact I might never have known about my abuse if my first hypnotherapist had not asked the questions which led to its discovery. I would have continued to be plagued by a variety of problems without understanding the cause and I would have continued to think I was crazy.

But perhaps my main reason for going to a therapist was to have a safety net. I wanted to be sure I had someone I trusted to help me, and who was familiar with sexual abuse problems, so I would have someone I could count on if I felt I could not handle things myself.

The events and emotions in abuse cases can be devastating. For people uncovering blocked memories, recalling the acts of abuse can be a horrifying experience. Sometimes your mind can flash back to a grisly childhood scene which for a moment can seem almost real to you. The emotions which may explode as memories are uncovered or merely discussed can be frightening in their savagery and power.

Even your friends or family may become immobilized if you begin to scream in terror or shout repeatedly that you want to kill your mother or whoever your abuser was. They will not know how to handle the situation and will not be of much help to you. In addition, your friends and family may want to stop your emotions as quickly as possible, while you need to release your emotions if you are to heal. If you work on the difficult situations in your therapist's office, you will be with someone who understands your emotions and knows how to help you deal with them. Your therapist will also be available for telephone consultations if you need help at home.

Frequently survivors of abuse suffer from extreme depression. A seemingly insignificant event can remind you of your abuse and you may tumble without warning into a well of despair. In some cases you may have suicidal thoughts. If you have a therapist, you have someone with whom to explore these thoughts immediately, before they get out of control.

In a very few instances, you may want or need to go into a hospital. Jennie is a therapist who was brutally raped by an intruder as a child but had repressed the memories into adulthood. She asked her own therapist to check her into a hospital because she felt she would only be able to let the memories out if she was in a totally safe place. If you have a therapist, you have someone who is available to arrange for your admission to the hospital which best meets your needs. Some hospitals have excellent psychiatric facilities and allow private therapists to treat their clients during hospitalization; others emphasize the use of psychotropic drugs and ignore therapy. Your therapist will be familiar with local hospitals and can help you choose one where you will be the most comfortable. He or she can also monitor your progress and make sure that you are in the hospital for the shortest period of time.

Unwinding all of the problems related to child abuse, whether physical or sexual, is a complicated business. Merely discovering that you have been abused and knowing that you are angry is just the tip of the iceberg. You may not have the skills to let go of that anger and put it behind you. You also may have difficulty coping alone with all of the other powerful emotions that you have experienced and repressed during the abuse.

Some emotions which are trapped inside you may be totally hidden from your conscious mind and you will need help to uncover them. For example, I discovered through hypnosis that below my anger and fear was an overpowering subconscious feeling of helplessness. At this buried level of my unconscious, I thought that nothing I did would ever go right and that I would always be at the mercy of other people. I needed someone who had the knowledge to foresee that I might feel helpless, who could help me dig until I exposed this pain, so I could reach the source of my anger and release it.

Joe, a resident of the adolescent mental health unit, was surprised to discover an unsuspected feeling while he was in therapy. Joe was angry and took it out on the staff and on his peers with sarcasm, obscenity, insults and physical violence. With help, he discovered that beneath his smoke screen of anger was a very hurt little boy who sobbed uncontrollably for hours when he unearthed deeply hidden feelings of loss and betrayal by his mother who beat and neglected him and allowed her boyfriends to torment and sexually abuse him. Once he released his childhood anguish, Joe's anger vanished.

Our feelings are not always what they seem; sometimes it takes a professional to help us sort it all out. The way we react to events today is determined by choices we made as a frightened child. Our childhood reactions usually were the best choices we had at the time, but they frequently are not the best decisions available to us today.

For instance, after Rita was abandoned by her father, she was raped and physically abused by her stepfather. Her mother knew of her new husband's acts but did nothing because she was afraid she could not support herself and her children alone. Rita came to the logical conclusion that people were inherently untrustworthy and treacherous and decided to protect herself by keeping people as far away from her as possible. When she arrived at the adolescent unit, she had perfected a personality of bullying and criticism. She boasted that she did not care whether anyone liked her or not, and she did her best to make sure that they did not.

Underneath this facade, Rita was a normal teenager who wanted the love and approval of her peers, but her behavior pushed everyone away. Even with therapy, it took many months for Rita to recognize what she was doing. Without help it would have taken many years of loneliness for her to recognize her behavior and change her conduct.

Preventing the cycle of child abuse is an equally complex problem. If you want to be sure that you will not repeat the pattern of abuse, you need a therapist to guide you. You simply are in no position to judge whether or not you have unconscious impulses resulting from your own abuse that will compel you to abuse your children. (The question of whether or not you will abuse your children is discussed in Question 22, *If I have been abused, will I abuse my child?*) A skilled therapist can help determine if you have worked through all of the memories, emotions and patterns necessary to free you from any danger of hurting your children.

I do not intend to condemn you to a life of expensive weekly or biweekly sessions with a therapist. *You* control your therapy and you decide when you are finished. I believe that you should be able to finish in a couple of years. For some people with prolonged abuse who are suffering from multiple personality disorder (MPD), it may be longer. But I believe even people with multiple personality disorders can consciously control the amount of time they will need to be in therapy by setting goals and that the average length of time will become substantially shorter than it has been in the last decade.

You should stop your therapy when you feel it is time for you to stop. Remember, nothing is irrevocable. You can always change your mind and go back if you want. All you have to do is make an appointment. But you will have someone to call who knows you and understands what is going on so you can pick up where you left off without a great deal of explanation or lost time.

You can also control how often you see your therapist. In most cases, visits of once or twice a week are ideal to get the fastest results. This schedule gives you the opportunity to talk to your therapist often enough to establish continuity so that you can easily pick up where you left off from week to week. If you go less frequently than once a week, it is easy for both you and the therapist to forget what you should be working on next. So much will have happened to you in the interim that you will waste much of the hour trying to bring your therapist up to date on past events, rather than working on significant problems.

However, if money or time appear to be insurmountable problems, you can still benefit from infrequent visits to a therapist if you are exceptionally self-disciplined. You and your therapist must decide what you will work on by yourself and make sure that during your office visits, you work only on the most important issues. You will have to resist the temptation to bring your therapist "up to date" during each visit. Some therapists will agree to read material you have written between your sessions, and this can be an acceptable substitute for verbal discussions. Other therapists use this technique for saving time even when they see the client on a weekly basis. But it means the therapist must work extra hours outside of the sessions, and many do not want to do it.

Most important, your therapist should be a friend you can rely on, as well as an expert who has the training to help rescue you if you get into trouble. You should should feel comfortable with your therapist, at least at the beginning of your relationship. There may be times when patterns created by your abuse cause you to distrust your therapist or make you angry, and you will need the patience to work these problems through. But you should feel that your therapist cares about you and is available for emergencies. By providing a safety net, your therapist can help you feel more secure so that you can more easily face the problems of your abuse.

Although I believe that we have the answers to our problems inside us and the ability to cure ourselves, my experience is that therapists can help us more easily find our way, make us feel more comfortable during ney and show us techniques for arriving at our destination more quickly and safely.

But your healing is up to you. It took me a long time to realize the truth of a poster in my former therapist's office that said:

> *You are the only problem you will ever have*
> *and, baby, you are the only solution.*

4. I just want to get on with my life. I don't want to spend years in therapy.

An Australian friend of mine, also a therapist, found out in her late thirties—when she began to have flashbacks about her father raping her—that she had been abused as a child. She had three children, had put herself through college and graduate school, had a master's degree and was about to finish her doctorate in psychology. When I talked to her, she was terribly upset because she wanted to get on with her life and did not want to spend the time or money on therapy, even though she knew it would be helpful. I pointed out her not-insignificant accomplishments and asked her why she thought she could not be as productive while in therapy as she had been during all the years when she had lived with her unconscious turmoil.

She said she was afraid she would be miserable facing what her father did to her and thought she would have to put off enjoying her achievements. I acknowledged the truth, that it is no fun reliving the abuse and facing the fact that someone you loved did it to you. But she was not being abused now and, as an adult, she *could* have fun and enjoy her adult accomplishments in her present situation. Her children and her studies were her creations and she could take pride in them and enjoy them now because she created them *in spite of what was done to her*.

When we parted, I was not sure what she would do. But she called me later that night and said that she realized she could go on living despite the therapy and that she intended to do so. She said she felt it was a turning point in her life and that she was choosing to be happy no matter what.

Your fear of being stuck in an interminable nightmare is very real and common to abuse victims. The prospect of long years of therapy may seem overwhelming. You have already spent too much of your life in misery and horror and you want it to end. You want to put your abusive and violent past behind you and start a new life, one which will bring you peace and satisfaction. The idea of having to relive those terrible past events is frightening and abhorrent. You want it to be over once and for all.

I am familiar with those feelings because I had them myself; I even screamed them more than once at my therapist, in much cruder language. And I know that the desire to be healed and whole is very healthy. Some people have been so badly hurt that they have no desire to get well. They only want to die. The first step for them is to help them realize that they are alive because they are strong and worthwhile and that they can overcome their pain and find something to live for. But those of you who want to get on with your lives have already chosen to live. Even more important, you have decided it is time for you to have a good life. That is a major leap toward making your life good for yourself.

Many people do not believe they deserve happiness. In fact, the most common mental illness in the United States is happiness anxiety. Many people experience this anxiety, even those who have not been abused in childhood. They all want happiness and they all strive to achieve it, but just when they almost have it, or sometimes when they really do have it for a brief time, they destroy it for themselves. You have seen many examples of this: the rock star who, at the peak of success, overdoses on drugs; the student who starts to get straight A's and then blows an exam; and the couple who picks a fight when-ever things are really going well. These are all part of our inability to accept happiness and success. We feel we do not deserve it; we feel it will not last; we feel something awful will happen; the gods will be jealous. So we destroy our own happiness before it is destroyed by the gods or someone else. By destroying our happiness ourselves, we have the illusion of controlling our fate.

It is difficult for people to believe that we were born to be happy. I convinced myself by watching animals. Despite their struggle for survival, they have fun, they enjoy their lives. Birds fly for fun at times, not food; they soar and swoop just for the joy of it. Squirrels and chipmunks bask in the sun and play games with each other. Otters and seals are the most fun to watch; they play games all the time. Cats snooze and love to be petted, and dogs are joyous creatures who adore any kind of attention. Why should we deny ourselves what animals take as a matter of right?

I also convinced myself by my idea of God. I believe in a loving, compassionate, forgiving God. If you believe as I do, can you believe that

29

S/He would want any of us to be miserable?

So the fact that you are now choosing a happier life for yourself is a very healthy decision. And there is no reason why you cannot have that life even while you are going through therapy. Your life does not have to be placed on hold. You can be happy even though you are learning more about yourself and how to avoid repeating the patterns of the past.

The fact that you may recall unpleasant past events in therapy does not have to taint the rest of your life. The unfortunate fact is that life works the other way around. If you do not face the past, understand it and resolve it, it will haunt you for the rest of your life. You will make decisions based on past pain rather than present reality. And since your past was negative, you will make many negative decisions—without knowing why.

Life does not have to stop while you are in therapy. Of course there will be difficult times and you may feel angry, depressed, confused, etc. But there are two main parts to your healing. One part is clarifying and understanding what was done to you and identifying the decisions you made about yourself and others based on those events. You can then analyze whether those decisions are still correct now or if you should change them. You also need to release the emotions you repressed so that they do not come out at inappropriate times now.

But the second part is learning to feel good about yourself. That is something you can work on by yourself as well as with your therapist. You don't have to feel miserable to heal; you can learn to have fun, control your emotions, find inner peace and experience joy, all while you are dealing with your abuse issues. You can learn to care for yourself, love yourself, and make your life what you want it to be *right now*. You not only do not have to wait to do this, but you should not wait one more minute to get started.

There are many ways that you can help yourself and make your life happier without a therapist, many of them are described in Part IV, *Healing—Finding a Therapist*. Unfortunately, these methods are not a substitute for therapy if you have not worked out the pain and other emotions from your abuse. But they are vital for helping you to recognize and use your strengths and for restructuring your life so that it works for you.

I tell my clients that they are allowed to be miserable for a maximum of two hours per day. Then they have to do something they enjoy, call a friend or work on some of the techniques in Part IV. You can have a good life right now; you don't have to wait to be "cured."

Is therapy going to take years out of your life? I cannot give you a definitive answer because the answer depends on you. It depends on how hard you work, how regularly you attend, your willingness to face past events and your honesty and commitment to recognize and attack your own problems. You can do a great deal of the work on your own outside of your therapeutic sessions. If you are willing to invest the time, your therapy will proceed faster.

You have control over your therapy just as you have control over your life. You can speed up your emotional healing the way other people speed up their physical healing—with a positive attitude. Some people are up and around working and playing three weeks after surgery, while after the same surgery it may take takes other people six or eight weeks to do even simple tasks. And I am sure you have heard patients who recovered quickly say things like: "This is not very serious." or "I'll be up in no time. I'm not going to let this get me down." or "I'll fool that doctor; doctors don't know what they are talking about."

Your attitude determines how long you will take to work through the effects of your sexual abuse. It could take six months or several years, depending on how long you choose to have it take. How long do you want it to go on? Pick a time limit you feel is reasonable. Then keep telling yourself that you will be finished in that amount of time. *You* know what happened to you and how long it will help you to heal better than anyone, including your therapist.

My therapist told me my therapy would be finished in six months. I felt very uncomfortable about that limit; I was tense and anxious inside. I later uncovered more memories that showed that my abuse had occurred over a period of five years and that there were many events that had not yet surfaced when my therapist set the limit. My intuition and my body told me that six months was not realistic. It took approximately a year longer than my therapist's estimate because I had so many repressed events to bring to consciousness—or perhaps because I hung on to the pain longer than necessary.

As impossible as it may seem now, you can reach a stage I call "So what." During my therapy, I consulted the head of the psychiatric department of a major hospital in Salt Lake City for a second opinion because I was so distressed. He told me that I needed to continue to release the emotions and that I would reach a point where I could just say "So what" about my abuse. "So what!" I screamed at him. "How can I ever say 'So what' to having been raped, beaten and tortured by my own father? It's very easy for you to say but you haven't been through it." He calmly pointed out that my abuse happened over thirty years ago and said that the memories were coming out because it was long past time for me to let it all go.

I was furious at his callousness. But he turned out to be right. A little over a year later, I told my therapist I was *bored* by the stream of abusive memories I was still uncovering. Even though they were each somewhat different, the horror and fear were gone. I had released my fury, my hatred, my pain, my sadness and my fear, and I could truly say, "So what" to the whole business. While I continued to work on some of the residual patterns, I could be calm and analytical, even if an unpleasant memory popped up.

I am not the only one to whom this has happened. I promise you that with work and the passage of time, it will happen to you too.

Only you can tell how long it will take to heal to the point where you can continue growing on your own. And while you should never push yourself beyond what feels safe for you, you should set a reasonable goal with your therapist and work towards it. Your therapy will become easier as you progress, and the revelations and emotions will become less painful. The quality of your life will improve, and one day you will realize you are really living for the first time.

> *It is better to light one small candle*
> *than to curse the darkness.*
> Confucius

5. I keep having flashbacks about my abuse. Will they ever stop?

Yes. Your flashbacks will disappear when enough of your memory of the abuse has returned to allow you to deal with the repressed emotions and to accept the truth of what happened to you.

Flashbacks are perhaps the most frightening aftermath of physical and sexual abuse, especially if the survivor does not understand what is happening. During a flashback, the survivor reexperiences a traumatic event that has been repressed, wiped from memory, because of extreme emotional stress.

Ellen, one of my clients, is a stunning blond executive in her mid-thirties with a wonderful sense of humor who came to therapy certain that she was crazy. She had begun to have vivid mental images of her father abusing her when she was three years old. She had never suspected that she had been abused and was terrified by the visions and the feelings they aroused in her. She described the flashbacks as pictures that would force themselves into her head, usually in the evening, while she was still awake. At first they were just brief flashes, as if she were looking at a still photo, and she sometimes was not even sure what she was seeing. But after a couple of months the visions became more distinct, lasted longer and portrayed the movement and the words of her father's rape.

When she started therapy, Ellen did not want to believe that her visions were real because she would have to give up the myth she had created of having parents who loved her. But as the flashbacks supplied more of the pieces of the abuse she had repressed, she could no longer deny the reality of what her mind was telling her. And as she accepted the truth and began to assimilate it into her understanding, Ellen's flashbacks started to disappear.

Ellen's condition is a classic example of post-traumatic stress syndrome. Post traumatic stress syndrome was originally diagnosed during wartime when soldiers, subjected to extreme stress during battle, would forget all or part of their combat experiences only to recall those experiences through flashbacks months or years later. Prisoners of war who were tortured, such as those in Vietnam, frequently repressed the horror until they returned home. Then their minds brought it to consciousness through flashbacks and nightmares. People may experience this syndrome who are subjected to so much stress that their minds cannot cope, such as victims of natural disasters, witnesses to gruesome accidents, and victims of violent crimes.

Recently therapists have found that victims of child physical or sexual abuse exhibit symptoms of post-traumatic stress syndrome and many have started use this diagnosis for insurance purposes, instead of using labels which carry a more damaging stigma. The only difference in the symptoms between tortured prisoners of war and abused children is that children's memories seem to be repressed for a longer time, probably because childhood events have a more traumatic effect, so the memories do not surface until the children are old enough to cope with them.

When people experience such intense fear, terror and helplessness that their minds are unable to cope, the mind shuts off and provides a temporary oblivion from the feelings and the memory until a time when they are able to handle them. This defense mechanism is a healthy one; the person is saved from insanity and is able to continue functioning. This "time-out" gives the person a chance to grow stronger and to obtain some distance from the traumatic event so that the impact is not as overpowering.

During the period of amnesia, the mind heals unconsciously even though the person is not aware of the repressed event. When I was about fourteen, I read the book *Sybil*, the story of a girl tortured by her mother until she could only cope by creating multiple personalities. I read that book over and over, fascinated, even though I could not remember my own torture. I believe that book had a substantial impact on my subconscious; my mind knew that if Sybil could get better, so could I. I can see that many things in my life prepared me subconsciously to recover the memories of my abuse and healed me so that I could face the horror with less disruption in my adult life.

When the flashbacks come, it means you are ready to handle the memories. Although flashbacks can be frightening, they are a healthy sign that you are now prepared to cope with the trauma. Our minds are wonderful mechanisms; they know when we are strong enough to face repressed events and they provide us with bits and pieces of those events small enough for our conscious minds to digest a little at a time. Although some people see an entire event in flashback, most experience only small segments at first and do not recover the whole picture until much of the emotional impact has already been released.

While the impact of flashbacks varies from person to person, many people describe the sensation as one of "reliving" the experience. They feel as though they are actually back in the situation. This does not mean you will feel the physical pain to the same extent that you felt it when it was happening. But you may feel the emotions you felt—the fear, the anger, the betrayal, the sadness, the helplessness—just as you did when you were being abused. It is the emotional impact of these flashbacks that victims find so threatening.

You may be asking whether you "need" to have flashbacks. No, flashbacks are not an essential part of the healing process and many victims never have them. You can recover the memories and emotions of your abuse through hypnosis or dreams, or by remembering your abuse in therapy or by yourself. However, flashbacks are a natural process and are safe because your mind is telling you that you no longer need the defense of amnesia. Whatever method you use to uncover the trauma, you must recover enough of the memories and the emotions that accompanied your abuse to understand what happened, to accept the reality and to release the emotions so that they will not continue to affect your life.

The most harmful effect of having repressed memories and emotions is the fact that they "leak" out in ways that damage your relationships and your life without your knowing it. Your suppressed sadness and wish to die when you were being abused may make you depressed and suicidal in your adult life and you will not know why. The repressed fear and helplessness during your abuse may subconsciously impel you to repeat the pattern of your abuse by marrying someone who abuses you, by putting yourself in a position to be raped as an adult, or by abusing your own child.

Your subconscious mind will be trying to control the fear and the feeling of powerlessness you felt as a child, but you will not be aware of it. Even though you are not aware of the memories and emotions you have repressed, they affect your behavior. Repression is an unnatural state of mind and what is repressed is a poison which festers until it is released. Your suppressed memories must be released from your mind, just as a physical infection must be expelled from your body if you are to reach a state of health.

It takes a tremendous amount of energy to repress memories and emotions. People who recover their memories and deal with the emotions report that their minds are clearer and that they feel lighter and have more energy. When people with multiple personality disorder are integrated, they find that they can think in ways they never could before; it takes them a while to cope with the fact that they no longer feel "heavy" and tired. The energy used to keep memories out of your consciousness is energy that is lost for other purposes. Many survivors of abuse discover a creative energy they never knew they had once their minds no longer have to conceal old memories. They cultivate unsuspected talents in art and music and embark on university studies or graduate programs they never considered before. I doubt that I would have written this book or any other book if I had not released the memories of my abuse.

Survivors frequently ask whether it is necessary for them to see every detail of every abusive incident. The answer is *no* for most people. But the number and intensity of the memories you have to expose is totally individual and there is no right or wrong. If you have endured many abusive incidents over a period of years, it is usually sufficient to recover memories of several incidents that exemplify the course of abuse. Some survivors are able to heal by seeing only indistinct visions of what happened, as long as they are able to discharge the emotions. Others experience lifelike memories in vivid color, complete with sounds and smells.

You will be able to tell when you have recovered enough because the flashbacks will diminish and the painful emotions will subside. Even if you have an occasional flashback later on, you will not experience the violent emotions but will say to yourself, "Oh, that again. What can I learn from it?" It will just be an additional piece of information you can plug into the puzzle of your life.

How long the flashbacks continue depends on your own situation—how long you were abused, how old you were, how quickly you are able to adapt to the knowledge of your situation: how easily you can deal with the repressed emotions. In most cases, the flashbacks may occur over a few months or a couple of years. Although a few people who have been abused for several years find that the flashbacks continue for a longer time, they report that the emotional impact of the flashbacks diminishes considerably. Each person is different; your own mind will provide what you need to know and what you can handle in a time frame that is right for you. Trust in the ability of your mind to protect you—it has for a long time.

There are ways to help you handle the flashbacks. If you realize that flashbacks are a natural part of your healing process, they will not seem as frightening. Each flashback has something to teach you which you need to know, either about what happened to you or how you felt about it. So when they come, even though what you are seeing is certainly not pleasant, do your best to relax. Prepare yourself by telling yourself several times every day: "I let go of the past quickly and easily. I have survived the past and my abuse. I don't live there any more. I am an adult and I can help the child part of me through this. I have survived and I will survive this."

Know that you can control the flashback and that you can cut it off if you want. But if your mind has decided that you are ready to see something, it is better to just let it flow. Although the time may seem long while the flashback is going on, you will find that the actual time is very short, only seconds, like a dream. The most important thing to remember is that the flashback is only a *thought*. You have already survived the reality, when you were a child and far weaker than you are now. You can survive the thought.

Sometimes children faint or feel as if they are having a heart attack while they are being abused. I had convulsions from the beatings and torture my father inflicted. I was terrified that if I relived the memory of those convulsions I would have them again. It took a long time for me to allow myself to relive that experience, but when I relived it, I did not have the convulsions.

Geri, who was beaten, raped and turned into a child prostitute by her father, had an even more frightening experience to face. Her father had beaten her to a point of unconsciousness so that she was actually dead for a couple of minutes. She was terrified of reliving that experience because she feared she might never come out of it. But Geri had multiple personality disorder and needed to relive that experience in order to integrate one of her personalities. She finally summoned the courage to relive it with the help of her therapist, and she survived.

I do not know of any case where someone died of a flashback. I do know that our fear of reexperiencing past pain is always far worse than the experience itself. We have an incredibly strong survival instinct and our minds will not allow us to see or relive anything that would kill us. Does it make sense that our minds would protect us from the reality and then allow us to perish from recovering the memory?

After you experience the flashback, write down everything you remember about what happened and how you felt about it. Writing it down is a good way to release your emotions and will help you put it into perspective. If you are seeing a therapist, you will have a record of what occurred to discuss at your next session. And if you are only receiving incomplete flashes of incidents, you will be better able to piece them together if you have written the details down.

It also helps to discuss the flashback with your therapist, and/or your partner or friend. Your emotional reaction to what you have experienced may be powerful and it is helpful to have someone with whom you can talk. I strongly advise against keeping it all to yourself and isolating yourself from sources of help. The emotions evoked by flashbacks can be overwhelming, especially those of depression and rage. You should not try to handle those feelings alone.

The most important thing to remember is that the flashbacks will not last forever. They will stop, and they will stop in much less time than the actual abuse you have already survived. You are dealing with a thought of a long-past event that is trapped in your mind. Once that thought is released, it can no longer hurt you; you will be free.

There's only one corner of the universe
you can be certain of improving;
and that's your own self.
Aldous Huxley

6. Will I ever be able to enjoy sex?

Happily, the answer is an unequivocal "Yes," although it may not seem possible to you right now.

If you have been sexually abused, you have been through a terrible experience which may have made you feel that any sexual act is ugly and repulsive. For most victims, their abuse is their first experience with sex, and so their only picture of an act that should be beautiful and loving is smeared with violence, anger and hate. Many victims have an intense fear and aversion to being touched. Others see the face of their abuser whenever they try to make love. Many women experience pain with intercourse, even though their doctors can find no physical cause for it. Female victims may be frigid and males impotent.

Some victims unknowingly take their anger and fear out on them-selves. A large number of victims, male and female, try to control their overpowering anxiety about sex by being the aggressors, the ones in control. Nancy lived near me in an expensive Brentwood house and became a close friend when we started junior high school. She was sweet and loving, movie star attractive, and I felt lucky to have her as a friend. I knew something was wrong in her family. I had seen her father brutally beat her, sometimes in front of me when I was spending the night, and other times she would telephone, sobbing. Her mother was a would-be actress who pushed Nancy to attain the success that she had never achieved and who often screamed in front of anyone present that Nancy was stupid, a slut and a whore. I could not understand why she said such things about Nancy, but I do now.

I should have known by the way Nancy and I were drawn to each other what her father was doing to her; we shared similar experiences. But because I could not remember my own abuse, I was blind to what was happening with Nancy. When I went to college, Nancy went to New York and I later heard that she was a call girl. I refused to believe the rumors. I could not imagine my friend, the girl with whom I shared my innermost secrets, who sat up with me until all hours fantasizing about our boyfriends and the lives we would have when we escaped from our homes, who was always there when I needed her, selling herself on the other side of the country.

When I became aware of my own abuse in my early forties and became a therapist, I began to learn more about women who shared Nancy's reaction to sexual abuse. I learned that *all* of the girls who were runaways and prostitutes in two separate Utah institutions had been sexually abused and that similar statistics are being reported all over the country.

In Barbra Streisand's powerful movie *Nuts,* she portrays a woman from a wealthy background who becomes a call girl. When she kills a client while he is attempting to rape her, her mother and stepfather try to convince a court to declare her insane in order to avoid the publicity of a murder trial. During Barbra's fight to prove her sanity, her lawyer, played by Richard Dreyfus, suddenly guesses what happened to her and forces her stepfather to admit that he sexually abused her from the time she was five years old. The film made it clear that the woman played by Streisand became a prostitute so that *she* could control sex, she could have it when she wanted to and with whom—she was rather choosey— and under her conditions. And she did not have to become emotionally involved with anyone; that would be too threatening. After all, she had loved her stepfather and look what *he* did.

Sadly, this movie is based on too many true life situations. Many young boys and girls escape from their abusive homes and become prostitutes, trying to overcome the feelings of helplessness they felt when they were being raped. Some women do not go quite so far as to sell their bodies but, instead, find a string of men who dominate and hurt them, mentally if not physically, and who remind them unconsciously of their abusers. These women obtain no pleasure from sex; they are reenacting their childhood abuse.

We are destined to repeat the patterns of our most painful experiences unless we look them clearly in the face and release our blocked feelings about them. We walk into the same traps, the same horrors, unconsciously thinking that if we can just do it again, we can make it come out differently. Our minds believe that somehow if we have a chance to relive the experience, we will be in control and we can master the anxiety we carry with us. I also suspect that replaying our abuse is a way to remind us of the facts we refuse to face.

Rebecca was a survivor of Auschwitz, one of the worst of the Nazi death camps. As a Jewish child, she was beaten and used sexually by any Nazi who wanted her. After her release, she was brought to New York where she put her past behind her. She married well, had children, and I would like to say "lived happily ever after." But she has been raped *five* times, which is extreme, even for New York. Rebecca never talks of her concentration camp experiences, but they live within her and eat away her pretense of contentment. Until she deals with the memories of her past, she can expect the acts which terrorized her to be repeated.

It is difficult to understand why we would place ourselves in situations which repeat the worst part of our experiences. But Freud and more modern therapists say that by repeating frightening events, we are trying to control them, and by controlling them we control our anxiety. We can only put these patterns to rest if we are aware of them and if we can release the emotions stored with our blocked-out memories.

Most women do not have such extreme reactions to their abuse and outwardly appear to live fairly normal lives. But they may fight with their husbands after intercourse, or accuse their lovers of wanting only their bodies, or have pain related to intercourse or their menstrual periods that baffles their gynecologists. Men may find women who use them, thus confirming their image of how they were used before, or, if they were abused by a male, they may find themselves attracted to other men or become the object of homosexual advances.

Whatever the ways you have unconsciously devised to cover up the effects of your abuse, you can change the patterns and you can be free. You can free yourself from the prison of your patterns by understanding what you are doing and by examining the emotions and memories of your past. You can do this in therapy or by yourself by looking closely and objectively at your harmful behavior and deciding to stop it. You have control over your conduct and you can decide to eliminate actions you do not like. Your own work, coupled with therapy, can help you break out of the patterns which affect your relationships.

So how long will it be before you can eradicate your old patterns and enjoy your sexual relationships? There are no definitive answers as to how long it will take before your relationships and your sex life will be enjoyable. I have seen abuse victims work through their feelings about their abuse and change their attitudes toward sex in six months, and I have seen people hang on to their pain for several years.

But you don't have to wait to enjoy sex until you have worked out all of your problems. There are some practical things you can do on your own to improve your lovemaking while you are going through therapy or even before. If thoughts of your abuse invade your mind or if you sometimes see your lover as your abuser—a common phenomenon—you need to work on putting your lover and your abuser into separate boxes in your mind.

First of all, you will want to try a desensitization process, one that will make you view lovemaking as something totally different from sexual abuse. Just by calling the two acts by different names can help you make a distinction in your mind. *Abuse* is an act which is forced on you, either physically or psychologically. It is performed by people who are not equals; the one who is dominant and powerful takes advantage of someone who is weaker and helpless. On the other hand, *lovemaking* is a voluntary, joyful act between equals who want to give and receive pleasure mutually. It is an act of tenderness, gentleness, kindness and caring, rather than an act of violence and coercion. Sometimes abuse victims have a hard time making these distinctions because they have only known abuse.

If you have problems differentiating between lovemaking and abuse, then you might try the technique introduced by sex therapists Masters and Johnson: stop having sex and start learning to be affectionate and tender. Explain to your partner that you are having trouble with sex because of your abuse and that you want to experiment with some ways which will make it more comfortable and enjoyable for you.

Whether you have a spouse or a new lover, if you want to improve your lovemaking, you must be able to talk to your partner and tell him or her what you are feeling. Your partner should be delighted that you are working on ways to improve your life and should understand that if you are able to find more joy in lovemaking, he or she will also experience more joy. If your partner is not understanding or is not willing to work to help you obtain more pleasure from lovemaking, then you are still in an abusive relationship and you should seriously consider finding another partner, or asking this partner to accompany you to your therapy sessions.

You and your partner should spend time kissing and caressing each other, giving each other massages and looking into each other's eyes, without worrying about intercourse for several weeks, or months if necessary. Listen to music, hug and kiss in a movie theatre, have picnics and fondle each other in the grass. Try to see how much pleasure you can give each other with just a gentle touch of your hand, your lips or your tongue. Your purpose is to *really* get to know each other, to know by feeling just what the other person likes. And the aim is also to have fun, to laugh, to tease, to play.

It is important that you and your partner talk about what you like and what you don't like. In fact, it is crucial for the survivor to describe specific acts, kisses or touches which ignite memories of the abuse, so they can be avoided. You must teach your partner to make love to you in a way that is special and unique so that you will not flash back on what you want to forget.

Later, when you feel really comfortable with your lover as an individual person and as someone who is really concerned with your pleasure, then you can go on to intercourse—but always under the same rules. Make sure your lover avoids positions that are painful or remind you of your abuse. Your goal is always to be gentle, loving and playful.

Sometimes people get a mental picture of their abuser while they are making love. Again this is a common phenomenon that will disappear over time. But for the present, you can avoid this problem by simply keeping a light on when you make love. By focusing on the face of the person you care for, you usually can block out any face from the past. An added benefit of using a light is that it allows you and your lover to watch each other's reactions and experience each other's pleasure, as well as making you both more sensitive to each other's needs and responses. You will find that your relationship will be closer and more sensual than if you are hidden by the dark.

If you continue to visualize your abuser's face, you should stop making love and tell your lover what is happening. Sometimes if you talk it out, it will stop. I also found it effective to have my husband talk to me sometimes while we were making love. It helped me focus on him and allowed me to separate what we were doing from what my father did. Sometimes I told myself mentally, "This is Jim. This is Jim." until I could bring my train of thought back into the present.

Another technique is to make love under circumstances that are completely different from those of your abuse. If you were abused at night, make love in the morning or during the day. If you were abused in bed, make love on the sofa or the floor. Set the scene so that you cannot connect anything that is happening now with what happened to you before.

Since most victims suffered intense feelings of helplessness during their sexual abuse, they may not feel comfortable with lovemaking unless they are in control. Instead of fighting these feelings, you can use them to make your love life more enjoyable. Again, you should discuss your concern with your partner and agree that, for a while, you will be on top. For variety, you can both lie on your sides or sit or stand up. But the victim should avoid being in a position of submission, of helplessness. When you have experienced pleasure for a couple of months and have more trust in your partner and the act of lovemaking, then you can try positions where you are not in control and see how you feel about them. But don't push yourself and don't feel that you have to like any particular position. The basic rule of lovemaking is never to do anything unless you *both* enjoy it.

Other powerful techniques such as meditation and mindfulness, described in Part V, are effective for learning to keep your mind focused on the here and now. Although these techniques are designed to improve all facets of your life, they should also be useful in maintaining your concentration on your present acts of lovemaking.

How much longer do you have to keep working on not remembering? Probably not very long. Once you establish a relationship of trust and intimacy with your partner, you will have already separated your partner from your abuser in your mind. You will begin to find that you *know* you are living in the present, that the past is really past, and that your lover is the one you love—a new and unique person who treats you with love and respect. You will know that now is different and that your abuser is an aberration, a sick and unhappy person who does not represent the majority of people in your world and is a relic of the past.

> *Enjoy yourself. This is the last and the most important suggestion. If you are not enjoying yourself, you are not doing a good job for yourself, your company or your family.*
> James Fadiman, *Be All That You Are*

7. Did I deserve to be abused?

Absolutely not. This is one question which has a definite answer. But your feelings of being bad or of having done something to deserve it are universal; people who have been abused feel that it would not have happened if they were good. You may feel ugly, dirty, worthless, shameful, cheap and even evil, but these feelings are based on your confusion and misperceptions of your abuse.

Although these feelings are totally without basis in fact, they are understandable. Being abused is so terrible, so shocking, so painful, that we have to try to make some sense of it. We ask: "Why is this happening to me?" There is no rational answer. If a parent or another relative is abusing us, the feelings of confusion are even stronger. We cannot understand why someone who is supposed to love and protect us is doing such destructive things to us. When we are being abused, we do not know that our abusers may also have been abused, and we do not know that the abuse comes from their own sickness. We try to figure out what *we* did to cause it. But there is no explanation. So we assume the reason is that we are bad. We don't know how, but we must be bad, or they would not be doing this to us. We draw the obvious conclusion that we must be so bad and so unlovable that we somehow deserve to be punished.

This explanation is our attempt to make sense out of chaos. Without an explanation, we must believe in a world so senseless, so arbitrary and out of control that we could not bear to live in it. If the world is that dangerous and without meaning, we must go crazy or die. The only alternative is to find a meaning—even if it is one that hurts us. Since these terrible acts seemed like punishment, and we have heard that bad children are punished, we draw the obvious conclusion.

Young children think that they are the center of the world and that they make everything happen. If they cry, mommy comes running. If they spit strained peas on daddy's tie, he yells. Even their toilet behavior is a big deal to their parents. So children believe that whatever happens, they are the cause. Children who are abused when they are young naturally think that did something to made it happen. Since the experience is so terrible, they assume that they must have done something equally terrible to deserve it. And so, when we grow up, we carry with us the subconscious conclusion that we did something terribly wrong or that we are terrible people.

Our irrational conclusion may be bolstered by what our abusers tell us. Most abusers shift the blame to others so that they can avoid looking at their own behavior. Often the easiest person to accuse is the victim. Abusers say things based on their own distorted feelings. Although what they say is untrue, we are all too ready to believe them because we already think we are bad. And so we are victimized both physically and mentally.

My father, being a writer, used very flowery language. He told me that his repeated sexual abuse of me was all my fault and that I lured him to his doom. He said the way I looked made him unable to resist me and that I was a "child of the devil." When I asked my mother, who was aware of the abuse, to take me away, *she* also told me that it was all my fault and that I was destroying the family. I believed them, after all they were my parents, the only ones I had. And for forty years deep down I really believed I was a child of the devil, beyond help or redemption.

A friend of mine, whom I will call Geri, is recovering from multiple personality disorder after fourteen years of severe sexual and physical abuse by her father. He constantly called her a slut and a whore, and he treated her like one, using her himself and selling her to his friends. She accepted his words as true and thought of herself as cheap and dirty.

As children, and sometimes even as adults, we tend to accept what our parents say as the truth. We have no reason to believe otherwise. When we are children, we are too young to understand that our parents have problems. We have to believe that our parents are O.K. and able to care for us, or we would be terrified because, as children, we cannot take care of ourselves. Or we may believe what our parents and other adults tell us because we look up to them and cannot believe that they would lie to us. But the sad fact is that they do. People say destructive things because of their own pain and problems. And abusers try to place the blame on anyone they can to avoid looking at their own behavior. (If I was a child of the devil, what did my father think *he* was?)

And so victims of abuse turn their anger on themselves. "There must have been something I did to make it happen." "There must have been something I could have done to prevent it or stop it." Brenda, an AMAC (Adults Molested As Children) in a therapy group, blamed herself for more than thirty years for not preventing or stopping her abuse, even though it started when she was *two years old!*

The truth is that there was absolutely nothing you could have done as a child, no matter what your age. You were coerced by someone more powerful. You did what you could. The most important thing is that *you survived*. Although the abuse I have described might seem too terrible to bear, the people involved did survive. We have not only survived, but we have gotten help and greatly improved our self-image and our lives.

Even though you could not stop the acts of your abusers, you can control your reactions to those acts now. Right now take the time to picture yourself at the time you were being abused. See whether there was really anything you did to make it happen or anything you could have done to prevent it. Remember, you must see yourself as you were then, not older and wiser as you are now.

I used this exercise when I was in therapy. I tried to picture how I could have seduced my father when I was four. I studied old family photographs of myself with my long red pigtails, freckles and spindly legs, so I could remember clearly how I looked. Then I exaggerated the situation in my mind, imagining that I had on makeup and a sexy nightgown and was vamping my father. Despite the pain, my mental pictures made me laugh. I saw clearly that there was no way I could have been sexy at four and that there was nothing I could have done to justify his conduct.

For women who may have been older and appeared to be actually sexy, I would like to clarify what I have said: Your appearance does not mean you caused your rape or abuse. If it did, no normally developed attractive woman would ever be allowed to walk down the street. It is up to abusers to control their impulses, and the responsibility for their acts rests solely on them.

If a friend, neighbor, teacher, relative or even a stranger is the abuser, our feelings of worthlessness may be the same as if our parents or stepparents were involved. We still tend to try to find a reason for the horror by blaming ourselves. These feelings are intensified if we tell our parents or someone else and they do not believe us, or if they tell us what happened is disgraceful and we should keep silent about it. We turn the shame we feel inward and see ourselves as shameful.

Later we make many adult decisions as the result of our abuse. Some survivors who were abused over a period of years become perfectionists and superachievers. They act on their childhood belief that "If only I can be good enough," "If only I can get it right," "If only I can please him, he'll love me and the abuse will stop." And in their adult life, they can never please themselves. No success is good enough.

Adult workaholics are trapped in a pattern established by abuse. When they were children, they were constantly watching their abuser, trying to keep the abuse from happening, keeping the abuse secret from their parents and desperately attempting to excel in school and go on with the "normal" part of their lives. Now as adults, these victims are terrified of not having enough to do. They think that only by keeping busy and constantly alert can they survive.

From their inability to stop their abuse, other victims conclude that they are helpless and that all their efforts in life will be worthless. They never try to get what they want because they decided, based on their abuse, that it is futile.

I lived for over forty years with the certainty that there was something wrong with me, some flaw that made my father abuse me. I was always looking for this flaw, always believing that other people saw it but I couldn't. If someone was rude to me, it was always my fault. I went through all of the possible explanations: I was bad, evil, a child of the devil; I didn't know how to act; I was too angry; I must have done something awful in a past life; I was being punished by God. I was haunted by a memory of my father saying he hated me and wanted me dead. There had to be a reason for all this. It took me a long time to realize that I had a very sick father and that there wasn't anything wrong with me. While I have accepted responsibility for my own life and work every day to make myself a better person, I now have placed the responsibility for my abuse where it belongs—on my abuser.

Victims make many other negative decisions. But the overall devastating result of abuse is that we develop low self-esteem. We believe we are bad, and we turn our pain and anger on ourselves, causing depression and sometimes explosions of rage. The side effects of low self-esteem are as damaging as the pain our feelings cause. When we feel we are bad or worthless, we usually act that way. Other people begin to see us the way we see ourselves and they treat us as worthless. Being treated as worthless only makes us feel worse about ourselves and so we act worse and the destructive cycle continues.

A woman who feels worthless and who is trying to find a job will probably do things that will defeat her attempts. She may arrive late for the interview, not because she plans to, but "because something absolutely unavoidable happened." Or she may be overly apologetic about her qualifications for the job: "Gee, what I did in my last job wasn't very important. I just did what they told me to do." Her low self-esteem makes her feel that she doesn't deserve the job she wants and keeps her from getting it.

Another symptom of low self-esteem is establishing disastrous relationships. A man who thinks he is worthless may go through a string of women who all cheat on him. He will not be able to understand why he keeps finding women who hurt him. The answer is that he is being treated exactly the way he sees himself, the way he expects to be treated.

It is a basic principle of psychology that good self-esteem is the key to a happy and successful life. All of the self-help books teach you ways to learn to love yourself. You can read the books and work on your self-esteem in therapy. Or you can start doing it right now yourself. Learning to love yourself is simple and you have a head start. You know *why* you feel worthless, and you can change your thinking about what happened to you and how you feel about yourself.

There are many ways of improving your self-esteem, but these are the basic ones:

- Recognize that you need to change what you think about yourself. Be clear in your mind what you really think about yourself and how you want to change it.
- Be aware of the thoughts you have about yourself. Learn to recognize the negative things you think and say to yourself so you can change them.
- Stop the negative thoughts by just saying "STOP!" to yourself whenever you put yourself down. Replace negative thoughts with positive ones, usually the exact opposite of the ones you started to think. Change "I can't do that," to "I can do that; it's easy." Or switch "That was a dumb thing to do" to "Hmmm, I made a mistake. Everybody makes mistakes. How can I learn from it?" And the "I am bad, evil, worthless" thoughts should immediately be turned off and replaced with "I am a good person" or "I am lovable." You don't have to believe the positive thoughts to make them work. Your mind accepts the truth of what you tell it.
- Spend some time each day giving yourself positive messages. These are sometimes called positive affirmations and several are listed in Part V. You can also pat yourself on the back for things that go well during the day and mentally review your successes at night. But be careful of placing too much emphasis on achievement. You are a valuable and worthwhile person no matter what you do. Everyone

makes mistakes. Everyone gets angry. Everyone does things they later regret. Give yourself a break. Forgive yourself and allow yourself to be human.

I do not know of any survivor of physical or sexual abuse who does not have low self-esteem. I also do not know of any child who did anything to deserve being abused. I do not think you are the unique exception. But you must carefully examine your situation after some time has passed and draw your own conclusion. You will come to the realization that you did nothing to cause your abuse; you really are a worthwhile person.

> *There is nothing either good or bad,*
> *but thinking makes it so.*
> William Shakespeare, *Hamlet*

8. What if I was abused by more than one person. I must have done something to deserve that?

The answer is still no. The amount of your suffering may be greater than someone who has been abused by one person and you may have greater problems trusting people, but you did not do anything to deserve it.

Unfortunately the tendency of victims to place the blame on themselves increases when more than one person has abused them. When victims of multiple abuse try to understand why it happened to them, they have a harder time understanding that several people were sick rather than just one. It is easier to believe that if all of these people are abusing you, it must be because you are bad or are doing something to deserve it. It is hard for a child who is being abused by several people to believe that the abuse is not a punishment, even when the child becomes an adult.

A child sees herself as the center of the universe. If most of the people she knows in her world hurt her, she concludes that she must somehow deserve it. She does not know that there is a larger, saner world outside. She only knows what she experiences and she learns to hate herself and to distrust others.

The tragedy is that cases where children have been sexually abused by more than one person are not uncommon. One reason is that people who have been abused attract other abused people to them, and abused parents often attract partners who continue the chain of abuse. It is not unusual for an abused woman to become involved with or to marry a string of wife-beaters. And it is also not unusual for a mother who was abused to marry men who abuse children. Cases of children being beaten and sexually abused by their own fathers and then by stepfathers are all too frequent. Mothers who divorce to escape an abusive marriage often find themselves in a similar situation with their next husband—unless they resolve their own problems in therapy.

Sadly, not enough parents resolve their own problems and thousands of children suffer abuse from more than one adult. Lori, a dark-haired, extremely intelligent pixy, was sent to the adolescent unit of the mental health center on several occasions. I especially liked her because of her mature insight into the problems of other teenagers in her group and her willingness to help them. Lori had been physically and sexually abused by two stepfathers, an uncle and a couple of other men. Her self-esteem was understandably at rock-bottom and her anger would burst into violence at the slightest provocation.

Often abuse is a family pattern in which all or most of the members participate. George who came from a family of 18 children had a father who physically and sexually abused all of the children almost from birth. As the children grew older, they began to abuse their younger siblings. So George was beaten and sodomized by his older brothers and sisters as well as by his father. He did not believe anything he did was very good and he was afraid he would be attacked when he walked down the street, even through his family was far away. He also had problems with his anger and violence. He was unaware that his family was not normal until he reached puberty and had a chance to see other families.

Steve was one of my favorites, perhaps because of his outrageous sense of humor. He cut his bright blond hair into a mohawk and swore obscenely with every breath. He carried knives, usually fake, and would do anything he could to offend and shock. He had been sodomized and abused by his father. He was taken out of his home when he was eight and placed for adoption. Because he was so appealing, a local television station selected Steve for one of its weekly spots on children available for adoption. He and a couple of other boys were adopted by a man who brutally beat and sodomized all of them.

How can this happen? The answer is certainly *not* that these children were bad. But part of the answer is that victims tend to be victimized. We have all seen children who are picked on by other children because they whine and kick up such a fuss when they are teased. The more they cry, the more they are picked on. This behavior certainly does not make them bad, but their conduct brings on the very acts they wish to avoid. Kids who are picked on usually have low self-esteem and do not know how to act differently. Once they are taught to ignore their tormentors or to fight back, they are no longer tormented and their role as a victim ends.

This situation is similar to that of the child who has been abused at a very young age. As a result of the initial abuse, the child develops low self-esteem and acts like a victim. People who think they are worthless are treated that way, and children who are victims behave in a very subtle, unconscious way that attracts abusers. The child is not bad. The child is not even aware of his or her actions. In most instances, no one would take advantage of such behavior. A healthy adult would try to help an abused child heal. But if the child is exposed to an adult who has a propensity for abuse, the child is vulnerable to being abused again.

I want to make it clear that the responsibility for the abuse is on the adult, not the child. The adult knows what is right and what is wrong and should have the control necessary to avoid abuse no matter what the child does. But the sad fact is that there are enough adults in the world who have been abused as children to provide opportunities for multiple abuse.

I used to wonder how anyone who had been through such repeated acts of violence could survive or ever get well. But in less than a year I have seen such tremendous improvement in these adolescents who experienced multiple abuse that I am now firmly convinced that love and therapy can heal any type of wound. These kids are learning to break the patterns of their abuse and to understand that they do not have to be victims anymore. As they gain confidence and feelings of self worth, they no longer send out signals of helplessness or victimization.

I believe that we have a mechanism inside us that heals us mentally just as we have a mechanism that heals our physical wounds and diseases. Anyone can be healed who wants to be, and survivors of sexual abuse are excellent subjects for healing. We have been through so much pain that we will take any positive step to reduce that pain. And our motivation pulls us through.

Healing is a matter of reprogramming, of replacing negative thoughts about yourself with good ones, and of learning to trust people. It means recognizing and breaking the negative patterns of victimization and replacing them with a positive self-image. It also depends on recognizing that it is your abusers who are sick and that you coped in the best way you could at the time. Whatever the number of people who abused you as a child, you were in situations from which you could not escape. When you cannot control a situation, you are not responsible for it. Only when you are an adult do you have control and responsibility. And no matter how much abuse you suffered as a child or how many people were part of it, you did not cause it to happen and you are not to blame.

At this time of your life, when you are aware of residual feelings caused by your abuse, it is extremely important for you to work out your problems in therapy. If you have been abused by more than one person, your subconscious mind becomes convinced that everyone in the world is an abuser. And so you act as though everyone is an abuser. You may even unconsciously recreate the patterns of your abuse so that you allow people to victimize you. Or you may abuse others. The best way to break out of these patterns and to change the direction of your life is to work with a counselor. You will be amazed to find how much nicer people seem and how much easier your life will be.

> *Nothing happens to anybody*
> *that he is not fitted to bear.*
> Marcus Aurelius Antonius, Emperor of Rome,
> A.D. 121-180, *Meditations*

9. Was God punishing me?

Absolutely not.

But most abused children believe it. Even AMACs like myself often discover that deep down they believe God chose them for punishment. They often are not consciously aware of this belief but find out in therapy that it has affected their lives in a destructive way. Many abused children grow up hating or denying God because they think God hated and denied them. Or they may believe in a punitive, vengeful God whom they must appease. They fear a God who may without warning wreak his wrath upon them, the wrath they experienced from their abusers. Their fear paralyzes them and prevents them from being able to enjoy life.

Jimmy is a fifteen-year-old who is funny and attractive but acts like a six-year-old. He was physically and sexually abused by his stepfather and neglected by his mother. When he was six, Jimmy was taken away from his mother by the state and placed with his real father. He loved his father, even though his father beat him, and was devastated when his father died six years later. One day in therapy, Jimmy blurted out that he thought God was going to punish him. A few questions elicited Jimmy's firm conviction that his abuse was a punishment from God and that he would continue to be punished for the rest of his life. Jimmy also believed that he was under a special divine curse. He had concluded—from the fact that he was taken away from his mother when he was six and from his father by death six years later—that God would do something dreadful to him every six years. He lived in mortal fear of what catastrophe would befall him at the end of the next six years.

Jimmy's case is not unusual. Many abused children believe that God is punishing them, and many adults have an abused child inside their minds giving them the same distorted message. Where do children obtain this belief? From what they hear all around them. Even children of atheistic parents hear from their friends, from teachers at school, from books, from the media and from numerous other sources that there is a God and S/He loves and protects *good* little children. If a child is abused, she quickly concludes that God is not protecting her. If God could let this happen, S/He must not love her. If God does not love her, it must be because she is bad. Only a really bad little girl deserves such a punishment. Children are very good at drawing the wrong conclusions because they do not have the ability to analyze the situation or the information to challenge their fears.

Our beliefs are created by our childhood experiences. One member of an AMAC group denied being angry at God until she remembered a picture of Christ that hung on the wall at the foot of her bed. She was furious and shouted, "There was that picture at the foot of my bed, the bed where my father raped me night after night. He (Christ) didn't do diddley. I believe in God but I never thought Christ counted for much."

Children also make bargains with God that may plague them later. I used to become very anxious whenever I was happy and used hypnosis to find out the reason. I discovered I had made a bargain with God that I would suffer all of my life, if S/He would just let me live. Even as an adult, it took quite a bit of talking to myself to convince me that God would not hold a child to that kind of bargain.

When we are children, our images of God are often based on the authority figures in our lives, usually our fathers and mothers, or stepparents. Actually our impressions of God are more frequently based on our fathers, because we usually hear people refer to God in the masculine gender, although that is changing in some religions today. To a child, a father is Godlike—huge, all-knowing and all-powerful. Even though a child may hear in his synagogue or church that God is good and kind, the child will form an image of God based on the actions of his father. If the father beats or sexually abuses him or punishes him in an arbitrary way, the child will picture God as punitive and capricious and will live in fear of God's wrath.

When I was seven and still being abused, I used to wear a small white felt pin in the shape of a purse on my clothes every day. Inside it my parents found my handwritten note, "Please God, don't let me die." Was I writing to God or to my father-god who I hoped would read the message and stop what he was doing?

Most religions teach that God is omnipotent, in total control of the world, and that what happens in the world is His/Her will and is thus fair. But abuse is not fair. Children are unable to accept the concept that the world is not fair. Even adults have a great deal of difficulty swallowing this painful truth. So again the conclusion is reached that God must have a reason for allowing these terrible acts to occur. And the only apparent reason is that the child must be at fault.

The beliefs resulting from abuse haunt victims for the rest of their lives unless they are unmasked and challenged. Therapists sometimes fail to explore their clients' irrational beliefs about God because they are reluctant to impose their own beliefs on their clients or to get into the seeming quagmire of religion and spirituality. I do not believe victims of abuse can be totally healed unless their erroneous beliefs about God are corrected. Therapists help their clients correct other less harmful irrational beliefs and they should certainly not neglect to address beliefs that so totally pervade and color their clients' view of the world.

It is important for therapists to question clients on their beliefs about God and to help them revise those views that are detrimental to their wellbeing. While I respect a client's values, I do not hesitate to point out those which are thwarting the client's efforts to achieve happiness and success. People should have the chance to form their beliefs about God based on their own analysis of everything they have learned rather than on the nightmares of their childhood. A person who has created a frightening image of God based on childhood abuse has made an important decision based upon inadequate information. It is the duty of therapists to help their clients understand how they came to have their beliefs and to provide them with additional information to consider in reevaluating that belief.

When one client was asked if he believed in God, he replied only half jokingly, "Yes, God is waiting for me right around the corner—and He's heavily armed." That is hardly a belief for a therapist to ignore.

I reformulated my ideas about God as an adult, with the help of my therapist and my own adult logic. I came to the conclusion that if God is good and kind and loving as the religions of the world teach, S/He could not be involved in anything as ugly and horrible as child abuse. I cannot picture any form of God sitting in heaven directing such a scenario. I can believe, however, that humans who have been hurt and humiliated could take their hurt out on other humans, especially ones who are smaller and more helpless than themselves. But I cannot believe that God condones such conduct or includes that conduct as part of a heavenly design.

I believe that God has evolved as we have and that the God of the *New Testament* has become even more loving and forgiving than the God in the *Old* one. The Bible, 3 John says, "He that loveth not knoweth not God; for God is love." My experience is that the world is getting better and that people are learning to care and help each other more. More and more books and television programs are describing a New Age spirituality which espouses love and service to each other as its central principle. God seems to be showing us in many ways that the way to heal each other is through love and kindness, a message that is totally inconsistent with a God who deliberately wreaks savagery and sexual abuse on defenseless children.

It is too easy to place the blame for abuse on God. I believe sexual abuse is a human problem we have created and which we have to solve for ourselves. *We* have to take the responsibility for our failure to intervene and help all of the children who were raped, sodomized and brutalized for so many years. We have to take the responsibility for our puritanical ideas that prevented us from talking about things involving sex or unpleasantness; when adults refuse to discuss abuse, children feel they have nowhere to turn for help. And we have to take responsibility for our strict code that says we should not interfere with how parents raise their children. Our willingness to look the other way has allowed abuse to be passed on from generation to generation.

We human beings create pain out of our own pain and it is up to us to get ourselves out of it. I prefer that explanation to the one that concocts an evil force which we cannot see and cannot control, or an explanation which says we must be evil or have done something wrong. The latter explanation certainly could not apply to people molested in infancy. It would be convenient to just blame the whole mess on God and wait for Him/Her to clean it up. But it's our mess and *we* have to clean it up.

Most people who have been severely abused will need to reexamine their ideas of God and how the universe works. If you are a member of a church or synagogue, it would be helpful to discuss your views with your minister, rabbi or priest. The Catholic Church and the Church of Jesus Christ of Latter-Day Saints have some of the strictest prohibitions on premarital sex of any religion. However, in working with church officials to help my clients, I have found that the doctrines of both religions recognize that victims of sexual abuse are not to blame, that they remain pure; they are loved by God.

Most religions now have programs to help victims of abuse. One local church is paying for the therapy of one of my AMAC clients even though her abuse took place in another state. Even if you are not affiliated with any particular religion, you might want to talk to these people anyway or to friends of various faiths and read books about the world's religions to see how others view God so you can form your own opinion. But be selective about the people you choose and don't rely on just one person's opinion.

Your present perceptions of God and the universe are based on the horrors of your abuse. It is important for your growth and happiness to give up your idea of God-the-Monster just as you have, hopefully, given up your childhood fear of the bogeyman under your bed.

You have a fascinating adventure before you; you have the chance to find out what *you* really believe, without anyone telling you what you *should* believe. Learning about God and the universe and forming your own philosophy of life is a challenge that will lead you to explore many new and ideas and introduce you to many new friends. It will certainly alter your childhood view of an abusing God.

> *He that loveth not knoweth not God;*
> *for God is love.*
> 3 John, *The Bible*

10. What if I sometimes enjoyed what my abuser did to me?

Many victims of sexual abuse have deep feelings of guilt because they enjoyed some or all of the things their abusers did to them. Some victims felt close to their abusers, usually a parent or other relative, and liked being touched and treated as someone special. Others experienced orgasms which they may not have understood at the time and which left them feeling confused and out of control. But all of these victims were left with the same ominous questions: Did I cause it to happen? Did I participate because I enjoyed it? Am I bad, evil, a whore, a homosexual because I enjoyed it? The answer to all of these questions is a resounding "NO"!

Let's consider the case of Judy who was molested by her father, a mechanical engineer and outwardly a rigid, disapproving and undemonstrative man. When he began to come into Judy's bedroom at night, she was seven years old. He would caress her and croon to her that she was his special little girl. Soon he was slipping his hand under her pajamas and stroking her private parts and later he made her play with his. During the daytime, he brought Judy little gifts and protected her from any punishment or discipline by her mother. At first Judy loved her father's caresses and all of the attention she was receiving from him that she had missed before. But as the years passed and he became more demanding sexually, Judy's enjoyment changed to fear, anger and repulsion.

As an adult today, Judy is in therapy and is beginning to understand that she was not responsible for her father's sexual abuse. Judy has lived for years with the pain and guilt of thinking she was to blame for what her father did to her. She did not even know that what her father did to her at first was abuse because she liked it. Judy had to learn as an adult that she was not accountable because she had no control over what was being done to her and did not understand it. A child who does something to please an adult or to obtain love and affection from a family member is not responsible for his or her behavior. By law, any time an older person engages a younger, less knowledgeable person in sexual acts, the older person's conduct is considered sexual abuse.

You cannot give your consent to something you are too young to understand, either in law or common sense. And if you are forced to do something or you do it through fear of what will happen if you don't, you are still a victim of abuse and are not responsible for your acts. No one has to put a gun to your head. It is enough if you are a child and fear that you will be hurt or that you will not receive the care and approval that you need.

Judy believed her father would not do anything wrong because he was her father. His stroking of her felt good and she liked the attention and gifts. What little girl wouldn't like those things? It is the adult who is supposed to know what is right, the adult who is supposed to protect the child, and the father who is supposed to take care of his daughter, not the other way around.

Children are vulnerable and want love, especially from their parents. They will do almost anything to please their parents and to win their approval. Children cannot survive on their own and they know it. So they are at the mercy of their parents and other adults in their family.

A child can never be responsible for sexual abuse. Even if you liked it or begged your abuser to do it, the adult has the duty to know what is right and should have the ability to control his or her urges. Your abuser was the one who initiated the acts and played on your lack of knowledge of what was appropriate. You were not bad, evil or a whore; you were just a child who happened to live with a person who had serious problems and took them out on you. (At this point you may want to reread Question 7, *Did I deserve to be abused?*) You wanted what everyone wants, love and closeness, but your abuser only took what he or she wanted without regard for your feelings or needs. It is not wrong to feel love and closeness for a relative, even one who used you. As an adult, you can retain love for the nice things your abuser did and still hate what your abuser did to you physically and sexually.

Perhaps now you will allow yourself to understand that you were filled with love. You wanted to believe the best about everyone, especially your family. And you wanted to be good and to please. How can these things have made you bad? You concluded that you were bad because you needed to find a reason for the terrible things which were being done to you, and what was being done seemed like punishment. But your conclusion was erroneous. Now, if you really think about what your abuser was like, you will see that he or she had severe problems and that what was done to you was only one symptom of a dysfunctional personality.

Children are never bad. They may act badly if they are mistreated or neglected, but they are not bad. Children are naturally loving and they need love. Studies have shown that infants who are deprived of love and, especially of touch, die even if they are given adequate food, water and shelter. Research also has shown that children need attention and touch so desperately that if they cannot get love and positive gestures of affection, they will try to elicit negative strokes from their parents because this form of recognition is better than being ignored.[5]

57

You are not bad because you wanted to be loved, you are only normal. You were also unlucky in being in a place where someone took advantage of your normal needs. Your abuser was to blame, not you.

All suffering comes from wrong beliefs.
Buddha

11. What if I had an orgasm?

One of the most frightening experiences for a victim, especially a child, is to have an orgasm during sexual abuse. At the time a child first has this experience, he or she is usually in a situation of intense humiliation and often pain, being forced to do acts which are horrifying and repulsive in a condition of total helplessness. A child who is being abused usually maintains his or her sanity through feelings of anger and hatred toward the abuser.

All of a sudden the child experiences an alien feeling of intense pleasure, a feeling that may possess her entire body, causing tremors and convulsions. The child is terrified and confused. She does not know what this feeling is or why it has taken over her body. The child only knows that her body has betrayed her, that somehow her body is giving its consent and approval to the unspeakable acts being committed by her abuser. She has lost control of her body and she has even lost control of the anger and hatred she used to provide an illusion of protection. She now feels that she is a coconspirator with her abuser. She is beyond redemption.

If the abuse is repeated and the child continues to experience orgasms, she becomes even further convinced that she is a participant and that she is to blame for what occurs.

This is the typical scenario for children who experience abuse, both male and female. Mickey was sodomized on two occasions by a friend of his father's, and the second time he had an orgasm. Because of that abuse, he was in the adolescent unit of a mental health facility, but he was primarily troubled by the orgasm he experienced. In addition to all of the other feelings I have described, Mickey thought that having an orgasm while being abused by a man meant that he was a homosexual. If a man did something to him and he liked it, Mickey assumed that he must have a sexual preference for men. Isn't that what his body told him?

The answer is "No." Mickey's body didn't tell Mickey he liked men any more than the body of the girl in our example told her than she liked her abuse. An orgasm is an involuntary reflex; it is a reaction of your body over which you have no control. Have you ever seen your leg jerk when your doctor hits your knee with a small hammer? Or have you ever sneezed when pepper or pollen gets into your nose? Those are reflex actions, just like an orgasm. Male or female, if someone rubs you in the right way in the right place, you will have an orgasm whether you want to or not. And it does not matter whether you like the person who is rubbing you or not. It does not even have to be a person—that's why some people use vibrators.

So your abuser rubbed you in a way that elicited an orgasm. Does that mean you are bad or that you participated in your abuse or that you have made an irrevocable choice about the sex of your future partners? No, it merely means your body was functioning in one of the ways it was designed to respond.

I had a lot of trouble with this issue because I had no one to talk to about it until I finally found my wonderful therapists in Utah. I had terrible guilt about having had a couple of orgasms during the later years of my abuse. My guilt was not diminished by the fact that my father knew when it happened and went into terrible rages, beating me and swearing at me that I was a whore, a slut and anything else he could think of. (And as a successful writer, he was quite creative.) So I not only thought I had done something terribly wrong, but I concluded that orgasms were bad. I had no memory of any of this until I was in my early forties and could never understand why I would have pain after I experienced an orgasm. When I started to recover my memories in therapy, I found out that I was punishing myself the way my father used to punish me. As soon as I realized that, the pain went away, happily never to return.

I now know that orgasms are a very nice part of love-making. Having an orgasm is a lovely thing to be able to do. It is a gift we were given to allow us to give pleasure to someone we love and to receive pleasure from them. It is also a gift to be able to let our partners know they have given us pleasure.

Since the ability to have orgasms is part of your natural design, you might as well enjoy them. It would be a shame to reject such a gift simply because someone in your past misused it.

> *You can clutch the past*
> *so tightly to your chest*
> *that it leaves your arms too full*
> *to embrace the present.*
> Jan Glidewell

12. Why didn't my mother protect me?

The simple answer is that she could not help you because she could not even help herself.

One of the most painful aspects an incest victim endures is her mother's failure to rescue her. Although mothers can be molesters, incest is usually committed in the home by a father, stepfather, brother or other close family relative.

If the mother was not the abuser, one should certainly ask, "Where was she while this was going on?" Earlier studies did not spend much time analyzing the role played by the mother in incest cases. But more recent research includes the mother as an indispensable part of the incestuous family triangle and reflects the obvious conclusion—that most of the mothers knew what was going on and either openly permitted the abuse or closed their eyes to it. Some mothers were told by their children but refused to believe it. And others believed but refused to help, blaming their daughters for the incest. There are some mothers who actually did not know what was going on. But most of these, when confronted by their daughters with the truth, realized that they should have known, recognizing too late the signs they chose not to question and the signals they chose to ignore.

One of the most difficult issues survivors of incest have to face is their mother's failure to protect them. Although she is not the active abuser, the mother's betrayal may be even more painful to the survivor because of the survivor's conflicting emotions and confusion about the mother's motives and feelings.

The abuser's role is clear—the victim can easily understand why she hates a relative who has betrayed and abused her. This betrayal by a father or stepfather is traumatic and exhausts the victim's emotional resources. The victim is warned not to tell and is often threatened with reprisal, but the fear that keeps her silent is the instinctive knowledge that "mommy" would not be happy. The victim is terribly torn; she wants to tell because she desperately wants help but she is terrified of having mommy find out how bad she is. She cannot afford to lose both parents. And so the abuse continues and the victim is forced to cope with the horror of her abuse alone.

Victims cannot face the thought that their mothers might have known of the abuse but refused to help; betrayal by both of the essential people in a child's life would be unbearable. It is the betrayal by the nonabusing parent that is that last straw, and victims will go to any length to avoid acknowledging that ultimate betrayal.

George was one of 18 children in a family where every child was physically and sexually abused by his father almost from infancy. George finally escaped when he was 14 by fighting with his father and had been in therapy almost a year when he was referred to the adolescent mental health unit. He had been working on controlling his violent temper, but he recognized that he still had a problem. He had spent a great deal of time focusing on his anger towards his father, so I asked if he would like to explore his feelings about his mother.

Since George was usually cooperative, I was surprised at the violence of his response: "NO! I don't need to work on feelings about my mother. I love her." When I suggested that he might have some anger because she did not protect him from the abuse, George started screaming: "She didn't know about it. She wasn't there!" I asked where she was, and he shouted, "She was in the bedroom. That's where she always went when one of us was being hurt. When she saw something happening to us, she would start crying and go in the bedroom. She couldn't help us. The door was closed. She never knew nothing!"

George could not face the truth about his mother, at least not consciously. But his subconscious knew what was going on; it was evident from the way George tried to manipulate women but did not trust or like them, and the way his anger raged just below the surface, at times exploding out of control. The horror of what his father had done to him during most of his life was all that he wanted to handle. Having to acknowledge betrayal by mother was just too painful.

But acknowledging betrayal by their mothers is exactly what most survivors must accept. One of the hardest parts of healing is accepting the terrible reality of total abandonment. At an age when they were truly helpless, many victims were totally alone, abused by their fathers or stepfathers and, literally, thrown to the wolves by their mothers. The terror of that aloneness is unbearable and haunts victims into their adult lives, making them possessive and dependent just as their mothers were before them. Is it any wonder that so many victims flinch from the truth through amnesia and denial?

Yet in order to heal, survivors must face their feelings about their mothers, recognize the pain and release the anger and hatred. The first step in healing is to recognize that *you survived.* Despite the fact that you were all alone and no one helped you, you survived. You were only a child, without any of the knowledge or resources you have now, and yet you survived. The terror of being alone is a child's terror and your fear is left over from the past. You survived the worst life can deliver at a time when you were helpless; so you know that you can survive the healing process now, when you have control over your life. As the memories of my abuse began to unfold, I kept telling myself that nothing could ever be that bad again—and it is true.

In spite of the research I have done, it is difficult for me to understand how mothers can allow their children to be abused. I watch the wildlife documentaries where wild animals of all species ferociously protect their young, and I wonder where human beings went wrong. Why do animals act so human and humans act without humanity? I feel such pain, it's hard to describe. Why didn't my mother protect me?

I have spent a great deal of time trying to understand my mother. She was the middle child, between a brilliant, beautiful older sister, a Ph.D. university professor, and a brilliant handsome younger brother, an M.D. surgeon and the shining star of this Jewish family. Although she was bright and attractive, my mother has admitted feeling insecure, dropping out of college, being bedridden with bouts of pneumonia. But she had talent, went to art school and became an accomplished painter. She married my father when he was a "starving" writer, and they lived in Europe while she painted and he wrote. When they returned to the United States, his novel sold and they were lured by the glitter of Hollywood. She claims that she always wanted a child, but he did not—perhaps he suspected his repressed hostile feelings. He finally agreed when my mother was thirty, quite old for a first child in the early 1940s.

My mother's world revolved around my father; he could do no wrong and she always defended him and covered up for him. She was codependent in the extreme. She claims that she realized about six months after they were married that he was dying his dark hair bright blond, over his entire body, but she did not think it odd. I know he hit her because I have some very early memories of that, as well as memories when I was a teenager.

Mother had a difficult time coping with me as an infant. I was a colicky baby and, as she always says with more blame than remorse, I would not drink her milk. When I broke my leg in my crib, she and my father were unaware of the injury, but they were both unnerved by my constant crying. Each of them separately hit me several times in frustration to stop my screams. The break was not discovered until they took me to the doctor several months later. Later, my mother started to withdraw from me and I have one distinct memory of her deliberately jabbing me with a safety pin because I was crying and squirming while she was trying to diaper me. I was two years old.

After that, there was little love left between us, and I turned even more to my father for affection. He was an affectionate and gentle man before the emergence of his multiple personality states. His brutal attack on me when I was almost four years old came as a complete shock to me. The rapes, coupled with beatings and later torture, totally changed me. As the family photographs show, I became a listless zombie, with vacant eyes. No one could have failed to notice the change, the bruises or the bloodstains. I tried to tell my mother at least once what was happening, but she hit me and said I was lying.

I don't know when my mother first discovered what my father was doing, but I have a clear memory when I was four and a half which shows unmistakably that she knew. She ran down the hall into my bedroom where my father was raping me. She was hysterically screaming for him to stop and she was crying, but my father didn't move and she ran out of the room. The next day I begged her to help me, to take me away, but she hit me several times and said I was to blame, that it was my fault, and that she had no place to go. Now I realize that she did not want to tell *her* parents the truth. How could she admit she had married such a man?

On another occasion, when my father was sticking a cold fire poker up me, she did try to help me, even when he hit her with the poker. She dragged me out of the room and helped me clean up, but she did not take me to a doctor or take me away from my father. When my father finally sought help and went to a clinic, she accused me of destroying my father and our family.

I have spent several years trying to fathom my mother's actions. I know her life was painful because I have recovered memories of her climbing the stone stairs in the garden to the patio and crying for a long time. I also have a vague memory where she told me in tears that I would go crazy because of my abuse. She mentioned something about "It's happening all over again," which led me to believe that she was also abused, but I can't be sure. Typical of abused children who have repressed their abuse, my mother portrays her childhood and parents as perfect.

Clinicians and researchers have only begun to study mothers who permit their children to be abused by father and stepfathers, and thus there are a number of only partially satisfactory theories as to why this phenomenon occurs. The main characteristic of mothers in incestuous families is codependency.

Codependency encompasses many factors, so there are many definitions. Melodie Beattie, in her helpful book *Codependent No More*, defines a codependent person as "one who has let another person's behavior affect him or her, and who is obsessed with controlling that person's behavior."[6]

Other definitions emphasize an inability to participate in loving relationships and having a dysfunctional dependence on someone else. While older definitions focus on people involved with someone addicted to drugs or alcohol, the term "codependency" today includes anyone enmeshed with someone who is destructive of themselves or others, whether mentally or physically. A comedian's definition may be the clearest: "You are codependent if you are drowning and you see someone else's life flashing before your eyes."

Codependents live for someone else; they put the welfare of others ahead of their own. According to Beattie, they feel responsible for other people's feelings, thoughts, actions, choices, wants, needs and well-being, and they are quick to give unsolicited advice. They do not believe that their needs are important, so they strive to please others instead of themselves. They think and talk mostly about other people. They are attracted to needy people and needy people are attracted to them. Codependents have low self-esteem and blame themselves for everything. Since they did not feel love and approval from their parents, they don't love themselves and do not believe others can love them. They want desperately to be loved and believe they cannot survive alone, so they endure abuse and the abuse of their children in order to keep their families intact. Codependents are overly concerned with winning the approval of others. Thus they may keep incest a secret because they are afraid of what people will say. Codependents live by an oppressive set of rules and repress their true feelings. They can be rigid and controlled. They don't trust themselves or their feelings and they don't trust other people. They usually try to trust untrustworthy people. And they lose faith and trust in God.

Codependents withdraw emotionally from their partners but will submit to sexual relations when they don't want to. They are frightened, hurt and angry and live with people who are frightened, hurt and angry. Their fear of anger makes them repress their angry feelings and try to avoid anger at all costs. However, this anger may start to come out in later years when they will become depressed, ill and even violent. They may begin to abuse and neglect their children.

One of the major characteristics of codependency is denial. Codependents ignore problems or pretend they are not happening. They deny reality, pretending that things are not so bad and convincing themselves that things will be better tomorrow. Other symptoms of denial include keeping busy, becoming a workaholic, getting sick or depressed, overeating—and ignoring these problems too. Codependents lie to themselves and others to cover up the painful reality they create for themselves. They often become martyrs, sacrificing their happiness and that of others for causes that don't require sacrifice.

Codependents are often victims of sexual or physical abuse. Recent studies of mothers in incestuous families revealed that a large percentage have been sexually abused as children. A study of mothers in a Long Beach, California, treatment program revealed that 90 percent had been sexually abused.[7] The figure could be even higher since some mothers may have repressed the fact of their abuse.

The large percentage of mothers who have been sexually abused provides an explanation for their failure to protect their children from abuse. Unless they work out the repressed emotions of their own abuse, women who have been abused seem to follow two patterns: they abuse their children or marry men who abuse their children. They are acting out a learned behavior, a pattern which was engraved into their minds at the time of their own abuse. During their own abuse, these women learn to relate to a particular kind of person—their abuser—and in later years they may choose this type of abusive person as their partner. (The nature of these patterns is described in Question 22, *If I have been abused, will I abuse my children?*) These mothers are acting out unconscious impulses created by their childhood abuse and these impulses override the bond between parent and child and the mother's protective instincts. The mother's own repressed fear, hatred, rage and shame destroy her sense of self-worth and create the conditions where she can tolerate the abuse of her children because she feels powerless to control the situation and is driven to placate her husband.

Another theory posited to explain a mother's permitting the abuse of her children is the rejection she felt from her own mother. One study found the maternal grandmothers of incestuous families to be stern, demanding, hostile women who rejected their daughters and pampered their sons.[8] These daughters spent the rest of their lives trying futilely to gain the love they were denied as children. Having been treated as worthless by their mothers, they become infantile, dependent women who reject their own daughters and permit them to be abused.

Although this study apparently did not consider whether the maternal grandmother or the mothers were sexually abused, later research documents the chain of abuse from maternal grandmother to mother to daughter. The chain of abuse makes these women "incest carriers" across generations.[9]

As a result of their own rejection and abuse, these women have a pervasive and childish need for nurturance and warmth. They live in fear of abandonment, but this very fear causes them to withdraw from their husbands and children. These mothers are jealous of their daughters, and to the extent that the daughters "win" their fathers, the mothers' love is lost.

A more recent theory attempts to explain the mother's role by linking sexual abuse to our cultural institutions and values. The dominance of men over women in our society is seen as creating a climate where females are rendered powerless over their environment and are exploited. It is true that incestuous families tend to rigidly follow the traditional male/female roles with the men dominant and the women submissive.[10] But while societal conditions certainly contribute to incest and sexual abuse, it is an oversimplification to attribute abuse to cultural conditions, ignoring the dynamics and abusive histories of the individuals involved.

Although the theories may vary, one fact emerges clearly from them all: mothers of incest victims are also victims. While I may not totally understand my mother's motivation and the motivations of other mothers who allow their children to be abused, I can empathize with the pain which torments them. These mothers have failed as women, as wives and as mothers. To endure the betrayal of your husband who sexually molests your child, to know your child is suffering, to betray your own child, and to be unable to help yourself or those you love must be the worst kind of hell.

The mother's role almost always involves some degree of denial.[11]

If your mother continues to deny the truth of your abuse, it is because she cannot bear to face her failures and her pain. She may have so deeply repressed what happened to you, along with her own childhood abuse, that she truly does not remember. Her denial may be so strong that she has erased the facts and replaced them with ones she can tolerate. My mother can talk about my father's hypnotherapy, but her only explanation for a treatment which was extraordinary in those days is that "he was depressed." Part of the syndrome of codependency is lying and covering up. And unless your mother is willing to go into therapy, she is probably not going to admit what happened.

Clinicians are pessimistic about the success of having children confront their mothers about the abuse, especially if the abuse is discovered several years after it occurred. If the abuse is exposed while it is occurring or shortly thereafter, the crisis makes mothers more willing to admit their knowledge and complicity and to accept help. But when the abuse is uncovered by the victims later in life, clinical experience is that the mothers become increasingly defensive and go to any lengths to maintain the family myth. The fear of uncovering the pain and their role in the abuse drives them to desperate measures to conceal the truth. When I was close to completing this book, my mother started telephoning our relatives to tell them I was crazy.

This section was the most difficult for me to write because I was still in the process of resolving issues about my own mother. Only as this book was about to go to press did I finally attain the understanding that released me at last from my hatred toward my mother. My process has been one of peeling off layer after layer of old emotions to get to the core of truth which can set me free.

Although I was able to let go of my anger toward my father fairly easily once I discovered that he had multiple personality disorder and I remembered his remorse, I could not find any explanation for my mother's conduct. Her denial of the truth and persistent rejection of me created a continuing anger which I had to sort out from my past feelings.

Because she never revealed anything in her life which would explain her conduct, I always felt my mother's actions were more deliberate, more a conscious choice than those of my father. I failed to recognize the essential truth: *no functional woman would marry—much less stay with—a man who would rape and torture her child.*

I was blinded by my mother's facade of the loyal wife who insisted over and over that she would not leave my father because she "loved him." I hated her for choosing him over me and abandoning me to his abuse. I always believed my mother was functional, but now I realize that a functional woman would have found ways to stop the abuse or to place her child out of harm's way. And as a friend pointed out, a truly functional woman would never have been attracted to my clearly dysfunctional father in the first place.

Once I realized my mother was dysfunctional, I began to see through her veneer of perfect clothes, perfect makeup and aristocratic manners to how isolated, alone and frightened she was and still is. She is not close to anyone. All her life she has pretended to be happy and that everything is wonderful. She repeats these phrases like an incantation to ward off evil spirits. But they never ring true.

Several years ago, before I was aware of my abuse, my mother's second husband asked me why she never talked about herself or her past. He said he really didn't know anything about her life or her feelings. He wondered how she could be happy when she never *did* anything.

My mother spends her days isolated in her home, gardening (although she has a professional gardener), reading and doing crossword puzzles. She is a talented artist but she rarely paints. She does not even keep house; a maid comes in every couple of weeks and her husband does most of the shopping and cooking. Although she has her husband and a few friends, her interaction with them is superficial, consisting of an exchange of impersonal anecdotes about people in the movie industry.

As I was growing up, I used to talk to her about some of my problems and received advice and encouragement. But I have never heard her ask for advice or admit to anyone that she had a personal problem or a negative feeling. Everything is always "fine." She has created a gold-plated fortress to keep out reality. But she is so *alone.*

I also began to understand how she could allow my father to abuse me. She felt so unworthy that she could not be close to anyone, even her own child. She began to detach herself from me when I was two years old, and she pulled farther away when the abuse began. She had to hate me or go insane. How could anyone watch someone she loved being raped and tortured?

Understanding that my mother was not rational, that she was just as sick in her own way as my father, and that she was and is in pain has released me from my anger. Now I know that her rejection of me was not my fault and it was not deliberate on her part, so I can forgive. I just feel intense sadness that my family was so dysfunctional and that we caused each other so much pain.

It is hard to cope with the fact that some people have been so hurt that they cannot love. But if you are to heal your own wounds, you have to accept the fact that you are seeking something your mother cannot give. It is not that you don't deserve your mother's love; you can't have it because your mother is incapable of loving you or anyone. She does not love herself and so she has no love to give to anyone else.

In order to save yourself, you may have to break off your relationship with your mother for a while, so that you can eliminate your feelings of dependence on her. If you are to heal, you must refuse to permit *anyone* to hurt or degrade you, and mothers who will not admit the truth usually treat their abused child with contempt and condescension. You need to surround yourself with people who accept and respect you and who make you feel good about yourself. But most important, you need to learn to love and depend on yourself, so that you no longer have an insatiable need for love and affection from others. Only if you love yourself can you truly feel loved.

When you have healed yourself, you may be able to begin a new relationship with your mother. Since you will have changed, she will have to treat you differently. If you can accept the fact that she is incapable of digging up the past and will never acknowledge the truth, your pain, or your recovery, and if you can simply accept her as she is now, then you may be able to be friends. But do not expect more than she can give. If you remember the hurt she has endured, perhaps you can let go of your pain and forgive.

> *The end of all our explorations*
> *will be to come back to where we began*
> *and discover the place for the first time.*
> T. S. Eliot

13. What if my mother sexually abused me?

You have been betrayed by the person who is closest to you psychologically and biologically and your pain and anger may feel overwhelming, but you are not alone. Although incest by mothers is less prevalent than incest by fathers, many thousands of children have been abused by their mothers, and the effects of such abuse can be treated successfully.

Most studies report that 90 percent of sexual offenders are men. However, some therapists believe that many cases of abuse by women are unreported. Even in general population surveys, where people reveal their own unreported childhood experiences, 95 percent of the adult contacts with girls and 80 percent of the adult contacts with boys are made by men.

Various theories have been proposed to explain this disparity between abuse by men and women, including the fact that women are not usually dominant in sexual relationships and do not generally act as initiators. Other hypotheses are that men are sexually aroused more easily than women and appear to be more interested in sex with a number of partners. Also women seem to be better able to distinguish between sexual and nonsexual affection, whereas men may confuse affection with sex and act accordingly. And sex appears to be more important to men and affects their self-esteem; if men are denied a sexual outlet, they are more likely to turn to children. Another possibility is that women are socialized to be more empathic.[12]

Whatever the reason for the differences between the rates of maternal and paternal incest, the fact is that women do become perpetrators in a large number of cases. In some instances, the mother is a co-offender or accomplice with her spouse; in such cases, her dependency on her spouse may be a major contributing factor. Where the mother is an independent abuser, she is frequently mentally ill or intellectually deficient. Other factors that seem to contribute to mother-child incest are a closeness in age between mother and child, incestuous victimization of the mother as a young girl, a history of promiscuity on the part of the mother, and a history of drug and alcohol abuse.[13]

Incest by a mother is often more traumatic than incest by a father because of the strong biological and psychological bond between mother and child. The injury to the child may be even greater than in father-daughter incest because the mother is the one who gives birth and usually is the nurturing parent. An infant is dependent on his mother during the early part of his life and focuses almost all of his attention on his mother during his first years.

When the nurturing parent becomes the abuser, the betrayal is greater because of the strength of the maternal bond and because the child's expectation of motherly love and protection is destroyed. The child is further torn apart by hate for the mother's abuse and the love created by the bond. In spite of abuse by the mother, the maternal bond remains strong, shackling the child psychologically to his tormentor. That bond is the reason why children are so reluctant to disclose maternal abuse.

Mothers are the center of a child's world. We are socialized by television, movies and magazines to accept the image of the madonna-like mother cradling and protecting her child. When a child is sexually abused by her mother, this image is shattered. The child becomes terribly confused because reality is so different from her expectations. And because the mother is the center of the child's world, the mother is a model for everyone in the world. The child concludes that if her mother could do something so horrible as sexually abusing her own child, no one is safe, everyone is a potential monster.

Abused children often assume that they somehow deserved the

abuse. (See Questions 7 and 9, *Did I deserve to be abused?* and *Was God punishing me?*) Children whose mothers have abused them are more prone to make this faulty assumption than other children because they know that mothers are supposed to love and protect their children—but theirs did not. Thus, since their abusive mothers obviously don't love them, despite the biological bond, these children become convinced that something must be wrong with *them*. Abused children have no frame of reference for perceiving that their mothers are mentally ill. They are plagued by our culture's childhood taunts such as, "Even a mother wouldn't love *him*." Self-hate is perhaps the most difficult issue children of maternal abuse must face, but it is one which can be overcome.

Abuse of a son by his mother has some additional negative consequences because the bond between mother and son seems to be even stronger than that between father and daughter. When a mother violates that bond by sexual abuse, the emotional effect on the son is devastating.

The son is left with enormous confusion as a result of the betrayal, not only as to the fusion of nurturing with abuse, but as to basic sex roles. The taboo against mother-son incest is powerful and an abused son feels overwhelming guilt and shame combined with rage toward his mother for the betrayal and for making him violate the taboo. Such feelings generate hatred toward his mother which must be repressed because, "It's not nice to hate your mother." So he turns the hatred on himself. These chaotic emotions are so painful that sometimes the son may cope by rejecting all women and choosing to become homosexual. This choice is made out of a terrifying ambivalence: the son wants to be close to his mother but knows she is forbidden. His natural love for his mother is mixed with intense hatred, and rather than deal with these overpowering emotions, he sometimes finds it easier to renounce all women.

Unfortunately such decisions are made under extreme emotional stress and are based on distorted information. For children, "mother" represents all women, just as "father" represents all men. So when boys are abused by their mothers, all women are seen as dangerous, both physically and emotionally. Abused boys are terribly afraid to acknowledge their violent love-hate conflict and find it easier to hide their revulsion for their mother behind revulsion for all women. The tragedy is that often sons refuse to reevaluate the decisions, even in therapy.

A therapist recently asked me what to do about a fifteen-year-old boy who had been sexually abused for nine years by his mother. The boy flaunted the fact that he was a transsexual transvestite and adamantly refused to discuss his sexual choice. I said that while everyone has a right to his sexual preferences, I did not think that a fifteen-year-old boy should make such a decision based on acts of abuse any more than children should conclude their abuse is a punishment from God.

Boys who have been abused by their mothers have no disposition, genetic or otherwise, to homosexuality. The choice is a decision made on the basis of the abuse, which is an unnatural and violent act. No rational decision can be made under such circumstances. Abused children and adults should be helped in therapy to release the repressed, tumultuous emotions of their abuse and to understand the reasons for the choices they made. Once they have all the facts, *then* they can decide what role to play for the rest of their lives.

Abused boys should be encouraged to experiment by cultivating friendly relationships with girls so they can get to know them as people. They need to learn that not all females are like their mother. Experiencing a good relationship with a female therapist can be helpful in building trust.

If you are a male abused by your mother, the situation is not hopeless. It may be difficult to explore the painful feelings and to sort out how you made some decisions, but therapy can help you. The fact is that many boys are abused by their mothers every year, so you are not alone. Clinical experience has shown that adolescent and adult victims of maternal abuse are able to heal and have fulfilling lives. Whatever sexual choice you finally make, you will be happier if you face your past and try to understand it than if you try to tough it out alone.

Although many of the examples in this book deal with abuse by men, the emotions and feelings you have experienced will be similar and the advice will apply to you too. If you had a father who failed to protect you, you can mentally substitute "father" for "mother." Often the characteristics of "nonoffending" fathers who permit or overlook the abuse are the same as those of the mothers. And all of the self-healing techniques will be useful, especially those which affect self-esteem. I recommend that you start with the affirmations in Part V, Section 8, *Reprogramming negative thoughts,* and Section 13, *How to nurture and reparent yourself* where you use photographs of your family to get a clearer picture of where the responsibility for your abuse lies.

While it may be true that your mother did not love you, it is because she was not capable of love—not because of anything you did. Just because you had a sick mother does not mean that no one will ever love you or that you are unlovable. You can learn to love yourself and once you do, you will find love all around you. Don't give up on yourself. Your path may be a little harder, but you will make it.

> *Experience is not what happens to a man.*
> *It is what a man does with what happens to him.*
> Aldous Huxley

14. It isn't fair! Why did it happen to me?

No, it isn't fair. What happened to us was terrible, but it's over and we have the rest of our lives to make up for it, if we let ourselves. But many of us get stuck ruminating over how unfairly we have been treated. It's not hard to keep focusing on how horrible it was, how much we were hurt, how we were betrayed and how it affected our lives. All those things are true. But thinking about them doesn't get us anywhere, it doesn't take away the horror, it doesn't stop the hurt, it doesn't negate our betrayal and it only continues to ruin our lives and keep us in the role of a victim. By hanging onto our injustice, we victimize ourselves.

The sad fact is that life is not fair. Tragedies afflict all of us no matter how good we may be. Author Dennis Wholey warns, "Expecting the world to treat you fairly because you are a good person is a little like expecting the bull not to attack you because you're a vegetarian." We want desperately to believe that there is some design to life and some reason for our pain. But often our attempts to make sense of our world brings us more pain.

Rabbi Harold Kushner has spent a great deal of his life pondering why tragedies occur and his answers are in his best-selling book, *When Bad Things Happen to Good People*. He explains,

> "It is tempting at one level to believe that bad things happen to people (especially other people) because God is a righteous judge who gives them exactly what they deserve. By believing that, we keep the world orderly and understandable. We give people the best possible reason for being good and for avoiding sin. And by believing that, we can maintain an image of God as all-loving, all-powerful and totally in control. Given the reality

73

of human nature, given the fact that none of us is perfect and that each of us can, without too much difficulty, think of things he has done which he should not have done, we can always find grounds for justifying what happens to us. But how comforting, how religiously adequate, is such an answer?

"The idea that God gives people what they deserve, that our misdeeds cause our misfortune, is a neat and attractive solution to the problem of evil at several levels, but it has a number of serious limitations. As we have seen, it teaches people to blame themselves. It creates guilt even where there is no basis for guilt. It makes people hate God, even as it makes them hate themselves. And most disturbing of all, it does not even fit the facts."

Kushner rejects this view and concludes that God is not in fact all-powerful, that there is randomness in the world. Thus, our pain is not the punishment of a wrathful God, but it is the result of acts of imperfect humans in an imperfect world and of events that even God cannot control.

If this explanation is too frightening, an alternative explanation of how the world works is being espoused by a growing number of people who call themselves the New Age spiritualists. You have probably heard of the works of Richard Bach, *Jonathan Livingston Seagull* and *Illusions*; Stephen Levine, *Who Dies?* and *Healing into Life and Death*; Ram Dass; Shakti Gawain; Carl Jung; Shirley MacLaine and many others.

The basis of spirituality is oneness, the belief that we are all created out of love by a benevolent God, power or universe and that we are all part of the same whole. Spirituality is a philosophy, not a religion, and does not have a church, but many churches are adopting more and more of its beliefs. There is no requirement that you have any particular belief, even in God. There is no belief that spirituality is "the only way" because since we are all unique, there is no "only way." And no one can ever be left out or damned because we are all part of the same whole.

Most people who follow this philosophy believe in the immortality of the soul. We never die; we merely continue on our journey of discovery and growth. We may do this in a different dimension, or, some believe, we may choose to come back to "earth school" to complete our lessons here. Our main lesson is to learn to love and be loved. We also learn to be ourselves and develop our potential—to be the best we can be. We are here to develop the collective consciousness and to help others. We are not judged, except by ourselves, and we choose what we believe is best for us in our lives according to our conscience. The crux of this philosophy is that we choose everything that happens to us because we have something to learn from it. So under this philosophy, we can look for the lesson in what we have suffered and seek the gain from the pain.

No answer is totally satisfactory. I personally do not believe there is an answer, at least not one we will know in this life. I am a pragmatist and I believe in doing what works. It does not work to believe victims of sexual abuse were punished by a vengeful God. I cannot believe in a God who would torture children. And I do not believe life is always fair. I like the comedian's line, "Who ever told you life was user friendly?"

It may not work for you to believe in the randomness of the universe or that you have chosen to suffer your abuse. You can develop your own philosophy. As an adult you are no longer bound by what your parents, teachers or preachers told you. You have the time to study and read about what people throughout the world believe, and to choose for yourself.

We all have a need for a context from which to view the world, as evidenced by humanity's perennial search for meaning and religion throughout the ages. But when you choose your own beliefs, choose ones that work for you, that make you feel better about yourself, that make you feel happy so that you can give joy to others. Reject ideas that fill you with guilt or point the finger of blame at yourself or others. Beliefs which make you unhappy should be discarded. After all, religions developed to help people live better lives, not to make people miserable. It is difficult to be kind and loving when you hurt. Choose a philosophy of love and happiness and you will find those qualities in your life.

The sad fact is that no one can make up for the pain you have suffered. If you keep trying to even the score, you will only hurt yourself. I found this out after many years of frustration and I am still working on changing my behavior. My abuse led me to expect and demand that people treat me fairly and that nothing should ever go wrong. When my expectations were not fulfilled, I dissolved into tantrums of fear and rage, fear at my feelings of helplessness to get what I want and rage fired by the irrational thought: "How dare he (the world) do that to me. It's not fair! After all I've been through, I should be treated better now." Despite the fact that this behavior got me even less of what I wanted, I pursued it for years, perhaps hoping subconsciously that one day, if I screamed loudly enough, everything would go right.

I learned that I not only had to forgive my abuser and myself, but I had to forgive *the whole situation* before I could let my anger go. I was angry at the world, stuck in the mire of "It's not fair." It took me a long time to realize I had to forgive God, the universe and my past, so I could truly live in the present.

I also figured out I was punishing people in the present for all the wrongs I suffered in the past. I fell into the trap of believing the world and people in it owed me something because of what I suffered. But they are not responsible for what happened to me and they are not obliged to make it up to me. It is up to *me* to make it up to myself. While I now realize how ridiculous it is to demand that everyone pay for what my father did to me, I still find the feelings popping up every so often, especially when I have to deal with utilities or government bureaucracies.

I know that if I want to be happy, I have to give up my childish ideas of black-and-white justice. I think one reason I became a lawyer was to find justice. But I learned there is no perfect justice in the law, and I have yet to find perfect justice in this world. Some say the world is perfect in its imperfection. All I know is that the world can be perfect if you can see it that way and if you can let go of your obsession with fairness. The old adage is still true: the best revenge is to live well. And you can only make up for past pain with present joy. If you can give up notions of fairness, you really can have it all.

> *As human beings, we are endowed with freedom of choice,*
> *and we cannot shuffle off our responsibility*
> *upon the shoulders of God or nature.*
> *We must shoulder it ourselves.*
> *It is up to us.*
> Arnold J. Toynbee

15. I am afraid people will find out I have been sexually abused. What should I do?

Bring it out in the open and talk about it.

That is probably not the answer you expected. Perhaps you thought I would say, "Keep it secret. It's nobody's business but your own." Many of the teenagers I have worked with go to extraordinary lengths to keep their experiences secret, despite the fact that they are all participants in a program for adolescents who have been severely abused and 90 percent of them have been abused sexually. They are sure that no one has ever had a similar experience and that no one could possibly understand. And, surprisingly, some adults also react with terror when they contemplate disclosing what happened to them many years earlier as children.

Many victims are unwilling to disclose the fact that they have been sexually abused, fearing their friends and colleagues will react with horror and disgust. They live in terror that they will be tarred with the stigma of "incest." At worst, these victims think they will be ridiculed and ostracized and, at best, pitied and the target of whispers behind their backs. But their real fear is that people will think that they are somehow responsible for their abuse and that they are bad or cheap or ruined for life. Their fear condemns them to the very isolation they believe would result from disclosure of their abuse.

The crux of the problem is that victims project their own negative feelings about themselves onto others. Since they feel bad about themselves, they think others will think they are bad. Because they fear that they caused their abuse to occur, they believe others will blame them. As we discussed in Question 7, *Did I deserve to be abused?*, survivors must face these irrational fears in order to heal. Once these fears are extinguished, survivors can decide objectively whether or not they want to disclose their past by assessing each situation on its merits.

There is an important therapeutic reason for disclosing your abuse. In order to heal, you must be relieved of the terrible burden of keeping your abuse a secret. Past of the trauma of sexual abuse is not being able to tell. Keeping sexual abuse a secret tends to make it "dirty." And many victims conclude from the secrecy that *they* are dirty. It is important for children and adults to have people to whom they can talk freely about the abuse because verbalizing what happened reduces their anxiety and pain.

I did not remember my abuse until I was in my forties. I was in a state of shock and could not cope with the revelation of incest in my "happy," upper class, intellectual family. I even wondered if my husband would want to stay around me since we had not been married very long. I was amazed that he took my calamity so calmly and was so sympathetic; his strongest emotion was the anger he felt toward my father for having caused me so much pain.

At first I could not tell anyone else because I thought people would think it was my fault and that I was bad and tainted by the experience. But once I worked through my negative feelings about myself in therapy, I began to have more confidence in myself and in my friends. When I dared to tell my closest friends the truth, I was again surprised at the compassion and understanding I received from them. But what was even more astonishing was that they responded by revealing their own stories of abuse. The result was that I developed even closer relationships with my friends than I had before.

However, not all of my friends responded in the same way. I found that some people had difficulty handling the concept of sexual abuse. One new friend in particular, I will call her Dorothy, reacted stiffly when I told her about the abuse I was trying to overcome and cut short our lunch. She was a buyer in a large department store and we had been meeting for lunch at the mall where she worked at least once a month. But after my disclosure, she would not accept or return my telephone calls. I didn't see her for almost a year, but when I ran into her in the store one day, she greeted me like a long lost friend. She told me that my revelation of abuse had upset her so much that she had gone to a therapist and learned that she too had been abused as a child!

We all need friendships where we don't have to put on an act and where we will be accepted for ourselves—with all our faults. The choice to tell someone is often the choice to see if that relationship can be such a friendship. Not all of our relationships necessarily have that potential, and there may be people who we choose not to tell. Once I had support from my husband and a couple of close friends, I decided to bring my story out in the open because I did not want to have friends who would shun me because of something in my past. But that was my choice, and yours may be different.

I will not tell you that everyone will react with sympathy and compassion when you tell them that you were abused, but my experience is that the majority will. And I have found that those people who respond negatively have some incidents of abuse either in their past or their present lives. People who have no experience with abuse may be slightly uncomfortable and embarrassed because they find abuse difficult to understand. But most will not reject your friendship and will not think that anything is wrong with you. Of course you do not want to bore them with excessive details.

I have had almost exclusively positive experiences since I have been talking openly about my abuse. My law practice has not been adversely affected, although more of my clients tend to have been abused. And my social work clients who have been abused are more comfortable with me because they know I understand their pain. I have become friends with some wonderful new people who have also been abused and I have embarked on a new career to help survivors of abuse. I have even begun to give speeches about abuse in which I describe my own experience.

When I taught a course at the University of Utah on "Women and the Law," which included a section on spouse and child abuse, I briefly described my experience and said I would be happy to talk to anyone who had had the same problem. *One-third* of the class came to me during the semester and said, "I never told anyone, but . . . " That was a line I was to hear repeated by the head of one of the departments on campus and several other students who heard about my lecture from members of my class. By being forthright about what happened to me, I have been able to encourage victims to begin therapy, answer questions they have been afraid to ask, and educate people who might be able to help solve the problem if they had more information.

My friends and people I have seen in therapy have had similar experiences after disclosing their abuse. The adolescents who were encouraged to tell their stories to their peers in the mental health unit have been delighted by the reactions of their outwardly tough, "bad" friends. Steve, who proudly wore an outrageous mohawk as a symbol of his defiance, told Bonnie, a girl he liked, about his sodomy by his real and adopted fathers. Their relationship became even closer and they were able to give each other support and understanding because she too was a victim of incest. In a month, her depression and his violent conduct improved dramatically. To me their new found happiness was indisputable proof that love and sharing painful memories are the best remedies in the world.

This lesson was repeated for me many times in combined group therapy sessions for adolescent sexual abuse survivors and perpetrators. Every group member was initially terrified to discuss his or her particular abusive experience. But each time a group member disclosed details of the experience, the other members were supportive and compassionate. I was also surprised to see that the survivors consistently expressed sympathy for other adolescent perpetrators who had been abused. I think they understood that the perpetrators' abusive acts were a response to the abuse they had endured as children. The most healing effect of the group was a member's experience of being accepted after disclosing events which he expected would bring a reaction of disgust and ridicule. The reactions they received were totally opposite from what they expected and so they learned, as Franklin Roosevelt said, "The only thing we have to fear is fear itself."

One exception may be with children who are too young to comprehend sexual abuse and who have not yet developed a sense of empathy. Becky, a spunky eleven-year-old who was raped by her older brother, confided her experience to her best friend. The friend taunted Becky and told the entire school that Becky was "making it with her brother every night." Becky was devastated by this betrayal and considered changing schools. But in therapy, Becky began to recognize that not all of the children participated in tormenting her. One girl in particular seemed to be kind and Becky decided to try to be friends with her and to stay at her school. Although it was a painful lesson, Becky learned what friendship means and to choose her friends carefully. And by staying at her school, she learned how to deal with adversity and with gossip. She discovered that both blow over and that she had the strength to survive them. She did not need much more therapy to help her out of the victim role; she was already there. But Becky made me realize that perhaps it is better for children *not* to tell their friends, because most children are too immature to understand sexual abuse or to empathize with victims.

The other exceptions to the general rule of disclosure are based on a victim's motives. If the motive is to have someone to talk to and to develop further intimacy with a friend, disclosure may be beneficial. But sometimes victims flaunt their abuse in order to get attention. Or they focus on their abuse to the exclusion of other topics of conversation. Neither of these motives is healthy for the victims. They soon find that people grow tired of the repetitious and detailed accounts of their abuse and drift away, leaving the victims feeling more betrayed than ever. You should consider your motives carefully and choose with caution those people you trust with the vulnerability of your abuse.

You *must* disclose your abuse to some people. One is your spouse or lover. You must tell your partner because he or she is affected by the abuse in all aspects of your relationship. If you jump when your partner tries to touch you or reject his advances because they remind you of your past abuse, he may start to feel that he is doing something wrong or that you don't love him. One night my husband thought I was awake and he leaned over me in bed and started to kiss me. His reward was the most piercing shriek that either of us have ever heard. My father used to wake me up and rape me and what my husband did brought back the memories. Luckily my husband knew about my abuse so he could help me stop screaming once he got over his own shock. Reactions like this are why you must discuss your abuse with your spouse or lover so he or she will not touch you without warning and can avoid other behavior which makes you uncomfortable.

Your own sexual pleasure will be enhanced if you can openly tell your partner that you want him to avoid certain behavior which may remind you of your abuse. Ask him to approach you gently and to make love with the light on if that helps you concentrate on him and forget your abuse. (See Question 6 on enjoying sex.) Even more importantly, if you tell your partner, you will have someone important in your life with whom to share your feelings. I think you will find that your partner will be more considerate and will become a true partner in helping you overcome the effects of your abuse.

Other people you must tell are your physician and your gynecologist. Your doctors must know about your abuse so that they will be able to treat you properly. Doctors are finding that an increasing number of physical and mental symptoms are due to past physical and sexual abuse. Pain with intercourse, pain and excessive bleeding with menstrual periods, and even premenstrual syndrome are now being connected with sexual abuse. You do not want to have an unnecessary operation, as I did, or be put on drugs with harmful side effects if you can resolve your problem in therapy or through hypnosis.

Symptoms such as headaches, backaches and other physical pains may also be directly connected to your abuse. I found that I had headaches in the areas where my father hit me in the head. Once I recovered the memories about the blows, the headaches disappeared. Most people with multiple personality disorder have blinding headaches when they change personalities, and even people who have ego states may experience pains in their heads when the ego states are being discovered and they are releasing their memories and feelings.

You may also experience anxiety attacks where you have difficulty breathing or where you feel your heart pounding so hard you think you are having a heart attack. These may come because you are afraid of uncovering a painful memory or because you are reexperiencing the fear you felt when you were being abused. If your doctors know about your abuse, they can help you deal with these feelings of anxiety. Doctors have heard it all and they are legally bound to keep what you tell them confidential. It is important that you begin to trust people who can help you and confiding in your doctor is a good place to start.

Disclosures of sexual abuse are more readily accepted today due to the increased public awareness of the problem and its prevalence in our society. The media has made incest and abuse a matter for public discussion. The news routinely covers vivid stories of child abuse and realistic enactments of abuse are dramatized in detail in motion pictures and on television. Solutions for the growing problem of abuse are debated openly in school and government meetings. Because the public is becoming educated, the old stigma of incest and sexual abuse is diminishing rapidly.

The things you hide always haunt you. Why live your life in the fear that someone will find out about what happened to you? Have you noticed that most of the drama on daytime soap operas is created by situations where someone decides to hide the truth? The characters' lives are invariably complicated by keeping the information secret and they live in constant fear of exposure or blackmail. It is always obvious that their lives would have been much simpler if they had only told the truth. But then, of course, the producers would not sell soap.

If you want to live in a soap opera and cut yourself off from the support and understanding your friends could give you, by all means continue to keep your abuse secret. Otherwise take the plunge and trust your friends to react with compassion and respond with secrets of their own.

Whatever you decide is best for you, I believe it is important for the subject of sexual abuse to be candidly and openly discussed in our country. Only if people can be made to see that the problem does not just affect "those people," but their friends, their neighbors and even their own families, will we be able to mobilize the support and understanding needed to stop the chain of abuse.

The problem of abuse is not a personal experience; it affects our entire nation. Mental and physical illness caused by abuse are depleting the resources of this country. Abuse can lead to depression, joblessness, welfare, crime and even murder, placing a staggering burden on our economy. But the greatest loss to our country is the loss of human potential, of creativity, of productivity. People must speak out so that others become aware that abuse affects someone they know. It is not *their* problem, but *our* problem.

> *Love is an act of sharing our reality -*
> *who we are - with another person.*
> Unknown

16. Was it wrong to tell?
Did I destroy my family?

No! Emphatically no, to both questions.

The situation you are probably in is extremely painful. You were being abused by a relative—a father, mother, sister, brother, aunt, uncle, grandparent, stepparent or a combination of people. No one in your family protected you while you were suffering the pain and humiliation of these brutal acts. You finally marshalled the courage to ask for help. Perhaps your social service agency stepped in and removed you from your family. Your abuser(s) may be facing criminal charges. And at least one member of your family may be accusing you of destroying them.

Your situation is frightening and unstable, and you are finding it difficult to stand up to the attacks of your own family members. Our relatives know very well how to make us feel guilty. But where were they when you were being injured? Would you rather go back to what was happening before you told, when you were being abused, and no one would help? Would you rather have allowed your abuse to continue? It would only have gotten worse. Could you have survived that?

The real issue here is survival, *your* survival. You did what you had to do to protect yourself, to survive. The most fundamental instinct of all animals, including humans, is to survive. Our bodies are programmed to protect us. Our eyelids close if something gets too close to our eyes. If we are wounded, our bodies send out special cells to fight infection and create new skin to cover the cuts. If we are in danger, our bodies manufacture adrenalin so will we have extra energy to escape. The first principle of life is to protect yourself. When you told about your abuse, you were only following the basic law of survival. You were being harmed, seriously harmed, and you chose a sensible and humane way of saving yourself. Some victims of abuse are pushed beyond the limits of reason and kill their parents. You did not. You used a system that was established to help you *and* your family.

Lest we quibble over whether survival is only a law for the lower animals, I would like to point out an often misquoted and little understood sentence in the *Bible*: "Love thy neighbor *as* thyself." The *Bible* does not say that we are to love others *more* than ourselves. We have to love ourselves *first*. Psychologists now recognize that it is impossible for us to love someone else if we don't first love ourselves. You must love and take care of yourself before you can love or take care of anyone else. You followed the first rule of survival and cared for yourself enough to protect yourself from abuse, one of the worst kinds of harm. Your decision was a healthy one.

You ask about the effects on your family. First of all, did your abuser care about you, about the effects of the abuse on your feelings and on your body? Did anyone consider the harm that would result to you psychologically? Although their callousness to your needs does not justify a similar callousness on your part, it should make you see that their present protestations of righteousness are not worth much weight.

Let's look at the effects on your family. Did you really destroy it? Think back to what was going on before you told. Did all of your family members love and respect each other? Did they treat each other with kindness, give each other the freedom to grow and support each other? Were their lives successful and fulfilling? It would surprise me if you could answer yes to any of these questions.

Abuse does not occur in happy families; it occurs in dysfunctional families where the members' needs are not being met. And it occurs in families where one or more members have themselves been abused in childhood but have not worked out their past pain. So your family, like mine, was probably a far cry from *Leave it to Beaver* or *The Brady Bunch*. Those television shows were so popular because they portrayed an ideal family life that most of us wished for but never had.

Picture each of the members of your family. Were they happy and cheerful most of the time, or were they sullen, angry, depressed or drunk? Did you really destroy their happiness or did you perhaps give them a chance to get help for their problems and discover their first opportunity for happiness? They may not have sought help yet, but if any of them are facing criminal charges, in most states they will also receive therapy. And that is the only chance your abuser will have to resolve the problems that are causing unhappiness and abuse.

Certainly the first reaction of your abuser and other family members will be anger. People generally hate change, and the lives of your relatives have been disrupted because the abuse has been discovered. Your brothers and sisters will be angry because they do not want to be associated with an abusive family. If they have not also been abused, they may be shocked and say you are lying. They will not want to believe the truth and have their images of their parents tarnished. And if they have been abused, they may not be ready to face the truth.

If your abusive relatives have not been willing to face their behavior before, they are certainly not going to be happy about being forced to look in the mirror now. Since they will not take responsibility for their acts, they will try to place the blame elsewhere, and you are the most likely target. It is easy to focus on your act of "snitching" as a betrayal of them. Then they don't have to look at their own far more serious betrayal of their duty to love and protect you and at the fact that they were committing a felony.

You may not want your abuser to go to jail. In a few states like Wisconsin, an enlightened system realizes that people who abuse children are sick, and they are treated that way. In Wisconsin, the abuser is taken out of the family and sent to a halfway house where he or she can receive intensive therapy and still continue to work. All family members are given therapy and the family is reunited when the abuser has worked through his or her problems and family members agree that the abuser can return. Other states are not as enlightened and do send the abuser to jail. However, most of these states provide therapy for inmates, so these abusers also have a chance to change.

The reality of having sent your abuser to jail is painful. But the fact is that she or he committed a serious crime. While I would prefer to see abusers receive counselling, I would rather have them in jail than untreated and continuing their abuse. Maybe they would no longer abuse you, but what about one of your sisters or brothers? Or perhaps your parents would divorce and the abuser would remarry and become part of another family where he or she would abuse the children. Or sometimes when the victim leaves or grows up, the abuser begins to molest other children in the neighborhood. Suppose you did not tell, could you live with the knowledge that others have been abused because of your silence?

Although everything may be tumultuous when the abuse is first revealed, the situation often changes after a few months or a year. In one case, April was molested by her father who touched her sexually and masturbated in front of her. He refused to allowed her to date and bought her a vibrator, directing her to use it so that she would not feel any urges to go out with boys. In spite of his strange conduct, April loved her father but, after much soul-searching, she went to her school counselor and reported him. She testified against him at the trial and he was found guilty of child abuse. He was sent to therapy rather than prison, but he was furious and refused to speak to April at all for several months. When April first entered therapy, she was desolate. She sat huddled in a corner and could not talk about what had happened. It took four or five months for April to understand that what she had done was right. I didn't realize April's feelings had changed until I heard her reassuring another group member that she had done the right thing by turning her father in.

April's story had a happy ending. Through therapy her father understood the need for April's action and started communicating with her. April left her foster home and returned to her father after they both completed therapy. She was very firm in her belief that if her father ever started to molest her again, she would leave, call for help and turn him in.

Another adolescent I will call Edie was raped for several years by her stepfather. Edie was terrified of him and afraid to tell anyone. When she was fourteen, she finally told a sympathetic teacher. After her stepfather was prosecuted, Edie was devastated. Her mother accused her of lying, a typical reaction, and her stepfather renounced her in very ugly terms. Edie was all alone and was placed in a home for abused girls. She condemned herself bitterly for what she had done and said that she wished she had kept her mouth shut.

After a few months of family therapy and of repeatedly confronting her mother to acknowledge the truth, Edie was surprised when her mother broke down and said she believed Edie and that she should have known what was going on. Her mother accepted her responsibility for what happened and she and Edie were reconciled.

Less than a year later, Edie was allowed to go home on an overnight visit. Both her mother and stepfather were there. After a day, Edie telephoned me in tears, saying that her stepfather hardly spoke to her and that he must hate her. I said that she could not know what was in his mind and that she should ask him. I told her that sometimes when people were feeling unhappy about something, they were quiet and that what her stepfather was feeling might have nothing to do with her.

I did not hear from Edie until she returned to the girls' residence at the end of the weekend. She was radiant and said she had spoken to her stepfather. He had told her he felt awkward about what he had done and that he still loved her. He said that she had done the right thing in turning him in, that he had been unable to control himself, and that he now felt much happier.

I am not saying it will always turn out as it did for April and Edie. But if you tell, *you* have a chance for a better life. Whether the rest of your family accepts the opportunity to help themselves is up to them.

> *The best mind altering drug is the truth.*
> Lily Tomlin

17. People tell me I should have done something to stop my abuse. Is that true?

No. Your inaction is a common symptom of abuse, and many factors may have made it impossible for you to do anything.

It is common for victims of sexual abuse to be abused for years and never attempt to stop it or to escape. People who do not understand the dynamics of abuse cannot comprehend how this could occur; they cavalierly admonish victims that they "should have done something." A few insensitive people even go so far as to say, "It's your fault, you let it happen." The truth is that it is not that simple.

Some people do not realize that victims of sexual or physical abuse are usually in a state of shock, the same type of shock as victims of accidents, holocausts and natural disasters. Victims often have the same vacant stares as the starving children you see in magazine ads soliciting donations for famine relief. I have that look in all of my early family photos, never smiling, totally expressionless. A kind of numbness envelops victims, mercifully dulling their senses and making their world of horror a little less real. But this mental protection also makes it more difficult for the victim to think clearly or to devise a rational plan of escape.

Even more than numbness, victims are immobilized by fear. People who have been physically or sexually abused live in a state of unrelieved terror. This terror arises from the initial abuse, where they are forced to give up all control and to endure pain and suffer unspeakable acts against their will. At the first moment of abuse, they become victims, totally at the mercy of their abusers, unable to control their lives, their bodies or the emotions raging through them. They are completely helpless. And losing all control is the most terrifying feeling in the world. From that moment on, the terrible feeling of helplessness is burned indelibly into their brains. They will do anything to avoid that feeling, including appeasing and subjugating themselves to their abusers.

But there is an even more ominous side to the feeling of helplessness. Victims begin to believe that they are, in fact, helpless and that they have no power to control their lives. Although some fight everything in order to survive, many victims give up and become utterly passive. They have no hope and so they do not seek help because they believe there is none to be had. They are trapped by their situation and by their own feelings of despair. And this feeling of helplessness will haunt them until they work it out in therapy or their own way.

When children are little, they are at the mercy of their parents; they literally cannot survive without them. They want desperately to please their parents in order to obtain love and the care they need to sustain their lives. When they are small, the thought that they could survive in their parents' absence is inconceivable. If the abuse begins in adolescence, or later, some victims may be mature enough to know that they can survive without their parents or abusers. They are no longer dependent for their very existence on their abusers. But if abuse begins in childhood, it is a very different story. Children are unaware of the existence of child protection agencies or the laws prohibiting child abuse. They believe that if they are abandoned by their parents they will die. So they protect the relationship, despite the abuse, because they believe that in shielding their parents, they are insuring their survival.

Abused children are also victims of the bond which is formed with their parents at birth. This bonding, evident also in the animal kingdom, causes children to love blindly those who care for them as infants. This bond occurs between parent and child and insures that the child will receive adequate food and care. Usually the primary caretakers are the parents, but sometimes mishaps occur, such as the case of a wild duck whose mother was killed. The duck egg was taken to a bird sanctuary where it was incubated by the staff. When the egg hatched, the tiny duckling imprinted on a male member of the staff and followed him everywhere, ignoring other ducks, convinced that the staff member was his mother. The bond was so strong it overcame the differences in size, sex and species.

Bonding is still a mysterious phenomenon, but we know that it involves powerful psychological and biological forces. And human children retain a strong attachment to their parents no matter how abusive or neglectful those parents may be. Sadly, this attachment often prevents them from turning their parents in, even when the children are suffering serious injuries. The biological bond programs a child to love the abusive parent even though a more rational part may hate the abuser intensely. So the victim is cruelly torn between the conflicting emotions of love and hate and is paralyzed to act.

And as if the natural attachment were not enough to immobilize victims, psychologists have recently discovered that the abusive situation itself establishes a bond between abuser and victim. This bond chains victim to abuser even if the abuser is completely unrelated to the victim. This grim phenomenon is known as the "Stockholm" syndrome, and it was first detected in hostage situations where hostages were found to experience positive feelings toward their captors and negative feelings toward the police.[14] The captors reciprocated by developing positive feelings toward the hostages. This syndrome is more likely to develop in hostage situations which last for prolonged periods of time.

An abusive situation is similar in many ways to a hostage situation. If the abuse is occurring to a child within the family, the victim is effectively a hostage, without means of escape. Abusers often show a preference for their victims within the family unit and protect them from any interference or punishment by other family members. It is common for children who have been abused to protect their abusers and to even display affection toward them. This behavior was vividly demonstrated on a recent network television program in which a social worker was trying to discover which parent was abusing a child, since neither the child nor the parents would tell. She took the child into a room and then asked the parents to enter. The child ran immediately to the father and hugged him tightly. The social worker knew instantly from this reaction that the father was the abuser.

This behavior may seem puzzling. Why would an abused child cling to her abuser? Because of the Stockholm syndrome and because the child was attempting to achieve some control over her life. Children believe that if they are good enough or loving enough or can please their abuser enough, then they can end the abuse. They are also often so dependent on their abusers for survival that they must please them in any way they can.

Often abusers take advantage of their victims' extreme dependency and threaten their victims with all types of dire consequences if they tell anyone about the abuse. Some abusers actually tell children that if they disclose the abuse, they will be abandoned and they will die. My father warned me that if I told anyone, I would destroy the family and I would have nowhere to go. Other abusers threaten to punish or kill their victims for telling. Children who have been severely abused are all too ready to believe these threats and to feel that they cannot escape, especially if the abuser is a family member.

One of the more vicious threats is that the abuser will injure another family member if the victim divulges the truth. One stepfather warned his stepdaughter that if she told her mother, he would kill her baby sister. Is it any wonder why victims do not run for help?

Most people have no trouble understanding the barrage of television police scenarios where the bad guys extort money or force their victims to do something against their will by threatening to kill them or someone close to them. The victims usually have many opportunities to go to the police, but they don't because they are protecting themselves or their loved ones. Why is it so difficult then for some people to understand that the same situation exists where a child is being abused, especially when the child is so much more defenseless?

The sad fact is that threats of violence are not even necessary to subjugate a child. A child who loves her father and trusts him will do what he says because she wants to please him and does not want him to be mad at her. Many parents manipulate children into sexual abuse by playing on their affections, bribing them with gifts and assuring them that nothing is wrong with the sexual conduct. Children do not think their parents will lie to them, and thus they may not know for years what their parents are doing is wrong.

The parent may be able to insure silence merely by telling the child to keep the conduct a secret or by saying that the other parent will be angry. But just because there is no *overt* coercion does not make the conduct any less abusive. The psychological coercion, based on the biological bond and manipulation of the child's love, is every bit as forceful and reprehensible as the threat of physical harm.

So the fact that some of you did not protest is no reason to think you participated or to blame yourselves for what happened. You exhibited two very positive qualities, love and trust, and someone who was sick took advantage of that love and trust. You were not at fault and, in time, you will realize that there are people in the world who will cherish and respect those qualities.

Another reason victims are afraid to seek help is that they fear that no one will believe them if they do tell. That fear was certainly justified a decade or so ago. No one wanted to hear about child abuse, and many denied that it was even real. (See Question 26, *When I was abused many years ago as a child, I asked people to help me but no one believed me.* But today, with all of the publicity about child abuse and the creation of agencies to deal with the problem, that fear should diminish. People are beginning to recognize that children do not make up stories about sexual abuse.

However, each time a child is prematurely returned to an abusive family, the child's fear of seeking help increases. If abused children are to be encouraged to ask for help, it is essential for child protective agencies to take the reports of children and others seriously and to insure that children will not be sent back to a harmful environment. It is also important for schools to educate children at a very early age about reporting abuse and to continue to create an atmosphere of trust throughout the school years in order to encourage children to seek help.

Many good reasons prevent children from reporting their abuse. Some of these may apply to you, and all of them can be used to educate people who accuse you of failing to help yourself. Even adults can be paralyzed by abuse, as the men and women who allow their spouses to abuse them can attest. It is important to realize that given your circumstances at the time, you could not have acted differently. You did what you could and you made the best choices you could have made then. They were clearly the right choices because you have survived. You are no longer that helpless child; you can help yourself and receive help from others. You now have control of your life, you can take care of yourself, and you do not have to put up with abuse of any kind anymore.

A human being is a part of the whole, called the universe - a part limited in time and space. He experiences himself, his thoughts and feelings, as something separated from the rest, a kind of optical delusion of his consciousness. This delusion is a kind of

prison for us, restricting us to our personal desires, and to affection for a few persons nearest to us. Our task must be to free ourselves from this prison, by widening our circle of compassion to embrace all living creatures and the whole of nature in its beauty.
Albert Einstein

18. Is it O.K. to hate the person who abused me even if that person is a close relative?

People who have been sexually abused are overwhelmed by violent emotions, but the most frightening one they experience is hatred. They hate what their abuser did to them, they hate the helplessness and other emotions they felt during their abuse, and they hate their abuser. But most of all, they hate themselves.

Our society discourages the expression of most emotions and hate is the most unacceptable. Children are punished for saying, "I hate you," and quickly pick up the fact that use of the word "hate" brings frowns of disapproval. Many survivors are frightened by their violent feelings and believe that they "shouldn't" feel so angry and hateful. Society says we are supposed to love our parents, so survivors feel guilty for hating their mothers who did not protect them and their fathers who abused them. Despite their hurt, they do not believe they have a right to be angry.

Victims of abuse have many reasons for repressing their hate and rage, and this repression masks their feelings—for a time. But hatred cannot remain dormant, and people who have repressed it find that it explodes at inconvenient times, it taints relationships, and it blackens their view of the world. Perhaps the worst part is that repressed hatred is turned inward on the victim. Victims who are not allowed to hate their abusers have only one person to hate—themselves. This self-hate does not fade and can only be healed if it is faced and worked through.

Many people believe that it is wrong to hate, especially if that hatred is directed at a close family member. They view hatred as psychologically destructive and contrary to religious doctrines which preach peace and brotherly love. But they may not understand the purpose hatred serves, and they usually have mistaken ideas about the role of hatred and anger in religion.

Hate and anger are natural emotions. Everything that is natural has a purpose and is part of a genetic design to protect and heal us. Hate and anger are important defenses; they give us adrenalin to help us fight our enemies and the strength to surmount incredible obstacles.

Lien Cheng became an executive in an American company in Shanghai after her husband's death and was falsely arrested during the turbulent Chinese Cultural Revolution. Her gripping account of her years of imprisonment and torture during the Cultural Revolution, described in her book *Life and Death in Shanghai,* vividly illustrates the benefits of hate and anger. Lien Cheng survived because of these feelings; at times she even deliberately baited her tormentors in order to release her anger. Without her hatred, she claims she could not have endured her years of abuse. It fueled her will to continue living.

The emotion of hatred is not something humans artificially create. It is a natural spontaneous feeling that grows from actions we find reprehensible and from hurt we find unbearable. What is *not* natural is to abuse someone, especially where the victim is a relative or a child. Natural law is to protect our young. We get angry when we believe something is wrong or against natural law. Without anger, we might never try to correct injustice or to improve our world. Hatred gives us the courage and strength to stand up to our abusers and to resist their efforts to subdue us.

There are countless examples of anger being used for good. Ralph Nader, the consumer activist, has saved millions of lives because his anger led him to challenge the indifference of the business community to safety and quality. And the Incredible Hulk dramatized for TV viewers the strength rage can give an ordinary man to enable him to help the powerless and overcome the bad guys.

The hatred and anger generated by victims of abuse give them the will to survive. When I complained about my inability to control my anger after I discovered my abuse, my therapist said, "Lynne, your anger saved you. If you had not been able to stay so angry, you would have been destroyed." She was right. My anger had helped me achieve in school, get jobs, and support myself despite years of abuse. Even though I had blanked out my childhood abuse, my anger made me vow that no one would ever hurt me again or stop me from getting what I wanted. I would never depend on anyone or let anyone get close to me. I may have gone a bit too far and I have modified a few of these vows since I discovered my abuse, but they served me well in terms of what I viewed as my survival. And they enabled me to reach the place where I am today.

Hatred has saved many abuse victims from injury and even death. George was brutally sexually and physically abused by his father and older siblings from the time he was an infant. As George grew up, the beatings and abuse grew worse, and so did his anger. When he was thirteen, George began to steal and get into fights. And when he was fourteen, his anger gave him the courage to fight his father. He lost the first time, but when he tried again, his father called the police. And George told his story and was taken out of that house of horrors.

During our therapy sessions, I told George that I thought he had showed a lot of courage in finding a way out for himself. He gave me a surprised smile and said that he would have done anything to escape. For George, like so many other abused teenagers, antisocial and even criminal behavior were the only routes of escape. Now that he is safe, he is ready to work on controlling his anger.

George's anger served him well, and anger has been the salvation of many abuse victims. Unfortunately, victims are frequently made to feel guilty about their anger and hatred by people who fail to recognize that anger and hatred are natural tools for survival. If victims are deprived of these emotions, they may become totally hopeless and passive, thereby condemning themselves to continued abuse. People often need hatred and anger to mobilize them so they can help themselves.

Some people condemn anger and hatred on the ground that these emotions violate religious principles. However, the *Bible* is full of examples of God's wrath and even Jesus destroys the temple in righteous anger. Anger is not a sin, according to the Apostle Paul. "Be ye angry, and sin not; let not the sun go down upon your wrath." Paul acknowledged that anger is an acceptable part of being human; the "sin" is to hold onto it and let it fester. Anger is a reaction to injustice and falseness, it gives us the courage to right wrongs, and it is not "sinful" as long we use it to help ourselves or others.

Anger only becomes destructive when we fail to confront the problems that cause it. When we swallow our anger, it grows within us, feeding on our recurrent thoughts of how we were wronged. As our anger grows, we become angry at ourselves for failing to act and for allowing ourselves to be victimized. Since it is safer to be angry at ourselves than at our abusers, we begin to blame ourselves and our self-esteem declines. And when we hate ourselves, we begin to hate others, even if they have done us no wrong. And so the circle of anger feeds on itself and increases over time until we become consumed by anger and obsessed by revenge for the most minor of trespasses.

Turning our anger inward produces physical as well as emotional damage. Repressed anger causes headaches, backaches, and even cancer. Several clinics across the United States are successfully helping cancer patients by teaching them to release repressed anger, anger which is literally eating away at them.

Although anger and hatred can be positive forces to help us initially, if repressed they can become poisons which eat at our souls. Our objective should not be to eliminate anger, but to use and express it constructively. Feelings only cause harm when they arise in response to acts which we misinterpret or when we hang onto feelings too long so that they adversely affect our lives. Since powerful emotions are a normal response to acts of abuse, your feelings cannot hurt you unless you cling to them when they no longer serve their purpose. Your feelings of hate and rage saved you from severe psychological damage and gave you the strength to survive.

But now you are no longer being abused. You no longer need to feel these emotions fomenting inside you; they serve no purpose. Now they are ruining your life by making you angry at people you may not want to offend or by causing you to destroy your own success and happiness because you feel unworthy. This is the time to let go of your anger, when it is no longer useful and when it is hurting you.

The way to release these feelings is to recognize them, understand the reasons for them and express them. A first step is to obtain the help of a hypnotherapist in recovering the memories of your abuse. It is important to recover and experience the *emotions* which accompanied your abuse, not just the mental pictures or knowledge of the acts. Until you experience these emotions and release them, you will never be free of them. Some people have problems freeing their childhood emotions because they are trapped in ego states that have to be uncovered separately. (See the description of "dissociative" states in Question 28, *Can you explain multiple personality disorder?*) Once you have again felt the repressed emotions, as painful as they are, you will experience a sense of relief, because the tremendous burden you have been carrying will have been lifted from you.

Other therapeutic tools can be used to release the feelings. Some of them can be done at home. An exercise frequently used by therapists to release emotions is a Gestalt technique called the "Empty Chair." You face an empty chair and imagine your abuser sitting in it while you tell your abuser all the things you wanted to say but didn't. You tell your abuser how you felt when you were being abused, how you felt about him or her, and how you felt afterwards. You have to be totally honest, holding nothing back. And you can scream and swear as much as you like. When you begin, you will probably be rather timid, but as you get going, with the help of your therapist, you should be able to really let go and experience your anger, hatred and perhaps, sadness and fear.

Another version of the Empty Chair technique is to pound a pillow that represents your abuser. However, any exercise which involves violence should be done with a therapist or at the direction of a therapist. Your feelings may be fairly strong and you will feel safer and better able to release them if someone you trust is present. When you pound the pillow, you yell whatever you want to at your abuser, as in the Empty Chair exercise. Sometimes the action of pounding a pillow can stimulate a release of rage more effectively than merely yelling at a chair.

One technique you can do safely at home by yourself is to write a letter to your abuser. This letter is not to be sent; it is only a vehicle to help you remember and express all of your feelings. This letter should be as complete and detailed as possible. Write everything that you feel about your abuser, your abuse and what it has done to you. Don't leave anything out. When you think you have finished, put it away until the next day. Then add whatever you may have forgotten.

Do this for a week and put the letter away for another week. Then take the letter out and read it carefully two or three times. Make sure you have included everything you want to say: all of the anger, all of the hatred, all of the betrayal, all of the grief, all of the guilt, all of the fear, all of the pain. Add anything you may have omitted.

When you are sure that you have written everything you have to say, take the letter and destroy it in whatever way is most satisfying to you. You are destroying the hold your abuser has over you, so chop up the letter, burn it, or shred it—flush what is left down the toilet where it belongs.

Sometimes people find it difficult to express their anger. We block our feelings because we are afraid that if we let go, our feelings will erupt in an uncontrollable explosion that may hurt us or someone else. When we are angry, it is sometimes difficult to separate the anger from our behavior. But anger and behavior are separate and we do have control over our behavior. Sometimes venting our anger in safe ways can convince us that even when angry we have the power to choose our behavior. Pounding pillows or throwing eggs at trees can be useful in proving that anger does not have to be harmful.

One of the most imaginative techniques for helping people who are afraid they can't think when they are angry is used by therapists Mary and Bob Goulding. They urge clients to pound a stool and, when they are really angry, screaming and pounding, Mary asks them to come up with two creative ideas on how to handle the situation. The clients are amazed to find that they can think clearly, even though they are in a rage.

Try it sometime when you are really furious. Have someone ask you to answer a question, or stop yourself and see it you can think of a question and answer it. You will find that you are still in control. You rule your anger, it does not rule you.

We may find it difficult to express our anger and hatred because we have ambivalent feelings toward our abuser. Our abuser may be a parent for whom we have a bond of love despite the abuse. We may hate our parent and love him or her at the same time. This is a tremendous dilemma which paralyzes us from expressing or even acknowledging our hatred. If the abuser was also the nurturing parent, as is often the case, the victim experiences even greater conflict.

Sandra could express her anger at her mother but continued to protect her perpetrator father for many sessions of an AMAC group because as she said, "He gave me only pitiful crumbs of love, but those were the only crumbs I had." She had difficulty facing the fact that she had received no real love and was alone during the long period of her abuse. When she finally was able to see the crumbs for what they were, she realized that she "... had learned to hate my own needs and weakness instead of hating my father." By refusing to place her hatred where it belonged, she ended up hating herself.

Some authorities say that one way of dealing with this love-hate conflict is to separate the acts of abuse from the abuser. You can hate what your parent did to you and make sure it will never happen again— without hating your parent. Thus you can rage at what your parent *did* and not at your parent. My therapist suggested this way of divorcing conflicting feelings about my father, but it did not work for me. I had to work through my rage because I could not separate my feelings about what he did to me from my feelings about him.

Frankly, I have never seen anyone who could successfully sever their feelings about their abuser's conduct from the person. I believe that we have to go through a period of hate before we can recognize and accept the feelings of love. After I expressed my rage, I found that I could still love my father for the kindness and love he gave me later in life. The important thing is to recognize that you may have conflicting feelings and that you must deal with them all.

There are also ways to control feelings of anger and hatred. When we are really angry, it is because we have engaged in a lot of negative self-talk which increases our anger. Some of this self-talk is usually based upon feelings we had and conclusions we drew during our abuse.

For example, if we ask a friend to come over and he declines, we can look at the refusal two ways. We can say, "He is never around when I need him," and, based on our abusive experience, "He probably doesn't like me. He can't be trusted. He'll only hurt me. He really is a..." Or, we can say STOP to ourselves and replace those thoughts, which are fueling our anger, with positive ones. "Gee, I'm sorry he can't come over tonight, but I know he's busy and I gave him very little notice. I know he likes me, he's a good friend, and I'll see him soon. Now who else can I call or what else can I do to make tonight enjoyable?" It is when we think the same angry thought over and over in our minds that our anger feels uncontrollable. But we can control our thoughts.

I used to get furious for hours and even days when something relatively minor went wrong. When I stopped to analyze my thoughts, I found that I was thinking, "I'm so angry, I'm so furious. They shouldn't do that to me." By repeatedly telling myself that I was angry, I was stirring up anger within me. I learned to replace those thoughts with positive ones, "I am calm. I am peaceful." At first I found it very artificial, but as I kept repeating the positive thoughts, my anger began to diminish. With some practice, I am now able to cut off my anger before it ruins my day.

I also replaced the "They shouldn't..." thought with "They are doing the best they can." Once I stopped thinking people were out to get me, a belief based on true facts from my childhood, my life became a lot easier. (For more information on thought stopping and positive thoughts, see Part V, Section 8, *Reprogramming negative thoughts or affirmations.*)

One of the most powerful ways to release anger is through understanding. If you understand the person you hate, you may begin to see that the person had very few choices.

Many abuse victims hate their mothers for failing to protect them. I despised my mother because she was aware of my brutal abuse and, when I begged her to take me away, she hit me and told me it was all my fault. I was six years old. But when more memories started coming back, I saw her running out to the patio to cry. I also remembered that she said something about my situation being like what happened to her, so I suspect that her father also abused her. And after studying psychology, I know that she is a textbook example of the codependent wife and was psychologically incapable of leaving my father. I have begun to feel sorry for her and the hatred is gone because I understand that her life must have been as much of a hell as mine was.

Understanding your abuser may appear to be more difficult. But it may help to know that almost all abusers have themselves been victims of abuse. (I believe that *all* abusers have been physically or sexually abused, but the statistics cannot show it because in some cases the abuse may have been so severe that the abusers repressed their memories and thus cannot be counted in a survey.) Surveys do show that at least 80 percent of incestuous fathers have been sexually or physically abused as children.[15]

Sexual abuse appears to be a learned behavior. If you know that your abuser was also a victim and experienced similar pain, fear, anguish, rage and hate as you, you may begin to understand that perhaps he or she was unable to control unconscious impulses which led to your abuse and that you were not the cause. Of course, being abused does not excuse abusing others. Your abuser is still responsible for getting help and controlling the impulses and you have every right to be angry that he or she did not do so. But the knowledge that your abuser acted out of past pain may help you understand so you can forgive yourself and your abuser.

Understanding can aid forgiveness in other situations involving abuse. Emily was the youngest of four daughters. All of her older sisters were abused at puberty by their father, but they never told anyone. And so the abuse was passed down to Emily when she came of age. She blew the whistle on her father, and now her sisters are condemning her. Emily's rage is understandably great. "I *hate* my sisters for not telling and for letting it happen to me. Why didn't they protect me?"

First, Emily needs to feel and express her anger at her sisters, and, of course, her father. She has been harmed by their actions and she needs to know her anger is justified. After she has vented her anger about her sisters, it would be helpful for her to understand why they never told anyone. In this case a therapy session for all the sisters where the therapist could moderate and keep the discussion on track may be best way to help the sisters understand each other. But, if you have a similar problem and are able to talk to your siblings without rancor and with sensitivity, you could do it yourself.

In Emily's case, her sisters were terrified of their father who had threatened to punish them if they told. When the sisters were being abused, there was not as much publicity about sexual abuse as there is now and the sisters were afraid no one would believe them. The sisters condemned Emily for telling because they felt so guilty for not telling themselves and for letting it happen to her. They hated what they had done, condemned themselves for it and turned their condemnation on her. They also envied and hated Emily for having the courage that they lacked. People generally hate those they wrong, so the sisters hated Emily for that reason too.

The reasons why people do what they do are many, and when we wade through this complexity, we can see that they really did the best they could with the understanding and resources they had at the time.

Which brings us to the next step in the process—forgiveness. The subject of forgiveness is treated in Question 20, *Do I have to forgive my abuser?* I refer you to that section for this important step. Forgiveness is critical because it is a letting go of what happened. If you want your life to be happy from now on, you must let go of the pain and blame. What happened to you does not exist any more, except in your mind. You are letting a thought ruin your life. To hang on to something that no longer exists when there is so much in the world to enjoy, does not make much sense.

Your anger served you well once. It is not serving you well now. Now is the time to let it out and let it go. You do not need to fear your anger or any other feeling. Our feelings give us gifts—we need our feelings. Accept your feelings and make them your friends. They have helped you when you needed it and they will continue to guide you and to point out problems. You do not have to save your ancient anger; it has served its purpose. Now is the time to learn to use your anger constructively so that you can make the best use of the strength it provides.

Most abuse victims need assertiveness training. We know how to be angry and we know how to be aggressive. But we need to learn how to channel our anger and strength in ways so that we can get what we want without offending people or threatening them. We need to learn that we can achieve more through softness—even men need to learn this—than through demands and power plays. I strongly recommend that you enroll in an assertiveness training course, or at least get some books on the subject. Then you will have completed the last step in making your anger work for you in a positive way.

> *To be wronged or robbed is nothing*
> *unless you continue to remember it.*
> Confucius

19. I often think about killing the person who abused me. Is that wrong?

People often have violent fantasies about taking revenge on their abusers. These fantasies can include killing their abusers in a variety of unique and creative ways. Some therapists even advocate using fantasies of revenge to help their clients release repressed anger. Therapists

Mary and Robert Goulding use fantasy to give their clients permission to enjoy their anger rather than be afraid of it. They help clients learn that fantasies are acceptable as long as they are not acted out, and the Gouldings encourage their clients to devise unusual and humorous ways to express their thoughts of revenge.[16]

It is natural to have strong feelings about your abuser, and it is even more natural to think about revenge. The thought of revenge is a way of obtaining control over what happened and of relieving the terror of helplessness you experienced. Many therapists help clients who have been abused by guiding them under hypnosis to obtain a sense of control over their abusers and the situation. Thus victims go back under hypnosis to the scene of their abuse and push their abusers away, hit them, or take control of the situation in some other way. When I was hypnotized, I imagined going back as an adult to the house of horrors where I was abused, and I hugged and comforted myself as a little girl. I took her by the hand and led her out of the house, telling her that she *never* had to go back. Then, at my therapist's suggestion, I mentally went back and burned the house to the ground. It gave me a sense of control and a wonderful feeling of relief.

However, fantasies of revenge must be handled carefully because they can be dangerous if they become a repetitive part of a person's daily pattern of thought. Fantasies which become obsessions can inflame anger instead of releasing it. And if they become too real, they could motivate action and become reality. Violent thoughts can be therapeutic only if they remain thoughts and if they are worked out with the support of a therapist. Your concern about the violence of your thoughts or your ability to control your anger may be a warning signal that you need professional help to let go of your anger and hatred. We know ourselves better than anyone, and when we are concerned, we usually have a reason to be.

Carrying out an act of revenge is not generally useful. Although revenge seems more than justified in cases of abuse, the sad fact is that revenge never brings the hoped for satisfaction. Suppose you did kill your abuser for victimizing you. What then? No one gets away with murder these days, and you would be tried, sentenced and either imprisoned or put to death. What would you accomplish? You would have made yourself the ultimate victim. Even if you only injure your abuser, the results would be similar. Violence only breeds violence, and revenge only brings further retaliation. Do you want to spend the rest of your life in an endless battle with your abuser? Do you even want to spend the rest of your life *thinking* about your abuser? Are you willing to let your abuser ruin the rest of your life?

You may be thinking that you can't let your abuser get away with it. He has to be punished for the anguish he caused. You may even be thinking that if you don't take revenge, you will be a wimp or remain a victim. Many victims of abuse have similar thoughts.

How do you know what your abuser has suffered? He or she was probably severely abused as a child. Do you know what guilt and pain your abuser feels? Is he living a happy, carefree life? I am not saying that your abuser's pain justifies your abuse. Of course it doesn't. I am also not implying that you do not have a right to your anger, rage and hatred over what was done to you. I am only saying that abusers are sick people in need of help. If you kill your abuser you may deprive him of the chance to fully appreciate what he has done and feel the guilt and sorrow that may enable him to change. And if you injure him you may add to the pain that is imprisoning him in his role of abuser. Given a rational conscious choice, unaffected by past pain and abuse, do you really think anyone would consciously *choose* to abuse a child?

We don't have knowledge of all the facts which would enable us to decide what punishment to impose on our abusers, nor do we really have the power. The *Bible* says, "Vengeance is mine; I will repay, saith the Lord." Romans:19. If that is what you believe, God is the only one who has the knowledge, understanding, and the power.

I have come to believe the maxim, "What goes around, comes around." I used to scoff at that idea, but no more. I have seen too many people who have hurt others being hurt or, more often, hurting themselves.

My father is a good example. After he became aware of what he was doing to me, he immediately went to a clinic and received help from a hypnotherapist. He never sexually abused me again, and he felt tremendous guilt and remorse over what he had done to me. When I was a teenager, he used to cry and tell me he was so sorry he wanted to kill himself because he had been such a terrible father and done such terrible things to me.

By that time I had repressed everything and I ran to my mother who, in her typical denial reaction, covered up the truth by telling me that Daddy was just worried because his career was not going well. Only after he died and I discovered my abuse did I realize the pain my father lived with for the rest of his life.

And my mother who denies everything to this day is one of the most unhappy women I have ever seen. She goes around with a childlike desperation telling everyone over and over again how happy she is and how lucky she is, as though by repeating the magic words she can make them true. But when she does not think anyone is looking and her forced smile falls from her face, the pain and grief are so obvious it hurts to look at her. The irony is that I am the only person who has seen behind her facade. I know exactly what she is and what she has done and I have forgiven her. I am the only person who can accept her as she really is, but her fear forces her to reject me. She has made herself so alone.

My mother has created her own suffering beyond anything I could possibly have wished for her even when I hated her most. I have tears in my eyes as I write this because it hurts to think of her living in such pain. I hope that someday, before she dies, she will allow someone to love her as she is. I would like to be her friend but I no longer have any expectation that things will change between us. I know I cannot change her, so I continue to send her love and hope for her healing.

I believe people engineer their own revenge. Why did Jim and Tammy Baker get caught so blatantly with their hands in the till? Why did Richard Nixon keep the tapes? Sometimes we even have enough awareness to recognize that we cause our own downfalls. Napoleon said at St. Helena, "No one but myself can be blamed for my fall. I have been my own greatest enemy—the cause of my own disastrous fate." We seem to find ways to punish ourselves if we refuse to change or make amends. No one really has to do it for us.

You can consume what remains of your life in an endless quest for revenge and spend your days and nights raging at your abuser and ruminating over past wrongs, if that is your choice. I chose a different path. With help, I decided to let go of the past, to work through the pain of my abuse as quickly as possible, to surround myself with people who make me feel good, and to make up for all my misery with happiness. Instead of punishing my tormentors, I let them go; I refused to give them any more control over me or to let them ruin one more day of my life. And the more content I became, the less I desired revenge.

Since I could not find a reason for the horror I had endured, I decided something good had to come out of it. I had so many questions when my memories started coming back, and I felt so alone that I decided to go back to graduate school to become a therapist and write this book in the hope that my experience would help someone else feel better. You may be able to use your abuse to prevent someone else's or to make someone's life a little happier. I know my way works for me because when I follow the path of letting go and choosing happiness, I feel peaceful, and when my thoughts return to anger and bitterness, I feel turmoil and pain. My angry thoughts are infrequent now, so I can assure you that it is possible to let them go.

Nothing that you can do to your abuser can erase your suffering or bring back the happiness you have lost. Your abuser cannot make up for what is past. Only you can make your future. You can only go on and work to make the rest of your life as full of joy and peace as you can. "The best revenge is living well."

> *Blood stains cannot be removed by more blood;*
> *resentment cannot be removed by more resentment;*
> *resentment can be removed only by forgetting it.*
> The Teachings of Buddha

20. Do I have to forgive my abuser?

Certainly not, if by "forgive" you mean condone what your abuser did to you. "Condone" means to overlook, and you can never overlook conduct that caused the magnitude of suffering you have endured. Nor can you forget it. Those acts are irrevocable and have affected your life just as your height and coloring affect your life.

But that does not mean that your abuse has to haunt you or be the focus of the rest of your life. You can let go of what happened and you can let go of the bitterness, anger and pain you feel about the what happened and about your abusers without condoning what they did. "Letting go" is the true meaning of forgiveness. You are not a God who absolves people of their "sins." You can only refuse to harbor the hate and bitterness which will ruin the rest of your life. Forgiveness is not for your abuser, it is for you.

Merle Shain says in *Hearts That We Broke Long Ago,* "When you forgive, you take your enemy's power over you away, you defang them and change the atmosphere between you from highly charged to neutral, and sometimes even to rosy hued. And people, who had the power to control you just by being, can no longer command your emotions, or suck you into the vortex with a word. They cease to be the eye of your storm, and once you forgive them, they become people like any other, human and flawed and misguided on occasion, and hence rather like the rest of us."

"Letting go" does not mean that you would ever permit what happened to you to happen again. You are an adult now and you can take care of yourself. Forgiveness does not mean putting yourself in a position where someone can harm you. And "letting go" does not mean you have talk to the people you forgive again, unless you want to. It is your choice. You can see them if *you* really want to and if you feel safe. The purpose of forgiveness is to help *you* feel better so you will allow yourself to be happy.

One of the best books I have read on healing and forgiving is *You Can Heal Your Life* by Louise Hay. She emphasizes what the medical profession is beginning to acknowledge—that disease comes from the repressed emotions that are festering in our minds and bodies. The word "disease" itself informs us that illness is a result of "dis-ease" or an unresolved problem within us. Hay asserts that we can release our harmful thoughts and emotions by forgiving, or letting go of our negative feelings toward the people who have hurt us.

If disease comes from a state of unforgiveness, then whenever we are ill, we need to look around to see who we most need to forgive. We have all heard the phrase "being eaten up by hate or anger." In her list of various diseases, Hay lists the probable cause of cancer as the feeling of "deep hurt. Long standing resentment. Deep secret or grief eating away at the self. Carrying hatreds. What's the use."

There is no longer any question that the emotions and resentments we store in our minds affect our bodies. Survivors are often amazed to find that in recovering the memories of their childhood abuse, they recall sensations of the pain they felt in their bodies at time they were abused. They actually feel mild pain in the places where they were hit or wounded or raped, and this pain moves to different spots as each memory is brought to consciousness. Once a memory is recovered, the pain disappears.

Our minds and our bodies are inextricably interconnected. So we must release the negative feelings from our abuse if we are to attain physical health and mental contentment. We cannot do this without letting go of the rage and hatred we feel for our abusers. Hay was speaking to all victims when she wrote, ". . . the very person that you find hardest to forgive is the one YOU NEED TO LET GO OF THE MOST. Forgiveness means giving up, letting go. It has nothing to do with condoning behavior. It's just letting the whole thing go. We do not have to know HOW to forgive. All we need to do is to be WILLING to forgive. The Universe will take care of the hows."[17]

While forgiving is essential to a complete healing, victims should not be pressed to forgive their abusers too soon in the healing process. It is clear from clinical experience that healing cannot take place unless survivors' repressed emotions are released and all of the survivors' feelings of rage, hatred, betrayal, sadness and fear are experienced and understood. This is especially true for AMACs who may have repressed memories of their abuse so thoroughly that they are still carrying all of their pain inside them. This pain must rise to the surface of consciousness before a survivor can let it go, and forgive.

Some therapists make the mistake of counseling forgiveness before victims have had a sufficient opportunity to experience their feelings and deal with them, thereby making it more difficult to release repressed emotions and recover other painful memories. This error usually occurs where victims have been severely abused and experience a great deal of distress when recalling savage events. Therapists may find it hard to see their clients in so much pain. They may try to rescue their clients by prematurely cutting off the pain. These well-meaning therapists fail to recognize that people know intuitively how much they need to recall about their past traumas and will stop themselves when they have completed what they need to accomplish.

Victims will find it difficult if not impossible to let go of their feelings and forgive if they are urged to forgive before they have a complete understanding of the abusive events and emotions they need to examine. It is hard to forgive someone for something you do not remember. Moreover, if therapists encourage clients to forgive before examining strong emotions about abuses, the clients may interpret the therapists' actions as disapproval of their feelings and may repress them still further.

Lori is a dramatic example of the damage caused by urging forgiveness too soon. Having been viciously abused physically and sexually by two stepfathers, an uncle and a couple of their friends, Lori, filled with rage, had been treated in a hospital and in the adolescent unit of the county mental health facility on more than one occasion. Before her most recent stay at the unit, someone had advised her that the answer to her problems was to forgive her abusers and she would be cured.

Lori was extremely intelligent and wanted to get well. She also wanted to please her therapists so she would be discharged from the adolescent program. So Lori expounded constantly on the virtues of forgiveness. In group therapy sessions, she would preach forgiveness to anyone who expressed the slightest degree of anger. The tragedy is that she actually *believed* that she had forgiven those who abused her. When I said in group that I could believe that she had forgiven some of her relatives but not that she had forgiven one of their friends who had raped her, she insisted in a strange singsong voice that she had forgiven all of them. When she spoke, she was almost saintly. But later she punched out other kids and employees of the unit and had to be returned to the hospital.

105

Too many people today are trying to leap from hatred and rage to unconditional love without taking the time to unearth the buried fury from past abuse. It does not work. You cannot experience love until you love yourself and there is little room for love in a mind embalmed with ancient personal pain and emotions. There is too much of what I call "violent pacifism" in the world today. People preach peace and unconditional love while shooting at other drivers on freeways, ignoring the needs of their loved ones, stepping on their colleagues at work to get to the top, and killing forests and animals that get in the way of their desires or their profits. True enlightenment is elusive and its end is unconditional love. Unconditional love is unconditional caring and respect for all life because we are all one. Realization of this concept known as "enlightenment," is difficult to achieve because we have to erase the cobwebs of our past to attain it and that means dealing with all of the spiders.

You will know when you are ready to consider letting go of your past hurts and of the feelings you have toward your abusers. And in the meantime, it is important for you to recognize your right to your emotions, no matter how strong they are and no matter how vengeful your thoughts may be. As human beings, we come equipped with feelings which protect us from harm and inform us about the nature of our responses and of what is going on around us. It is natural for you to have strong feelings of anger and hatred toward your abusers and the people who failed to protect you. It would be unnatural if you had only positive feelings towards them or even no feelings at all.

The only danger is in holding on to your negative feelings for too long so they make you bitter and distrustful and poison the happiness which is available to you now. Once you have worked out your feelings, either by yourself or in therapy, you should feel substantially calmer. When you release the emotions, they usually evaporate. You won't have to work so hard to contain them anymore. This does not mean that you will never feel anger again. Of course you will, but you will feel an appropriate anger based on something that happens in your present environment. Your inappropriate explosions or depression, if you've turned your anger in on yourself, will be greatly diminished.

When you believe that you have released most of your emotions, then you can work in earnest on forgiveness. You may be able to start working on forgiveness affirmations or studying about forgiveness before you deal completely with your emotions, if that seems comfortable to you. You are the best judge of what is best for you. But I hope you will make a conscious promise to yourself to release your emotions and confront your painful feelings. Those feelings will disappear if you bring them to the light—and haunt you forever if you keep them in the dark.

A friend taught me an affirmation that I have repeated for many years to help me forgive. "I forgive all those who have hurt me intentionally and unintentionally. I forgive myself for all those I have hurt intentionally and unintentionally. And I accept the forgiveness of all those who have hurt me intentionally or unintentionally." By reminding me of the people I have hurt without meaning to, I get a clearer perspective on the people who have hurt me. It also makes me wonder if there isn't someone out there who is saying forgiveness affirmations about me!

I agree with Louise Hay that the desire to forgive someone is most of the battle. You are in control of whether or not you forgive, and what you want, you will cause to happen. The key is letting go. I learned this experience with my mother who at 78 years old is still burying the horror of my abuse under years of denial and amnesia. She refuses to admit or discuss my abuse and treats me as though it never happened. Despite the fact that my father's abuse was far more severe, I was able to forgive him and let go of my anger more easily because mother always said he was "sick." I could find no excuse for my mother's hitting me when I was only an infant, and, while she did try to save me a couple of times from the savagery of my father, she hit me when I asked her to take me away and left me to be abused.

My therapist suggested that I release my rage by cutting up a photograph of my mother or even chopping up one of her paintings. I followed my therapist's advice and was surprised by the depth of my fury. I took an ax and chopped to smithereens three paintings my mother had done, including the frames and a packing crate. I felt a peace I had never known after that act of rage. I still could not condone what she had done, but my therapist told me I did not have to. I could let go of the emotions and start fresh with my mother. I started to look at my mother as a new friend, one who cared about me and wished the best for me now. For a few months it seemed to work, but her continued denial and attacks on me prevented the friendship I had hoped for. Despite my sadness, I feel peaceful because, by letting go of my anger and hatred, I can overlook her actions and she cannot hurt me any more. I understand my mother better and can forgive her.

While I do not recommend that victims chop up mementos without the support of a therapist, it is essential to release the anger. People who try to paper over their rage with premature forgiveness find that their anger bursts out at a later time. The best way to release it is in therapy where it can be expressed safely. Only then should forgiveness be considered.

107

Forgiveness is a matter of understanding—understanding that deep down we are all abused children who hurt others when we feel hurt. Once we understand ourselves, we can understand our abusers and let go of the rage and pain that imprisons a happier child inside us.

> *Life's greatest achievement is the continual remaking of yourself so that at last you know how to live.*
> Unknown

21. Sometimes I feel life isn't worth living and I think about suicide. What should I do?

First you need to understand that your thoughts of suicide are not uncommon. While they seem frightening, thoughts about suicide are usual for people who have been abused. You have many valid reasons to feel hopeless, depressed and angry, and they all stem from how you felt while you were being abused. These feelings can be changed and you can begin to enjoy life once you understand the origin of your feelings and work on releasing them.

If you have thoughts about suicide, you need support. But people usually think about suicide when they feel most alone and have little energy for doing anything. And based on their past experience, abuse victims are often convinced that no one will help them, so they do not seek the help they need.

Before I remembered I had been abused as a child, I thought I was hopeless. No one, not even highly recommended therapists, had been able to understand the turmoil raging inside me. They thought I was just hysterical, and I was terrified because I knew it had to be more than that but I didn't know what it could be. I was so unhappy that I stockpiled pills for several years and hid them wherever I moved. I had to know that I had a way out if I couldn't stand the pain anymore. I would get the pills out and look at them every few months to decide whether it was time to take them, but somehow I always decided to try life just a little longer. Sometimes I even decided to keep trying for one more year. The pills finally ended up hidden under a floorboard of the attic in my Maryland home.

One night, I decided I had really had it. I was miserable, things were not getting better, and I really didn't care about anything anymore. I got the pill bottles and lined them up on the floor. I was always a perfectionist and whatever I did, I was going to do it right. I had collected more than enough pills to kill me ten times over. I don't even know how I would have swallowed them all.

I looked at those pills and thought about all the times I had sat looking at them. I decided it was time to either do it or stop playing this game. And then I remembered all of the things I had walked away from in my life and later regretted. It hit me that if I walked away from life, I would never get a chance to try again.

I sat on the floor for a long time staring at the pills and getting angry. A tiny kernel somewhere in me believed there had to be a way I could change my life, and I was going to keep going until I found that way. The rage I felt as a child enveloped me—they were *not* going to lick me. I had made it alone all of my life and I was not going to give up now. I dumped bottle after bottle of brightly colored poison down the toilet. After that, suicide was no longer an option for me. And I now realize that if I had decided differently, I would have missed all the happiness I have known in the last few years.

Although I somehow managed to reach a positive conclusion by myself, it would have been much easier to have had some help. At the time I threw the pills away, I had not uncovered my abuse so I had no idea what was wrong with me. I had been going to a psychoanalyst for almost three years who had not discovered the problem; he had not helped me because he hardly ever spoke to me. I never told him about my struggle with suicide because I would never have dreamed of telephoning that cold, unresponsive man at night to ask for help, nor did I trust him to help me. But if I had known that I had been sexually abused, I would have known what to do. I would have run to an experienced sexual abuse therapist where I could have been sure of receiving understanding and help.

Since I have started counseling survivors of abuse and working with other counselors, I realize the difference just over a decade has made in the quality of treatment for sexual abuse. Cases of sexual abuse have become commonplace, and therapists have become increasingly familiar with the issues involved and have devised more effective methods of treatment. If you carefully determine whether your therapist has experience in handling cases of sexual abuse, you can be assured that the treatment you receive will help you. Things are no longer hopeless. No matter how unbearable your life appears to be, you can be helped and you will get better.

A word of warning: Despite the gains in sexual abuse therapy, some therapists are still overly eager to suppress pain by prescribing drugs for depression and other symptoms of abuse. In extreme cases or for achieving short-term stability, drugs may be necessary, but the use of drugs can impede healing by making it more difficult to uncover the root cause of the problem. Some therapists believe that drugs may make a client calmer and more able to face problems in therapy. But sometimes the opposite result can occur. If an antidepressive drug knocks out depression, the client may lose her motivation for dealing with the underlying problems. In an abuse case, the depression will certainly be based on memories and emotions of the abuse. These must be brought to consciousness and resolved in order for the client to let go of the feelings and be free. Once the repressed emotions have been released, the depression will usually disappear. But can the cause of the depression be ascertained if the client is on drugs and cannot experience the depression? And the long term side effects of such drugs are still unknown. Are they worth the risk?

Drugs may be necessary if a client is truly suicidal and if there is no immediate way to work with the client to release some of the emotions causing the depression. If this is the case, antidepressants should only be used for a short time, until it is feasible to begin intensive therapy to uncover the problems that are causing the feelings. You are in charge of your own therapy and should make sure that you not are being given drugs without appropriate therapy. If you have doubts, get a second opinion.

The worst part of feeling suicidal is having such strong feelings of depression and hopelessness without really understanding where they come from. If you don't know what you are dealing with, you have no hope of ever changing it. You don't know whether there is a cure or if you are simply crazy. When you understand that your suicidal thoughts arise out of your abuse, you know that you have a logical reason for feeling as bad as you do.

No matter how terrible your life appears to be, most of your overwhelming feelings of depression and hopelessness are not coming from present events, but from the feelings you had when you were abused—feelings that were too painful for you to acknowledge then. When children are being abused, they feel trapped and totally hopeless. They often want to die. They may even beg to die or pray to God to let them die. These thoughts and feelings about death as the only possible means of escape are overwhelming and cause the mind to block them out. You detached yourself from these emotions to protect yourself as a

110

child, because you could not deal with so many violent emotions at once. But these emotions are stored within you. When events in your adult life trigger feelings similar to those you had when you were being abused, you get a double whammy: you are hit not just by today's feelings but by the old unresolved childhood feelings as well.

The fact that your old feelings are resurfacing is a signal that you are now ready to deal with these repressed emotions. Your mind is letting you know that you can uncover the memories and handle the emotions now. When you work with your therapist under hypnosis, you will find that the way you feel when you are depressed and suicidal is the way you felt as a child, when you were being abused and could not escape. Once these old feelings are released and you understand them, they will disappear as if by magic. This does not mean you will never be depressed; everyone has disappointments and you will still have to deal with today's feelings. But your emotions will not be as overpowering and you will find that you are able to cope with them.

Right now you may feel that you are helpless, but this feeling comes from your childhood and is probably the most overpowering feeling you had during your abuse. Then you were truly helpless, you had nowhere to go and no way to escape your abuser. Your abuser was bigger and older and could manipulate you; you could do nothing, you had no options. But is that the case today? With all of the support groups, therapists and people who want to help others, are there really no options? Are you truly trapped now, or are you merely seeing yourself as a little child who can't escape?

You survived severe abuse so you are very strong and you know how to protect yourself. You also have the strength to hold on a little longer and take the last couple of steps that will free you from the past and and move you toward happiness and peace.

Sometimes when we need help the most, we push it away. Our pain is so great that we cannot bear to have anyone see it, or we believe that we do not deserve help, that we are beyond redemption. But we also do not ever want to be hurt the way we were as children and we go to great lengths to protect ourselves.

Kim was a Korean whose father died and whose mother gave him up for adoption when he was four because she could not support him. She wanted him to come to the United States where she thought he would have a better life. Kim interpreted his mother's actions and his father's death as rejections of him and he internalized his pain. He could not bear to be rejected again and so he rejected everyone who tried to help or love him. The parents who adopted him gave him back to the state and his foster parents threw up their hands at his anger and rejection. He pushed everyone away, yet he insisted he was a victim of prejudice against Orientals. When the Korean Center tried to provide support, he refused to go. He made himself so alone that his isolation became unbearable and he cut his wrists. He barely survived.

All of Kim's actions were based on one premise: he did not want to be rejected ever again. Sometimes in our zeal to avoid pain, we inflict even greater pain on ourselves. Kim had some painful incidents in his life, but the emotions he felt as a child compelled him to reject love that was offered later.

We have to understand our childhood pain and the decisions we made as children if we are to be free to choose happiness today. Kim had to realize that the death of his father was not a rejection of him and that his mother simply was not strong enough to cope with raising a child in poverty. She thought she was doing what was best for him, but she made a mistake. So did Kim when he decided never to be close to anyone ever again. He had to realize that his earlier decision was based on a false childish view of the facts, a view that did not work for him as an adult.

People will hurt us and people will help us and we must learn to tell the difference. Not everyone is an abuser and not everyone will let you down. When you are an adult, you have the ability to distinguish between people who offer friendship from those who want to use you. You only have to listen to that little voice inside you which says, "Watch out!"

As an adult, you can realize that you are causing your own aloneness, and you can consciously allow yourself to give people a chance and give yourself permission to ask for help. If you have been abused and have suicidal thoughts, you can force yourself to find a group of abuse survivors who have had similar experiences so that you won't feel so alone. The immediate reaction of everyone who has ever joined a support group, especially sexual abuse groups, is, "This is wonderful, I never knew anyone else felt the way I do." (You may want to read Part V, Section 15, on support networks now.) You need friends and you need help. You have the desire to find help or you would not be reading this book. You do not have to be alone—unless you want to be.

You can take these steps right now to make yourself feel better. First, you can change the negative thoughts running through your head into positive ones. If you read the self-healing section on reprogramming your negative thoughts or affirmations, you will learn how to stop your negative thinking and consciously reprogram your mind so that you feel better. Our emotions are based on thoughts. If you are thinking, "Everything is hopeless, nothing will ever get any better. No one will help me, I just want to die," you will certainly be depressed. If you stand up, take three deep breaths and whistle or sing *Zip-a-dee-doo-dah* or a similar happy song, what happens? Go on, try it. No one's looking.

And how do you feel if you tell yourself, "I am really strong. I have gotten through the worst part of my life. Lots of people can help me. Other people have survived abuse and I'm a survivor too. I have control over my life. I choose to be happy and I am going to make myself happy." You will find with some practice that you have complete control over the way you feel right now.

You can avoid feeling hopeless by keeping busy. Sometimes survivors believe that they should quit their jobs and stay home so that they can concentrate on their therapy. They feel that they cannot cope with therapy and their jobs at the same time. This is a big mistake. You do not have to give up your life now to get rid of the past. In fact, the happier and more fulfilling your life is now, the easier it will be for you to cope with the painful memories. Sometimes it may be necessary to skip work if you are feeling particularly vulnerable, but these times should be kept at a minimum. I learned this lesson from painful experience. I stayed home too much thinking about my experiences and recovering memories through self-hypnosis and I ended up in the hospital. I discovered that I could only take three or four hours a week of therapy and self-analysis.

You do not have to live totally in the past to be able to let it go. You will feel better if you do not dwell on your past abuse. Focussing your mind on something else is another way of controlling your emotions. There is no benefit to feeling bad *now*. Your goal is to release past feelings—not to wallow in them. If you feel yourself spiraling into depression and hopelessness, *do something*. Call friends, clean the house, go to a movie, exercise, take a walk, buy something you have always wanted, help someone, fix something for a neighbor, but do something that will keep your mind off of your pain and make you feel better.

Other techniques to cope with depression are described in the self-healing section of this book. But what would really make your life worthwhile—give it meaning? We human beings have been searching for an answer to this question probably since we first stood up on two hairy feet and looked around. Philosophers have agonized over this question throughout recorded history, but no one has come up with a definitive answer—one that works for everyone.

Viktor Frankl, a survivor of a Nazi concentration camp who became a psychotherapist, tackled the question in *Man's Search for Meaning*. He concludes that there are three general categories of life meaning: 1) What one accomplishes or creates during a lifetime; 2) what one takes from the world in terms of knowledge and experiences; and 3) one's attitude toward life, how one bears suffering and handles challenges. He rejects the Freudian notion that meaning for man is based on seeking pleasure because he points out that when you look for pleasure, it eludes you. According to Frankl, pleasure is not the final goal of life but a by-product of one's search for meaning. "Happiness ensues; it cannot be pursued."

How does this apply to survivors of abuse? First, you can be proud of the fact that you survived your abuse. Frankl decided in Auschwitz that only by surviving could he give meaning to his anguish. Others survived for the sake of children or a spouse, or to tell the world about the death camps, or for revenge. But Frankl found meaning in a quotation from Nietzsche: "That which does not kill me makes me stronger." And although it may be hard for you to recognize now, *you* are stronger because of your abuse.

Frankl also chose to survive because he knew that he could use his experience to become a therapist and help others; he wanted to make something good come out of his horror. People who suffer usually become more sensitive to the suffering of others. And you will be able to recognize suffering and help others because of your increased sensitivity. It does not have to be a big thing. Your kind word to someone, even a smile of encouragement, may change that person's life.

Frankl observed that people found meaning in creativity. Whether you paint a portrait or a wall, run for Congress or concoct a new idea for a daycare center, erect a building or change a diaper, you are adding something unique to the world. And if you have a child, you have created life itself. There are many ways in which you have been and will be creative; you have only to choose the ones most meaningful to you.

Even in Auschwitz, Frankl discovered that other prisoners found meaning in beauty, truth and especially from love. One lone wildflower in the barren camp provided pleasure to those who could see beyond their pain. You will see only what you focus on. If you can grasp the moments of beauty, revere truth and accept the offers of love, life will have meaning for you.

Many people have found that the quickest way to happiness and meaning in life is to help others. The famous psychiatrist Alfred Adler used to tell his depressed patients, "You can be cured in fourteen days if you follow this prescription. Try to think every day how you can please someone." Dale Carnegie, whose advice has been followed by millions for almost a half century, recommended taking an interest in others and doing a good deed each day that will put a smile of joy on someone's face as a "sure-fire" way to happiness.

I read Carnegie's book, *How to Stop Worrying and Start Living*, just after I had decided that suicide was not the answer for me. I had made a pact with myself that I would follow the advice in every self-help book I read. If the advice worked, I would continue and if not I would go on to the next book. And so I started looking around for a way I could help someone. My friends warned me not to be a martyr but to choose something I felt I would enjoy. Happily, I took their advice and decided I wanted to help a young girl who needed a friend.

As has usually been the case in my life, as soon as I made this decision, an answer came to me. I learned of the Pals Program in Maryland. Pals is a Big Sister-Big Brother program for boys and girls who need extra help or cultural enrichment. After the training program, I was assigned to an eight-year-old girl who lived in subsidized housing near my home.

At first I was afraid we might not be able to relate to each other because she was black, and her mother felt threatened because she had expected a teenaged pal for her daughter, not a 40-year-old white woman. Her mother and I decided that it might be better to find another match, but Jackie and I liked each other so much that I wrote to her while I worked in Israel for a month. When I returned, all of the doubts were gone and Jackie and I and the rest of her family have been close friends ever since. I have always felt Jackie has helped me much more than I have helped her—she has given me such joy. I believe Ben Franklin's words: "When you are good to others, you are best to yourself."

You can easily find some type of service you can do in your neighborhood because there is always so much to be done. Choose something you enjoy, not something you think you *ought* to do. This is not a punishment. Working in a campaign for a candidate you believe in or raising money for the symphony are just as useful as working in a hospital or cleaning up your neighborhood. And just smiling at someone who looks unhappy or angry may be the most valuable gift you can give.

When you think of suicide, think about what you really want. There were a suicide attempts almost twice a month at the adolescent mental health unit where I worked. Some were serious and others were pleas by abuse victims for attention from their insensitive family members. Sometimes the teenagers wanted revenge, sometimes to prove they were hurting, sometimes to end their pain and loneliness. There are many motives for suicide.

Most therapists believe that depression is anger turned inward and that suicide is a type of murder. People filled with rage they cannot express turn it on themselves. Anyone who has been abused has some anger inside, and usually a substantial amount. People who deny having any feelings of anger often have a lot and are internalizing it. They are afraid of the force of their anger and so they take it out on themselves instead of those who deserve it. (This misunderstanding of anger is covered in Question 18, *Is it O.K. to hate the person who abused me, even if that person is a close relative?*)

Sometimes abuse victims wished their abusers were dead or wanted to kill them. These are natural feelings for someone who is totally helpless and being hurt. But in our society, people often make us feel that such feelings are unacceptable, thereby causing guilt as well as pain. Since we cannot express our wish to kill our abusers, we again turn the unacceptable feelings inside and we may decide to kill ourselves instead. The way to avoid perverting our justifiable feelings into self-punishment is to acknowledge and release them.

There are better ways of expressing anger than ending your own life. Are you clear about what you really want? Do you want someone to feel sorry for you or do you want someone to be sorry for what they did to you? Do you want to end it all and stop living or do you really want happiness that you think you can't obtain? Are you angry at your abuser and people who failed to help you? Are you angry at yourself? Whatever your motive, killing yourself may end the problem but does not solve it. If you are reading this book, you really want a solution. You want to end your pain but not your existence. You would surely trade death for happiness.

If you kill yourself, you will never have a chance for happiness. You've been through the worst life has to offer. And you survived. Why bow out now, just when you have the chance to have the better part? I hope you will realize you can heal and that you will give life one more chance. Allow yourself to try for two more years, and if you still feel the same way at the end of that time, you can end it. And during those two years, get the best help you can and cram as much living into your life as you can so that you will not feel you have missed anything if you decide to die. I hope you will wait to make your life decision when you see that you have some choices—rather than when you have blinded yourself to them all.

In writing this, I realized that at my lowest moments someone or something always helped me change my mind. Perhaps this book will help you, but somehow I know in the deepest part of me that, if you allow it, something or someone will help you—or you will help yourself.

I carried the following quote in my wallet for many years:

When you get into a tight place,
and everything goes against you
till it seems as if you couldn't hold on a minute longer,
never give up then,
for that's the time and place that the tide will turn.
Harriet Beecher Stowe

22. If I have been abused, will I abuse my children?

It is unfortunately true that abused children can become child abusers or can fail to protect their children from abuse by others. But abuse can easily be prevented through therapy.

The reason therapy is so important is that it makes you aware of what you are feeling and, once you are aware, you have control. When you are aware that you have been abused, you can begin to examine the emotions you have about what happened and release them. The release of these emotions will release you from unconscious impulses that might lead you to abuse your children. When you understand how you reacted emotionally to your abuse, you will find that your emotions will diminish and you will begin to feel differently about yourself and about events around you.

If you bring your now unconscious memories and emotions to consciousness where you can work on them, the chance of abusing your children will be greatly reduced. It is only when the memories and emotions are still unconscious that a high probability of child abuse exists because it is the old rage, hatred, fear and pain still trapped in your mind which cause the present overwhelming emotions leading to child abuse.

If these powerful emotions remain repressed, the normal crying or crankiness of a child may lead you to feel a loss of control that, in turn may remind you unconsciously of the desperate helplessness you felt as a child. Often this feeling is covered up by intense rage. In order to overcome these feelings, the child-part of the adult's mind wants desperately to exercise the control the child did not have. The child-part of the adult's mind enjoys the abuser's control and believes this control can be obtained by becoming like the child's abuser and former authority figure. This need for control may be manifested by carrying out abusive physical or sexual acts on another child "who needs to be punished."

I want to emphasize that none of this is conscious; former victims are unaware of their reasoning or acts. The sad fact is that we repeat the patterns we experienced as children, especially the patterns established out of misery and horror. Pain seems to imprint these patterns in our brains like a computer program, and we have to be aware of the program in order to replace it with a new one.

However, as adults, we have conscious control over our acts. Despite the patterns in our brains, if we are aware that we might have a problem, in some instances we can consciously control our behavior and change it. This applies to physically or sexually abusing children. Even now you have a important protection against abusing your children: awareness. You know that abuse is a possibility, so you can be on guard against it. You can monitor your feelings and actions and learn to walk away when you begin to feel angry or helpless with your children—before you get out of control. Others who abuse children often are not aware of what they are doing at the time. *You* are aware that abuse could be a problem so you have an excellent chance of preventing it.

A number of survivors of abuse have avoided abusing their children even before finishing therapy. Geri, a friend of mine with MPD, multiple personality disorder, had one of the worst histories of abuse I have ever heard. Her father began raping her when she was two years old and added torture soon afterwards. The rape and torture continued throughout her childhood. When she was only seven years old, her father sold her for use in pornographic photographs and to his friends for their perverted pleasure. By the time she was fourteen, she had already had an abortion and a child that her father sold to an adoption agency. The horror ended when she was fourteen or fifteen. By then, she had totally suppressed her memory of any of her childhood up to that time.

In her twenties, she began to have nightmares and flashbacks about having a baby in her childhood. She was baffled by these images and, when she began seeing a therapist, she also found that she had multiple personality disorder. By that time she was married and had two young children. She had never hit or hurt her children and has been very careful to avoid any situation when she might. If she feels she is becoming angry, she leaves the room. Geri is one of several women I know who has been able to consciously control herself and avoid the chain of abuse even before completing therapy.

In most cities there are support groups for families who are prone to child abuse. These groups teach parents a variety of techniques for controlling and disciplining children. Learning these skills is essential for those of us who were abused by family members because we lacked useful role models for loving discipline in our own homes. We did not learn how to cope lovingly with crying babies or how to deal with childhood tantrums without violence. By teaching parenting techniques, these groups provide parents with effective ways of coping with the continual and sometimes overwhelming problems children present. Moreover, they provide the support and understanding of other parents in similar situations. If you join one of these groups, you will always have someone to call if you need help.

These support groups can also be effective for survivors of sexual abuse even though they do not focus specifically on problems of sexual abuse. The unconscious impulses and emotions that impel parents to batter children are often the same as those which lead to sexual abuse. Parents who feel good about themselves and who have some confidence in their ability to handle their children are less likely to abuse them.

Child abuse is a learned pattern which is usually passed down from generation to generation. The way to break the chain is through awareness. Since you are aware that you might have a problem with abuse, you are already halfway to the solution. The next step is to start therapy so that you can be freed of the violent feelings which might explode into abuse. You may also want to immediately join a support group or form one with your close friends so that you have someone to turn to when the pressure builds up and you feel you cannot cope with your child. You do not have to abuse your child if you are willing to take the steps necessary to prevent it.

The only path away from our suffering
is to embrace our suffering.
Scott Peck, *The Road Less Traveled*

23. Is it O.K. to spank my child?

No. It is never appropriate to hit a child, and particularly not for survivors of abuse.

People who were abused experienced intense frustration, helplessness, pain, rage and hatred during their abuse and are probably still repressing an excessive amount of unresolved anger. If you were abused and your child causes you frustration and anger, you may intend to discipline the child by merely "spanking," but your anger can easily get out of control and lead to abuse without your intending it and sometimes without your even being aware of what you are doing at the time. This is particularly true for the thousands of adults who were so severely abused that they have repressed their abuse to the point that they cannot even remember it. These people are like walking time bombs; any act of their child or their spouse can set off a reaction of uncontrollable rage.

There is no safe way to spank a child, whether you have been abused or not. Once you start hitting a child, you may not be able to stop. And how do you know exactly how hard to hit a small child? It has to be hard enough to have an effect, and what effect is that? Do you want the child to stop, to realize he or she has done something wrong, to cry, to plead, to apologize, to cower before your authority and power? And how hard do you have to hit a child to obtain one or more of those results without injury?

Merely shaking an infant or small child can cause permanent brain damage. Blows to the head can cause death. And what if your child has an abnormal internal condition of which you are unaware so that even a soft slap can cause serious injury? What if your swat to the child's behind causes him or her to jerk away in fright, fall and be injured? Hundreds of children in this country sustain permanent brain damage or die every year due to "gentle" spankings? The only safe way to spank a child is not to do it.

Hitting is not a minor punishment. It is violence. It is the act of a bully, the use of force by someone larger against someone totally unable to defend himself. Hitting is a show of power. That is why abuse victims often abuse their children. They have experienced total helplessness and it is such a terrible feeling that they want to replace it with power. If they cannot make even their small child do what they say, the old feeling of helplessness sweeps over them, and they are terrified. They react to this terror by trying to prove that they are in control, by beating their children into submission to demonstrate their power. But the end result is not control nor power. Children who are beaten act worse than before, because they are frightened and confused. And parents who beat their children feel more helpless than ever, knowing that they are unable to control their children or themselves.

Violence is a learned behavior. When you hit a child, you are teaching the child that physical violence is acceptable. You are instilling a pattern which they will pass on to their children who will pass it on to their children. Once children learn violence, it is difficult to teach them more effective responses.

Research shows that punishment is not an effective way to change a child's behavior. Punishment elicits a negative response in the child so that the child may start to dislike the learning situation and may even lose interest in learning in general. For example, if a child is punished for mistakes in arithmetic, the child may never want to learn mathematics again.

The child may also develop a negative attitude toward the person administering the punishment. Sometimes a child will try to avoid the punishing person by staying away from home or by lying. Punishment can also teach children to become aggressive.[18] If you have been abused, you may recognize your own rebellious tendencies which resulted from the ways you chose to fight back and survive. Children who have been hit learn that the way to handle their frustration for not getting their way is by screaming or hitting. And if children are physically punished when they are small, they grow up to be physically aggressive with their peers and their parents when they reach adolescence. The rebellious, abusive adolescents we see come from violent and abusive families. Violence is a learned response; it does not come naturally.

Another reason punishment does not work is because it usually only shows children what they should *not* do; it does not teach them how to do something properly. Children want and need to be shown how to act in a way that is acceptable. If you want to change your child's behavior, you have to patiently explain and show the child what you want the child to do, probably many times.

And the most important reason for not using punishment is that it usually does not work. How many people have stopped speeding because they received a ticket? Studies have shown that punishment, especially physical punishment, is equally ineffective with children. In fact, physical punishment and yelling have been demonstrated to *increase* a child's offensive behavior, rather than stopping it. Surely you have seen children who will throw tantrums to gain their parent's attention, even if that means a spanking. If children do not receive positive reinforcement and attention, they will seek negative attention.

In 1979, Sweden passed a law banning the physical punishment of children. As a result of the law and social control, spanking has essentially disappeared in that country. Most American child psychologists are now recommending corporal punishment only to stop self-destructive behavior which is dangerous to the child, such as swallowing poison or head banging by an autistic child.

The modern prohibition on spanking may seem to be a dramatic change from the old adage, "Spare the rod and spoil the child." You may be thinking, "Well, I was spanked by my parents and it didn't hurt *me*." But if you sit down quietly and remember how you felt as a child when you were spanked and how it made you feel about yourself, you may come to a different conclusion. If you cannot feel anything at all, it means your mental pain was so great that you blocked it out. No one who is hit can escape the confusion, pain, anger and shame which result. If someone you love strikes you, the feelings are worse than if a teacher hits you; you usually conclude that you must be a bad person. Physical punishment teaches poor self-esteem, a lesson which will impair a child's personal relationships throughout her life. The very fact that you believe it is necessary to hit your child is a result of your own spankings and the negative feelings you developed about yourself.

Less than a century ago we allowed young children to work twelve and fourteen hour days in workhouses and factories. Now we have child labor laws to protect children. We used to allow parents to abuse their children physically, mentally and sexually because we believed parents had the right to do what they wished with their children. Now we have laws and agencies to prevent child abuse. We used to believe that sparing the rod would spoil the child. But modern research has demonstrated that the opposite is true. As a society, we are becoming more enlightened about the effects of our actions, and as we become more knowledgeable, we become more humane. We have learned that physical force damages a child; it does not teach him.

So how do you discipline your child lovingly and effectively? The best ways to discipline your child are positive ways. Demonstrating warmth and interest in your child and praising behavior you want to encourage are probably the most effective ways to obtain acceptable behavior. Remember how much you wanted the approval of your parents when you were small? That is how much your child wants to please you.

Many useful techniques been developed to help parents teach their children appropriate behavior and you can find them in dozens of helpful books in your local bookstore or library. Books on child development may be especially useful in helping you understand what to expect of your child at a certain age.

Since many of us never had the chance to be children, it is important to understand the developmental stages so we can allow our children to grow and act in a way appropriate to their age. In addition, most communities now sponsor parenting classes and have established support groups so that parents can help each other.

Most of us never received the nurturing we needed as children, so we lack role models for fulfilling our own children's needs. If we are to be effective parents, we must reparent ourselves because only by loving ourselves do we have love to give to others. We have to learn what it is to be nurtured, if we are to be nurturing. There is a section on nurturing and reparenting in this book, and there are many other books and courses on the subject which you may find helpful. Once you feel loved yourself, it is easy to train your children in a loving way.

No one wants to beat or scream at a child. The recent techniques can help you teach your child while you are both having fun. And if you attend the support groups, you will find that you are not alone; that others are struggling with the same feelings and problems. Experiment and find the methods that work best for you and your child. But most of all, remember that your child is your creation, something perfect and wonderful created by you. Your child is worth the time you spend learning new ways to help him or her develop in the gentlest way to be the best person possible.

Children need love, especially when they don't deserve it.
Harold S. Hulbert

24. What if I am doing sexual things to my child or to a younger sister, brother or friend?

I suspect you are carrying a heavy burden of guilt and pain over what you are doing, and you would give anything to stop. Sadly, many victims of sexual abuse are in your situation and have become perpetrators, repeating the patterns they learned through their own abuse. Recent studies report that *80 percent* of fathers who commit incest have been sexually or physically abused as children.[19] And this number is probably much larger because many victims block out memories of their abuse. But perpetrators are not only adults, they are also older children and teenagers who have learned to abuse through being abused. These victims victimize younger children in their families or in their neighborhoods. Many of them may not even know that they are doing anything wrong.

If you are aware of what you are doing, you well on the way to being healed. Some victim-perpetrators are not even aware that they are abusing others; they may have multiple personality disorder or a type of amnesia that blocks out their knowledge of their sexual acts. Other victim-perpetrators are aware of what they are doing but make excuses about it, saying that they love their child and the child likes what they do or that what they are doing is harmless.

If you were a victim of sexual abuse yourself, your actions are caused by unresolved issues of your own abuse. We have discussed patterns created by past pain throughout this book, and your actions are a vivid illustration of those patterns. When you were abused, you were helpless so now you try to control others. Your mind is trying to erase the terrible fear and impotence you felt by putting you in a position of power. Since you still carry feelings of fear, rage, hate, guilt, shame and helplessness within you, these feelings are impelling you to repeat what happened to you as a child.

Abuse is a learned behavior. Nora was raped by her stepfather from the time she was six years old. Sometimes her mother watched. When Nora was 13, she molested her five-year-old cousin and an eight-year-old neighbor. Nora did not know that there was anything wrong with what she had done and protested being included in a therapy group for perpetrators. She was horrified when she finally understood that she had taken advantage of the younger children in the same way that her stepfather had taken advantage of her.

The difference between normal sexual exploration of children and sexual abuse is one of age and dominance. If two five-year-olds play doctor, that is normal exploration. If a ten-year-old plays doctor with a four-year-old, coercion may come into play making the behavior sexual abuse. The distinction is becoming harder to draw and many children are now being accused of abuse in cases where the behavior may well be normal exploration.

Some children do not know what appropriate behavior is. George, the young man who grew up in an abusive family of 18 children, thought his family was normal. Living in the country, he did not see any other families until he entered high school and found out that his doubts about his family's normalcy were justified. But he had to be taught. He had to have a model of what was appropriate.

Since both Nora and George remembered their abuse and were able to deal with their emotions about it, they could unlearn their behavior very quickly. Jack was not so lucky. With his mother's knowledge, he was sodomized by his father for several years. When he became a preteenager, he began molesting young boys around his neighborhood. Jack had difficulty changing his behavior because he had repressed all of his emotions and most of his memories about his abuse which occurred when he was very young. Since he was not being treated with hypnosis, he did not uncover his emotions and did not make much progress. His counselor anticipated that he would end up in prison.

These three perpetrators learned their behavior from their own sexual abuse; later they were faced with the task of understanding their emotions and their actions and of changing them. Studies show that sexual abuse can be unlearned. With the proper treatment, perpetrators can be healed.[20]

While most animal behavior is instinctive, most human behavior is not. Although many animal babies are almost independent from birth, human babies would die without long term care and training. We have to be taught nearly everything.

Human beings even have to learn how to make love. Although one would expect sex to be a natural instinct to propagate the species, humans learn this art. Some acts we Americans consider to be basic responses are different in other cultures. For example, while Caucasians kiss each others' lips to show affection, Eskimos rub their noses together.

Personality traits are also learned. Why is the stereotype of the Italian warm and demonstrative and the Anglo-Saxon Protestant cool and reserved? Because we learn from our parents.

So it is not difficult to understand that abuse can be learned. And anything that can be learned can be unlearned. But it does take work and constant vigilance. And it does take recalling the memories and emotions of your own abuse and coming to terms with what happened to you. If you want to stop abusing others, you have to make a commitment to the treatment process and stick with it until you break the patterns established by your abuse.

One of the most difficult parts of healing is to let go of your hatred for your abuser. (See Question 20, *Do I have to forgive my abuser?*) An ancient Chinese proverb warns us to choose carefully those who we hate, because we will become like them. Victims of abuse often find that they have adopted characteristics of their abusers and even become the abuser. There are only three possible roles for victims unless they get help to extricate themselves from this triangle: victim, victimizer and rescuer, and all three have their pitfalls. Instead of remaining a helpless victim if you are abusing a child, you have chosen to adopt the role of victimizer as a way of coping with the horror and helplessness which still wreak havoc in your mind.

The good news is that since you know what is causing your anguish, you can do something about it. Wanting to stop is half the battle. The other half is finding a good therapist who can help you release all of the painful feelings and memories you may have been suppressing inside you so that you will no longer feel any compulsion to sexually abuse people. If you are abusing someone, it is essential that you find a therapist who is experienced in hypnotherapy because you may be driven by unconscious impulses from past events in your life, and you need the help of someone who can bring them to consciousness so that you can choose your behavior.

Attempts to change the behavior of perpetrators without the use of hypnosis, whether in individual sessions or groups, are usually not successful. Hypnosis is necessary because if victim/perpetrators were abused as children, they may have buried the memories through a process of self-hypnosis. Behavior modification techniques are not effective when a person is acting in a kind of trance emanating from past experiences. Only by uncovering the memories and emotions of past abuse can you be liberated from the impulses caused by these memories and emotions.

If you obtain the right kind of therapy, your chances of being healed are excellent. Therapists now have the ability to heal even the most difficult cases involving people with multiple personality disorder who have suffered the most unspeakable types of abuse and then have hurt themselves and others. Many of these people are now living normal lives. And every day, the techniques for helping people improve and the amount of time in therapy grows shorter. Today so many people are perpetrators—lawyers, doctors, therapists, housewives, business executives, teachers, artists, politicians, people from every walk of life— that a nationwide effort has been launched to find solutions and the trend is growing to treat victim-perpetrators in a humane way.

I have told you the good news, and I will be just as candid about the down side. In most states, when you go to a therapist, your therapist will be required by law to report that you are engaging in sexual abuse. This is one instance in which the therapist-client privilege of confidentiality does not apply. The rationale is that child abuse is so destructive, it should be stopped as quickly as possible. So in the case of child abuse, the rights of the abused child are placed ahead of those of the person undergoing therapy.

This means that your therapist will have to notify the police or the division of family or protective services in your community and report the fact that you are presently abusing a child. In most states, either you or the child will be removed from the home unless the therapist is convinced that there is no further danger to the child. In some enlightened states, such as Wisconsin, you would be placed in a halfway house until your therapy has been completed. As long as you continued therapy, there would be no criminal penalties. However, many states do not recognize the fact that abusers are also victims. So they make them victims again by prosecuting them criminally. These states destroy families and the lives of people who are still wounded by their past abuse and who could be healed to become productive members of society.

Despite my own abuse, I would prefer to see abusers cured rather than incarcerated. I believe that rather than abuse me, my father would have killed himself if he had known what he was doing. I do know that after he was healed by one of the earliest hypnotherapists, he never sexually abused me again and he lived the rest of his life in a state of painful awareness and guilt over what he had done to me. As I grew up, my father would come to me crying, telling me that he had done such terrible things to me, that he had been such a terrible father, and that he was so sorry for what he had done. He said I would be better off if he committed suicide. Sadly, I did not know what he was talking about— I had forgotten everything. But now that I remember, I am sure that he did not want to do what he did.

The system is beginning to treat perpetrators with more compassion. Some states that have criminal penalties for child abuse rarely impose them. If they do, the sentences are often stayed and the perpetrators placed on probation during the duration of their therapy. The truth is that we could not possibly incarcerate all of the child abusers in our country; our jails could not hold them all.

So, while some action may be taken, such as removing you from your home or removing your children temporarily while they receive treatment, you have a good chance of avoiding prison if you are following a treatment plan and remain in treatment. In fact, if you have started therapy and consent to being turned in, your attorney can make an excellent case that your rehabilitation has begun and you are no longer a danger to society. Such an argument is persuasive with most judges since they are aware that people who recognize that they have a problem and want help are most likely to be rehabilitated.

But let's look at your alternatives if you don't get help. You will go on doing what you are doing and you will be injuring the child you are abusing more and more each time. The other frightening fact is that the more you engage in abuse, the more brutal and destructive your acts may become. If you are now only touching a child sexually and having the child touch you, you may soon escalate to intercourse or sodomy or violence. The mental and physical damage you do to your victims will increase each time. And the damage you do to yourself will increase also. Can you live with the guilt of what you are doing, especially if it is your own child? I don't think so.

And if you are afraid of being turned in by your therapist, it will be far worse if you are turned in by your child, your neighbor or another family member. The days when abuse can remain hidden thankfully are over. Sooner or later your abuse will be reported, if not by someone at home then by someone at the child's school, a doctor or a friend. And when you are picked up by the police, you will not have a therapist or anyone on your side to help you. You are far more likely to go to jail, and you will be assigned a therapist you did not select. If you are aware enough to be reading this book, I suggest that you bite the bullet now and choose a therapist who can help you heal and see you through whatever proceedings are necessary.

If you were abused, you went through the worst pain you will endure in your life. You survived that pain and have been growing stronger since then. Whatever you have to face now is easy compared to what you have already survived. It is easier than living with the knowledge of the harm you will do to a child if you don't get help now. And it is much easier than living with the pain and anxiety which you are now feeling. The way to begin to feel better and to turn your life around is to start therapy now.

Try not to judge yourself harshly. All of us have abused others in some way. Be merciful with yourself; you have suffered enough—we all have.

> *With awareness, you give yourself*
> *the gift of an opening for growth and change.*
> *Do not criticize yourself because*
> *in darkness you could not see.*
> Emmanuel's Book

25. My family won't accept the changes from my therapy and seems to want me to be the way I used to be. Am I imagining this?

Probably not. The situation you have described is a frequently encountered psychological phenomenon and involves a universal resistance to change. You may have learned in school about the principle of homeostasis which means that things tend to return to a state of balance. If the state of balance is disrupted, there is a tendency to return to the balanced state as quickly as possible.

The principle of homeostasis applies to families and the relationship of one member to another. Family members learn to fulfill each others needs. For example, the husband may be shy and the wife outgoing, so she fulfills the family's social needs. In dysfunctional families, members are dependent on each other in unhealthy ways. You have seen families where one spouse is aggressively dominant, making all of the decisions and treating the other spouse like a child, and the other spouse is excessively submissive and acts like a child. Some women seek a mate who can be "Big Daddy" and some men may look for "the Big Breast." If this dominant-submissive pattern is carried to an extreme, the result will usually be spouse abuse. If the submissive partner obtains help, usually as a result of abuse, and becomes more independent, the partners will split up unless the dominant partner also obtains help and becomes less domineering.

Just as people find mates who complement their frailties, children may be forced to adapt to the needs they perceive in their families. For example, if the wife injures her back and no longer participates in activities with her husband, the husband may turn to his daughter to be a substitute wife and demand that she go on "dates" with him and give him the affection and attention he is no longer receiving from his wife. While she is young, the daughter may enjoy being "Daddy's emotional wife," but when she grows up she may find that having been forced into an inappropriate childhood role adversely affects her attempts to form healthy relationships with men.

But the most injurious pattern is where one family member plays the "sick role" or family scapegoat. In an extreme but true case, Anne was a normal healthy child. Her parents insisted on dressing her and having her sit on their laps when they fed her. When she was eight years old, they took her to a therapist because they were aghast that she wanted to tie her own shoes and eat at the table. During the sessions, Anne's parents told the therapist that Anne made up stories and that everything Anne said was untrue; they deliberately tried to make the therapist think that Anne was schizophrenic. Luckily, the therapist was able to see through their ploys. These parents needed Anne to be totally dependent on them and needed to see her as sick so that they could see themselves as well.

You may also have noticed families in which one member is designated as "the black sheep." One member acts out all of the unacceptable behavior for the family. This usually occurs in very rigid families where mistakes and imperfections are not tolerated and where family members will not admit that they might have problems.

Families involved in incest or severe sexual or physical abuse often follow these patterns of selecting a family member to represent their sickness and shoulder their blame. Obviously such families are dysfunctional or the abuse would not occur. But these families do not want to see themselves as dysfunctional or their behavior as sick or unacceptable. So they pick a member of the family to be their scapegoat and carry the burden for them. "Scapegoat" is a term derived from an ancient Jewish ritual in which a priest rubbed blood, representing all the sins of the people, on a goat and sent it into the wilderness. When families pick a scapegoat, they place all of their blame and sickness on the chosen person.

A friend recently pointed out that I was my family's scapegoat. I was shocked, although the evidence was obvious, but I had blinded myself to the facts. My father had blamed me for "luring him" into abusing me and my mother had accused me of destroying the family. Even though I blocked out the abuse, I noticed that my mother always treated me as though I were about to have a nervous breakdown. (When I discovered my abuse in my forties, I realized that my mother, an extremely intelligent woman, had good reason for expecting me to have a nervous breakdown—she knew what she and my father had done to me!) My family also stereotyped me as "emotional," "Sarah Bernhardt," "exaggerating," and most sentences about me began, "Oh, there goes Lynne again." My credibility was totally obliterated—perhaps because they were afraid I would reveal the truth.

Even my younger brother, who never participated in my abuse, unconsciously played out the family myth by treating me as an hysteric and not to be taken seriously. And because no one in my family would take me seriously, I compensated by screaming when I wanted to get my point across, unconsciously assuming that volume would make them believe me. And so the myth was perpetuated.

When I was in therapy and started to make substantial progress, I noticed that my mother and brother kept trying to treat me in the old ways. But because I acted differently, they had to respond to me differently. They countered this threat to the family equilibrium by trying to upset me and force me to act in my old ways. Both have a great deal to lose by changing the pattern. My mother does not want to admit that I am well because she might have to acknowledge the reality of my abuse. My brother has an even greater reason to maintain the status quo. He was also abused by my father as an infant and has blocked it out. If he acknowledges that I am well and have credibility, he will be forced to face his own demons. Since he loves me and wants to continue our relationship, he faces a painful dilemma: supporting my mother's denial or trying to adapt to my changes.

Survivors who obtain help and refuse to be victims anymore often find themselves being thrust back into the victim role by their families. Your change is a threat; it forces your family to acknowledge its own failings. You have disturbed the equilibrium. They want to return to "normal," to preserve the state of homeostasis. And you want a better life.

The answer is not to go back—you can't. To go back to a role which you now know is harmful to you would be devastating. You can only go on and be who you are. And you can only help your family by remaining well. They will never get well if you go back to being sick; they have no incentive to change if you return to the status quo. But they may get well in time if they can learn to accept you as a model of what is possible. If they see that you can get well in spite of the horror and abuse you have endured, they may seek help for themselves.

It is difficult to be strong and to remain true to yourself when you are besieged on all sides by members of your family. You have to distance yourself from their attempts to upset you and push you back into the mold, and you can do it by developing a new perspective on them. If you look, really look, at your family as though they were strangers, you will notice things you never saw before. I didn't see my mother for almost two years after I discovered my abuse. When I saw her at my brother's wedding, I studied her, wondering how she could have let such things happen to me. When she thought no one was watching, she dropped her ever-present cheery smile, and I saw a face of such sadness that it made me want to cry. It made me more able to forgive her and it also released any power she had over me.

You can learn to become a detached observer so that the behavior

131

and emotions of your family do not affect you. One way to practice being detached is to use the "mindfulness exercises" in Part V, Section 5, of this book. But you may have to face the fact, as I did, that your family will not take responsibility for your abuse. It is a terribly lonely feeling to know that your family has abandoned you. But the truth is that they abandoned you long ago when you needed them far more than you do now.

Perhaps the hardest thing I had to face about my abuse is that I was utterly alone—before I was four years old. Even as an adult that knowledge brought a terror which made it difficult to breathe. But after hours of panic, I was able to grasp the fact that I had survived in spite of my helplessness and my terrible aloneness. I began to comprehend that I would never be that alone again because *I now have control.* I may not have the support of my family, but I have the support of my friends and I can have as many friends as I want. I have also "adopted" parents who love me unconditionally. We fulfill healthy needs for each other: they love me unconditionally as my parents never did (perhaps because I am not really their child) and I love them unconditionally without blame or anger. My adopted mother acknowledges my abuse and shares my pain, and her acceptance of me almost makes up for my mother's rejection. I have also learned to be a parent to myself—by nurturing myself and treating myself with love and respect. (The exercises I used are in Part V, Section 13, on reparenting yourself.) So I will never be alone again.

The important thing is to be strong and to hold onto the positive changes you have made. You have to live the life which is right for you. You deserve happiness, and just as you are responsible for your happiness, your family is responsible for theirs. If you continue to act differently, your family may begin to treat you differently. Even if they don't, what good does it do if you revert to your old ways where everyone, including you, is unhappy?

This above all: to thine own self be true,
And it must follow, as the night the day,
Thou canst not then be false to any man.
William Shakespeare, *Hamlet*

26. When I was abused many years ago as a child, I asked people for help but no one believed me.
Why didn't they help me?

Thousands of men and women have asked this question. When they were children they were battered and sexually abused by their mothers, fathers, stepparents, grandparents and other people. In many cases, their abuse went on for years despite the fact that they begged people to help them. No one responded and they were left alone to cope with their own private hells.

In my own case, I told my school nurse, my pediatrician, and the parents of my best friend that my father was raping and torturing me. No one believed this incredible story coming from the mouth of a six-year-old. I believe that our maid knew or suspected what was going on. Although she was especially nice to me, she was afraid to interfere. She did take me to her fire-and-brimstone Baptist church to try to save my soul, but I would have preferred a little more concern with my body.

One day when I was seven, I saw a policewoman in our neighborhood park. I was sure she would have to help me, so I went to her and told her what was being done to me. She was shocked and promised to help me. She walked me to our expensive Westwood house and confronted my father. He was a well-known screenwriter who worked at home. He was also brilliant, handsome and articulate. In five minutes he had the policewoman eating out of his hand. She left, admonishing me not to make up any more ridiculous stories about my wonderful father. She was my last hope. When she left, she took with her all of the trust and respect I would have for anyone for a very long time.

Bill had similar experiences. He was severely battered by his father and had bruises, cuts and welts all over his body. His mother frequently had to take him to the doctor, especially when his father's brutality resulted in broken bones. After setting Bill's arm for the second time, the doctor asked Bill what had happened. Bill was terrified because his parents had told him that they would kill him if he told anyone. Seeing Bill's fear, the doctor assured him that no one would harm him. Bill blurted out his years of abuse. The doctor was horrified and called Bill's mother into his private office. Half an hour later, the doctor and Bill's mother came out smiling. The doctor sent Bill on his way, warning him not to climb so many trees or get into so many fights with his school-mates. Bill received brutal retribution from his father that night and for several years afterwards until he ran away from home.

How could this happen? There are laws, aren't there?

But no laws existed to protect children from abuse when these events occurred. Bill and I were among the millions of children who were abused before the 1960s when child abuse legislation was finally passed throughout the country. Until that time, child abuse was not a subject of discussion. Abuse described in books such as *Sybil* was thought to be an anomaly and beyond the comprehension of a civilized society. That same society tried to protect children from the degradations of poverty by taking children away from some indigent parents while it ignored abuse suffered by children of the rich and middle classes.

Traditionally children have been viewed as the possessions of their parents. People were reluctant to interfere with parental rights; what parents did to their children was their business. If parents severely punished or beat their children, they were not seen as behaving in a deviant manner; they were merely teaching their children obedience. "Spare the rod and spoil the child" was the rule of the day. The second rule about parental perogatives was, "It's none of your business."

It was not social reformers but pediatric radiologists who brought child abuse to public attention. Beginning in 1946, Dr. John Caffey searched for the cause of bone fractures in children and his work led to identifying the parents as the cause. Although pediatricians and family doctors saw the same children, they did not recognize the injuries as due to abuse because child abuse was not then a traditional diagnosis. Perhaps, too, these doctors did not believe that parents could abuse their children. If the doctor was treating the entire family, he may have thought reporting the abuse would violate the parents' confidentiality. In other cases, doctors may have refused to report abuse because they did not want to waste their time as witnesses in criminal proceedings.

Although radiologists were not hampered by the same concerns, they had problems because the medical profession wanted to keep child abuse under its control. According to Professors Diana M. DiNitto and Thomas R. Dye: "Child abuse had to be labeled a medical rather than a social or legal problem, or else physicians would be relegated to a subordinate role in its diagnosis and treatment. Child abuse was labeled 'the battered-child syndrome' in 1962. Labeling child abuse as a medical syndrome legitimated its recognition by physicians."[21]

As a result of media publicity about the problem, especially on television programs such as *Ben Casey* and *Dr. Kildare*, all states passed legislation on child abuse by 1965.

Early legislation made abuse a criminal offense. Today's legislation is more realistic; it recognizes that abusers are sick and need help. Most states, in an effort to rehabilitate abusers rather than punish them, provide individual and group therapy, often for all members of the family.

Even more important, states laws require mandatory reporting for anyone who becomes aware of possible child abuse. Failure to report suspected abuse is a criminal offense. And abuse victims have begun to successfully sue people in civil court for their failure to report the abuse as required by law.

Happily, we have witnessed an almost complete turnabout in the way our society perceives abuse and how it handles abuse. Although some victims continue to encounter disbelief, or worse, the efforts of their abusers to cover up their abuse, it is possible to find people who will help you today. If someone rejects your plea for help, try someone else. Ask for assistance from the abuse hotline in your area. *And don't give up.* I know how easy it is to become discouraged, but I also know that today you can find someone to help you if you keep trying. (See Question 34, *I am being abused. What should I do?* and Question 35, *Where can I get help?*)

However, the recent changes in policy do not ease the pain of the Adults Molested As Children (AMACs) living today who had nowhere to turn and no one to help them when they were children. Many of them are still bitter about the people who ignored their pleas for help. And many of them still find it difficult to believe that anyone would help them if they asked today. Those of us who were abandoned by the system are fiercely independent and find it difficult to accept help or even kindness.

Since I retain some vestiges of my childhood isolation and am still strug-gling with my own fear of trusting, I am unable to provide any quick cures for those of you who were also rebuffed by possible rescuers. I can only tell you what I am doing to overcome my old feeling and patterns.

First, I am trying to understand the people I approached and to com-prehend their actions within the context of the time. But most impor-tant, I am trying to focus on what is happening *now*. I see all around me that people *do* care and that there are people throughout the world devoting their lives to saving abused children. I remind myself that my friends would help me, just as I would help them, and I sometimes mentally review the times my friends and others have helped me since I became an adult. I firmly believe the world is getting better and that people are becoming more compassionate. I look for examples to support this belief, and I try to forget my earlier experiences. I know that if I am to enjoy the life I have now, I have to let go of the past. You may not share these beliefs, but they have proven true for me and I have found that they work.

I believe that with our present laws and social agencies and with all the people who care, if I called for help, someone would answer. Today the world is more humane, and I am learning to be content with that.

> *What do we live for, if it is not to make life*
> *less difficult to each other.*
> George Eliot

27. I went to a therapist who said my memories of sexual abuse are just fantasies. Is he correct?

Unfortunately, your experience is far from unique. Many women (and in this case it has been mostly women) have been seriously harmed by narrow-minded therapists who refuse to accept today's reality that a large number of children have been and still are victims of sexual abuse and incest. These individuals have failed to keep up with the news, let alone recent psychological and social developments.

Most of these therapists follow the teachings of Sigmund Freud (1856-1939), the Viennese founder of psychoanalytic theory. Many of Freud's principles and techniques—such as his concepts of the id, ego and superego; of the conscious and unconscious levels of our minds; and of ego-defense mechanisms—are still an integral part of modern psychology.[22] But even geniuses make mistakes and Freud was no exception.

Freud decided that those patients who claimed to have been sexually molested as children, were only fantasizing as a defense against their own sexual desires for their innocent parents. The absurdity of this conclusion is brilliantly demonstrated in the now classic book by Alice Miller, Ph.D., *Thou Shalt Not Be Aware*, in which she exposes how Freud's misconceptions have kept the Western world in the dark about sexual abuse. Dr. Miller uses Freud's papers to demonstrate how he based his fantasy supposition on his own theory of infantile sexuality, a theory which places the blame on the child rather than on the parents.

In Dr. Miller's words, "Only Freud had the courage to recognize the importance of sexuality, repressed as it was in the darkest reaches of forgotten childhood. But then, after discovering the prevalence of sexual abuse of children, he distanced himself from his findings and came to see the child as a source of sexual (and aggressive) desires directed at the adult. As a result, parents' sex play with their children could continue under cover of darkness."[23]

Despite the acceptance of Dr. Miller's research and widespread publicity about the prevalence of sexual abuse, a few irresponsible therapists still refuse to reevaluate their adherence to Freud's outdated views; they continue to injure their patients by denying the reality of sexual abuse. The harm that men and women have suffered by having their pain denied and their problems left unhealed is monumental. A friend of mine consulted one of these psychiatrists more than twenty years ago. She suffered two nervous breakdowns before she had the courage to leave him. It has taken her more than twenty years to be able to take a chance on another therapist. She is finally receiving the help she needs from a woman therapist who is experienced in treating sexual abuse cases. (I do not mean to imply that only men deny the existence of child sexual abuse. Although my personal knowledge of this is about men, I am sure there are women who can be equally myopic.)

I also had a painful experience which is still affecting me. My brother, also a lawyer, is impressed by titles and he went to a highly recommended, elderly psychiatrist in San Francisco.

After I discovered my abuse and uncovered memories of my father sexually abusing my brother when he was an infant, I telephoned my brother and told him what I had learned. He was shocked but interested in what I had to say. He arranged for me to talk to his psychiatrist by telephone. When I spoke to his psychiatrist, he listened but asked very few questions and made no comments. I told him that he was welcome to contact my therapist if he had any questions and I gave him the telephone number. He never contacted anyone. My brother called a couple of days later and told me his doctor said I was a liar and not to believe me. He said we women "just make those things up."

Nothing I said could change my brother's mind. Since I had always been labeled as hysterical by my family, even after obtaining a law degree and a White House appointment, my brother believed the doctor instead of me. To this day, my brother refuses to pursue the matter because "it just didn't happen." That psychiatrist's narrow mindedness and his refusal to call my therapist have prevented my brother from getting the help he needs and have seriously affected our relationship.

The majority of therapists, whether social workers, psychiatrists or psychologists, now recognize that children do not make up stories of sexual abuse. For one thing, children do not have sufficient knowledge of what constitutes sexual behavior to be able to manufacture a convincing scene. More significant is the fact that it is absolutely impossible for a child to fake the violent emotions engendered by sexual abuse. It simply can't be done.

When women discover their abuse as adults under hypnosis, their memories and experiences are sometimes discounted by outdated therapists who say that hypnosis is unreliable because the hypnotist can put ideas in the subject's mind. That allegation is nonsense. Experienced hypnotherapists know that you cannot put anything in a person's mind that he or she doesn't want there. And it is beyond belief that anyone would *want* to incorporate scenes of pain and horror into his or her subconscious. Skeptics do not explain the verifiable detail described by survivors. Moreover, memories of sexual abuse recalled by adults under hypnosis carry with them the same turbulent emotions that the abuse itself created when the person was a child. These emotions cannot be feigned, as anyone who has worked with abuse victims can attest. My research has not revealed one single case where a survivor has been proven to have made up incest or sexual abuse while in therapy. There is simply no motive for a person who seeks help to lie or to have someone else prepare them to fabricate a tale of abuse.

For those of you who have been subjected to the cruelty of these stubborn Freudians, I can only urge you to try another therapist. Thankfully, most of these adherents to an obsolete Freud are no longer around. Part IV, *Healing-Finding a Therapist*, emphasizes that it is important to interview more than one therapist and to question each therapist carefully about his or her beliefs and experiences. The number of therapists who are experienced in treating sexual abuse is increasing, so it should not be difficult to find a qualified therapist. My bias is to avoid therapists who are strictly Freudian because you may get one who does not believe in child sexual abuse and also because this psychoanalytic therapy is unnecessarily long and costly. But whatever your choice, if your therapist tells you that a memory of abuse you believe to be true is a fantasy or says that your experience is not real, get a second opinion. Trust your own instincts; do not ever take someone else's word as gospel just because she or he has a degree. And find another therapist if yours does not believe you.

The rigid never grow. They tend to do things the same way they've always done them. A colleague of mine who teaches graduate courses for teachers frequently asks the old timers, who have spent thirty years or more in the classroom, 'Have you really been teaching for thirty years or have you been teaching for one year, thirty times?
Wayne W. Dyer, Your Erroneous Zones

28. Can you explain multiple personality disorder and other dissociative states?

Multiple personality disorder (MPD) is a way of coping with severe sexual and physical abuse. Placed in a situation from which escape is impossible and subjected to traumatic and painful experiences over a period of time, people may be unable to deal with the pain and intense emotions and may protect themselves mentally by "dissociating" with what is happening. "Dissociating" means mentally shutting off from what is occuring.

Dissociation is the process by which we insulate ourselves from too much mental pain; our minds protect us by blocking emotions and events which are so horrible we are unable to mentally process them.

There are various degrees of dissociation. People can totally block out what is happening by becoming unconscious. They can block a traumatic event from their memory after it happens, (This is known as "amnesia.") or they can block out their emotions during the event and store the emotions in their unconscious minds.

If people unconsciously block out severely stressful events so they can continue to cope, the memories and emotions usually start to come back at a later time when the person is able to handle them. This can be a few months later in some cases or many years later in others. A woman in the AMAC (Adults Molested As Children) group I lead was sexually abused by her father as a child and, at the age of 59, was just recovering the memories of her abuse. However, most AMACs start to learn of their childhood abuse in their thirties or forties.

One of the most common types of dissociation that victims of abuse use to deal with trauma is known as "post-traumatic stress disorder." This disorder is more commonly found in soldiers during wartime, but it also affects people who experience natural disasters, such as earthquakes, large fires and gruesome automobile accidents. These people may have no conscious recollec-tion of the disaster, but they may have recurrent nightmares and flashbacks (daytime visions of their experiences) about the traumatic events.

Post-traumatic stress disorder was the subject of a great deal of media attention during and after the Vietnam War because many veterans of active combat and soldiers tortured in the Vietnamese prison camps suffered nightmares and flashbacks after they were safely home. They also experienced other symptoms of this disorder, such as the inability to have loving feelings, feeling detached from others, losing interest in things around them, irritability or anger and difficulty sleeping.[24]

Victims of childhood abuse experience the same disorder with the same symptoms. But since the soldiers are adults when they are subjected to trauma, they are better able to process and adapt to the events and to their emotions than people subjected to trauma as children. The soldiers thus regain their memories in a shorter period of time.

Many combat soldiers and prisoners of war diagnosed as having post traumatic stress disorder also report having out-of-body experiences during periods of extreme trauma and torture. Soldiers captured and tortured by the Vietnamese during the war in Vietnam frequently experienced this type of dissociation as part of the post-traumatic stress disorder. Until recently soldiers' reports of floating outside their bodies were given more credence than those of abuse victims. Now, however, therapists routinely diagnose victims of abuse as having post-traumatic stress syndrome, even where dissociation occurs, instead of some more serious condition such as schizophrenia.

The stress on young minds can create another dissociative condition—multiple personality disorder—which is less rare than previously believed. In cases of severe sexual abuse combined with physical abuse or torture, the intolerable stress may cause a child's mind to splinter the events into pieces because the mind is unable to cope with the pain and emotions which are generated. In such cases, multiple personality disorder results.

This disorder occurs when repeated abuse causes intolerable stress. The child cannot escape. The child does not know whether the abuse will ever stop. The child cannot even comprehend what is happening. The child has no one to talk to. Children's choices are to die (and many abused children do die of abuse), to become psychotic and dysfunctional or to find an alternative which will allow them to grow up and function.

The last choice is obviously the healthiest one, and the children who subconsciously choose it are intelligent and creative. They divide their minds into various personalities to deal with the continuing horror. Each personality seals off memories and feelings in neat little packages so that the child does not have to deal with too much pain at once. The child is insulated from the unbearable feelings and remembers nothing at the conscious level. The child is then able to continue living. One or more personalities deal with the abuse and protect the other personalities from knowledge of the abuse so that the child can continue to function on a day-to-day basis.

Depending on the severity of the abuse and how long it continues, a child's mind may create from two to a hundred distinct personalities. Studies have shown that these personalities may be of different ages and sexes and may even respond differently to psychological tests. What is more amazing is that the personalities may have different physical characteristics: eyeglass prescriptions, allergies and IQs, for example.[25] In one reported case, one of the personalities had diabetes, while the others were healthy.

Although multiple personality disorder is extremely painful and disruptive, the fact that people are able to create a variety of traits has some staggering positive implications for us all. The fact that people with multiple personality disorder have the capacity to develop totally different physical and psychological traits suggests that we all have the ability to create ourselves as we want to be. People with multiple personality disorder just have a head start.

Research indicates that while the multiple personalities are created in childhood, they usually do not begin to appear independently until after adolescence. Again this is a protective mechanism; the personalities and the memories they hold are not revealed until the person is old enough to deal with them.

As the child completes adolescence, the person's innate healing ability again becomes a factor. The personalities begin to come out. Where the personalities take full control, the person may experience periods of amnesia and not know what happened during the periods of blackout. Usually intense headaches accompany changes from one personality to another.

If you are experiencing these symptoms, it is important to immediately consult a therapist experienced in multiple personality disorder because you may be doing things that are embarrassing or harmful to

141

you during these blackout periods. I strongly recommend that you find a therapist who is familiar with this disorder and is trained in hypnotherapy to treat you. Research has shown that the personalities and ego states are created by self-hypnosis and that is why hypnosis is necessary for uncovering those ego states and bringing the memories to consciousness.[26] Clinicians recognize that hypnosis is the treatment of choice and you will save yourself a lot of time and grief if you insist on a hypnotherapist who has already successfully treated people with MPD.

Cases of MPD range from several fully developed personalities that take control to ego states that may contain only a single emotion. In the classic case of MPD, two or more personalities will take full control of the person's behavior. One personality may be shy and retiring and another may be flamboyant and promiscuous. You may have seen or read *The Three Faces of Eve* or *Sybil*. Those cases occurred long before therapists began discovering how common MPD is and before they learned how to recognize and treat it.

Therapists are finding that most people who have been abused more than once as young children have ego states. These are like personality states because they are sealed-off portions of a person's memory which may contain the emotions, pain, and/or picture memory but they do not take complete control over a person's actions. Some ego states may contain all of the memories of the child when the abuse first started. Another ego state may contain the memories of acts at another age. Although these ego states do not come out and take full control, they may affect the survivor's behavior when he or she feels threatened or perceives, usually inaccurately, that a situation is similar in some way to the abusive situation.

For example, if a woman is mildly criticized by her boss at work, she may become furious or tearful because she feels as though she is being put down by an authority figure. This may remind her of how her abusive stepfather made her feel and her child ego state may make her feel the emotions she felt during the abuse. The woman's reaction to her boss will then consist of her legitimate annoyance compounded by the rage and distress she felt when she was abused. Her reaction to her boss will obviously be more than the situation warrants. She will feel the exaggerated emotions and may even recognize that she is overreacting, but she will not know why because she does not remember the abuse.

I believe the child's solution of creating personality or ego states as insulation from the abuse is creative and intelligent because the child not only protects herself, but actually sets up a mental pattern or map to be used for healing later. When the child grows up, the adult can uncover each piece of the repressed abuse individually so that only a small bit has to be digested at once. The healing process becomes much easier when the person only has to deal with one memory or a portion of it at a time.

For those of you who have MPD or ego states, it is comforting to know that you have made a map for yourself. Your mind has all of the keys you need to heal yourself. You have a central part of your mind—I call it your "total intelligence"—which knows how you created these ego states and personalities and why you did. Your total intelligence also knows exactly which memories you need to see first and how they fit into the whole. You will not uncover personalities or memories before you are ready to do so. You will reveal to yourself only those pieces that are helpful to you at the time and that will help you along your path to health. It is important that you never let anyone push you into anything you do not think you are ready for. You know best what you need.

On the other hand, you should remember that the child in you will make you believe childhood memories are more frightening than they will actually be to you as an adult. Recovering the memories can seem very scary. The part of you that could not deal with childhood abuse tries to frighten your adult self into believing that as an adult you will be as overwhelmed as you were as a child. But it is not true. As real as the memory may seem, it is only a memory; it is not happening to you now. You are safe; you don't live there anymore.

My therapist used a device to make this point clear to me. Whenever I hypnotized myself, I'd take the adult part of myself along with me into my childhood memory to help my child self. Even when I was extremely upset, there was always a part of me that knew I was only seeing a memory and that I could stop it whenever I wanted. I also learned that I could take the child part of me out of that awful house and to a safe place. This is a very effective technique, but it should not be used until you have experienced all of the emotions you felt during the actual incident.

The worst part of what happened to you as a child was that you were totally helpless. But that is over. Now you are in control. You can determine when you will see a memory, what you want to see, how long you want to see it, and even how you will ultimately react to it. The important thing to remember is that *you are always in control*. I do not mean that you should control the emotions that come out with the memory; these are spontaneous and should be allowed to flow freely. But you can control how the memories will come out and, more important, you can decide as an adult how your childhood experiences will affect the rest of your life.

143

When I first learned of my incest, I was horrified. I was sure that anyone who had been through an experience like that could not ever be normal. After I got memories back of being tortured, I was convinced that I had to be defective and probably crazy for the rest of my life. How could I be anything other than defective? No one bothered to tell me the obvious: that I had survived and I was functioning—fairly well, in fact. It took me a long time to realize that I was really doing all right and a longer time to realize that if I could function this well given what I had been through, I must have a lot of strengths. I believe that those of you who are reading this book, particularly those of you who have multiple personality disorder, have had to be exceptionally strong to be where you are today. Your lives may not be perfect, but you are working hard to make them better.

Those of you who have multiple personality disorder have tapped abilities most of us don't even know exist. You know you can be and do anything you want to because you have done it. Moreover, you must have an incredible creativity to be able to invent a number of separate personalities to act for you. You created all of your own characters when you were just a child. Imagine what you can do now! You could write novels, plays, television shows or children's theatre.

And what is more amazing is the fact that you have the *abilities* of all of those personalities you created for yourself. You can do all of the things your personalities can do; you can choose the qualities of each personality that you want to use and those you want to discard. If there are some characteristics of your personalities that you would rather not have, don't be afraid of them; they helped you when you needed them.

Suppose you have a personality that is promiscuous and seductive. That personality expressed a part of you that wanted to have control over sexual actions. The seducer is the one who decides whether and when sex is to take place. So that part of you balanced the helplessness you felt because you were not in control. Perhaps that part is too strong now, but you can reeducate it and still use its strengths. You can let your seductive part help you be assertive so your sex life will be *your* choice and you will never be a victim again. That part of you can also help you be attractive to men when you want to be, as long as it knows that you are in control. You will find that no part of you is frightening; each part of you has a reason for being there. And each part, no matter how negative or primitive it seems, has a facet that is positive.

Your personalities are all parts of you. Sometimes they may do harmful things but they do not want to harm you, no matter what they say, because they were created to protect you. Although you are now an adult, they are still frightened children who may lash out in rage or who may want to hurt because they are hurt. But I have found that if you treat them as the hurt children they are, with love and understanding, they will respond very quickly. They are the wounded child part of you and they need to heal. As an adult, you have the power to give them the love they are starving for.

I had a particularly virulent ego state that called itself "Hatred." Most of my ego states were emotions or myself at certain ages rather than personalities, and each held memories which illustrated the source of the particular emotion. I apparently had so many overpowering emotions all at once that I had to split them up so I could stay sane. Hatred said that it hated everyone, including me, and that it wanted to destroy me. I was terrified, not only by these thoughts, but by the fact that when I called up this ego state, my view of the world was distorted. Under hypnosis, even my lovely therapist appeared misshapen and ugly when I looked at her through the eyes of this ego state. It was a vivid lesson in what hate can do to one's perceptions.

My therapist began to negotiate with Hatred and we found that Hatred contained memories of some of my worst abuse. My father chopped up my kitten in front of me while doing awful things to me at the same time. These events caused me to have convulsions. My feelings of hatred were so intense that I didn't think I could stand it. But I also learned that my hatred probably saved my life. Hatred gave me the courage to pick up a chisel my father had been using on me and stab him with it. He screamed so terribly that I thought I had killed him. Only when I relived the memory did I realize that I had shocked him out of his Nazi personality state and back to reality. He was so appalled when he saw what he had done that he went screaming out of the house. When he returned after treatment, he never sexually abused or tortured me again.

Every one of your personalities has much to teach you about your past and about yourself. It helps if you can see them as gifts, as teachers who have suffered much pain to spare you unbearable distress. My therapist always thanked my ego states whenever she talked to them and I learned to follow her example. When I began to see the horror my ego states hid from me so that I could grow up and function, I was overwhelmed with gratitude.

Most ego or personality states hold something valuable and can be reeducated and integrated into your total personality. A few others may want just to vanish. In my case, once Hatred had shown me its memories, it wanted to leave. Since we were unable to retrain it, my therapist and I thanked it and let it go. That does not mean I can never feel hatred again. It only means I have released those intense past feelings which could only hurt my life now.

Exploring yourself can be an exciting and challenging task. You may find it difficult to see it that way when you are overcome by pain and despair. But if you can recognize the creative and effective ways your mind devised to protect you when you needed it most, you will be able to thank yourself for your intelligence and your strength.

Some people view multiple personality disorder with fear and see it as a type of insanity. But even the official manual of mental diagnoses, the *Diagnostic and Statistical Manual of Mental Disorders*, does not view it that way. The manual calls it a "disorder." Many people who have multiple personality disorder believe that their condition is so serious and unique that they are beyond help. The truth is that multiple personality is much more common than was once believed; it just was not diagnosed before because therapists were not trained to recognize it. Now that therapists have more experience with MPD, it is becoming much easier to treat.

Researchers and therapists are even beginning to recognize that *everyone* has some aspects of multiple personality disorder. Have you ever heard someone say, "Part of me wants to try it, but part of me is afraid"? We talk about different "parts" of us all the time. And how about, "The child in me would like to do that." The theory of transactional analysis, a popular type of therapy, is based on various child and parent ego states. The trend toward recognizing that we all have aspects of multiple personality disorder is growing in many fields of study. In *Our Multiple Selves*, Dr. Richard Schwartz offers this view.

> "These researchers at the cutting edge of psychoneurology, computer science, and artificial intelligence, are converging on a new, multi-self view of people. In Ornstein's words, 'We are not a single person. We are many.' From this multi-self perspective, we not longer have to fear 'fragmenting'—we are already fragmented. *In a sense we are all multiple personalities. The condition we call multiple personality disorder only represents an extremely disengaged and polarized version of the ordinary operation of our internal system.* (My italics.) This is a very difficult proposition for most people to fully accept, but once it is accepted one's view of one's self and of human nature is profoundly altered."[27]

So if you have MPD, you do not have some strange and incurable disease. Your mind has created a condition where various parts of your personality have become exaggerated due to intense stress. This condition enabled you to survive.

People have so many misconceptions about MPD. Some therapists who do not have experience in this area still see multiple personality disorder as being extremely complicated, and they transmit their fear of being unable to cope to their patients. Therapists who have treated people with MPD know what to expect and do not find the condition overwhelming. That is why I have stressed the advisability of finding a therapist who has experience in successfully treating this condition.

Many people I know with MPD are trapped in a prison of fear, convinced that they are condemned to their condition forever. They do not understand the nature of their condition, and their therapists have not explained the facts to them. I believe that if more therapists would openly educate people with MPD about their condition at the beginning of therapy, their clients would have less anxiety and make faster progress. I want to reassure those of you who have MPD or suspect that you may have it that this condition is treatable and that you can live a "normal" life. Many men and women living in your own community have been through what you are experiencing and have learned to be happy. There is no reason why you cannot do it too, if you choose.

> *When the self has been confronted,*
> *when the hidden has been brought to the surface,*
> *the paradoxical result is not horror and paralysis*
> *but release and new birth.*
> A. J. Muste

29. If one of my parents had multiple personality disorder, will I have it too?

Not necessarily, although studies have demonstrated that the disorder is more prevalent in children of parents with the disorder than in the general population.[28] These studies make sense because multiple personality disorder (MPD) is a way people cope with traumatic events. As such it can be learned by example, just as children learn other behaviors from their parents. But no one learns this behavior unless they are subjected to events in their childhood that are too horrible for

147

their minds to assimilate. MPD has been found to only result from severe and prolonged sexual and/or physical abuse. It is not contagious like a disease. It also does not appear to be genetic.

Children of parents with MPD frequently acquire the disorder because they are abused by their parents who have never been treated. Their parents do not know that they have the disorder nor do they usually know of their own childhood abuse. These people may be aware that they have some strange behaviors and personality shifts, uncontrollable emotions, headaches, depression or other symptoms but ignore them because they think they can handle their own problems and "don't need a shrink." Or they may believe they cannot afford therapy. They may be totally unaware of the abusive acts they commit.

The unfortunate result of their failure to obtain help is a high probability that they will abuse their own children. This is not always the case, as was discussed in Question 22, *If I have been abused, will I abuse my children?* But these victims are driven by impulses that they are not aware of, unconscious impulses. The fact that these impulses are not conscious makes them very difficult to control. These parents do not *want* to injure their children but are unable to stop themselves. They are driven by the suppressed hurt and rage of their own abuse.

Children of parents with MPD cope with their own abuse through MPD when they are subjected to severe abuse *and* because they see the condition in their parents and copy it. This copying is not conscious. Children are very sensitive to their parents' behavior and often unconsciously pick up the physical and mental problems of their parents. This phenomenon is called "participation mystique" and is part of a child's attempt to adapt to the family. The child wants to participate in and fit into the family and so adopts the family's behaviors, whether they are positive or negative.

And so the cycle of abuse continues unless treatment is obtained. The number of reported MPD cases has increased dramatically during the past decade primarily because of increased awareness of therapists and increased knowledge of treatment. But the actual number of people with this condition has also increased and will continue to do so because parents are passing the condition on to their children through abuse and example. The cycle must be stopped. And the only way to stop it is to increase public awareness of the problem and to make treatment easy to obtain.

If one of your parents had MPD, you may have escaped the condition if your parent was able to control his or her abusive impulses. Even if you were abused, you may have coped in a different way than by creating different personalities. My father had a classic case of multiple personality disorder. He was abused by his mother and aunts and by students in the school he attended in pre-Nazi Austria. His Nazi-like personality took full control of his mind, and what I think of as "my real father," a gentle, loving man, did not know the "Nazi" existed. He was unaware of his acts of sexual abuse and torture and was horrified when he found out. My coping reaction was to create ego states, walling off memories of events and of the intense and destructive feelings I had about these events. But I never had blackouts or personalities that took over, even though my amnesia about my childhood was total.

I somehow rejected the classic multiple personality disorder, probably by deciding that I would not be like my father. In fact, I spent my life trying not to be like my father. I had heard somewhere that abused children could be child abusers, so even though I could not remember what had happened to me, I was terrified of babies and did not want to have any. I had a tubal ligation in my thirties to be sure I would not have children. I was never able to make a rational choice about having children because I was totally unaware of what the problem was. If I had suspected abuse, I would have gone to a therapist and found out the truth. I would have been healed much sooner and I would have been able to have a family without fear.

You have that opportunity now. If you suspect that you have MPD, you can find out the truth very quickly by one or two visits to a therapist who is experienced in hypnosis and the treatment of MPD. Under hypnosis, you will be able to tell yourself whether you have been abused and if you have extra personalities. Your unconscious mind cannot lie to you. If you have been abused and have coped by creating personalities or ego states, those conditions are curable and you can relax in the knowledge that you have spared your children the possibility of abuse. If you have been abused but do not have MPD, you will also need treatment to insure that you will not abuse your children.

Again, I want to repeat that MPD is curable. In fact, it is becoming easier and easier to heal as more cases are treated and more therapists become familiar with it. People who have been abused and had MPD or borderline MPD like myself are now becoming therapists and are speaking out about their experiences. Many of the old misconceptions are being demolished.

You have the key to your own mind and an experienced therapist can help you unlock all of your blocked pain. You can continue with your life while you undergo therapy. And I guarantee you will begin to feel better than you do now. If you obtain treatment, you can be healed. You do not have to fear that you will continue the chain of abuse or that your children will have MPD. If you get help, the chain can stop with you.

> *Your pain is the breaking of the shell*
> *that encloses your understanding.*
> Kahlil Gibran

30. What if I hear voices?

If you have been severely sexually or physically abused, you may have repressed memories of the abuse and you may hear voices that are associated with those memories. People with multiple personality disorder can sometimes hear voices of one or more personalities.[29] People who have suppressed traumatic events may also have flashbacks where visions, sounds, smells and other sensations are extremely vivid.

Hearing voices does NOT mean you are crazy or that you are incurable. It does mean that your abuse was probably severe and that you should have a therapist to support you and prevent you from getting confused. It is important that you find a therapist who is experienced in handling cases of severe abuse and multiple personality disorder because people who do not have this experience may not understand the voices and may misdiagnose you. If you are misdiagnosed, you may be placed on psychotropic drugs which you do not need. (This does not mean that someone who is abused or has multiple personality disorder may never need psychotropic drugs. In cases where a person becomes very distraught or confused, drugs may be necessary.) So, if you do hear voices, you should immediately consult an appropriate therapist who can help you make sense of them.

Confusion is the major problem when you hear voices. The confusion is much less if you know that the voices are coming from you rather than from outside you. Some people believe that the voices are coming from God, and many religions of the world support this belief.

But there is one cardinal rule for knowing whether or not these voices are reliable: **IF THE VOICE TELLS YOU TO HURT YOUR-SELF OR ANOTHER PERSON IN ANY WAY, IT IS *NOT* RELI-ABLE AND IT IS *NOT* COMING FROM GOD.**

If the message is to hurt yourself or someone else, call a therapist for help immediately. Knock on a neighbor's door, call a friend, but find someone who can talk to you and get help for you.

People who hear voices which tell them to hurt themselves have been severely abused. The abuse has made them feel very bad about themselves; they feel dirty, evil, worthless, unredeemable. If you tell these people that their feelings are distorted, they will not believe you. They believe deep down that if such awful things could happen to them, they must have done something to deserve it or cause it to happen. They believe they were being punished and that they must continue to be punished. Thus the voices may act as a means of self-punishment.

More often, however, people who hear voices and hurt themselves are repeating the pattern of their abuse. They may be repeating the pattern to let themselves and others know that the abuse really occurred. Suzanne stuck a knife in her stomach to tell herself and her therapist that her stepfather had stuck a knife up her. One of her child ego states wanted her to know what had been done to her.

Some abuse victims may hurt themselves because they are overwhelmed by strong negative emotions which they do not understand. They do not realize that their self-destructive feelings are coming from memories of childhood abuse rather than present events and so they act on those feelings. By acting in ways that make them victims again, they create an immediate reason for their turbulent feelings. Then they don't feel so crazy and out of control.

The repetition of conduct related to abuse used to seem unbelievable to me. In fact, I raged at the therapist who suggested that I was caught in a victim pattern: "Do you mean humans are dumber than Pavlov's dog? At least the dog stopped pressing the button when it was shocked. But we just keep pressing the button? I don't believe we are that stupid."

My ever-patient therapist calmly explained that we do not consciously do harmful things to deliberately hurt ourselves, but that the unconscious parts of our minds are attempting to make sense of our pain and control our anxiety. She used the example of a child who is taken to the doctor. The child waits with his mother in the waiting room and plays with toys and games. He is then taken to be weighed and measured. The doctor examines him and gives him a lollipop. The nurse then gives him a shot and he goes home. What happens when he is home? When he plays with his friends, he reenacts the giving of the shot over and over. If the child is female, she will gives shots to her dolls. The reenactment gives the child some control over the event so that the anxiety is controlled.

In this light, self-mutilation becomes understandable. It can be prevented if you call for help whenever you have the slightest hint that you might be tempted to hurt yourself or others. You do have control of yourself; it is the "hurt child" in your mind that is asking you to hurt yourself. You only have to tell it *no*, that you are in control and that you will find other ways to deal with the memories. If the thought comes back into your head, call for help and then tell yourself that you do not deserve to be punished, that you are a good person, that you are sorry the child in you was hurt, but you are now going to heal together. If you have not yet uncovered all of the memories, you can also tell yourself that you will let them come out and that you can and will deal with them as an adult.

Sometimes survivors also have visual hallucinations; they see things that are not there. Lettie, 15, was in therapy because of her stepfather's sexual abuse. It quickly became apparent to me that her abuse was more serious than she described, but pressure from her mother and stepfather made her afraid to reveal more. Lettie began to have hallucinations of a former childhood playmate who urged Lettie to kill her stepfather. Then she saw "ugly, troll-like men." When Lettie was hospitalized, away from her emotionally destructive mother and her violent stepfather, she was able to divulge her stepfather's brutal beatings and the earlier rape and torture by her mother's live-in boyfriend. Her hallucinations stopped—without drugs.

Hallucinations enabled Lettie to find a safe place where she could receive help. More important, they signalled that something was wrong—that she had repressed traumatic memories which she needed to release. The hallucinations also provided clues about her abuse.

Hallucinations tell you that your mind is in distress and that you need to go immediately to a therapist or a hospital so you don't confuse your visions with reality

Voices and visions are frightening and confusing but they are merely symptoms of what you have suffered. They are certainly not as bad as the real events. These hallucinations and voices are your creation and are there to give you information about yourself. You can use them to obtain more information about what happened to you and what you feel about your abuse. If you use the voices to understand what your mind is trying to tell you about how you feel about yourself and past events, you will find your fear and confusion diminishing.

It is important to remember that once the memories are brought to consciousness and dealt with, the voices and visions will disappear. They will not be with you forever and you will not go crazy. Discuss them with your therapist and use them as another tool to help you learn more about your mind and yourself. Think of your voices as a way of talking to yourself, use what is helpful and ignore the nonsense.

> *Be like the bird, who*
> *Halting in his flight*
> *On limb too slight*
> *Feels it give way beneath him,*
> *Yet sings,*
> *Knowing he has wings.*
> Victor Hugo

31. I have had some strange mystical experiences. Am I crazy?

"I can't stand this another minute. I feel like I'm dying. I want to die. Oh, please, let me die. What's happening? I can't feel the pain anymore. Why don't I feel the pain? I don't feel anything. I feel so peaceful. I'm floating, floating up to the ceiling. What is happening? I can see my father's naked body on the bed below me. I can see his back and the back of his legs. He's on top of a little girl, a girl with long dark hair like me. That *is* me! I'm so confused. I don't understand. How can I be down there and up here on the ceiling at the same time? I can see my father and the girl— me moving on the bed, but my feelings and the pain are gone. I don't feel anything, but I can hear her crying. I'm glad I'm not there anymore. I don't want to go back there."

These words were sobbed in the voice of a seven-year-old, but they emerged from the mouth of a thirty-two-year-old woman. The woman, we shall call her Jane, was in her therapist's office recalling under hypnosis one incident of her father's rape that had occurred during an eight-year period of abuse. After she came out of her hypnotic state, Jane expressed surprise about the memory. She knew she had repressed her emotions about the repeated rapes; the fact that she could not consciously remember her father's acts had necessitated the use of hypnotherapy for her treatment. But Jane was totally baffled by her vision of floating up to the ceiling. She had never heard of out-of-body experiences before and was quite distressed by this recollection of

153

leaving her body.

Is she crazy? No. Jane and others like her lack the accepted characteristics of psychosis. Having a mystical experience does not mean you are psychotic as long as you remain otherwise grounded in reality and able to function rationally on a day-to-day basis. It should be emphasized that some people have these experiences and some people do not. Having mystical experiences does not mean you are crazy. Not having them does not mean you have missed something. We each grow in our own way and follow our own path.

Many victims of abuse have had mystical experiences but some therapists and psychological researchers are reluctant to discuss them because they are afraid their colleagues will think *they* are crazy. The boundary between spiritual experiences and psychosis is a fine one, and therapists are frequently unwilling to discuss their clinical cases involving mysticism because they do not want to expose themselves to ridicule. But the fact is that many therapists, especially those who specialize in sexual abuse cases, routinely use crystals and energy balancing techniques along with gestalt, behavior modification, hypnotherapy, and Jungian techniques to heal their clients. However, research in parapsychology and transpersonal psychology has revealed the fact that *most* people have had at least one mystical experience, but fear and awe render them silent because they think they are the only ones to have had such an experience and that no one will understand.

I debated with myself for a long time whether to "go public" with these experiences for the same reasons, but I finally concluded that since so many survivors of abuse have had mystical experiences, I should include these case histories to help them deal with their fears and questions. Every experience should be used as a step towards healing, and I believe that experiences which may be frightening should be demystified so that healing can continue.

Mystical experiences can take as many forms as there are people to have them. Three types appear to be common among victims of sexual abuse. The first is a phenomenon commonly known as an out-of-body experience, labelled "dissociation" by psychologists. Dissociation is the process by which we insulate ourselves from too much mental pain; our minds protect us by blocking emotions and events which are so horrible we are unable to mentally process them.

There are various degrees of dissociation. People can totally block out what is happening by becoming unconscious. They can block a traumatic event from their memory, a psychological reaction known as "amnesia." They can also block out their emotions during the event and store the emotions in their unconscious minds.[30] If people unconsciously block out severely stressful events so they can continue to cope, the memories and emotions usually start to come back at a later time, when the person is able to handle them. This can be a few months later in some cases or many years later in others. When people repress their memories to cope with extreme stress and pain, they may develop post-traumatic stress disorder or create multiple personalities to protect their sanity. (See Question 28.)

The "mystical" way people dissociate themselves from traumatic events while they are happening is by mentally floating outside of their bodies and watching from the ceiling or somewhere else. These experiences are sometimes called out-of-body experiences and many who are pursuing a spiritual path actively seek to achieve this state. Richard Bach describes his efforts to learn "astral projection," another name for out-of-body experiences, in his recent bestseller, *Bridge Across Forever*. Although Bach and others seek these experiences through methods such as meditation in order to seemingly travel to distant places without leaving their homes, victims of abuse stumble on this phenomenon in their desperation to escape from rape and brutality.

A Canadian woman, interviewed for a PBS TV documentary on sexual abuse, was raped by her father for several years when she was a child. On the program, she pointed to a solid concrete wall across the room from the bed on which she was raped and described floating out of her body and going into the wall to escape. She said she would sit inside the wall and watch what was happening to her body on the bed. She did not feel what her father was doing to her. It was as if she watched her father abusing someone else. She did not remember any of these painful events for many years, and only as an adult did she begin to recover her memory and deal with the painful feelings she had suppressed.

Out-of-body experiences are frequently encountered by therapists who treat combat soldiers or prisoners of war subjected to torture. These soldiers relate episodes where they have left their bodies in order to cope with the horrors of battle or the pain and terror of torture. Soldiers captured and tortured by the Vietnamese experienced this type of dissociation.

Are the experiences of leaving one's body real or imagined? Of course no one really knows. People who have these out-of-body experiences believe they are real, that part of them, their soul, actually leaves their bodies. And some recent research seems to support the possibility that some portion of a person's soul or consciousness can separate from or expand out of our physic-al form. For example, surgeons report that patients who are anesthetized can recall what occurs in the operating room and can describe people who entered the room while they were unconscious. In his bestseller, *Love, Medicine and Miracles*, Dr. Bernie Siegel, a surgeon and professor at Yale Medical School, discusses his own experiences and various studies which indicate that patients under anesthesia hear and recall everything that is said during their surgery.

Another phenomenon which suggests an ability to stretch our consciousness far beyond the walls of our bodies is "remote viewing." For several years the military has financed research on remote viewing, a phenomenon enabling people to mentally "see" what is happening thousands of miles away without equipment of any kind. Subjects are able to describe in detail an area that is only defined for them by a certain latitude and longitude on a map. If part of us can know what is happening miles away, perhaps our consciousness can leave our bodies during stress or even at will.

No one has a definitive explanation for these phenomena. But for sexual abuse victims the explanation is less important than the fact that dissociation of any kind—leaving one's body, creating multiple personality disorder or blocking the event with amnesia—provides protection from unbearable pain and overwhelming emotions. These protections are created by the victim's mind in order to confine the stress of the traumatic event to an amount that can be tolerated and processed at the time. Dissociation is a positive defense against intolerable stress, similar to the body's creating cells to combat an invasion by germs from outside. What is amazing about dissociation is that the mind also lets the survivor know when he or she is ready to tolerate the stressful event by creating symptoms, flashbacks, dreams and other behaviors which alert the victim to the existence of suppressed events so they can be remembered and put to rest.

A second type of mystical experience common to victims of severe sexual and physical abuse is the "white light experience." Victims have described being visited by beings of white light during severe abuse, often at the worst moment of prolonged episodes. The victim is often unaware of these experiences until they emerge while the victim is under hypnosis, usually while the victim is disclosing details of the abusive act at a later time.

Revelations of communications with a white light being are often a complete surprise to the victim and to those therapists who may not have encountered such revelations before. Many victims who have had these experiences are either nonreligious or overtly atheistic, so recovering memories of white lights can be extremely perplexing and even frightening, although the events themselves are universally positive.

The reports generally have similar features; the victim sees a white light which begins to grow larger and brighter. The victim knows instantly that the white light is a power for good and love and under-stands what the white light is saying even though it does not actually speak. The light informs the victim that the victim is loved, that there is a reason for what is happening and that the victim will survive the abuse. Some victims are given elaborate information about the universe and their lives and futures. Victims report feeling intense love and peace in the presence of the light unlike anything they have known before.

There are, of course, variations on this theme. Geri was raped by her father from infancy; he sold her to friends and relatives as a child, used her in pornography and turned her into a child prostitute. She had two abortions and a child before she was fourteen. All this was "forgotten" by her as an adult. She survived by splitting her mind into many person-alities. When she was in her twenties, Geri began to have flashbacks of babies being killed and, fearing she was insane, started therapy.

One day, during her regular hypnotherapy session, Geri described a white light which appeared during a certain gruesome incident of rape and violence by her father. The light radiated warmth and love. Al-though Geri could not see a form in the light, she concluded that the light was an angel who had come to comfort her. She was not frightened even when the light enabled her to fly to a distant place. Geri recounted moving very fast and believes she travelled a long way. The light took Geri to see Jesus. She described him as a beautiful man, filled with love and surrounded by light. She was a young child at the time, so she sat on Jesus' lap and sang songs to him. She was told that she was loved and would survive to live a happy life later on. Then the light took her back.

Geri believes her white light experience gave her the courage and strength to survive her fourteen years of abuse even though she did not consciously remember the experience as an adult. The love she felt from the light and from the figure of Jesus instilled in her an unshakable belief that she was loved by God and would survive, despite her father's continuing abuse.

Although she repressed her memories, including the memory of the white light, Geri retained her faith in God and Jesus as an adult. She claims that her faith in God and her recollection of his intervention through the white light helped her through the years of therapy and enabled her to bear recalling the brutal memories of her childhood. Geri believes that God has healed her for a higher purpose and plans to help others.

I had an experience with white light which I recalled under hypnosis when I was exploring with my therapist a particularly grisly incident that took place in the basement workshop of our house. As the memory returned, I described to my therapist how my father, after beating and raping me, killed my black and white kitten and dismembered it in front of me. Things got worse from there and, after I had convulsions, I picked up a chisel my father had been using on me and stabbed him with it. I thought I had killed him because he screamed so loudly, but I realized when I discussed the incident with my therapist that I had really only given him a flesh wound. The shock of the wound apparently was enough to knock him out of his multiple personality state, so he became aware of what he had been doing. The horror of this realization sent him screaming out of the house and to a clinic.

But at seven years old, I believed that I had killed my father, that I was evil and that I had no further reason to live. I crawled, covered with blood, onto the dirt of the foundation under the boards of the main floor of the house to die. I could feel bugs, attracted by the blood, biting my naked body as I lay in the darkened space less than two feet high. My eyes were closed but it seemed to be getting brighter. There were vents along the side of the crawlspace and I thought dawn had come. But when I opened my eyes, I was nearly blinded by a whiteness and brilliance I had never seen before. I was enveloped in a light that told me, without words, not to be afraid, that my abuse was over.

I was narrating this memory to my therapist, but at this point I could stand it no longer. I broke off and came out of hypnosis saying, "This is nonsense. What in the world is going on?"

"Go back. Go back. I want to hear the rest," my therapist ordered, and so I returned to my hypnotic state. The light informed me that I would forget everything that had happened until I was old enough to handle it and that I would be happy later in my life and help other people. It made a couple of other predictions, all of which have come true, including one about saving a cat to make up for the kitten that was killed. A few months before recovering this memory, I had rescued a cat which had been abandoned by the former owners of the house I had purchased. I ignored pressure from my husband, who is allergic to cats, to take it to the pound, and I found a home for it after several anxious weeks of searching. The light was also accurate about my losing my memory about my abuse. I had lost my memory of those years of my childhood and my memories did not return until I was over forty, which was the first time I could have handled it.

I cannot explain what I experienced. I only know that it came out as a memory, just as countless other memories have returned under hypnosis. My therapist and I did all kinds of tests to determine the veracity of this memory, and we were never able to find anything to lead us to believe it was false. My therapist had encountered several of these experiences with her abused clients so she did not find it as extraordinary or as suspect as I did. All my life I had been an agnostic and my family was not only atheistic but ridiculed faith and religion. No one ever talked about white lights.

My mind could have concocted the events I recalled. The predictions had already come true when the memory returned, except perhaps the one about being happy. Did my mind make up this story to make me feel better as I struggled to understand the truth of my abuse and overcome the damage it had done to me?

Are these experiences "real," or are they illusions created in the minds of people tormented beyond endurance in order to survive? Again, I can only say, after several years of study, I don't know. My research introduced me to a whole new world of spirituality which contends that we are all beings of white light. I have read numerous accounts by physicians and others of the "near-death experiences" of people who "died" according to the medical definition of death, but who were later resuscitated.[31] These people of all religions and backgrounds described similar encounters with beings of white light who were filled with love or were love itself and who "spoke" without words. In some of these cases, the lights revealed the person's life and asked if the person had completed everything he wanted to, so the person could decide whether or not to return to life.

Although the people who had "near-death" experiences were physically dying, they were undergoing extreme mental and physical stress, stress similar to that experienced by victims of abuse. Perhaps all people have a similar mechanism which is triggered by proximity to death, or perhaps there are souls which watch over us and help us in times of need so we can choose whether or not to live.

Loving beings of white light are reported to have appeared in many religions, and the visualization of white light itself is used for healing. Beings of white light have been reported so frequently throughout history that one might conclude that they are real or that all humans, regardless of race, nationality or religion, experience the same vision when subjected to severe stress. However, the incredible coincidence of people with different backgrounds and beliefs creating identical hallucinations strengthens the case for their reality.

For purposes of healing or therapy it does not matter whether or not these beings are real. What matters is that they bring love and hope to victims of abuse in a time of dire need. Whether the light comes from our own soul or mind to give us strength or from an outside force that loves us and is watching over us, we can take comfort from the knowledge that there is a power which sustains and supports us. Rather than being frightened of an occurrence which is certainly beyond our usual experience, we can draw strength from the knowledge that a power exists, whether outside us or within, to comfort us in our worst moments and to help us survive and grow. The positive reaction of my own therapist reinforced the beneficial effect of my white light experience and added to my healing.

Despite the benevolent nature of white light beings, some people are frightened because they misconstrue the implications of these experiences. They think if they are helped by mystical forces, something scary and painful will be expected of them. Whether we are religious or not, we have been influenced by the story of Jesus and we immediately fear that we may have been chosen for some painful task. This is not the case. According to tradition, Jesus chose to do what He did in His own way for His own purposes. Having one of these experiences does not mean that you have been chosen by God for some overwhelming and terrible task. We are all leading ourselves out of our personal hells and whether the help comes from ourselves or from outside, there are no strings attached. We have inside us a genetic program which pushes us toward health, toward healing, toward happiness, toward love. Help is always available in the universe.

Some sexual abuse victims go through yet a third type of mystical experience during their healing process, one which may be frightening. People with multiple personality disorder and those with less complicated ego states may discover under hypnosis the existence of a certain "personality" that wants to hurt them or has destructive or bizarre aspects. Such personalities may indicate that they are not part of the victim at all but separate souls of people who have died and have remained on earth. These personalities, which I call "independent personalities," may come out under hypnosis and express extremely hostile feelings towards the victim and sometimes the therapist. In such cases, a person with multiple personality disorder may believe that she is possessed.[32] If client and therapist are not aware that this phenomenon is a possibility, uncovering such a personality can be a very disconcerting experience, to say the least.

Most people's first reaction to hostility is either fear or to retaliate in kind. Abuse victims and their therapists are no exception. Although these personalities can be expelled quite easily, therapists have been known to struggle with them, to argue with them and to even attempt to expel them by exorcism. But so far, no one has ever been harmed by this phenomenon.

Some therapists have found that such personalities are more easily expelled with kindness. In cases of multiple personality, the personalities are usually parts of the victim's own personality and contain memories and feelings that the victim has experienced. Since the personality is part of the victim's experience, the therapist normally integrates the fragmented personality back into the victim's minds. But independent personalities do not acknowledge any connection with the victim; they indicate that they are unhappy and do not want to stay in the body they inhabit but would rather be guided to wherever they are supposed to go. Since these personalities have no traits or information that would be helpful to the victim and may be hostile, therapists may choose to let them go rather than integrate them. Acknowledging the pain of the personality immediately reduces its hostility and having victim and therapist say a prayer for a guide to lead it away usually ends its existence in the client.

How does it feel to have an independent personality inside you? Jennifer, a forty-four-year-old attorney and victim of sexual and physical abuse, described feeling "jittery, almost as if low voltage electricity was going through me."

Barbara, a first-grade teacher similarly abused, said she felt a kind of nervousness, different from ordinary nervousness, which kept her from sleeping. Barbara was able to bargain with her personality to be calm and let her sleep during the night on the condition that she find a way to help the personality on its journey in a painless way. Barbara and her therapist induced the personality to leave by praying for a guide to take the personality where it needed to go. As soon as the personality indicated that it saw the guide, it left Barbara's body and Barbara's "nervousness" disappeared.

Some abuse victims experience more than one independent personality in their bodies. Sally, a thirty-six-year-old writer, grew frustrated with coaxing several personalities to leave. She shouted at her therapist, "Will you tell them I am not a damn hotel!"

Where do these personalities go? No one knows. But under hypnosis, abuse victims uniformly assert that their personalities must leave earth to go where they need to go to progress in the development of their souls.

As fantastic as all of this may seem, many therapists who deal with multiple personality disorder and ego states encounter this phenomenon. We would all like to know whether these personalities are really independent or, like multiple personalities, creations of the minds of abuse victims. If we can create distinct multiple personalities, our minds certainly have the ability to create these personalities. However, unlike the usual multiple personalities or ego states which contain past memories and feelings, independent personalities do not appear to serve any purpose; they do not contain memories or feelings of the victim and often reveal information which is inconsistent with the victim's history.

For example, some independent personalities say they are older than the victim or a different sex. Although some of a victim's multiple personalities may be the opposite sex or a different age, these personalities can usually be traced to events and people in the victim's life. Independent personalities reveal little and only request help in leaving; they seem to be totally unconcerned with the victim's condition. Since mental creations usually have a function, it seems strange that these personalities would be so superfluous to the healing process of the victims.

One psychological explanation is that these personalities may be created to express hostility a victim is afraid to consciously acknowledge. By placing hostility in "another soul," the victim does not have to own his or her anger and destructive feelings. If the therapist treats the personality kindly in spite of its hostility, the victim learns that negative feelings are acceptable, and he can begin to accept his own negative feelings and heal.

On the other hand, some people believe that these personalities are who they say they are. The theory is that when we die, we go through a type of tunnel to our next place of learning. Some people believe that souls may become confused and are unable to go through the tunnel, usually due to drugs or alcohol, or they may choose to stay on earth because they want to watch over loved ones, obtain revenge or other misguided reasons. Since they no longer have a body, they use the bodies of others, not in the sense that they control those bodies because they have no control, but rather like a hotel.

Whether any of this can be scientifically proven does not matter; what matters is how you handle it if you encounter it. The most important thing to realize is that there is nothing to fear. If in fact you have created this phenomenon mentally, you have total control over it and can do with it what you like. It has no separate power to hurt anyone.

If a personality really is indeed "a lost soul," it also cannot hurt you because it has no body and cannot affect the physical plane. A personality cannot hurt its host or the therapist unless the patient or the therapist reacts with extreme fear; we can sometimes hurt ourselves through our own fear. It is important to the victim's well-being for the therapist to avoid exacerbating the victim's fears about such phenomena. If the appearance of an independent personality is treated calmly and with kindness, my experience is that the personality will lose its hostility and can be easily removed.

These personalities can teach us one of the major truths of life—that fear is an illusion. Only our own fear can hurt us; the personality, however inexplicable, cannot. I believe these "independent personalities" may appear to teach us a valuable lesson: If we face our fears and act with love rather than hate, we will see that our fears are illusory. Fear can harm us by making us act in irrational ways. But if we look behind our fear, we will always find a way out.

We all have fears. You may fear that you are hopeless, that you will never get well, but such fears are an illusion. We all have the power to heal ourselves. You may be terrified of facing the memories of your abuse, but that fear is also an illusion. The abuse happened long ago; it is not happening now.

Whatever you face during therapy or other parts of your life, remember when you are frightened that what you fear is always much worse than the truth. "Independent personalities" can teach us that there is no evil, only fear. What we call "evil" is what human beings create out of pain. And if you treat "evil" with kindness, it disappears.

Although the three types of phenomena experienced by survivors of sexual abuse have both positive and negative aspects, I believe the ultimate results in all cases are predominantly beneficial. These experiences enable victims of abuse to survive overwhelming mental stress, retain their sanity and heal themselves. If victims create these experiences within their own minds, such creations demonstrate an ingenuity and intelligence beyond anything we now recognize. If we create our own mystical experiences to heal us, we may truly have the answers to all we need to know inside us. And if we create white lights, the way we create imaginary childhood playmates, then we must have a part of ourselves that is more developed than our everyday personalities, one which protects us and strives for a higher purpose.

Whether you believe these experiences are psychological or spiritual, there is much to learn from them. Out of body experiences show us that we have the power to control pain—both physical and mental—and if we can escape from the agony of abuse, we can certainly control more minor pain. We should also continue to explore the possibility that we can expand our consciousness far beyond the confines of our bodies.

Experiences with white light may teach us that we have an infinite source of love inside ourselves which nurtures us and helps us to heal. We can call on this inner strength to aid us in times of trial and give us the courage to continue. White light experiences also show us that we have more wisdom inside us than we realize; our "inner guides" are actually the infinite power of our own minds.

Independent personalities can also be powerful instructors. They show us that we can be hurt by our negative feelings because those feelings make us fearful and nervous. But we can expel negative feelings, just as we banish independent personalities. And the fact that gentle treatment is more effective for expelling personalities than fighting them illustrates that we should treat ourselves and our feelings, both positive and negative, with kindness and acceptance. No emotion is good or bad; each is all a part of being human.

Perhaps the most powerful lesson of these mystical experiences is that we have the unlimited power of choice. We can choose how we want ourselves and our lives to be. We can choose whether to survive or give up, whether to continue to be a victim or not, and if so, for how long. We can choose to let our pasts destroy the present, or we can choose to be happy now.

We have only begun to scratch the surface of what our minds have to teach us. If we face the mystical and the inexplicable with curiosity rather than fear and hostility, we may uncover a new world of wonderful possibilities.

> *He that will believe only what he can fully comprehend,*
> *must have a very long head or a very short creed.*
> Caleb C. Colton

32. The person who abused me is dead. How can I ever resolve my feelings now?

Sometimes an important person in your life dies before you are able to express your feelings to him. You are left with a sense of loss, of incompleteness, of regret. Your unexpressed feelings of resentment, rage, hate, pain, hurt, anxiety, guilt and grief are shoved beneath the surface of your consciousness where they continue to fester until you resolve them. This is called "unfinished business" and if you do not deal with it, it will interfere with your life until you do. Your repressed emotions will pop out at inappropriate times and affect the nature and intensity of your responses to present events.

You can have unfinished business whether you loved or hated the person who died. Unfinished business merely means that you did not express intense emotions at the time they were evoked or that you did not say something to the deceased that you wanted to say. If you loved the person, you might regret not having told her before her death. You may also have a lot of anger at the person for dying, anger that you are afraid to express because "It's not nice to be angry at the dead." So you keep it quietly inside you where it builds up until it explodes. And if you hate the person, you have been deprived of an opportunity to express that hate. You've been told it's wrong to hate and it's worse to hate someone who is dead, so your hatred is stuck inside you where it can only turn inward.

Death freezes our emotions for the deceased where they were at the moment of death. If we have been open and honest about our feelings, we have few regrets and little to repress. Then our emotions have been appropriately expressed, not necessarily to the deceased, but in a way that has released them so that we do not feel incomplete. But we still must go through the stages of grief—shock and denial, anger, bargaining, depression and acceptance. Repression of emotion at any of these stages will also cause pain later on. In fact, repression of any intense emotion causes problems until it is released. Death merely makes it necessary to deal with what we have repressed in a different way.

Even if we have not been open about our emotions, we still have a chance to deal with them. People often believe that death makes it difficult to resolve repressed feelings about the deceased and impossible to change the relationship. But they are wrong. The crux of the problem is to release emotions that have gotten stuck and the same therapeutic techniques can be used whether the object of these emotions is dead or alive. The aim of these techniques is to evoke the old emotions so that they can be experienced and understood. The techniques are mechanisms for helping people feel what they should have let themselves feel before. Once the emotions are released, the relationship with the deceased can be experienced in a different way.

So, the fact that you did not express your feelings to or about your abuser before he or she died does not mean that you never can. There are many techniques you can use with a therapist or by yourself to vent violent emotions, and the person who generated them does not have to be present. Some of these techniques are described in Question 18, *Is it O.K. to hate the person who abused me?* Although these examples relate to anger and hatred, the principles apply to other feelings too, such as grief, fear, pain, guilt and sadness. By giving you permission to let go of old feelings, these techniques enable you to talk to your deceased in a way which will bring out the emotions you felt but did not express. Often someone has to tell us that it O.K. to feel—to grieve, to rage, to hate— before we allow ourselves to break down the barriers we have erected so

165

that we can appear to be in control. When will we learn that our feelings are a natural part of our existence, and that when we deny our human responses, we suffer?

One technique which is designed expressly for situations where someone has died is to mentally recreate your abuser's funeral. There are a number of variations on this and you can use your imagination, but the basic exercise is to visualize your abuser's funeral as if it were happening now. Start by using the relaxation techniques described Part V, Section 6. As with most visualizations, this one is more effective if done under self-hypnosis. When you are relaxed, let yourself picture your abuser being placed in a coffin, using as much detail as you can. Your vision does not have to be accurate; research has shown that your subconscious mind accepts what you say and what you visualize as true, just as though it were real. You are creating a scene for your own benefit and you can make it any way you like.

When you have placed your abuser in the coffin, you can close it or keep it open. You may want to talk to your abuser now or later on during the funeral, or perhaps when he or she is buried. But when you talk, give yourself permission to let go and say everything you always wanted to say, about how your abuser treated you, how you felt and what you think of him. This is the time to let all of your emotions come out; you can cry, swear and scream as loudly as you want. You may want to imagine what your abuser would say to you and discuss what happened. You could even do this in a mental deathbed scene *before* you place him or her in the coffin. The aim is to make it all as real as possible so that you know how you really *feel* about it.

Next, mentally follow the funeral procession to the grave. Even if your abuser was not buried, visualizing a burial helps to make the death final. The funeral I envisioned for my father bore no resemblance to reality. My father was cremated in Mexico and I pictured an old-fashioned wooden coffin on a horse-drawn cart in what appeared to be farm country in the midwest.

When you are at the gravesite, tell your abuser how you intend to live the rest of your life and say goodbye. Will you let your abuser continue to have control over you from the grave by allowing him or her to hold your feelings captive and inflame your rage? Or will you break free of your abuser's hold on you, and tell him or her that you are letting your anger go, that he or she is really dead and can't hurt or affect you anymore, and that *you* are in control now? Now walk away from the grave, knowing that your abuser is dead and that you are totally free.

One of the most damaging fallacies about death is the attitude that it not proper to be angry at the deceased. There are many appropriate reasons to be angry at someone who dies, most of which are based on the deceased's acts while living. But death itself is a cogent reason for intense anger, even if the deceased is beloved. By dying, the person has abandoned us, leaving us alone, cut off from communication. Even though part of us may think the person had no control over dying, another part holds the deceased responsible. We are angry at having been left to deal with life without the deceased and this anger is an important stage of the grief process through which we all pass. I should emphasize that we go through a grief process even if the deceased is someone we hate—because we have lost a person who has played a significant role in our lives. Whether the deceased was loved or hated, we must deal with those feelings now, or we will be forced to deal with them later.

Another common phenomenon is for a victim to hate her abuser so much she wishes him dead—and he dies. The victim believes deep down that she somehow caused her abuser's death. Children engage in magical thinking; they believe that they cause what happens around them and they think even their thoughts can even kill. People who have been abused tend to be emotionally frozen at a childhood stage and they react as children to traumatic events.

When I was twenty-seven years old, long before I discovered my abuse, I had a terrible fight with my father. Although he no longer beat me up, he yelled and screamed and used his brilliant intellect to make me feel as worthless as possible. Something in me snapped and said "NO! He is *never* going to do this to me again." I told him that he was a horrible father and that I was never going to see him again, and I left. He died a month later.

I had described the fight to my psychiatrist and said that while I did not want to see my father again, I would never forgive myself if he died. And I didn't, not for many years. Since he died when his screenwriting career had hit rock bottom and our house was in foreclosure, I blamed myself for causing him more pain at a time when he had enough already. He died of a heart attack and I felt responsible for his stress and sorrow. My psychiatrist tried to point out that my father had abused me mentally and physically (we did not then know of the sexual abuse) and that I needed to break away from him. But it was to no avail. I still idealized my father and was unable to see that he was to blame for his troubles and for his death. I could not forgive myself and I punished myself by allowing my marriage and my life to deteriorate.

My father died in Mexico and my mother did not let me know until she was on her way to the funeral, so even though I flew to Mexico, I did not arrive in time for the funeral. So I never was able to grasp the reality

167

of his death. I was totally numb. I could not grieve and I could not cry. For years I had dreams about my father coming back, saying he was not really dead. Only now do I understand why Elizabeth Kubler-Ross, the Swiss expert on death and dying, emphasized the importance of attending funerals so that the death becomes real and grief is possible. After I worked out my feelings about my father's abuse of me, the funeral exercise finally laid him to rest.

Your abuser and others who have hurt you must be laid to rest, or you will have no peace. Whether you work with a therapist or by yourself, you must let your abuser go by releasing your feelings so that you can go on with your life. Until you do, your abuser will live in you. If your abuser is dead, you have a chance to free yourself once and for all. Your feelings, no matter how violent, can no longer hurt anyone but you. If you let them out, they will be gone forever, and so will the hold your abuser has on you.

I don't mind dying.
I just don't want to be around when it happens.
Woody Allen

33. What if I suspect I was abused but I can't remember?

As you grow older and are better able to cope with your childhood abuse, hints of what happened may begin to creep into your consciousness. You may have nightmares of being raped or beaten, of dying or of being chased. You may have flashbacks of your experience, slivers of frightening mental pictures you do not understand. You may start to notice destructive patterns in your behavior and your relationships. Or you may find yourself drawn to books, articles and television shows about abuse.

Other signs may indicate past abuse, such as gaps in your childhood memories. My situation was extreme: my earliest childhood memories began when I was eleven years old. Other survivors have selective amnesia; they may recall the less threatening incidents of their childhood but not the abusive ones. And some remember the acts of their abuse, but they have repressed the emotions that accompanied it.

Bob remembered many incidents of his childhood, such as the antics of his English bull dog and arguing with his younger sister. He insisted that he had a happy childhood until his sister reminded him of numerous incidents of abuse by his alcoholic mother and several occasions on which he was beaten almost unconscious by his father. After his sister's disclosure, Bob began to acknowledge that he might have had a problem. But a few weeks after the discussion with his sister, Bob *again* forgot everything she had told him and denied that she had ever mentioned any beatings! This is an example of how far our minds will go to protect us from painful memories. Fortunately, Bob talked to his sister again, realized that his lapses of memory meant that he needed treatment, and went into therapy to work through his abuse.

Another telltale sign of possible abuse is a serious problem with relationships, especially where you can discern destructive, repetitive patterns when you analyze your relationships objectively. Of course, all problems with relationships are not due to sexual or physical abuse. But if people frequently take advantage of you, if you often feel betrayed, and particularly if you find yourself repeatedly playing the role of a victim, you would do well to seek help.

If your lovers or spouses beat you, you could be playing out the role you played as a child, and you would also benefit from therapy.

Unexplained pain with intercourse and painful menstrual periods can be indications of sexual abuse.[33] Recent studies have shown that sexual abuse can cause pain even where there is no evidence of physical injury from the abuse. And clinical evidence is beginning to demonstrate that premenstrual syndrome may also be caused by sexual abuse. Men and women who have been sexually abused may also have frequent urinary tract and bladder infections. It is as if our bodies are signaling us to remember our abuse.

These physical symptoms appear because we store traumatic memories not only in our minds but in our bodies. This phenomenon has been brought home vividly to victims of abuse who have experienced body memories where they feel a vestige of the pain they felt as a child when they recall the traumatic event. The pain of a body memory will appear briefly exactly where the person felt it when it was inflicted, although the pain is far less than the original pain. So if a person was whipped with a belt on his back, he may feel slight pains on his back where the belt hit. If he was also kicked in his head, he may feel the pain in his head at another time. Women who have been sexually abused may feel pains in various areas of their pelvis. Once the corresponding memory is retrieved, the body sensation disappears. When a memory of rape surfaces, a woman may feel pain in a certain area of her pelvis. After she reexperiences the incident and the accompanying emotions, the body memory will disappear, usually forever. Sometimes more permanent conditions or pains also disappear or diminish as victims recall memories and resolve the tumultuous feelings of past abuse.

Certain types of behavior are frequently indicators of abuse. Criminal behavior, especially among adolescents, is commonly linked to either severe physical or sexual abuse. At the Salt Lake Valley Mental Health Center, all of the adolescent residents had suffered serious abuse and most of them, male and female, were victims of sexual abuse. And in another local program, all of the teenage girls who were runaways and prostitutes were victims of sexual abuse. Barbra Streisand's sensitive movie, *Nuts,* portrayed the story of a prostitute from a wealthy family who had been sexually abused as a child by her step-father.

Not all abuse victims rebel against the law. Some take the opposite route and become superachievers. They feel that if only they can do a little better, maybe they will be worthy of love. After I discovered my abuse and started to speak openly about it, I was astonished to learn how many of my female friends and colleagues who were lawyers had also been abused. I could not understand the connection until I analyzed my reasons for choosing law as a profession.

At the time I made the decision, I was unaware of my abuse and I thought that I just kind of fell into law school. But when people asked me why I became a lawyer, I would respond: "I did it to protect myself." I never really understood what that meant until I started seeing a hypnotherapist and recovered my memories. Then I knew that I wanted to make sure that no one could ever abuse me again. And I realized that I had continued to push myself academically and professionally thinking that accomplishment was the way to gain love and approval. I only recently learned that the percentage of female victims of sexual abuse is so high in law schools that some schools are employing counselors to help them.

Certain professions seem to attract more survivors of abuse. Police officers and prison wardens include a high percentage of abuse victims who have chosen to be in a role where they can punish offenders just as they would like to punish their abusers. I have also met many therapists who have been abused, as well as those who are recovering alcoholics or drug addicts. They picked counseling for a profession as a way of working out their own problems, in addition to their desire to use their experience to help others. Men who chose the military as a profession frequently endured severe physical abuse as children and are working out their fear and aggression on the "enemy" as a substitute for their abusers. And many dictators, such as Hitler, were abused children. The potential implications of the connection between certain occupations and abuse are impressive and the area is a fertile one for further research.

Just because you are in one of these occupations does not mean you have been abused, nor can you exclude the possibility of abuse because you read meters for the gas company. Obviously, not all lawyers or soldiers have been abused, and not all people who have been abused become therapists or police officers. These connections are merely trends and, like the other indicators I have mentioned, may be evidence of abuse or may be purely coincidental.

If anything I have said rings a bell or if you feel anxious about the possibility of past abuse, there is only one fairly reliable way to be certain: make an appointment with a reliable sex abuse psychotherapist who is experienced in hypnotherapy and use hypnosis to find out the truth. Your subconscious mind has stored everything that has ever happened to you and, under hypnosis, your subconscious is able to provide information that is not available to your conscious mind. Your subconscious will immediately be able to provide an answer to the question of whether you have been physically or sexually abused without your having to recover the memories. You can also have your therapist ask the question a different way: Has anyone ever harmed you or done sexual things to you that were so painful that you do not remember them consciously?

I was amazed at how quickly I found out that I had been abused. It was in the second session with my therapist; it could have easily been in the first session except I did not go under hypnosis until the second session. I learned more in two sessions of hypnotherapy than I had in ten years of "talk therapy!" Many people have taken years to uncover the fact of their abuse without hypnosis, and some never do. You can't talk about what you don't remember. Only with hypnosis can you get to the heart of the matter quickly.

You do not have to worry about not being able to hypnotize yourself. (See Part V, Section 12 on self-hypnosis, where I explain how hypnosis works and the fact that all hypnosis is self-hypnosis.) Most people can easily achieve a state of hypnosis. And if you have repressed your abuse, you have probably done so through an hypnotic process, so you will be more susceptible to hypnosis than the average person. You may prevent yourself from attaining an hypnotic state through fear, but a competent hypnotherapist should be able to help you overcome that barrier.

Now that you know you *can* find out the truth, the big question is whether you *want* to. The prospect of finding out that someone violated you, beat you or tortured you, possibly even a parent or other close relative, is frightening. Your mind blocked out your abuse because when you were a child you could not deal with the pain and violent emotions you experienced. But you are no longer a child, and what was overwhelming to you as a child can be understood and processed by an adult. The question is whether you should dig it up again.

If you were not ready to find out the truth, you would probably not be interested in reading this book. Our minds and bodies are incredible mechanisms which are designed to heal us and bring us to a state of perfect health and contentment. When we are little, our minds protect us from trauma by blocking it out. When we get older and can deal with those memories, our minds allow them to seep into our consciousness.

Many victims of abuse in early childhood begin to recover memories in their thirties and forties. Victims who experienced abuse in their preteens may have flashbacks or dreams about their abuse when they are in their twenties. But the truth begins to emerge when you are able to deal with it. If you are seeking answers, you are probably ready for them. And the amazing protection hypnosis provides is that your mind will not reveal any more than you are ready to absorb.

I wrestled with the question of whether I needed to uncover all of the memories of being raped and tortured by my father. I had already discovered the fact of my abuse, but the details of what had occurred were more grisly than I could have ever imagined. I did not want to know any more, and I needed some advice, so I went to see the head of the department of psychiatry at a local hospital for a second opinion. He said I should go on, that the memories would come out sooner or later anyway. He compared my situation to that of a woman having a baby. If the head is sticking out, you cannot push the baby back in. And since the knowledge of my abuse had started to filter through to my consciousness, I could not push it back.

I believe knowledge of abuse usually does come out sooner or later, and that in those few instances where it may not, it festers and causes pain throughout the person's life. Despite the distress I experienced recovering the memories, I knew I could not stop because the peace and understanding I achieved through each revelation more than made up for the pain. As I released the emotions from each memory, I began to feel lighter; the anguish, depression and fear I had thought were natural states of being began to disappear.

The relief of releasing the memories was best described by 28-year-old Georgia who was raped and tortured for eight years by her older brother. She said she had felt throughout her entire life as though her insides were being torn apart by wolves. When she finished her therapy, she was filled with wonder at the sense of peace that pervaded her body. I believe such changes are worth the effort.

The understanding you will gain of yourself also justifies exposing your past abuse. I discovered that so many things I had done in my life, so many of my thoughts and dreams, so many of my choices were all explained by my abuse. I learned that I refused to have children and had my tubes tied because I was afraid I might abuse my children. I understood why I was never able to sleep through the night and awakened at the slightest sound, even when I wore ear plugs. My father used to enter my room in the middle of the night.

But most important, I began to understand the self-defeating patterns of my relationships. I saw how I was continuing to replay the victim role which began with my father and how I sabotaged my own happiness. I recognized how I was repeating my father's betrayal of me by expecting betrayal from everyone and in fact causing it to happen, usually by testing people beyond the limits of their tolerance.

I learned something new from each memory I uncovered and as my therapy progressed, I began to experience more moments of happiness. Feeling so much better in every aspect of my life has more than made up for what I have endured in therapy. I do not want to minimize what I experienced, but I would do it again to achieve the changes in my life.

I believe that knowing is better than not knowing. If you avoid learning the truth, your fear will always be like the Sword of Damocles hanging over your head. The worst that can happen is that you find out that you were abused, something you already suspect, but you will have the support of a hypnotherapist and you will be on your way to making your life infinitely better. You will also be secure in the knowledge that by dealing with your abuse, you will not abuse your own children. And you will have explanations for many unexplained events in your life.

If you find that you have not been physically or sexually abused, you can let go of your fear and perhaps work with your therapist on other issues that are preventing you from having a totally satisfying life.

> *Here is a fact*
> *that should help you fight*
> *a bit longer:*
> *Things that don't act-*
> *ually kill you outright*
> *leave you stronger.*
> Piet Hein

34. I am being abused.
What should I do?

The obvious answer is to tell someone and ask for help. If you are under 18 years of age, call your local child protective service agency or social services agency. Talk to your school counselor, nurse or teacher. Report your situation to a police officer or go to your nearest police station. These people are required by law to investigate your report. Telephone numbers for reporting sexual abuse in every state are listed in Question 35, *Where can I get help?*

But the issues that may be of more concern to you are the emotional issues. Will anyone believe you? What will happen to you if they do? What will happen to your family? What will happen to your relationships with family members?

Victims of sexual abuse are often afraid that people will think they are making it up, especially if the abuser is a parent and a pillar of the community. Some of the most difficult cases therapists and social service agencies encounter are those where the abuser is a lawyer, doctor or some other highly respected member of the community because the abuser often vigorously resists the allegations and uses influence to try to have the proceedings dismissed.

Abusers often defend themselves by lying and charging their victims with fabrication, especially if those victims are children and more vulnerable as witnesses. Perpetrators use the youth of their victims against them, claiming their therapists brainwashed them. However, research contradicts these charges; the fact is that children almost never make up stories about being sexually abused. Children do not have the knowledge to realistically describe being molested and they could not possibly feign the violent emotions of abuse. Although a few children may be coached by their parents or attorneys in divorce cases, these instances are rare and the children's stories can be easily challenged by competent therapists. Children rarely lie in child protection cases, a fact acknowledged by most unbiased mental health professionals. And Adults Molested As Children certainly do not make up their abuse; they have no possible motive to lie—in many cases their abuser is dead. They only want to heal.

A few frightened people have formed vigilante groups to repeal the laws on sexual abuse, but they lack proof and credibility. Although these vigilantes are trying to confuse the public, most mental health professionals ignore them, recognizing that they are protecting their own self-interests and their own guilty secrets. Why would anyone fight so vehemently to deny abused children legal protection unless he had something to hide himself?

Most people will believe you these days. If you call one of the sexual abuse hotlines, you will be referred to professionals who see hundreds of abuse cases and will help you. A few decades ago, no one talked about sexual abuse and there were no laws to protect abused children. But today laws in every state protect children and require reports of abuse to be investigated. At times the investigations may be less than adequate because the child protection agencies in every state are so overloaded with cases. But there are ways you can insure that your case will receive proper attention.

First, the most effective way to insure that your case will receive attention is to enlist the support of as many people to help you as you can. Tell a teacher or coach about your situation and ask them to help. School counselors can be especially helpful because they may know workers in child protection agencies. The school nurse and your doctor can help.

What about your friends? Would any of their parents be willing to go to bat for you? Think of everyone you know who might help you through these proceedings. They do not have to know any details about your abuse. They only have to keep calling the child protection agency to make sure your case is properly handled. They might also testify that in their experience you have been trustworthy and would not make up stories.

Most people want to be helpful, and even though they may be reluctant to get involved, I have found that if you ask enough people, you will find some who will help. Do not be discouraged by a few rejections, just keep asking. Because of your abuse, it may be difficult to believe that anyone will help you. Considering what you've been through, this is a natural feeling. But ask for help anyway because the more support you have the easier the whole process will be for you.

Second, if you are fairly *sure*, not just *afraid*, that you may not be believed, collect as much evidence about your abuse as you can. This step can be difficult because your abuser obviously wants to keep it a secret. If you cannot escape immediately, you might be able to hide a small tape recorder in the area where your abuse is taking place. Obviously, you should report your abuse as quickly as possible and not suffer through more abuse just to obtain evidence.

Another possibility is to hide a tape recorder in a pocket, purse or notebook so you can record a conversation with your abuser. In order to get your abuser to admit what is happening, start the conversation by asking him or her to stop—and describe the conduct. Your abuser does not actually have to say, "Yes, I am abusing you." It is enough if you say what your abuser is doing and he or she does not deny it. We've all seen enough detective shows on television to be able to set things up. Just make sure you don't use a tape recorder which beeps when it runs out of tape. Even if the quality of your recording is not terribly good, it can be enhanced by the police or at a local recording studio. *Never give anyone the only copy of your tape.* Make several copies and give at least one copy to a friend or teacher so if one is lost, you will have duplicates.

Other evidence is your abuser's sperm on your sheets or clothing which can be analyzed in a laboratory. Both sperm and blood type can identify your abuser. Save anything with your blood on it so that you will have evidence of what is happening. Take pictures of any bruises or cuts, or have a friend help you. You will have to take people into your confidence because you will need help and support.

Once you report your abuse, you may be taken out of your home and placed in a temporary home or agency pending an investigation of your case. Several people from your child protection agency will want to hear what happened and give you tests. They will all be on you side, so you should tell them everything you can remember, with as much detail as possible.

As part of the investigation, your caseworker will talk to your family and to your abuser. If the abuser is a member of your family, the whole family may try to deny the truth. But caseworkers are used to these attempted coverups and will usually not be fooled into believing your family's story.

In most cases you will be returned to your home once the investigation is over, and your abuser will be removed until therapy is completed. In those cases where it is not safe for you to go home, you may be placed in a foster home or some other facility. In some states a hearing or full court trial will be held to determine if your abuser is guilty of violating the laws prohibiting sexual abuse. If so, you will have to testify in court and be cross-examined by your abuser's attorney. Have no fear, real courtrooms are *not* like what you may have seen on *Perry Mason.* Judges will not permit an attorney to intimidate a child, and few lawyers are clever enough to pounce on witnesses the way professional actors reciting a script can do. The legal trend is toward protecting minors in trials, especially in cases of sexual abuse. Some enlightened courts attempt to reduce children's trauma by permitting them to testify on closed circuit television from a more comfortable room than a courtroom. However, a recent United States Supreme Court decision has cast doubt on such procedures by declaring use of a screen between the abuser and child victims to be unconstitutional. The Court expanded the Sixth

Amendment to require face-to-face confrontation between the abuser and the witnesses.[34]

Even if your abuser is not convicted, child protection services still has the legal authority to prevent your return to the abuser's house. You will be helped by therapists until they determine you are able to go home safely. Some victims are afraid *they* will be put in jail. This is definitely not the case. You may be placed with other victims your age in a supervised living situation but it will not be a jail or anything close to it.

Your other questions about what will happen to your abuser and your family are answered in Question 16, *Was it wrong to tell? Did I destroy my family?*

If you are over eighteen and being abused, your situation is somewhat different. Adults who are being abused are usually trapped in a pattern of abuse based on their childhood experiences. If you have been abused earlier in your life, you have adapted to being a victim and you may not know how to play any other role. You may feel so helpless and dependent that you are afraid you cannot survive alone, and abuse seems preferable to isolation. If this is the case, you need support so that you can develop the confidence to leave. Most cities and towns have programs and shelters for battered men and women where you can find counselors and people who have shared your experience and who can give you the support and protection you need to escape from your situation. If you cannot find a shelter, contact your local social service agency or a therapist to assist you.

If you are in immediate danger, call your local sheriff or police department. The laws of all states prohibit spouse abuse. Although some law enforcement officers have been reluctant to intervene in family quarrels in the past, they now respond more quickly because the courts have recently awarded huge damages to women injured because the police failed to protect them.

If you are not related to your abuser, you are protected by the criminal laws against assault and battery and rape. You will have to contact the police or sheriff and make a criminal complaint against your abuser. The sheriff or police may be reluctant to take a complaint if you are living with your abuser because many men and women later reconcile with their abusers and refuse to act as witnesses for the prosecution. The law enforcement system is already overloaded and officers do not want to spend time on complaints which will not be carried through to conviction. If you pursue this route, and I recommend that you do, you should be sure that you are willing to be a witness and help convict your abuser, and you must convince the officers of your intention to follow through.

The best route for adult victims to follow is the legal process. A criminal conviction is the only way you can insure that your abuse will stop. Even if you are not willing to protect yourself, could you live with yourself if you had done nothing and learned that your abuser had injured or even killed someone else?

Whether you are a minor or an adult, reporting your abuse takes courage. Change can be frightening, even if that change is for the better. But if you think about what you have already survived, can anything be as bad? You already have proved that you have tremendous courage and strength just to be able to endure your abuse. Your life may be unstable for a while after you tell, but you will have people to help you. They will make sure you receive the therapy you need so that your abuse will not destroy the rest of your life. If your family is involved, their situation cannot get worse. Their only chance for help is to have the truth come out so that they can get the help they need.

> *Courage is not the absence of fear,*
> *it is the triumph of the will over fear.*
> Jim Kennicott

35. Where can I get help?

The following lists of resources were compiled by The Clearinghouse on Child Abuse and Neglect Information and by the U.S. Department of Health and Human Services, Offices of Human Development Services, Administration for Children, Youth and Families, Children's Bureau, P.O. Box 1182, Washington, D.C. 20013, (703) 821-2086.

State child protection agencies: reporting procedures

Because the responsibility for investigating reports of suspected child abuse and neglect rests at the state level, each state has established a Child Protective Services (CPS) reporting system. Listed below is the name and address of the CPS agency in each state, followed by the procedures for reporting suspected child maltreatment. A number of states have toll-free (800) numbers that can be used for reporting. Some states have two numbers, one for individuals calling within the state and the other for those calling outside of the state. Normal business hours vary from agency to agency, but are typically from 8 or 9 a.m. to 4:30 or 5 p.m. on weekdays.

Alabama
Department of Human Resources
Division of Family and Children's Services
Office of Protective Services
64 North Union Street
Montgomery, AL 36130-1801
During business hours, make reports to your County Department of Human Resources, Child Protective Services Unit. After business hours, make reports to local police.

Alaska
Department of Health and Social Services
Division of Family and Youth Services
Box H-05,
Juneau, AK 99811
Ask the operator for Zenith 4444 to make reports in-state. Out-of-state, add area code 907. This telephone number is toll free.

American Samoa
Government of American Samoa
Office of the Attorney General
Pago Pago, AS 96799
Make reports to the Department of Human Resources at (684) 633-4485.

Arizona
Department of Economic Security Administration for Children, Youth and Families
P.O. Box 6123
Site COE 9404
Phoenix, AZ 85005
Make reports to Department of Economic Security local offices.

Arkansas
Arkansas Department of Human Services
Division of Children and Family Services
P.O. Box 1437
Little Rock, AR 72203
Make reports in-sate to (800) 482-5964.

California
Office for Child Abuse Prevention
Department of Social Services
714-744 P Street, Room 950
Sacramento, CA 95814
Make reports to County Department of Welfare and the Central Registry of Child Abuse, maintained by the Department of Justice (916) 445-7546.

Colorado
Department of Social Services Central Registry
P.O. Box 181000
Denver, CO 80218-0899
Make reports to County Department of Social Services.

Connecticut
Connecticut Department of Children and Youth Services
Division of Children and Protective Services
170 Sigourney Street
Hartford, CT 06105
Make reports in-state to (800) 842-2288 or out-of-state to (203) 344-2599.

Delaware
Delaware Department of Services for Children, Youth and Their Families
Division of Child Protective Services
330 East 30th Street
Wilmington, DE 19802
Make reports in-state to (800) 292-9582.

District of Columbia
District of Columbia Department of Human Services
Commission on Social Services
Family Services Administration
Child and Family Services Division
500 First Street N.W.
Washington, DC 20001
Make reports to (202) 727-0995.

Florida
Florida Child Abuse Registry
1317 Winewood Boulevard
Tallahassee, FL 32301
Make reports in-state to (800) 342-9152 or out-of-state to (904) 487-2625.

Georgia
Georgia Department of Human Resources
Division of Family and Children Services
878 Peachtree Street, N.W.
Atlanta, GA 30309
Make reports to County Department of Family and Children Services.

Guam
Department of Public Health and Social Services
Child Welfare Services
Child Protective Services
P.O. Box 2816
Agana, GU 96910
Make reports to the State Child Protective Services Agency at (671) 646-8417.

Hawaii
Department of Social Services and Housing
Public Welfare Division
Family and Children's Services
P.O. Box 339
Honolulu, HI 96809
Make reports to your Island's Department of Social Services and Housing CPS reporting hotline.

Idaho
Department of Welfare
Field Operations Bureau of Social Services and Child Protection
450 West State, 10th Floor
Boise, ID 83720
Make reports to Department of Health and Welfare regional offices.

Illinois
Illinois Department of Children and Family Services
Station 75
State Administrative Offices
406 East Monroe Street
Springfield, IL 62701
Make reports in-state to (800) 25-ABUSE or out-of-state to (217) 785-4010.

Indiana
Indiana Department of Public Welfare-Child Abuse and Neglect
Division of Child Welfare Social Services
Sixth Floor
141 South Meridian Street
Indianapolis, IN 46225
Make reports to County Department of Public Welfare.

Iowa
Iowa Department of Human Services
Division of Social Services
Central Child Abuse Registry
Fifth Floor
Hoover State Office Building
Des Moines, IA 50319
Make reports in-state to (800) 362-2178 or out-of-state to (515) 281-5581.

Kansas
Kansas Department of Social and Rehabilitation Services
Division of Social Services
Child Protection and Family Services Section
Smith-Wilson Building
700 West Sixth Street
Topeka, KS 66606
Make reports to Department of Social and Rehabilitation Service area offices.

Kentucky
Kentucky Cabinet of Human Resources Division of Family Services
Children and Youth Services Branch
275 East Main Street
Frankfort, KY 40621
Make reports to your district office, one of 14 in the state.

Louisiana
Louisiana Department of Health and Human Resources
Office of Human Development
Division of Children,Youth, and Family Services
P.O. Box 3318
Baton Rouge, LA 70821
Make reports to your Parish Protective Service unit.

Maine
Maine Department of Human Services
Child Protective Services
State House, Station 1
Augusta, ME 04333
Make reports to your region'sOffice of Human Services; in-state to (800) 452-1999 or out-of-state to (207) 289-2983. Both operate 24 hours a day.

Maryland
Maryland Department of Human Resources
Social Services Administration
Saratoga State Center
11 West Saratoga Street
Baltimore, MD 21201
Make reports to County Department of Social Services or to the local law enforcement agency.

Massachusetts
Massachusetts Department of Social Services
Protective Services
11th Floor
150 Causeway Street
Boston, MA 02114
Make reports to your area office, to the Protective Screening unit or in-state to (800) 792-5200.

Michigan
Michigan Department of Social Services
Office of Children and Youth Services
Protective Services Division
Ninth Floor
300 South Capitol Avenue
Lansing, MI 48926
Make reports to your county's Department of Social Services.

182

Minnesota
Minnesota Department of Human Services
Protective Services Division
Centennial Office Building
St. Paul, MN 55155
Make reports to your county's Department of Human Services.

Mississippi
Mississippi Department of Public Welfare
Bureau of Family and Children's Services
Protection Department
P.O. Box 352
Jackson, MS 39205
Make reports in-state to (800) 222-8000 or out-of-state to (601) 354-0341.

Missouri
Missouri Child Abuse and Neglect Hotline
Department of Social Service
Division of Family Services
DFS, P.O. Box 88
Broadway Building
Jefferson City, MO 65103
Make reports in-state to (800) 392-3738 or out-of-state to (314) 751-3448. Both operate 24 hours a day.

Montana
Department of Family Services
Child Protective Services
P.O. Box 8005
Helena, MT 59604
Make reports to your county's Department of Family Services.

Nebraska
Nebraska Department of Social Services
Human Services Division
301 Centennial Mall South
P.O. Box 95026
Lincoln, NE 68509
Make reports to your local law enforcement agency, or to your local social services office or in-state to (800) 652-1999.

Nevada
Department of Human Resources
Welfare Division
2527 North Carson Street
Carson City, NV 89710
Make reports to your local Division of Welfare office.

New Hampshire
New Hampshire Department of Health and Welfare
Division for Children and Youth Services
6 Hazen Drive
Concord, NH 03301-6522
Make reports to your district's Division for Children and Youth Services office or in-state to (800) 852-3345 (Ext. 4455).

New Jersey
New Jersey Division of Youth and Family Services
P.O. Box CN717
One South Montgomery Street
Trenton, NJ 08625
Make reports in-state to (800) 792-8610. Phones operate 24 hours a day.

New Mexico
New Mexico Department of Human Services
Social Services Division
P.O. Box 2348
Santa Fe, NM 87504
Make reports to your county's Social Services office or in-state to (800) 432-6217.

New York
New York State Department of Social Services
Division of Family and Children Services
State Central Register of Child Abuse and Maltreatment
40 North Pearl Street
Albany, NY 12243
Make reports in-state to (800) 342-3720 or out-of-state to (518) 474-9448.

North Carolina
North Carolina Department of Human Resources
Division of Social Services Child Protective Services
325 North Salisbury Street
Raleigh, NC 27611
Make reports in-state to (800) 662-7030.

North Dakota
North Dakota Department of Human Services
Division of Children and Family Services
Child Abuse and Neglect Program
State Capitol
Bismarck, ND 58505
Make reports to your county's Social Services Office.

Ohio
Ohio Department of Human Services
Bureau of Children's Protective Services
30 East Broad Street
Columbus, OH 43266-0423
Make reports to County Department of Human Services.

Oklahoma
Oklahoma Department of Human Services
Division of Children and Youth Services Child Abuse/Neglect Section
P.O. Box 25352
Oklahoma City, OK 73125
Make reports in-state to (800) 522-3511.

Oregon
Department of Human Resources
Children's Services Division
Child Protective Services
198 Commercial Street, S.E.
Salem, OR 97310
Make reports to your local Children's Services Division office or to (503) 378-4722.

Pennsylvania
Pennsylvania Department of Public Welfare
Office of Children, Youth and Families
Child Line and Abuse Registry
Lanco Lodge, P.O. Box 2675
Harrisburg, PA 17105
Make reports in-state to CHILDLINE (800) 932-0313 or out-of-state to (713) 783-8744.

Puerto Rico
Puerto Rico Department of Social Services
Services to Families with Children
P.O. Box 11398
Fernandez Juncos Station
Santurez, PR 00910
Make reports to (809) 724-1333.

Rhode Island
Rhode Island Department for Children and Their Families
Division of Child Protective Services
Bldg. #9, 610 Mt. Pleasant Avenue
Providence, RI 02908
Make reports in-state to (800) RI-CHILD or 742-4453 or out-of-state to (401) 457-4996.

South Carolina
South Carolina Department of Social Services
1535 Confederate Avenue
P.O. Box 1520
Columbia, SC 29202-1520
Make reports to your county's Department of Social Services.

South Dakota
Department of Social Services
Child Protection Services
Richard F. Kneip Building
700 Governors Drive
Pierre, SD 57501
Make reports to your local social services office.

Tennessee
Tennessee Department of Human Services
Child Protective Services
Citizen Bank Plaza
Deadrick Street
Nashville, TN 37219
Make reports to your county's Department of Human Services.

Texas
Texas Department of Human Services
Protective Services for Families and Children Branch
P.O. Box 2960, MC 537-W
Austin, TX 78769
Make reports in-state to (800) 252-5400 or out-of-state to (512) 450-3360.

Utah
Department of Social Services
Division of Family Services
P.O. Box 45500
Salt Lake City, UT 84110
Make reports to your district's Division of Family Services office.

Vermont
Vermont Department of Social and Rehabilitative Services
Division of Social Services
103 South Main Street
Waterbury, VT 05676
Make reports to your district office or to (802) 241- 2131.

Virgin Islands
Virgin Islands Department of Human Services
Division of Social Services
P.O. Box 550
St. Thomas, VI 00801
Make reports to the Division of Social Services (809) 774-9030.

Virginia
Commonwealth of Virginia
Department of Social Services
Bureau of Child Protective Services
Blair Building
8007 Discovery Drive
Richmond, VA 23229-8699
Make reports in-state to (800) 552-7096 or out-of-state to (804) 281-9081.

Washington
Department of Social and Health Services
Division of Children and Family Services
Child Protective Services
Mail Stop OB 41-D
Olympia, WA 98504
Make reports in-state to (800) 562-5624 or to your local Social and Health Services office.

West Virginia
West Virginia Department of Human Services
Division of Social Services
Child Protective Services
State Office Building
1900 Washington Street East
Charleston, WV 25305
Make reports in-state to (800) 352-6513.

Wisconsin
Wisconsin Department of Health and Social Services
Division of Community Services
Bureau for Children, Youth, and Families
1 West Wilson Street
Madison, WI 53707
Make reports to your county's Social Services Offices.

Wyoming
Department of Health and Social Services
Division of Public Assistance and Social Services
Hathaway Building
Cheyenne, WY 82002
Make reports to your county's Department of Public Assistance and Social Services.

National organizations concerned with child maltreatment

Action for Child Protection
428 Fourth Street, Suite 5B
Annapolis, MD 21403
(301) 263-2509
Professional and institutional inquiries only.

American Academy of Pediatrics
141 Northwest Point Boulevard
P.O. Box 927
Elk Grove Village, IL 60009-0927
(800) 533-9016
For professional and public educational materials contact the Publications Department on activities of the AAP Task Force on Child Abuse and Neglect.

American Bar Association
National Legal Resource Center for Child Advocacy and Protection
1800 M Street, N.W., Suite 200
Washington, DC 20036
(202) 331-2250
Professional and institutional inquiries only.

American Humane Association
American Association for Protecting Children
9725 East Hampden Avenue
Denver, CO 80231
(301) 695-0811 or (800) 227-5242
Professional publications and public inquiries regarding child protective services and child abuse and neglect.

American Medical Association
Health and Human Behavior Department
535 North Dearborn
Chicago, IL 60610
(312) 645-5066

American Public Welfare Association
1125 15th Street, N.W.
Suite 300
Washington, DC 20005
(202) 293-7550

Association of Junior Leagues
660 First Avenue
New York, NY 10016
(212) 355-4380
For legislative information, contact Public Policy Director; for individual Junior League programs and child abuse and neglect information, contact the League Services Department.

Boys Clubs of America
Government Relations Office
611 Rockville Pike, Suite 230
Rockville, MD 20852
(301) 251-6676
1,100 clubs nationwide serving 1.3 million boys and girls. Offers child safety curriculum.

**C. Henry Kempe Center for Prevention and Treatment
of Child Abuse and Neglect**
1205 Oneida Street
Denver, CO 80220
(303) 321-3963

Child Welfare League of America
440 First Street, N.W.
Suite 310
Washington, DC 20001
(202) 638-2952
Professional and institutional inquiries only.

Childhelp USA
6463 Independence Avenue
Woodland Hills, CA 91367
Hotline: (800) 4-A-CHILD or (800) 422-4453
Provides comprehensive crisis counseling by mental health professionals for adult and child victims of child abuse and neglect, offenders, parents who are fearful of abusing or who want information on how to be effective parents. The Survivors of Childhood Abuse Program (SCAP) disseminates materials, makes treatment referrals, trains professionals and conducts research.

General Federation of Women's Clubs
1734 N Street, N.W.
Washington, DC 20036
(202) 347-3163
10,000 clubs nationwide. Provides child abuse and neglect prevention and education programs, nonprofessional support and legislative activities. Programs are based on needs of community. Contact: Program Office

Military Family Resource Center
Ballston Centre Tower Three
Ninth Floor
4015 Wilson Boulevard
Arlington, VA 22203
(202) 696-4555
Recommends policy and program guidance to the Assistant Secretary of Defense (Force Management and Personnel) on family violence issues and assists the military services to establish, develop and maintain comprehensive family violence programs.

National Association of Social Workers
7981 Eastern Avenue
Silver Spring, MD 20910
(301) 565-0333
Professional and institutional inquiries only.

National Association of State VOCAL Organizations
VOCAL, Inc. of Florida
P.O. Box 40460
St. Petersburg, FL 33743
Provides advocacy and support to develop balance and professionalism in the child protection system in order to protect the rights of children and families.

National Black Child Development Institute
1463 Rhode Island Avenue, N.W.
Washington, DC 20005
(202) 387-1281
Provides newsletters, annual conference and answers to public inquiries regarding issues facing black children and youth.

National Center for Child Abuse and Neglect
Children's Bureau Administration for Children, Youth and Families
Office of Human Development Services
Department of Health and Human Services
P.O. Box 1182
Washington, DC 20013
Responsible for the federal government's child abuse and neglect activities. Administers grant programs to States and organizations to further research and demonstration projects, service programs, and other activities related to the identification, treatment and prevention of child abuse and neglect. Clearinghouse provides selected publications and information services on child abuse and neglect. (703) 821-2086

National Center for Missing and Exploited Children
1835 K Street N.W., Suite 700
Washington, DC 20006
(202) 634-9821 or (800) 843-5678
Toll-free number for reporting missing children, sightings of missing children, or report-ing cases of child pornography. Provides free written materials for the general public on child victimization as well as technical documents for professionals.

National Committee for Prevention of Child Abuse
332 South Michigan Avenue
Chicago, IL 60604
(312) 663-3520
68 local chapters in all 50 states. Provides information and statistics on child abuse and maintains an extensive publications list. The National Research Center provides informa-tion for professionals on promising programs, methods for evaluating programs and research findings.

National Council of Juvenile and Family Court Judges
P.O. Box 8970
Reno, NV 89507
(702) 784-6012
Primarily professional and institutional inquiries.

National Council on Child Abuse and Family Violence
1050 Connecticut Ave. N.W.,
Suite 300
Washington, DC 20036
(800) 222-2000

National Crime Prevention Council
733 15th Street N.W., Rm. 540
Washington, DC 20005
(202) 393-7141
Provides personal safety curricula, including child abuse and neglect prevention education for elementary school children and model prevention programs for adolescents. Educa-tional materials for parents, children, and community groups are available.

National Education Association
Human and Civil Rights Unit
1201 16th Street N.W., Rm. 714
Washington, DC 20036
(202) 822-7711
Offers training to NEA members. Sells child abuse and neglect training kits and supplemental materials to professionals and the general public.

National Exchange Club
Foundation for Prevention of Child Abuse
3050 Central Avenue
Toledo, OH 43606
(419) 535-3232

National Network of Runaway and Youth Services
905 Sixth St. N.W., Suite 411
Washington, DC 20024
(202) 488-0739
Provides written materials, responds to general inquiries regarding runaways and adolescent abuse, and serves as a referral source for runaways and parents.

National Organization for Victim Assistance
717 D Street N.W.
Washington, DC 20004
(202) 393-NOVA
Provides information and referral for child victims as well as crisis counseling.

National Runaway Switchboard Metro-Help, Inc.
2080 N. Lincoln
Chicago, IL 60657
800-621-4000 (toll-free) or (312) 880-9860 (business phone)
Provides toll-free information, referral, and crisis counseling services to runaway and homeless youth and their families. Also serves as the National Youth Suicide Hotline.

Parents Anonymous
7120 Franklin Avenue
Los Angeles, CA 90046
(800) 421-0353 (toll-free) or (213) 410-9732 (business phone)
1,200 chapters nationwide. National program of professionally facilitated self-help groups. Each state has different program components.

Parents United/Daughters and Sons United/
Adults Molested as Children United
P.O. Box 952
San Jose, CA 95108
(408) 280-5055
150 chapters nationwide. Provides guided self-help for sexually abusive parents as well as child and adult victims of sexual abuse.

36. How do I tell if my child is being abused?

One of the worst fears most parents have is discovering their child been sexually abused. Many parents cannot bear to think about it and assure themselves that it could not happen to *their* child. But the conservative statistics show that one in every three or four children is sexually abused, and some studies indicate even greater numbers of children have been molested.

Despite the odds, some parents disregard the facts and refuse to believe their child could be a victim of abuse, even when the evidence is overwhelming. Although denial is clearly harmful to the child, parents often use this defense because they are unable to cope with the painful reality.

There are many reasons why parents delude themselves and reject the fact of their child's abuse. Sometimes the perpetrator is a family member, usually the father or stepfather, but sometimes an older sibling, the mother, a grandparent, or an uncle. Parents may be unable to cope with the fact that a member of the family is molesting their child and may thus refuse to believe such a horrible situation could be true. If another sibling is the perpetrator, the parents may be unable to admit that a child of theirs might have problems that cause him or her to abuse others. Parents tend to blame themselves for their children's problems and their sense of guilt may cause them to ignore the situation, thus denying help to both the abuser and the victim. If a husband is the perpetrator, the wife may be afraid to confront her mate out of fear of physical harm or abandonment. Spouses may be so codependent on their mates that they cover up for them and allow the abuse to continue. (See Question 12, *Why didn't my mother protect me?*) The possibility of the family being split apart is so terrifying that some parents cannot acknowledge the truth.

Parents may also deny their children's abuse because the parents themselves have been sexually abused. Since abused parents often repress memories of their own abuse, they cannot deal with a situation that reminds them subconsciously of their own trauma. They are unable to help their children because acknowledging the abuse would force them to open up their own wounds. So they deny their children's pain, just as they deny their own.

Parents often use a defense commonly employed by people in a variety of unpleasant or threatening situations: "If we don't talk about it, it doesn't exist," or "It will go away." The technique of blocking out reality is used by alcoholics and their spouses, by spouses who do not want to learn their partners are unfaithful, by women who find lumps in their breasts, and by many other people who do not want to deal with unpleasant truths. Parents of abused children do not want to believe that the abuse is serious, that their child has been severely hurt, that the effects will go on for a long time. They want to believe the abuse is merely an incident that can just be put behind them so everyone can go on with their lives as before. So they deny the abuse, or tell their children to keep it a secret, thereby denying them the support and help they need.

Studies have shown that the sooner the abuse is discovered, the less trauma there is and the easier it is for the victim to heal. And the earlier the child receives therapy for the abuse, the less damaging are the effects on the child later in life. Equally important, if the child has parental support and love, the effects of the abuse, especially on the child's self-esteem, are greatly diminished. Your validation of the truth of the abuse and the support you give to your child make a tremendous difference in your child's ability to love himself, to trust others, to trust the world, and to heal.

On the other hand, if you deny the truth and fail to support your child, your child's life will be permanently damaged. As she becomes a teenager, she may be promiscuous, take drugs, run away, attempt suicide, mutilate herself or do other self-destructive acts. As an adult, unless she receives therapy, your child will engage in destructive relationships, be chronically depressed, attempt suicide, and may even abuse her own children.

Annie, an attractive teenager even with too much make-up and her hair teased six inches over her head, was a runaway and promiscuous with boys and men. She always chose boyfriends who treated her badly or dumped her. Her parents were despairing and sent her to therapy to have her conduct changed. They refused to believe she had been raped when she was six years old by an uncle who had been her babysitter for a night. Despite the fact that violent emotions about the abuse came out during Annie's hypnotherapy sessions, they continued to believe she was making it up.

Annie's parents could not face the fact that anything so terrible could happen in their family or that they might have contributed to it, so they clung to the diagnosis of a doctor who saw Annie in the hospital after she tried to kill herself. The diagnosis was that Annie had a personality disorder which accounted for her behavior. The problem with such an overly simplistic and misleading diagnosis is that fails to take into consideration the *cause* for the personality disorder. In this

193

case, the parents were using the diagnosis to delude themselves into believing that Annie made up her abuse, and that her "lies" were just another facet of her "personality disorder."

A basic truth about sexual abuse is that children do not lie. Studies show that all but a minute percentage of children tell the truth about their abuse. Those few cases where children do lie usually involve divorces where one of the parents has coached the child to fabricate sexual abuse in order to obtain custody. Children simply do not have any motivation to concoct a story of sexual abuse nor do they have the knowledge or experience to make up a credible story.

Therapists specializing in sex abuse therapy can easily determine if a child is telling the truth. Although a child might be able to fabricate details, it is almost impossible for a child to feign the profound emotional reactions of an abuse victim. A child who could simulate the fear, confusion, pain, shame and anger experienced by a victim of abuse would certainly deserve an Academy Award.

But you do not have to be a therapist to determine if your child is being abused. Some signs are fairly obvious. If your child begins to scream when a certain babysitter comes or when you take her to a day-care center, do not assume that she is just fussing because she does not want to leave you. While separation anxiety is a possibility in small children, children usually adjust to a pleasant situation away from their parents. If a child is screaming with fear, something is wrong.

In a recent infamous criminal case, a "highly respected" choir leader in California molested boys in the choir who were sent with him to summer camp to receive special training. After it was revealed that a large number of boys had been seriously abused, one of the parents was interviewed about the effect on his son. This father related his son's fear of sleeping alone, how he would crawl into his parents' bedroom at night and sleep on the floor, and the devastating effect on his academic performance. And this father was close to tears as he described how, when his son begged not to return to camp, the father attributed it to homesickness and weakness and had made the son return.

Sometimes we think we know the reason for our child's behavior and we act on that assumption without checking it out. It is so simple to ask, "What's wrong? What's bothering you? I want to help you." If we really want to understand, our children will open up and talk to us. But we have to want to take the time to listen. Children know the difference between our listening attentively and not listening but going through the motions. Saying you want to talk when you are taking a pan out of the oven or grabbing your briefcase to walk out the door makes your words meaningless. The most important way of finding out if your child is being abused is by establishing good habits of communication early so that you have your child's trust if something happens.

Even if you have your child's trust, it may be difficult for your child to talk about sexual abuse. One way to overcome the child's embarrassment is to talk about sexual abuse *before* it happens. Even at a very early age, you can tell your child that he has a right to say *no*, that his body is special and that he can always come to you if someone does something to him he does not like.

Impress on your child that she does not have to be nice to grownups who try to touch her, that she can go to a teacher or a neighbor if you are not there, and that you will always understand and love her no matter what. Several prevention books are available that tell you how to talk to children of all ages about sexual abuse.

It is important to understand how difficult it is for children to tell about the abuse. (See Question 17, *People tell me I should have done something to stop my abuse. Is that true?*) Children eventually sense that sexual abuse is wrong and become afraid that their parents will think they are bad if it happens. Because children think in a cause-and-effect pattern, they also may believe they have somehow caused the abuse and are being punished. They may be afraid you will stop loving them. Or they may be afraid you will not believe them. These barriers make it essential for you to be sensitive and open about discussing sexual concerns with your child so that your child feels comfortable coming to you to discuss sexual events.

Other symptoms that may indicate sexual abuse and should be investigated are the use of sexual terms a child of that age would not ordinarily know. One little boy started using the words "pee pee" and "pussy" when he returned from visiting his father and stepmother, words which were never used in his mother's home. He also screamed in the car on the way to his father's house. An evaluation indicated that he was being sexually abused.

Excessive masturbation and playing in a sexual way may also be the result of molestation. Young children often act their traumas out on themselves, their friends, their dolls or other toys. One mother noticed her three-year-old girl was rubbing the genital areas of two dolls together. She was being abused by her teenaged babysitter.

Recent studies show that sexual abuse frequently causes promiscuity, abuse of alcohol and drugs, shoplifting and other criminal acts, truancy, running away, poor grades and other acting out behavior among adolescents. Eating disorders, such as anorexia nervosa and bulimia, also have been connected to sexual abuse. If you see this behavior in your child, the possibility of sexual abuse, as well as other factors, should be explored.

Changes in your child's behavior, such as depression, sleeping more than usual, withdrawal from family and friends, declining grades, anger and acting may be manifestations of serious problems and may be evidence of molestation. Such behavior should not be ignored. Whatever the reason, children do not simply "outgrow" such behavior but need help in working out the underlying problem.

If your child does not tell you, how do you know if your suspicions about sexual abuse are accurate? The most reliable way is to have your child evaluated at a children's hospital or sexual abuse treatment center with an established program for evaluating sexual abuse. If you take your child to a hospital or to doctors that lack the necessary experience, you may not obtain an accurate answer and you may increase your child's trauma. In most cases, the results of the tests and interviews will be conclusive, especially if the abuse is recent.

However, if the abuse occurred several years before, the child may have repressed it and an evaluation may not be able to uncover the blocked memories even under hypnosis. Victims of sexual abuse have sometimes been so traumatized that it takes weeks or months of therapy before the facts emerge. If you suspect sexual abuse, you should take your child to a therapist experienced in sexual abuse. The therapist can work on behavioral issues until your child is ready to face the sexual ones.

Facing the possibility that your child has been sexually abused is frightening, but you can handle the situation if it arises by understanding your own reactions. If you have strong emotions about the abuse which make you want to avoid dealing with the problem, you should explore your feelings with a sexual abuse counselor and get advice on how best to handle the situation. Fortunately all states have centers for the prevention and treatment of sexual abuse and these centers can provide you with assistance in obtaining a reliable assessment of your child's experience.

There is no way to protect your child from all of the world's dangers. You can only do your best to see that your child knows she is loved and can come to you with her problems. If you have open lines of communication, you can help your child solve the problems as they arise. The best advice I can give you is to put aside your fears and preconceptions and listen to your child. And believe what she says.

> *Worrying about the future is like trying to eat the hole*
> *of a doughnut. It's like munching on what isn't.*
> Jerry Braza

37. Can I sue my abuser?

Yes, you can sue your abuser in all states, if your abuser is not a parent. If your abuser is a parent, most states will not permit a suit; only a few of the more enlightened states have begun to recognize a child's right to sue for physical and sexual abuse by a parent. The more important question is whether it is in your best interest to sue.

Although the law is clear that you can sue a stranger who rapes or hits you, the law becomes muddy when that person is a parent. In the United States, children have been traditionally treated as the property of their parents and their parents' rights to raise them and discipline them have been sacrosanct. Court rulings have given parents the right to use corporal punishment in disciplining their children.[35] This right has been extended to anyone who stands in the shoes of the parents and includes school officials, stepparents and other caretakers.

In our country, children are chattels. Even basic Constitutional rights do not apply to them. In its infamous decision in *Ingraham v. Wright*, a divided United States Supreme Court held "paddling" by school officials did not constitute cruel and unusual punishment and was not a violation of the Eighth Amendment. The majority ignored the fact that one of the students was paddled so severely he was out of school for eleven days and the other lost the use of his arm for a week. The Court ruled that school officials had the same right to use corporal punishment as parents because they had custody of children during school hours.[36]

The results of applying these principles to actual cases are shocking. A leading Oregon Supreme Court case recently held that a father could not be indicted even for involuntary manslaughter where he had killed his 12-year-old son "by striking him about the head and face with his hand." The decision was based on a statute which recognized homicide as excusable when committed by "accident or misfortune in correcting a child . . . with usual and ordinary caution and without unlawful intent."[37] The court did not allow a jury to decide whether or not the father used ordinary caution or had an unlawful intent, even though the death of the child would seem to be persuasive evidence that the "punishment" went far beyond what was reasonable. Thus parents can literally get away with murder, as long as their victims are their own children.

Although the general rule is that children cannot sue their parents even for conduct which is excessive and cruel,[38] some states have recently begun to allow children to recover money from their parents for injuries due to intentional acts, such as hitting, and even negligent acts.[39] But the courts are still having difficulty with suits against parents for sexual abuse, probably because no one has dared to broach the subject in open court until recently.

Certainly no court could find that sexual abuse was reasonable or proper corporal punishment. But courts have managed to find other legal obstacles to thwart suits by victims of sexual abuse against their parents. In a cavalier and poorly reasoned opinion, the Court of Appeals of Washington recently held that there is no separate cause of action for sexual abuse and that none is needed because such cases can be adequately prosecuted under conventional doctrines,[40] and then proceeded to bar all of the victim's "conventional" causes of action because the victim failed to comply with the conventional statute of limitations, the deadline for filing suit. The victim was sexually abused as a child, the last incident occurring when she was 8 or 9 years old. She filed her complaint just before her 21st birthday. Although the court acknowledged that the statute of limitations was stayed until the victim reached 18, the age of majority, she still could not comply with the two-year statute of limitations imposed by the court because she was unaware of the nature of her abuse and its effect on her until later.

In many instances, victims of sexual abuse may not be aware of their abuse until long after they reach majority. They repress memories of their abuse and suffer from post-traumatic stress syndrome[41] or multiple personality disorder.[42] Although the average age of abuse is eleven, victims generally do not begin to discover their abuse until they are in their third or fourth decade of life.[43] Survivors of abuse also need time to overcome the pattern of victimization which often makes it impossible for them to assert their rights. To require them to file suit within two or three years of their majority is to deprive them of legal justice.

Where people have sued for injuries discovered long after the negligent act, such as cancer caused by toxic products, the courts have created an exception to the statute of limitations and have allowed it to run not from the date of the act, but from *discovery* of the injury—the cancer. It would seem logical to apply this discovery principle to cases of sexual abuse, especially since sexual abuse involves an intentional act, one which is recognized by law as more serious than mere negligence.

However, a divided Supreme Court of Washington refused to apply this discovery rule in a case of sexual abuse even though the victim could not remember the acts until she began therapy eight years after her 18th birthday. The majority of the court thought that the action was "based solely on an alleged recollection of events which were repressed from her consciousness and there is no means of independently verifying her allegations in whole or in part."[44] The majority ignored the fact that in most cases the jury has to rely solely on the word of the plaintiff and defendant, and that, as the judges pointed out, courts routinely rely on the testimony of experts, including psychotherapists, and could easily do so in cases of sexual abuse. (Videotapes of victims recalling memories under hypnosis or uncovering personalities would certainly be sufficient proof to convince a judge or jury.)

One enlightened court recently recognized a separate cause of action for incestuous abuse. The Wisconsin Court of Appeals held that for purposes of determining the limitations period, the time does not begin until the victim discovers, or in the exercise of reasonable diligence should have discovered, the fact and the cause of the injury. The Court of Appeals ordered a trial in the case of a woman who was sexually abused by her father three times a week, beginning in 1969, when she was five years old, and ending in 1978, when she was fifteen. At fifteen, she told her mother about the abuse, but her mother and father trivialized it. Her father convinced her that she was not injured by the conduct and that she was at fault for her problems and for those of her family. In 1985, as a result of her distress when her father attempted to obtain custody of her younger sister, she began to consider the relationship between his acts and her continuing psychological and emotional problems. She then began therapy and filed the suit. Even though she knew of her abuse all along, the Court of Appeals held that she had the right to her day in court.[45] The statute of limitations did not run until she fully understood the connection between her problems and her abuse.

More cases are being filed by sexual abuse victims in trial courts every day and the law is gradually changing as more judges become aware of the realities of abuse. While suits in some states may still be dismissed, I believe judges will be increasingly inclined to follow the reasoning in the Wisconsin case and to give victims a remedy against their parents for physical and sexual abuse.

Children should be allowed to sue their parents, and the outmoded policy permitting corporal punishment should be eliminated. The policy considerations in favor of such changes are overwhelming. The long-term physical, psychological, emotional and social effects of corporal punishment on children are devastating. Corporal punishment has been shown to increase aggression and to be a precursor to juvenile delinquency.[46] And abused children often become child abusers. If the cost in human terms is not enough, the monetary costs to society are staggering. A higher percentage of abused children drop out of school; end up on welfare; become criminals, prostitutes, drug addicts and alcoholics; and commit suicide. The loss of human potential is incalculable.

Even if we ignore the human and social factors, the fact is that corporal punishment should be eliminated because it is outdated and *it does not work*. Just as we have learned not to use radiation for thyroid problems because it can kill, we have learned not only that corporal punishment is an ineffective way to discipline children, but that it may have the opposite effect. Studies have demonstrated that physical punishment *increases* a child's offensive behavior rather than stops it. And physical punishment can teach children to become violent. They learn by the example of their parents that the way to cope with frustration or not getting their way is by hitting.

Based on current research, a policy supporting parent's "rights" to corporal punishment is no longer justified. Children are not property; they do not belong to their parents like a house or a car. Society has a stake in its children; they are our future. Instead of allowing children to be treated as their parents' property, our policy should be to make children's care our top priority and to protect each one to the greatest extent possible. They are our country's most important resource.

Children are human beings and should have the same rights to life, liberty and the pursuit of happiness and the protection of those rights by law. We have just begun to reject the notion that wives are the property of their husbands and to accord women the same rights as men. The law has finally abolished the "right" of a husband to beat his wife. We should go further and acknowledge that all human beings regardless of age, sex, color or creed are valuable and should receive our respect and protection through our laws and our policies.

All states have child abuse legislation enabling children to be removed from unsafe homes and providing penalties for abusers. The policy allowing corporal punishment is inconsistent with laws protecting children from abuse, and from our recently acquired knowledge about the detrimental effects of corporal punishment. If children can be removed from their homes and their parents can be prosecuted for child abuse, it does not make sense to prevent those children from suing their parents for support and the expenses of their physical and mental injuries. A child who is sexually abused may need years of therapy. Should the state pay for that therapy or should the abusive parent?

How can corporal punishment be legally protected while the physical abuse of a child is a crime?

If you believe that the policy in favor of corporal punishment should be changed and that victims should be able to sue their parents, write to your state representatives and work for changes in your state law. By helping to change these laws, you will be helping yourself and others to shed the victim role by placing the responsibility where it belongs—on the abuser.

If you live in a state that permits suits for physical or sexual abuse against parents or in one where your attorney believes a court will adopt the more enlightened view, or if you are suing an abuser who is not a parent, you are then faced with a more important personal question: Whether suing your abuser is in your best interest—emotionally, psychologically and financially.

Perhaps we should start with the bleak facts about filing lawsuits, facts which are even bleaker for suits involving sexual abuse. First, no case is a sure thing. No matter how much proof you have, no matter how one-sided in your favor your case seems to be, you can always lose. No one likes to think of losing when contemplating a lawsuit. Many attorneys will not tell you the truth, but the hard fact is that you may not win. Even if all the evidence is on your side, and it never is, the judge or jury may be in a bad mood or may not like the clothes you wear and may find against you. So you must always take into consideration the fact that you may lose.

Your chances of winning a sex abuse case are not encouraging, especially if your abuser has not admitted the abuse. It will be your word and that of your therapist against your abuser and his or her expert—unless you have an independent witness. (Videotapes of sessions in your therapist's office can often be very persuasive, but they are not a substitute for a witness to the actual abuse.) That does not mean your suit is hopeless, only that it is difficult. You will have to rely heavily on your therapist's testimony and ability to educate the jurors on such complicated matters as post-traumatic stress syndrome or multiple personality disorder. And you will have to overcome the jury's reluctance and even revulsion about sexual abuse.

Even if you do win, will you be able to collect any money damages from your abuser? Many people think that once the jury renders its decision, the loser hands over the money, but this is not the case. Your attorney must use legally approved collection procedures to collect the money, and many losers use every trick they can think of to hide their money and prevent collection. And are you sure that your abuser has anything to collect? Does he or she have stock, a large bank account, investment property, jewelry, expensive cars without loans on them, a well-paying job so that you can garnish the salary? In most states, homes are exempt from execution unless they have an extremely high equity, and the expenses of sale are high. If you want more than a moral vindication, you should investigate your abuser's financial condition *before* you file your lawsuit.

The worst part of bringing a lawsuit is what you will have to face as a witness. You will be suing for your "mental distress," and that means everything in your therapy sessions and everything you have ever done is fair game for the defense attorney. If you have anything to hide or anything you do not want the court, or the press, to know, do not bring a suit. Not all courts will close the trial to the public. Once you file a suit, you waive all of your rights to confidentiality for any information that even remotely pertains to the case. You will be forced to bare your soul to strangers, some of them hostile, and you have to be prepared to do so.

You must also be prepared for hostile and abusive questioning by the defense. Unfortunately, my colleagues are not always kind or ethical. In fairness, their job is to defend your abuser to the best of their ability, but some go for the jugular. You can expect them to try to show that you are, at best, hysterical and, at worst crazy, and not to be believed. They will use the evidence you present to show the effects of your sexual abuse to persuade the jury that you are unstable. They will try to convince the jury that the abuse never occurred; that it is all in your mind.

The defense may try to prove that your attempts break free of the abuse are the hostile acts of a vindictive child.

One of the most painful things they will do is try to place the blame on you. They will play on the ignorance and prejudices of jurors to prove that you seduced your abuser, that you liked the sexual acts, and that you could have stopped the abuse at any time but you did nothing. If you have ever had an affair, they will use it to show that you are promiscuous. Everything that you have ever done which you are ashamed of—and we all have our share—will be dragged out and used against you. And they will try to rattle you, to make you angry, so that you will contradict yourself and lose credibility.

Unless you have reached a point where you have made peace with your feelings about the abuse, the stage I call "So What," and you are strong enough to undergo the kind of vicious, humiliating cross-examination I have outlined, I do not recommend putting yourself through the ordeal of a lawsuit. The strain of any lawsuit is devastating, but a suit which involves so much of an emotional investment is worse. In most states, it takes from one-and-a-half years to five years to bring a lawsuit to trial. During that time there are depositions (testimony taken under oath in the lawyers' offices), interrogatories (lengthy written questions to be answered under oath), medical and psychiatric examinations, and many other procedures that may cause emotional stress. You will not be able to forget your abuse because the lawsuit will constantly force you to remember. Your abuser will lie and do other things that will constitute new forms of emotional abuse. Can you stand up to all of this? Do you want to?

Although I was a trial lawyer for many years, I always tried to talk my clients out of suing. I felt that the emotional strain was such that most lawsuits were just not worth the agony. I believe this even more strongly in cases of sexual abuse where the emotional investment is infinitely greater than the usual civil case. As a therapist, I do not believe it helps victims to become enmeshed in a lengthy lawsuit which keeps them fixated on their abuse. I prefer to see survivors live happy lives, free of the debilitating emotional strain of a lawsuit. I really believe that the best revenge is to live well.

I do not want to spend one more minute of my life reliving the pain of my abuse. If you are wondering whether I would give up the money I might win, I did. My father is dead, but I considered suing my mother who knew of the abuse and did not stop it, and who engaged in her own physical and emotional abuse. I rejected the idea because it would have meant prolonging my pain. I also felt that she had been through enough pain and I did not want to add any more to her life; I just wanted my own life and my freedom.

The costs of a lawsuit are also prohibitive. The most experienced attorneys usually require payment on an hourly basis, and the fee ranges from $100 to $250 per hour. A sexual abuse case would cost a minimum of $10,000 to try, and a more realistic estimate would be between $15,000 and $50,000 to take the case to trial. Even if you can find an attorney to take the case on a contingent fee—where the fee is a percentage of what you win and collect—you will usually have to pay the court costs. These costs include the filing fee, reporters' fees for depositions, the cost of your expert witness, jury fees, etc., and will usually total a minimum of $2,000 and can run into the tens of thousands. If you lose, you pay not only your own costs, but those of your abuser.

There are some circumstances where it might be worthwhile to sue, but I urge you to carefully weigh the pros and cons and the effect on your life before you decide to devote your time, energy and money to a lawsuit. Some therapists believe that suing your abuser can be therapeutic because you are confronting your abuser and placing the responsibility where it ought to be. A victory is a public vindication of all that you have suffered. Even if your abuser continues to deny your allegations, when your abuser is held liable by the jury, the world knows the truth. The law recognizes you have been wronged. But if your abuser has some degree of amnesia, he may believe that *he* is the victim of injustice. Do not expect an apology or reconciliation; all you probably will receive is more hostility.

More important, if you are counting on a vindication, how are you going to feel if you lose? Can you brush it off or will you feel like a victim all over again—a victim not only of your abuser but of the whole system! Is that therapeutic?

One arguable situation where it might be worthwhile to sue your abuser is where your abuser is wealthy and you are unable to support yourself or pay for therapy. Perhaps you have been in a hospital, or you are divorced with children and do not have enough money. The costs of therapy can be devastating and if your abuser can be forced to take responsibility for your rehabilitation, a suit might be warranted. But a suit should only be a last resort.

In some cases the threat of suit may induce a substantial settlement. Some abusers will pay you a settlement to avoid the publicity of a trial. Others may have repressed their memories about abusing you and will fight you to the Supreme Court.

The way to escape from the victim role is to be able to support *yourself* and give *yourself* what you need. It may be healthier to spend your energy on training for a job you really want rather than wasting it on a lawsuit you may not win. Even if it is a real struggle, being able to make your own money instead of trying to get it from your abuser puts you in control. It shows that you can take care of yourself and are no longer dependent on your abuser.

If you decide to bring a lawsuit, you need to have a healthy attitude about it. Plan your life as though you are going to lose. Work on making your life the way you want it to be without relying on winning the suit. If you win, it's gravy; if you lose, you've gone on with your life and you're doing what you want to do. Put yourself in a position where you don't *need* to win.

While I am skeptical about the overall benefits of filing suit against abusers, I strongly believe that victims should have the right to compensation for their rehabilitation, whether or not the abuser is a parent. It is a national disgrace that women and children are not accorded the basic protections of our legal system. I look forward to the day when our country will recognize that all people, big or small, are valuable and have the right to be protected and treated gently.

A political victory, a rise in rents, the recovery of your sick, or the return of your absent friend, or some other quite external event, raises your spirits, and you think good days are preparing for you. Do not believe it. It can never be so. Nothing can bring you peace but yourself.
Ralph Waldo Emerson

IV HEALING –
FINDING A THERAPIST

Finding a therapist can be a bewildering task because of the wide range of therapeutic theories, the confusing array of titles and endless differences in personalities, beliefs and techniques. *Consumer Reports* would never undertake the challenge of trying to rate therapists the way they rate cars and home appliances because evaluating the effectiveness of therapy is so inherently subjective.

Although researchers are trying to devise accurate ways of measuring the success of therapeutic interventions, the helping professions acknowledge that it is almost impossible to control enough factors to make the studies even remotely reliable. So there is no way for you to find out that therapist A "cured" eight out of ten clients, while therapist B "cured" only sex out of ten.

But even if you cannot find any accurate ratings, there are still ways you can increase your chances of finding a therapist who can help you. First of all, there is no "right therapist." There are many different therapists who will be able to help you in different ways. If your goal is to recover from your sexual abuse, increase your self-esteem and trust, release your repressed emotions, and establish new patterns for a happier life, a large pool of candidates is available.

There is no one magic cure. Beware of any therapist who tells you, "You can only do it my way. My way is the only way." It's nonsense and it's false. Leave immediately if a therapist ever tells you, "I am the only one who can help you. You will fall apart without me." What ego! Some therapists try to make you believe that they are indispensable out of their own neurotic insecurity; it gives them a feeling of power. Don't ever believe it and don't stay to listen to any more. There are lots and lots of people who are qualified to help you; the challenge is narrowing down the list to one who you feel is right for you.

The most important thing to remember in choosing a therapist is that *the therapist works for you.* You are hiring this person to give you what you need; you set the goals. And you decide if you think what you are getting is valuable. It's a little like hiring a contractor to build a house. You give him the plans and he builds according to your specifications. But he works for you, and so does your therapist.

People who hire professionals, such as doctors, lawyers and therapists, are often intimidated by their education and fancy titles. They think someone who has spent more years in school must know more about what is good for them than they do. And if they are paying large fees for services, they often leave their common sense in the parking garage and accept at face value whatever the professional has to say.

You are even more vulnerable when you go to a therapist than when you go to a lawyer or doctor. People usually seek a therapist only when they are really in pain. Your emotions may feel overwhelming, your life seems out of control and you may even believe you are going crazy. You want someone to take the pain away and to tell you what to do.

Unfortunately, as in all professions, there are good therapists and there are bad therapists, just as there are good and bad plumbers, dentists and auto mechanics. And you will usually be faced with the task of finding a good therapist while you are in a bad mental state. However, there are ways to succeed even against these odds—by making sure you have adequate information and keeping in mind that *you* are in charge and *you* must be satisfied with your choice.

Your relationship with your therapist is the most important single factor in determining the progress you will make in therapy. If you have a good relationship, your therapy will be easier and faster than if you have a negative or neutral one. Research indicates that clients show substantial improvement when they have warm, caring relationships with their therapists, even if the therapist does nothing! It is essential that you feel warmth, respect and caring from your therapist because it is difficult to let your emotions pour out and to discuss sensitive issues about your sexual abuse unless you trust the person who is listening to you.

If you are working under hypnosis, and many of you will be, your relationship with your therapist is even more important. Hypnosis is an intense state of concentration which makes you acutely sensitive to attitudes of people around you. Under hypnosis you will notice a tone of voice or a turn of phrase that you would not ordinarily catch, and your mind will react to it, sometimes without your being aware of it.

I had an experience which brought this phenomenon home to me vividly. The therapist who first discovered my repressed childhood sexual abuse was a man with a great deal of experience in hypnotherapy. The first time I hypnotized myself, he quickly discovered my abuse by asking questions that could be answered either "yes" or "no." I answered by allowing one of two fingers to rise by themselves, one designated for "yes" answers and one for "no" answers. We were able to find out a great deal about the abuse by drafting more specific questions which could be answered either "yes" or "no."

However, as the months passed, my therapist and I became increasingly frustrated because no memories were coming out. Even after we discovered the existence of an ego state, very little emerged. But when I went home and hypnotized myself, I recalled all kinds of memories. Fortunately, at about this time, my husband accompanied me to one of the sessions because we were also having marital problems. After the session, I hesitantly asked whether my husband thought the therapist was hostile towards me. His emphatic "Yes, he sure is!" helped me realize that the reason I could not let the memories out was that my therapist made me feel like an experimental animal rather than a person, and his hostility was preventing me from exposing my deepest secrets. After I changed therapists, I found out that my therapist had been going through a bitter divorce and had negative feelings toward women.

If a therapist has a problem he or she does not recognize, that problem may interfere with your therapy. For example, if your therapist repeatedly tells you to forgive your abuser and will not permit you to express your anger, your therapist may have a problem with his own unresolved anger and is doing you a disservice by forcing you to keep yours repressed. Obviously you cannot discover all of these things before you start therapy, but you should be aware of them so that you can discuss them if they arise.

You are hiring a therapist to help *you*. The fees you have to pay should help you to remember this fact, if nothing else does. You are not in therapy to help your therapist. Some abuse victims take on the role of rescuers and try to rescue their therapists. If you find yourself giving your therapist advice or comfort or trying to avoid upsetting him or her, you should point this out to your therapist. It may be your problem, but it may also be the therapist's problem. If you do not receive a satisfactory answer, you should change therapists.

Do not assume that because you are the one going to a therapist that you must have all of the problems. In many cases, people who have the ability to recognize that they need help and the courage to get it are far healthier than people who do not get help. Use your common sense when selecting a therapist and remember that you may be the healthier person.

You will never find a therapist who is perfect. Therapists are only human, with all of the human frailties. If you are looking for a therapist who "has it all together" and has resolved all possible problems, you will be looking for a long time. Analytic psychiatrists of the old Freudian school go through a few years of analysis themselves before they can practice, and even they have neuroses. They may be more aware of some of their hangups than therapists who have not been through therapy, but they still have the hangups.

Some people think therapists are useless if they have not solved all of their own problems. I heard a woman say of a therapist who lived in her neighborhood: "I'd never go to her; she can't even control her own kids." I, on the other hand, would never go to a therapist who did *not* have problems. How could such a paragon possibly understand my pain?

Sometimes therapists may have problems that actually increase their effectiveness in treating similar problems. Most alcohol and drug abuse counselors are recovering alcoholics and addicts. They have a clear understanding of the causes of addiction and the difficulties of facing addiction and overcoming it. The same is true of sexual abuse. More and more people who have been abused themselves are becoming therapists and are bringing with them a sharper knowledge of the patterns of reactions to abuse, the ways the mind works to repress memories, how ego states and multiple personalities function and how to best unravel the tangle. This does not mean that a therapist who has not been sexually abused is not competent to help you. The specifics of the therapist's personal experience may not be as crucial as the therapist's self-awareness and understanding of human emotions. Only a therapist who has experienced pain and loss and is comfortable with the depth of these feelings can be helpful.

While it is imperative that you have a warm, caring, friendly relationship with your therapist when you begin your sessions, your relationship will not always appear to be that way during the course of treatment. You will become angry, even furious with your therapist. I guarantee that if you have been sexually abused, you will accuse your therapist of doing something untrustworthy and, at some time, probably more than once, you will be convinced your therapist does not really care about you. And I know with certainty that you will find other faults with your therapist. I have done all of the above as a client and I have had all of them done to me by my clients.

Your reactions of anger and mistrust are normal and are based on what is called "transference." Transference means that you transfer the feelings you had about important people in your life—your mother, father, abuser—onto your therapist. For example, if one of your parents betrayed you, you will see your therapist as untrustworthy. You must be careful to distinguish between what you are transferring onto your therapist because of your past experiences, and what is the present behavior of your therapist. If you are in doubt, ask a friend for an objective opinion.

Once you have found a therapist with whom you are comfortable during the first couple of sessions, be careful about changing that therapist later in the process without a great deal of discussion and thought. There are times when therapy is difficult and painful and it is all too easy to dump your therapist to avoid facing the hard issues. At this stage, your therapist may very appropriately question your urge to change therapists and may suggest that remaining in treatment is the best course, which may sound like "only *I* can help you." One of the hardest things for both therapist and client to sort out is whether the problem is transference or a real conflict with the therapist. If you walk away without carefully exploring the situation with your therapist, you will be depriving yourself of a valuable opportunity to work out a detrimental pattern that may continue to hurt your personal relationships.

Finally, your therapist should be a loving friend. This sentence from *How to Be Your Own Best Friend* by therapists Mildred Newman and Bernard Berkowitz changed my therapist, my confidence in my ability to choose someone who would help me and my life: ". . . one of the most important things an analyst can give is his loving interest." Keep looking until you find someone you can think of as a friend.

1. How do I find a therapist I will like?

One way to find potential therapists is to obtain as many recommendations as possible from as many people you know and trust. Talk to your friends, your minister, your lawyer, school counselors, your company personnel office, your doctor, and anyone you know who is currently in therapy. Visit the agency in your area that handles cases of child sexual abuse and ask specifically for the names of therapists who have experience in treating cases of multiple personality and do hypnotherapy. Your community sexual abuse treatment center could be an excellent source of referrals. Although these centers often have therapists with the greatest experience in sexual abuse cases, do not feel that you have to go to one of their therapists. Simply add the names to your list.

Your local Mental Health Association may have some recommendations. You might also contact various professional organizations in your area for social workers, family therapists, psychologists and psychiatrists. However, I do not believe professional association referral services are very useful because they do not rate the ability or expertise of their members and often will not even specify whether the member even treats cases of sexual abuse. You merely get the next available name on the list. If you use these recommendations, be sure to confirm the person's ability by talking to at least one other source.

Make your list as exhaustive as you can and be sure to write down the names of people who referred each therapist and what they said. Then read over your list. If a couple of names keep popping up, you may want to put those on your list to be interviewed. If you particularly like what one person said about a therapist, put that therapist on your interview list. You will probably want to narrow the list down to a half dozen possibilities. You will not have to interview all of them. At least a couple of them may not be able to take you right away. And you may eliminate one or two because of the way you were treated when you set up an appointment. Special financial arrangements may be a factor where you may have to make your list longer.

Once you have your list of potential therapists, you can begin the process of making your choice. Determine if you will like your therapist by watching, listening and questioning. Your first conversation when you call to make an appointment can be revealing. How long did it take you to reach the therapist? If the therapist had a secretary, answering machine or answering service, how long did it take for the therapist to get back to you? This is an important question because it gives you an idea of what may happen if you try to reach the therapist in an emergency. You will not want to wait a week for a response. Whether the secretary or answering service is polite to you or rude should also be considered. A therapist who permits employees to be rude to clients may not have much concern for their feelings. You should consider how you felt about the way the therapist talked to you when you finally made contact. Although phone conversations are sometimes awkward, the therapist should not be abrupt or overbearing, but should put *you* at ease, and give you the feeling that your problem is important.

You should ask yourself similar questions at your first meeting with the therapist. Was the therapist on time? Being on time is always important but even more so at the first session because the client is

210

nervous and in a strange environment. If the therapist does not have a secretary who can welcome a new client, and many therapists don't, the therapist should make sure to be on time to meet the client when he or she first arrives. Therapists should be aware that new clients are usually apprehensive about the first meeting. Those who permit new clients to sit alone in unfamiliar surroundings demonstrate a lack of sensitivity to these feelings. Of course, therapists can have emergencies which make tardiness excusable; in that case they should provide an explanation and an apology.

In the initial interview, notice whether the therapist listens to you or interrupts frequently? While a therapist may want to obtain certain information, continual interruption indicates a lack of respect for your feelings and for your judgment in deciding what is important. Does the therapist respond to what you say in a way that indicates he or she has heard what you said? Do you feel comfortable talking to this therapist?

One of the most important questions you can ask yourself is whether you like this therapist as a person? You are going to be spending a lot of time with your therapist. If you do not like this person, you will be miserable and probably find excuses to miss appointments or you may quit altogether. It is harder to start again with someone new and you will have lost the time and money you spent on someone you did not like. No matter how highly recommended and qualified someone appears to be, *do not start therapy with someone you do not like.*

In deciding whether or not you like the therapist, you must trust yourself. This will be a new experience for some of you. But your feeling of comfort with your therapist is something no one can help you with. If others think a certain therapist is a saint, but you are uncomfortable and want to get out of the office, leave. Do not try to be rational or think what you *should* do. Think with your gut. Trust your instincts—those vague little feelings you've ignored for so much of your life. Only *you* can decide.

It is often easier to make a decision if you can make a comparison. You may interview at least three or four therapists before you make your choice. Yes, it will cost you perhaps $200 to $300, but if it prevents you from making a mistake and helps you find a therapist you really like, it will be well worth the effort and the price. If you have a run of bad luck, you may have to interview a few more than three or four. But if you look hard enough, you will find what you want. If you begin to feel that you have interviewed too many therapists and perhaps the problem stems from you, then it may be time to make a choice.

Making the wrong choice is not a disaster. No choice is irrevocable. You can always change your mind. You can always find another therapist or switch to a group. Remember you are totally in control of

211

your own therapy and only you can know if you are getting what you need. You may lose some money and time in the progress of your therapy, but sometimes it is better to cut your losses than stay with a therapist you do not like. If you trust your instincts and rely on what you *feel* about your therapist rather than what you think or what you think you should think, you will make a wise choice, one that will work for you.

2. Qualifications to look for in a therapist

A qualified therapist has the knowledge, training and experience to help you deal with your problem. These qualifications can be easily ascertained during the initial interview. You will want to find out whether the person has a license. In most states, therapists are licensed and regulated which tends to insure a minimally greater chance for competency than if therapists are unlicensed. As a practical matter, however, licensing is of dubious value because most states do not have much money to follow up on complaints or to police their licenses, which means that incompetent therapists rarely lose their licenses. A license only demonstrates that the person holding it had the ability to memorize facts and theories and pass a somewhat rigorous test.

Then you will want to evaluate the type of training the therapist has. You will first have to distinguish among the various types of therapists: social workers, psychiatrists, psychologists, psychiatric nurse specialists, and pastoral counselors. Psychologists usually have a Ph.D. (Doctor of Philosophy) degree; they have written a research paper but do not have medical degrees. Their education includes therapeutic theories and techniques and is heavily weighted in favor of psychological research, testing and experimentation.

Psychiatrists, on the other hand, have completed medical school and have a specialty in psychiatry. Their emphasis is on the physical causes of mental illness and the medications that can cure them. They are trained in therapeutic techniques, but their training may lead them to perceive their therapeutic relationships in a rigid doctor-patient mode where you are sick and they have the power to make you well. You should explore whether this is the case before making your decision. Only psychiatrists can prescribe drugs, but other types of therapists have access to psychiatrists so their clients can obtain medication if necessary.

Clinical social workers have an M.S.W., a master's degree, and have completed a graduate program which is specifically designed to emphasize the most comprehensive theories, techniques and practices of therapy. This discipline often stresses short-term therapy and the focus is not on research or medicine, although social workers learn some of both subjects, but on developing an equal partnership relationship with a client which will facilitate maximum disclosure and discussion and on using a variety of techniques to help people heal and learn to take control of their lives. As a social worker, I have an obvious bias in favor of social workers if they have the appropriate experience. I chose the social work program to treat abuse because it was the most comprehensive in addressing theories and techniques that could be used in clinical practice.

Some states license psychiatric nurses to do therapy. My favorite and most effective therapist, a woman skilled in hypnotherapy and sexual abuse cases, was a nurse practitioner who practiced under the supervision of a psychiatrist. She had more sensitivity and ability than any other therapist I have encountered and is certainly proof that the person, not the license or type of training, is what counts.

Two of the most respected family therapists, psychologist Augustus Napier, Ph.D. and psychiatrist Carl Whitaker, M.D., authors of *The Family Crucible*, view the requisite training in much the same way I do. They wrote,

> ". . . the psychiatrist spends an inordinate amount of time learning medical skills that are of little use in any psychotherapy. He becomes biased to thinking in terms of illness and symptomatology, attitudes that must be unlearned as he tries to understand and work with social systems. We still speak of the family as our 'patient' largely out of habit, but it is a bad habit. The tendency to compare human psychological distress with physical illness is an often destructive use of metaphor.
>
> "The psychologist who becomes a family therapist also finds that much of his training was peripheral or irrelevant. The hours spent studying statistics, research design, neurophysiology, and learning theory may have an occasional relevance to the family, but I have to strain to find it. . . . But the skills I need in order to be able to work effectively with families had to be acquired largely at my own initiative and after the 'necessary' training was over.

"It is possible that the social worker's training is the most appropriate education of all for family therapy since social systems are the direct focus of this field."

In spite of my personal preferences, it really does not make any difference whether you choose a psychiatric nurse, psychiatrist, social worker, psychologist or a member of the clergy, as long as the therapist meets your needs for a therapeutic relationship and has the necessary expertise and experience in handling sexual abuse cases. Expertise and experience are important concerns and are areas where you should ask very specific questions and demand very specific answers. Sexual abuse is a complicated condition and, although I believe anyone can learn anything, I would not want to be a therapists's first case of sexual abuse. Someone experienced in the field can quickly cut through defenses and the tangled web of memories and emotions which might take many times as long for a novice to figure out.

If you use the services of a public or nonprofit agency, you may be assigned to a trainee under the supervision of an experienced practitioner. This can be successful *if* the trainee is receiving ample and appropriate supervision by someone experienced in sexual abuse cases. I encourage you to ask such questions if you find yourself in this position. And if you are not satisfied, do not keep quiet in order to spare the trainee's feelings. You are entitled to competent, effective therapy.

Sadly, some therapists really are ignorant about sexual abuse but will take the cases anyway. I sat in on a mental health provider meeting where various heads of divisions were discussing the fact that they were getting an increasing number of sexual abuse cases and were overwhelmed because the facility did not have enough therapists with the experience to treat them. One official suggested that the cases be transferred to other mental health facilities in the area. But a more senior official responded that the facility should keep the cases because the facility needed the business and because "sexual abuse cases are just like any other problem and any therapist can handle them."

I was astonished that anyone would fail to recognize the special knowledge and skills needed to adequately deal with sexual abuse cases. Many states are studying legislation to require additional training and a special license for sexual abuse therapists because of the complexity of the issues and methods of treatment. The official's comment was a little like asserting that a mechanic trained to repair bicycles could just as easily fix a Ferrari. I don't know many Ferrari owners who would be willing to take that risk. Since I was still getting my degree and was only an observer at the meeting, there was little I could do to prevent the senior official from imposing his decision on the facility and making guinea pigs of its clients. I can only hope that therapists will speak out in the future and ensure that clients obtain better treatment.

You can avoid being the "first," by simply asking how many cases of sexual abuse your prospective therapist has handled. Do not feel that someone has to be the first. Therapists can obtain appropriate training under an experienced supervisor. That way the therapist is able to learn and the client is protected. But I strongly recommend that you select a therapist who has handled several cases of sexual abuse and who has seen at least one of those cases through to a successful termination. A therapist who has been sexually abused and has completed treatment may have special insights and understanding to help you.

Next, if you know or suspect that you have repressed all or part of your memories of the abuse, it is essential that you find a therapist who has had experience with multiple personality disorder (MPD) and with hypnotherapy. Because you have repressed some memories this does not mean you have multiple personality disorder. But certain types of repression resemble some of the features of MPD and if your therapist is familiar with the more severe cases of MPD, she or he will certainly have the skills to help with less complex symptoms.

The most effective techniques for MPD and other types of amnesia are highly specialized and demand that the therapist have adequate training and experience. Studies have shown that MPD and other amnesia states are created by abuse victims through self-hypnosis.[47] Since these states of amnesia are created by hypnosis, it stands to reason that they can be treated by hypnosis. And, in fact, research has substantiated this hypothesis; hypnosis is now recognized as the treatment of choice for MPD and other amnesia states.[48] Common sense leads to the conclusion that forgotten memories cannot be restored through the more usual therapeutic process of just talking, and yet that is what some uninformed therapists attempt to do. How can you talk about something that you cannot remember?

Jane, a lawyer friend of mine, went to a therapist because she had a vague suspicion that she had been abused as a child. After three years of traditional "talk" therapy, she knew only that she had been abused by her father, but not how long, in what way, or any of the details. Most of her emotions remained repressed. After three years, she knew less about her abuse than I did after two sessions of hypnotherapy. After we talked about our experiences, she changed therapists.

Jane's therapist should have referred Jane to someone else, or perhaps called in an experienced hypnotherapist to help. But therapists unfortunately do not always do what they should do, so it is up to you to protect yourself. If you suspect that you may have forgotten memories or portions of memories having to do with your abuse, or if you find out during therapy that this is the case, your therapy will proceed faster and more effectively if you find a therapist skilled in hypnotherapy.

One word of warning: Do not confuse a hypnotherapist with a hypnotist. Hypnotists are not trained to treat the psychological and emotional problems of your abuse. Make sure that you choose someone who has a degree and a license in therapy or psychological counseling who is also trained in using hypnosis as a therapeutic tool.

3. Theories of therapy

Therapy is based on a wide variety of psychological theories from psychodynamic following the work of Freud, to psychodrama, where emotions and experiences are acted out usually in a group setting, to existential which focuses on the meaning of life. There are far too many theories to discuss them in detail here. As long as the therapist you choose has experience with sexual abuse cases, MPD and hypnotherapy, you will be able to work out your abuse problems and it really does not matter what other theories the therapist follows. However you should be aware of a few general principles.

First, I have found the better therapists to be eclectic, which means they use techniques from a number of theories. Every person is unique and a technique which may work for one will not work for another. The treatment plan must be tailored to fit the client; the client should not be squeezed into an unsuitable theory.

No therapist is skilled in all areas. My most successful therapist was excellent in hypnotherapy and brilliant at helping me analyze what I discovered but did not use the behavioral techniques I needed to acquire the communication and assertiveness skills I never learned as a child. You may have to use more than one therapist to work on different areas. Your first priority should be to deal with the memories and emotions of your abuse.

You also have to consider whether you want your therapy to be passive or active. Therapists' styles range from saying very little and letting you struggle for all of the answers yourself to being very directive and confrontive. As with most things in life, the extremes do not work as well for the majority of people as a balanced approach. You probably do not want a therapist who does all the thinking for you, just as you do not want a therapist who wastes your time letting you flounder when you could be making progress if someone pointed out other alternatives. If you do not want a passive therapist, the psychoanalytic model is not for you.

When I first lived in Washington, D.C., I went to the head of the psychoanalytic association, a psychiatrist who was highly recommended and respected. Although he was also expensive, I wanted "the best." For three years I lay on his couch, freely associated and cried. He never said more to me than "Um hum!," "What are your thoughts on that?" and "Your time is up." Despite all of my free associations, he never suspected my childhood sexual abuse or any other reason for my depression and he never provided any guidance, advice or alternatives whatsoever to make me feel better. I actually felt worse while he put his kids through college on my money. After three years, my best friends finally decided they couldn't stand seeing what this doctor was doing to me any longer. They sat me down and told me that I should be getting better, not worse, and argued with me until I finally began to believe that the problem was my doctor's and not mine. I am so glad they "interfered," because they gave me the courage to leave that analyst. When I announced my decision, he said he didn't think I had made any progress for a long time. I asked him why he never told me that before, and he replied, "Because I kept thinking you might."

As a result of my experience, I would not recommend someone who only sits, listens and does nothing else. If you want that, you can designate an hour a day to sit in front of a mirror and talk to yourself and put your money in the bank.

The newer theories where the therapist is more directive, are far more effective in resolving your problems than those where the therapist just sits there. Directive therapists help you out when you are stuck by providing alternative ways of seeing situations and alternative ways of reacting and behaving. They have tested techniques for helping you release repressed emotions and for recognizing your harmful patterns of behavior. Therapists who follow the newer theories also base their practices on current research demonstrating that a warm therapeutic relationship alone can help clients heal. These therapists will help you learn trust by being someone you can like and trust. You will find that you can improve very quickly if you have a friendly relationship with your therapist and if that therapist will answer your questions and provide some direction for you. That's what you are paying for; you can wallow in misery by yourself.

In your initial interview ask what the therapist believes about the therapist-client relationship. (If the therapist refers to you as a "patient." you already know that you are seen as sick and not as an equal.) Find out whether the therapist is active or passive. Your therapist should answer these questions candidly. If not, then you know that you will probably face the same type of evasion when you ask other questions later.

Beware of "quick cures" or long ones

Another principle is to beware of "the quick cure." A number of enterprises advertise instant cures and transformational miracles during "marathon" courses lasting a week or a weekend. Cases of severe sexual or physical abuse raise so many difficult issues that it is impossible to resolve them in such a short period of time. No one can wave a magic wand and heal you in a week.

These courses may actually be dangerous to you if you have repressed memories about your abuse. Some of these courses use techniques similar to brainwashing—long hours, constant tension, and extreme psychological pressure to "get to your issues"—which are designed to break down your defenses and expose your problems. Your defenses are there for a purpose; you built them to protect you and if they are ripped away too violently or rapidly, you could find yourself in real trouble. A number of people who have taken these courses have had a psychotic breaks and have ended up in hospitals. These courses are not run by therapists; no one does a psychological interview or evaluation of the applicants; and there is little or no followup. You are on your own after all or your defenses are torn away, unless, of course, you fall for the next slick pitch and sign up for another more expensive course. But none of these courses has the ability to put Humpty Dumpty together again if repressed memories are exposed too abruptly.

Your friends may tell you how wonderful these courses are and that they "changed their lives." It is true that some people obtain helpful insights from such courses and may make changes in their lives, but your friends' problems may be ones they were consciously aware of and fully remembered. There is a big difference between "My mother loved my sister better," and being raped by your stepfather for several years. Also, your friends may believe they have changed. But watch those friends for a few months and decide if the changes are permanent. Overnight changes usually last little longer than overnight. In therapy, you take each piece of the problem only when you are ready to handle it. You have a chance to digest what you learn and incorporate it into your daily behavior.

I would never say absolutely not to do something that you believe will be helpful to you because I believe people heal in many different ways. What has worked for me may not work for you.

If you really believe you could profit from these courses, I strongly urge you to wait until your therapist is satisfied that you have recovered all or most of your memories and emotions. At least then you will not be in danger of having your pain exposed before you can deal with it. Many of these courses require that you obtain your therapist's written permission if you are in therapy. This is an important recognition that the course may not be safe for people with certain problems. I hope you will follow this warning.

Lest you feel that you are being shut out of a special club, let me assure you that all of the principles that are taught in these marathon courses are readily available in self-help, religious and spiritual books; from your own therapist; and in the self-help materials and bibliography at the end of this book. Many of these marathon courses make all of their participants swear that they will not tell anyone what occurs in the course on the pretext that disclosure would ruin the experience for potential applicants. The truth is that the companies producing these courses want to create a mystique of secrecy because they don't want people to know that the techniques and principles have been around for a long time and can be easily discovered at your local bookstore. You can get the same information at your own pace in a safer way.

These "quick cure" courses should be distinguished from workshops, sometimes also called "marathons," conducted by licensed therapists. Therapists often hold therapy weekends that may cover specific issues such as being divorced or improving marriages. Sometimes therapists give short courses on self-help techniques, such as assertiveness training, communications skills or mental imagery. The difference is in the expertise of the leader and the care that you will get if you need help. But most important, no legitimate workshop will claim to cure you in a week or a weekend. Instead, you will learn some skills and techniques that may improve your life, and you will learn what you can handle and absorb without the risk of severe emotional distress.

My only other warning when you are considering a therapist's theory is with respect to Freudian analytic psychiatry. Traditional psychoanalysis is an intensive, long-term process involving several weekly sessions for three to five years, or, as some researchers believe, four to eight years or more. Clients lie on the couch for "free-association activity," which involves saying whatever comes into their minds. They report their feelings, experiences, associations, memories and fantasies.[49] I do not recommend this therapeutic model because of its unrealistic time and cost, its unequal treatment of women and the tendency of some of its adherents to negate the reality of sexual abuse. This problem is discussed in Question 27, *I went to a therapist who said my memories of sexual abuse were just fantasies. Is he correct?* If you are considering going to a Freudian analyst, please reread that section now. Newer theories incorporate the best of Freud's ideas with more effective techniques that achieve therapeutic results far more rapidly.

"Strategic therapy" is a powerful type of short-term therapy for incest families when the abuse is recent and the perpetrator is a family member. This involves the entire family and lasts from six to eight weeks. The perpetrator is helped to see the seriousness of the abuse and apologizes to the victim. Other members of the family recognize their failure to protect the victim and promise to protect her in the future. The emphasis is on the family unit as a whole and the family is helped to break out of dysfunctional patterns to insure that the situation cannot reoccur. While this type of treatment may not be appropriate for past abuse where the victim has repressed memories and emotions, it is extremely effective where the abuse has just occurred and the victim can deal with her feelings about herself and her family in the sessions. You can obtain more information about this program from the Family Therapy Institute in Washington, D.C.

Spiritual theories

No discussion of theories would be complete without mentioning the growing number of theories and programs that emphasize spiritual healing. These theories may focus exclusively on spiritual issues or may combine spiritual and psychological techniques. Some sexual abuse victims are able to use religious and spiritual beliefs to leap over all of their psychological problems to a complete healing. Other people must go through a long course of psychological counseling before they heal.

No one can tell if you have the ability to heal through spiritual means alone, just as no one can tell why some people are miraculously cured at Lourdes in France while others with the same ailments are not. However, the successes of religious and spiritual methods for healing abuse warrant serious consideration especially when used with more traditional therapy. In severe cases of abuse, spiritual methods alone may be confusing, especially when a victim is just beginning to face abuse issues, and may not provide the support necessary if problems arise. But spiritual issues inevitably arise in the treatment of sexual abuse and must be addressed.

An enormous number of traditional religions and spiritual options exist and many even have programs specifically designed for survivors of sexual abuse. Many religions now provide counseling for abuse survivors, and others make funds available for therapy. Even if you choose to go to a therapist not connected to your church, it is still comforting to know that your church supports you rather than condemns you, as you may fear. And survivors who truly believe that their God loves them and regards them as good heal faster than those who have no such belief.

The twelve-step programs started by Alcoholics Anonymous are perhaps the best known and most established examples of a mixture of spiritual and psychological principles. These programs have demonstrated their effectiveness not only for alcoholics and their children, but they have expanded to include anyone from a dysfunctional family. Now groups exist expressly for survivors of sexual abuse, since most victims come from severely dysfunctional families. The twelve-step formula of sharing experiences, group support, recognizing present defects, forgiveness and turning over one's life to God or a higher power have had beneficial effects on thousands of people. A major advantage is that these programs are free and available in most communities.

A major drawback is that no trained therapist is present to help if you are severely distressed or recover a particularly unpleasant memory. The absence of a therapist also means that the meetings may lack direction. Some groups are very formal and follow the rigid rules of Alcoholics Anonymous which do not permit group members to comment on each other's statements or to confront each other. Some groups are more flexible and are conducted like other support groups and group therapy sessions, permitting members to point out each other's self-defeating behavior in supportive ways.

While the twelve-step groups for alcoholics have been extremely successful—in fact Alcoholics Anonymous is *the* most successful program for alcoholics, the sexual abuse groups are still in the developmental stage. Whether the success rate is less because abuse groups are new or because abuse survivors need a greater degree of therapeutic support is unclear. But since the twelve-step program is free, you have nothing to lose by trying it. You can even choose individual therapy and *also* join a twelve-step program. I believe in trying *everything* until you find what works best for you.

Another program I have found to be particularly effective for abuse survivors is that of Stephen and Ondrea Levine. The Levines have skillfully combined spiritual philosophy and traditional psychological precepts into various meditations to deal with abuse issues. These meditations include a type of mindfulness meditation for reaching repressed memories, which is similar in some ways to self-hypnosis but appears to be more gentle. Other meditations are for loving kindness, forgiveness and a powerful "Opening the Heart of the Womb Meditation" which appears in Part V, Section 10. All of the meditations can be found in Levine's book, *Healing into Life and Death.* The Levines give workshops around the country that are very effective and one-third or more of the participants tend to be sexual abuse survivors.

I have only mentioned those spiritual programs of which I have some personal knowledge. Certainly other useful programs exist and you will find those that are helpful to you. One warning: Abuse survivors should avoid anything that looks at all like a cult. People who have been victimized often have a tendency to become victims again, to allow others to run their lives and to let others control them. If people start telling you how to think, how to live, to spend all your time with them, to sign up for additional, more expensive courses or to otherwise give them lots of money, *run.* You were a victim once—you don't have to do *that* again.

I believe we are physical, mental and spiritual. I pooh-poohed the spiritual part for many years—until I learned how potent it could be. Now I know we can heal through any or all of these aspects. Explore spiritual healing when you are comfortable with the idea. It's a part of us that's too wonderful to overlook.

In the long run, the choice of a theory is not as important as whether you like your therapist. Any theory or technique is more likely to work if you feel comfortable with the person who is using it. If one technique does not work, most therapists have many others they can try. Reputable therapists will refer you to someone else if they are unable to make any headway with your problem. Be assured that there are many theories and many techniques and many therapists—and there will always be someone who can help you.

4. Decisions you will need to make

Individual or group sessions

Whether you should have individual sessions or join a group for therapy is difficult to answer in cases of sexual abuse. Each is helpful in different ways and both would be beneficial if you could afford them in terms of time and money. If you have to choose, you should probably decide in favor of individual therapy, especially if you suspect there are emotions and memories you may have repressed. If you have multiple personality disorder, ego states or any type of amnesia about your childhood or aspects of your abuse, hypnosis is the treatment of choice and therefore you must be treated individually. If you have been sexually abused, your first priority has to be to deal with the abuse, and you have to recall it in order to deal with it.

On the other hand, group therapy has some powerful effects. It makes you know deep down in your gut, beyond any doubt, that you are not alone, that you were not picked for some terrible punishment and that you are not bad. You can tell yourself these things, you can hear them from your therapist, you can read them in this book, and sooner or later you will begin to believe them. But nothing brings those facts home as fast and convincingly as being in a group with other people who have also suffered abuse and seeing with your own eyes that they are good, nice, kind, decent people. You will quickly understand that they did not cause their abuse and neither did you cause yours.

When you hear other victims in a group express their feelings of rage, hatred and fear, you will know that your own violent feelings are normal and that you are not crazy. By listening to others talk about their problems and fears, you can gain new insights into your own, and you will even find yourself helping other members of the group based on your own experiences. By helping other members, you not only bring the lesson home to yourself but you increase your feelings of self-esteem.

The drawbacks of group therapy are that you do not receive the individual attention you would have in private sessions and your therapy may take longer because the focus of the group will not always be on you. The group leader may sometimes cut you off before you have a resolved an issue if she or he believes that the focus has remained on you too long and other members are getting restless. There may also be times when you simply do not want to raise an issue in front of a group, although in a well-run group, once trust develops, members are usually able to share even their worst fears and experiences. However, some group therapists do not encourage members to let out the depth of feeling expected in individual therapy because they believe the group will become too unruly. This reluctance to allow members to experience emotions is one of the major defects in some groups because it deprives member of the catharsis that they desperately need.

There are benefits and drawbacks to either choice. Starting with individual therapy does not mean you can never have the benefits of a group. Many abuse victims join groups after they have been in individual therapy for a while. If you cannot afford both, you may be able to find or form a support group of abuse survivors your age. Although you would not have a therapist in the group, you probably do not need one if most of the members have been through some therapy. If a majority of the group has had some therapy, you should have enough knowledge to run it yourselves. You might even ask or hire a therapist to get the group started. Once the group gets going, most groups run themselves anyway.

There are many ways to get the group support you need. I talked to friends about my abuse and got the names of other Adults Molested As Children (AMACs) in my state. We formed a telephone support network and we call each other when we need someone to talk to. The important thing is that we know we are not alone and that there is always someone we can go to if we are in trouble or need to ask a question we are afraid to ask anyone else.

Once you feel as though you have a handle on some of your pain and problems, you can consider trying other types of therapy. If you are pleased with your progress, stick with what you are doing. If you want to move more quickly or you are not satisfied, change. Every group and every therapist is different and somewhere out there is the right one for you. You only have to search for it.

Special note for adolescents

If you are an adolescent, group therapy is clearly the best choice for you.[50] Since most adolescents find it difficult to sit still for an hour and talk to a stranger about feelings and sexual matters, they often find individual therapy uncomfortable and may not attend regularly. On the other hand, you are at an age where the influence of your peers is exceptionally strong and the peer pressure of a therapy group can greatly accelerate healing. When adolescents work together on each others' problems, they tend to stay interested and committed to the group. You can improve your self-esteem by listening to your peers reveal feelings about their abuse and by experiencing the acceptance of those peers when you disclose your situation. Being accepted by a group that understands what you have suffered can increase your confidence and your feelings of self-worth.

A group can also help teenagers with behavior problems. Sexual abuse can cause antisocial behavior in teenagers, ranging from acting out, defiance, fighting, drugs, alcohol, sexual promiscuity, prostitution and other criminal behavior. Abused adolescents are often labeled "ungovernable" or are diagnosed as having conduct disorders. The negative labeling only further damages the teenager's self-esteem. But this behavior is caused by the self-hatred and anger resulting from sexual abuse. When the abuse is appropriately treated, the offensive behavior usually subsides. The label does not mean that you are hopeless.

An active therapy group where teenagers confront each other and point out each other's self-defeating behavior can be more effective than individual therapy. Although teenagers often do not recognize the harmful effects of their own behavior even when a therapist tells them, they can identify those consequences when they see them in their peers. My experience in leading adolescent groups is that teenagers are quite effective in helping each other and that they become supportive and protective of group members. The group solidarity promotes rapid therapeutic progress and significant behavioral changes occur in just a few months.

If you are an adolescent, you may be afraid of joining a group because you think your abuse is so terrible no one will understand. You may also fear rejection or ridicule by the group. Although I have never seen that happen, I know it may be difficult for you to believe that other kids could be nice and still be in the same boat as you. Perhaps it will help you to know that you don't have to tell your story or say anything the first day or even the first weeks unless you want to. Most groups have a formal rule that you don't have to participate unless you choose to. You can just sit back and listen to the other group members talk about their abuse until you feel comfortable sharing your experience.

If after a few sessions you want to leave, you can. You have the same control over your healing and your life that adults do. But I hope you won't reject the powerful support a group can give you. I believe it's worth trying a group to see if it will help you stop the pain you feel now.

A *male or female therapist*

In most situations where one is choosing among professionals, the question of gender does not matter; but whether a therapist is male or female can make a difference in cases of sexual abuse. If the sex of the therapist is the same as that of a victim's primary abuser, the therapy may be impeded. If you are a woman and you were sexually abused by a man, it may be difficult for you to develop a relationship of trust with a male therapist. It may also be harder for you to discuss the intimate details of your abuse with a man than it would be with a woman. Many women who have repressed memories find that they cannot recover them with a male therapist under hypnosis and have to switch to a woman. Most women tend to be more comfortable with a woman therapist and to feel that their emotions are understood more readily.

This does not mean that a male therapist cannot be effective for a woman or that a man cannot understand abuse experienced by a woman. In some respects having a male therapist can be an advantage for a woman. If a woman has difficulty in relationships with men and her lack of trust stems from abuse by a male, learning to trust and work with a male therapist can be a huge step toward healing. But it may take a very long time to take that step, and most abused women are in such pain that they need to work on their abuse immediately. They can often do that faster and develop trust more quickly with a woman. They can always work on issues of trust with a male therapist later, if they need to do so.

The same is true for males. Kent had been sodomized by a neighbor when he was a child and was very embarrassed talking to me about what had happened. He was candid enough to say that he felt uncomfortable discussing the situation, especially the subject of orgasm, even though he had questions about it which were extremely disturbing to him. I had his case transferred to a male therapist.

Most of us have not been brought up to openly discuss the intimate details of our sex lives with anyone, let alone a member of the opposite sex. It is not easy to talk to a stranger, and therapy is hard enough without adding additional obstacles. You should choose a therapist with whom you can be relaxed and open, one you can trust. Be aware of the potential problems of choosing a therapist of the same sex as your abuser, but choose the one, male or female, that you like the best.

Cost and how to pay for therapy

Therapy is expensive. A session usually lasts fifty minutes—to give therapists a chance to take notes, return phone calls and collect their thoughts in the ten minutes before the next client arrives. As this book is being written, the cost of an individual session is between $45 and $100. In most cities of reasonable size, it is difficult to find a therapist who charges less than $60 or $75 per session. Psychiatrists may charge $125 per hour or more because they have a medical degree. But if you do not need medicine, you are not going to use that expertise. Psychologists generally charge less than psychiatrists and clinical social workers sometimes charge less again.

How often do you have to attend sessions at these prices? Most therapists recommend a minimum of once an week—twice a week if you are in real distress. If you go less than once a week, it is difficult to maintain any kind of continuity. Both you and your therapist will have a hard time remembering where you left off at the last session. It is disruptive to have to stop your train of thought or emotional state at the end of 50 minutes, and it is difficult to pick up where you left off after more than a week has gone by.

A lot goes on in your life during a week and you may have many new events you want to talk about instead of returning to what you were working on at the last session. You will become frustrated because you never finish anything. If you are away for more than a week, you could find yourself spending your entire session just catching your therapist up on what has happened to you in the interim, with no time left to work on issues. You will make more progress if you see your therapist every week.

However, not everyone can or wants to fit into the traditional pattern. Some people who are sufficiently disciplined and knowledge-able about their own treatment may arrange to see a therapist twice a month or even once a month, usually after they have seen the therapist more often on a regular basis for a few months. These people work out a treatment program with their therapist and do a lot of the work themselves at home. They consult with their therapists on an "as needed" basis.

I believe we all have the ability to heal ourselves and have found there is a lot you can do on your own. I give my clients homework and encourage them to read self-help books and to work on issues by themselves. There are an infinite number of things you can do yourself if you want to. I do think, however, that it would be difficult for someone with MPD to work alone, at least initially, and the same is true of other abuse victims who have blocked memories. You should start on a regular weekly schedule for the first six months or so before you consider a lighter schedule.

On the other hand, I do not believe it is necessary to see your therapist four or five days a week unless you are in a period of extreme crisis. Most people cannot tolerate the stress of working on their problems with such intensity. They need some time to digest what they work on and to adjust to their new discoveries. You need some time off to escape from your problems, especially when you are delving into grim incidents from your past. You can't dwell on your abuse every day. You need an opportunity to rest, heal, relax, have fun and enjoy things in the present.

Most therapists recognize the financial and emotional problems of requiring clients to come to sessions five days a week on a regular basis. The only therapists I know of who demand that their patients come four or five days every week are psychoanalysts. Since analysts rarely direct their patients or even have conversations with them, the way analysts obtain information about their patients is by listening to their stream of consciousness, their uncensored speech and how they associate one idea with another. It is a laborious way of searching for tiny pieces of a jigsaw puzzle and trying to fit them together. That is why, despite the fact that analysts see their patients four or five times a week, analysis takes from two to five times longer to complete than other kinds of therapy. And there is no evidence that analysis is any more effective or lasting. Many celebrities choose analysis in the belief that because it is more expensive it must be better. The results can be seen in their lives and in their books. As I have discussed, analysis is not an appropriate treatment for sexual abuse cases, and the cost also makes it prohibitive.

So how do you do pay for your therapy if you are not an Arab sheik, Elizabeth Taylor or David Bowie?

First of all, it is important to get your priorities straight. Is it more important for you to have a new boat, car, house or dress, or to get rid of your abuse problems and feel better? What are you willing to give up to have a happier life, and what can you give up? What do you want most?

You have to place *your* wellbeing first. You can't be much help to your family if you don't help yourself. Your unresolved abuse issues, especially those of mistrust, anger, hatred and fear of loving, will get in the way of your relationships until you resolve them.

If you are willing to make your treatment a priority in your life, take some risks and make some compromises, there are ways to finance your therapy. If you do not have sufficient funds to pay for therapy, all states have publicly funded mental health programs, and most have programs specifically designed for cases of sexual abuse. Some public agencies charge no fee at all or have a very low minimum depending on your income.

Private voluntary agencies, such as local mental health centers and family service association centers, have well-trained therapists and sliding-fee scales. The availability, cost and expertise for therapy provided by public and nonprofit agencies vary greatly from state to state and community to community, but these agencies are certainly worth exploring if you are on a limited budget. The only drawback is that you may not be able to choose your therapist, although most programs will try to assign a therapist with whom you feel comfortable. This means you have to investigate the reputation of the agency you select. You should ask for a therapist experienced in cases of sexual abuse. In most agencies these days, you should be able to find someone with that experience.

One of the simplest ways of financing your therapy is through mental health insurance coverage. The policies of many large organizations provide insurance that covers their employees for therapy, although most have a substantial deductible and some have limitations on the number of visits and on the overall cost.

If you do not have mental health insurance where you work, you can find out what companies in your area have group health insurance plans that cover therapy and then change jobs so that you are covered for at least part of your therapy. Many group insurance plans do not have a waiting period for coverage, but you should check the plan so you know how soon your therapy will be covered. If you do not want to ask your employer about coverage for therapy, just obtain the name of the insurance company and the group number from your employer. Then you can telephone the insurance company directly to ask for details of coverage. Your employer will never know. Many state and local government entities and school districts also have excellent plans. The Federal Government used to have adequate coverage for mental health but has been reducing its benefits over the past decade.

It may seem strange to pick a job based on insurance coverage, but that may be your best alternative for financing your therapy, and you might be surprised at how many wonderful jobs there are that also have the insurance coverage you want. People in clerical jobs have the largest number of choices and can easily find an opening in government or a large company. If you need help in finding a job you like, I highly recommend Richard Bolles' classic guide to job hunting, *What Color is Your Parachute?*

You may already belong to groups or organizations that have insurance plans covering therapy. Almost all colleges and universities have either their own in-house counseling programs or student health insurance plans. You may be able to save money by enrolling in a class or two or even a part-time degree program in order to get the insurance coverage. And you may really enjoy the classes you take. You may even find, when you finish your therapy, that you have a new degree and a whole new career!

There are all kinds of groups and associations you can join that have group health insurance plans. Most professional groups have plans, as do associations of independent artists, writers, retired people and alumni associations, etc. My lawyer husband joined the local branch of the Farm Bureau to obtain his medical insurance and he has certainly never milked a cow. The possibilities are endless. You only have to be creative and find out what is available in your community. Your local mental health facility may have some suggestions and your public library and chamber of commerce could be fertile sources of information.

If you cannot find a job with adequate insurance, you still have other options. Depending on your credit record, you may also be able to obtain a loan to finance your therapy. It will be easier if you can use equity in your home or other assets for collateral. But if you have lived in your community for a while and know your banker or credit union executive, you may be able to obtain an unsecured loan. Again, whether or not you want to do this depends on how committed you are to getting help at whatever cost. I figured that I would enjoy whatever money I had more after I worked out my problems, so I might as well delay my gratification and devote my money to therapy.

What if you cannot find insurance or get a commercial loan? Most therapists are fairly understanding about the financial problems involved in therapy, especially since many insurance companies have reduced their mental health coverage over the last few years. Many therapists will try to work with you to find a mutually acceptable method of payment. Some mental health facilities and some therapists work on a sliding scale of fees that is based on the client's ability to pay. If your income meets the guidelines, you may be able to pay less for each session than the usual rate.

Another possibility is arranging for deferred payment. This is often easier if you have been working with the therapist for some time and have a record of making regular payments. If you know that you will be graduating and getting a job, getting a raise or receiving a large fee, some therapists will let you defer payment until you are able to pay. I have always been grateful to my therapist in Utah for waiting for a large portion of her fee until my house sold in Washington, D.C. It took more than a year and she never even mentioned it.

Some therapists reserve a couple of hours a week for clients who cannot afford to pay. These therapists have usually chosen the profession because they want to help people. I know a wonderful therapist who was very poor as a child and was given help when he needed it. The therapist vowed to do the same for others when he could,and has helped several clients who could not afford to pay. He says, "I'm just putting back in what I took out." He is finding now that some of his former patients are paying him back years later, and he is using the money to help more people. So if you are really in desperate straights and you look hard enough, you may find a therapist who will take you in a free slot.

But not all therapists can afford to be that generous. The only thing a therapist has to sell is time, and therapists have only a limited number of hours to see clients because the strain of helping people in emotional crisis is exhausting. Therapists cannot effectively treat clients 40 or even 30 hours a week or they burn out. A great deal of time is also consumed in paperwork, record keeping, and returning telephone calls for which there is usually no compensation. So you should not take it personally if a therapist cannot take you as a client for free or on the basis of deferred payment.

These are the most realistic alternatives for paying your therapist. There are certainly many others if you are creative. Perhaps you have something that your therapist would be willing to barter for. My husband had a beautiful cedar fence built for us in lieu of legal fees. You might find a way of working off your therapy fees. And if you are game for a really radical solution, you can follow in the footsteps of a few courageous souls I know and move to country that has national health insurance, like England, Australia or Scandinavia. If you meet the requirements, your therapy would be absolutely free for as long as you need it. But be sure to carefully check the country's work requirements and mental health insurance requirements before you hop on the plane.

If you want to obtain therapy badly enough, you will find a way. You will look hard enough, ask enough people for help, and a path will open up for you. In the end, obtaining the help of a therapist is not a question of money, it is a matter of commitment. If you are sufficiently committed and want to get help, you will find it.

Of all the people there are in your lifetime,
you are the only one you will never lose
and the only one who will never leave.
John Bradshaw

V SELF–HELP TECHNIQUES

When I browse in a bookstore, I am always amazed at the infinite variety of ways people around the world have found to help us feel better. These ideas, theories, philosophies and religions range from acupuncture to zen. I never know what to choose. Being a recovering perfectionist, I always want to choose the perfect answer for me.

Recently I have found that the universe is benevolent and gives you what you need when you need it. People who follow this philosophy also believe that you will be drawn instinctively to those books, records, tapes and people that will help you the most. Although I have not had the experience of books falling off the shelves at my feet as some people claim, by trusting my instincts when I look at the titles, I have always chosen books that are exactly what I need at the moment. I am not sure this is totally serendipitous; perhaps any new knowledge is bound to be helpful.

I have tried to give you a head start by selecting techniques that have been tested by abuse victims and found to be effective. The ones I have chosen are designed to alleviate specific problems experienced by the majority of victims, such as extreme anxiety, depression, fear, anger, feelings of worthlessness, uncontrollable emotions, and a sense of helplessness. A couple of exercises are designed especially for victims of sexual abuse. But these are just a start; the list is neither exclusive or exhaustive. There are hundreds—no, thousands—of ways to help you heal and be happy. You will find those which are right for you.

Some of you may feel too depressed, despairing or unmotivated to try some of these techniques. You may not even want to continue reading. I remember when it took too much effort to even get out of bed and the times when I hurt too much to move. I can only hope that you will take one small step toward healing yourself, either by finding a therapist or by trying one of these techniques for a week. I wish I could take your hand and pull you out of the hole, but I can't. You have to do it yourself. I can only promise you that there *is* a way out—if you will only open the door.

None of these techniques is very difficult and none requires more than a grammar school education. If you can read the instructions, you can do these techniques. You can do them in any order, but it helps to know a quick relaxation technique to put you in the proper frame of mind for meditation, visualization or hypnosis. Most of these techniques have been used by people all over the world for generations because they are relaxing and fun and because they make people feel better and more in control of their lives.

1. How to relieve stress

Stress reduction is perhaps the most useful method of self-help for survivors of sexual abuse. Sexual abuse creates stress of the most extreme and overwhelming magnitude. Abuse victims are subjected to intolerable stress at the time of their abuse, and they continue to carry that stress inside them as long as they suppress memories and emotions connected with their abuse. Stress can be stored just as memories and feelings are stored in various parts of the body. Techniques such as rolfing (a deep massage therapy) and acupuncture have been shown to release trauma stored in the body. When a certain spot is pressed or pierced with a needle, people vividly recall memories and reexperience emotions they had long repressed.

Women who have been raped as children may experience pain with intercourse or their menstrual cycles, even though their doctors are unable to detect any physical injury or cause, because they have stored their stress in their pelvic areas. Once these women recover repressed memories of childhood sexual abuse, the pain may mysteriously disappear. Many of these women find that when they become anxious even now, they feel the tension in their pelvic areas and store the tension there.

Survivors of abuse also have to deal with past stress in the present because the stressful feelings they felt at the time of their abuse—like repressed feelings of anger, fear and hatred—can be triggered by events resembling the past acts of abuse. If a victim was raped in the middle of the night, the slightest sound at night may precipitate an unconscious reawakening of memories of the rape and cause the victim to react with intense anxiety. The victim's heart may pound and the victim may shake uncontrollably for a long time. In fact, many stimuli that would provoke only a brief startle reaction in the majority of people can cause intense and prolonged fear reactions in victims of sexual abuse.

And if stress from the past is not enough, people who have been sexually abused are under intense stress every day of their lives trying to cope with the aftereffects of their abuse. Therapy itself is a strain which requires survivors to reexperience the emotions they felt during their abuse and face painful truths about their past and about present behavior patterns. And none of this takes into consideration the additional day to day stress of coping with modern society which sends many non-abuse victims to the hospital!

Most victims live in a constant state of anxiety and fear. Their thoughts race out of control and these thoughts are usually grim—fears of disasters occurring, of failing and of being hurt or betrayed. Most survivors have never experienced the sensation of inner calm or peace for any period of time. If any of this seems familiar to you, then you may be surprised to find that there are many simple ways you can learn to feel that inner peace and to control your thoughts and your stress.

A number of techniques will reduce your stress level. I will briefly describe the ones other abuse victims and I have found to be the most helpful. Choose the ones that most appeal to you and that you will enjoy doing on a regular basis. A list of references on exercise and stress reduction techniques is provided at the end of this book.

2. What is stress?

Stress is physical or mental pressure, and it can be positive or negative. Dr. Hans Selye defines stress as "the sum total of wear and tear on the person." Zerin see stress in a positive light as "your life energy to feel, think and act, seeking to express itself." Both can be true: stress can be a motivating or a destructive force, but we are concerned with eliminating the negative kind, the kind that causes disease and even death.

It is really not stress but "distress" or "stress gone bad" which causes heart attacks and other stress-related illnesses. Creative stress and hard work can actually prolong life; only negative stress kills. Exposure to a stressful stimulus creates a response in humans which we have had for millions of years. It is popularly called the "fight-or-flight" response, and it is a genetic mechanism that produces an increase in our blood pressure, muscle blood flow, rate of breathing, metabolism and heart rate. You have seen this response in other animals. Cats, for instance, arch their backs and their hair stands on end when they are frightened and ready to fight or run. The human response was designed to give us the ability to respond to danger by running away with extra energy or fighting with extra strength. But neither choice is socially acceptable in our technological society. Can you imagine a frightened employee sprinting away from an intimidating employer at a staff meeting?

Although we still have an abundance of fear, we respond in more "civilized" ways at least outwardly, but our bodies still react in the primitive way predetermined by our genetic programming. As a result, increased adrenalin remains unused in our systems and the physiological changes created by the fight-or flight response become dangerous to the very bodies they were designed to protect.

So what can we do to protect ourselves from the impact of stress?

3. Exercising to reduce stress

Exercise is one way of turning off the harmful effects of the fight-or-flight response and of using up our excess adrenalin. It is a substitute for running away or fighting. Our bodies don't care whether we are running from an assailant or in the New York marathon as long as the stress is released. And exercise is one of the best ways to release stress from our systems.

Studies have shown that health is substantially improved with a program of regular exercise. But I am not going to bore you with the details; I am sure you are already aware of all of the benefits of exercise on your physical health.

Are you aware, though, that exercise is now being prescribed by therapists as the single most effective way of combating depression? It outperforms drugs, shock treatment and even therapy itself. Exercise causes the brain to release endorphins, hormones which make you feel euphoric, the same hormones released during lovemaking. You may have heard of "runner's high," the state of bliss runners often experience, somewhat like a drug high, caused by the release of endorphins.

Runners often endure the painful aspects of running to reach this euphoric state. Other types of exercise may not produce such dramatic states of pleasure as running, but they also generate the production of endorphins and will make you feel noticeably better in a short period of time.

I don't know how I would have survived finding out about my childhood abuse without exercise. Exercise was a wonderful escape from the horror of thoughts from the past. I chose fast walking and hiking for my summer exercises and skiing in the winter. I decided against running because my gynecologist told me it places a strain on the pelvic region and I already had problems with painful periods.

If you are considering running, I urge you to read both the pros and cons of adopting this form of exercise. Many injuries have resulted from running; some women have developed pelvic problems and many runners have required knee operations. The same precautions apply to aerobics. Although aerobics are beneficial for conditioning your heart because your pulse is raised to an optimal rate, aerobics can cause injuries to your knees, feet and other parts of your body, especially if executed on an unsuitable surface. Aerobics should only be performed on a suspended wooden floor. Most experts now recommend only low impact aerobics for the majority of people in order to reduce the strain and danger of injury.

One half-hour to 45 minutes of brisk walking provides the same heart and general health benefits of jogging without any of the dangers. Walking also has some other advantages. You have an opportunity to be outside and, if you live near a park or wilderness area, you can watch birds, squirrels, chipmunks, potguts (in Utah) and even homo sapiens. They provide amusement with their antics as well as a diversion from your unpleasant thoughts.

If you want to avoid weather extremes, you might try an exercise bicycle. You can relieve the boredom by purchasing an inexpensive reading stand for your favorite novel or self-help book or by watching a video while you pedal. If you want to invest a substantial sum, you can bicycle down the Riviera and other exotic places by watching a television screen on an electronic bicycle.

I don't recommend commercial spas and fitness centers because they often promise more than they deliver, and I do not like the tactics some use to trap unsuspecting consumers into lengthy and expensive contracts which the consumers will seldom use and probably cannot afford. There are better ways to exercise that are free or much less expensive. Compare the costs and facilities of commercial clubs to those at your local community recreation center or the YWCA/YMCA. If you find the commercial centers more to your liking or more convenient, try one for a short time before signing any contract. Be sure to inspect the facility thoroughly before you sign anything and consider carefully whether you will really continue to use the facility for the entire term of the contact because you won't get your money back. Congress was so concerned by the large number of fraudulent practices perpetrated by the commercial spas and fitness centers, that it passed a federal law giving consumers the right to back out of their contracts within three days of signing. But you should also protect yourself; *do not sign any contract unless you read and understand it.*

Swimming is an excellent way to tone your body and get exercise. It does not put undue strain on any part of your body; you can even do it safely if you are pregnant.

There are dozens of other ways to exercise: mountain climbing, tennis, golf (if you avoid carts and walk fast), all types of dancing, team sports, trampoline jumping, and scuba diving. Anything that makes you move your body and increases your pulse rate is great. My favorite is skiing because you can meet people or be alone and you can fly through the sparkling snow, smell the pine trees, and feel the sun and the wind on your body. If you keep going and push yourself a bit, it is wonderful exercise. But you have to choose the method that is right for you.

Exercise for busy people or couch potatoes

If you are a confirmed couch potato and hate everything I have said about exercise, or if you are just too busy to add another thing to your day, have I got a deal for you. Could I convince you to try an exercise program for 10 minutes a day three times a week? Yes, that's 30 minutes for the entire week. And it works! I used this program for a couple of years when I was a diplomat because I was traveling so much and never had time to exercise. But I could do this program even in the Oriental Hotel in Bangkok.

The program is a combination of specific muscle building exercises coupled with a few minutes of aerobics. I used rock dancing because I could always find rock music on local stations, even in remote parts of India or the rural Philippines. The exercises are designed in three stages so you can work up to an optimal level. Yes, there is a catch but it is not what you think. It is just that I cannot give you the program because it is quite detailed, covering a series of exercises for three stages of advancement, and copyrighted by Laurence Morehouse and Leonard

Gross in their paperback book, *Total Fitness in 30 Minutes a Week*. I recommend it for improving your health and mental state although it is not as much fun as other forms of exercise, nor does it offer the opportunity to get out of your apartment or house and meet interesting people.

Whatever you choose, pick one or two things you really enjoy and then make a commitment to do them regularly. Do them especially when you don't feel like doing them. That is usually when you are depressed and need exercise the most. I guarantee that if you force yourself to exercise when you feel tired or blue, you will feel better.

Even if you have a cold, exercise will help; you will find yourself recovering faster. If you have been injured or have had surgery, check with a sports physical therapist to see whether there are exercises you can do to help you get back on your feet faster. The worst thing for your body is to lie in bed. Did you know that you can lose 50 percent of your muscle tone just by lying in bed for 24 hours? So if you are ill or injured, don't rely solely on your family physician to tell you what exercises you can do; doctors are not always aware of all of the techniques to make you heal faster. Consult a physical therapist too. When my doctor told me it would take a couple of months to heal after a ski injury, I was back on skis in four weeks with the help of a sports physical therapist. Many injured Olympic hopefuls are up and running almost immediately after sustaining serious injuries.

Exercise is essential for survivors of sexual abuse not only because it reduces stress, improves health and makes you feel better, as if that were not enough, but because it also improves your self-esteem. By exercising, you are taking care of yourself. You are acknowledging to yourself that you are important and you are demonstrating that you care for yourself. You are starting to give yourself the loving care that you missed as a child. And by exercising, you are proving to yourself that you can take control of your life, that you are in charge of how you look and how you feel. Exercise puts you well on the road to healing yourself.

Some people march to a different drummer,
and some people polka.
Unknown

239

4. Meditation –
How to achieve inner peace

How many times have you wished you could turn off your mind? How often have you prayed for just one moment of peace, a moment without pain, fear, sadness, anger or thoughts of your abuse? What would you give to have inner peace whenever you want? There is a way—it's easy and it's free. It's been around for hundreds of years, but we, in our fast-paced industrialized society, have ignored it until recently. It's called meditation.

The word "meditation" usually conjures up visions of saffron-colored robes, shaved heads, crossed legs and the slightly sickening scent of incense. Would you believe that thousands of bankers, lawyers and executives—men and women—meditate in their executive chairs every day while their secretaries hold their calls? Housewives, clerical workers, nurses, teachers and therapists find a quiet spot, slip off their shoes and slip into a state of peace every day. Some large corporations even hold meditation breaks twice a day instead of coffee breaks. And the Seattle-Tacoma International Airport has a clearly marked "Meditation Room" for frazzled travelers.

Meditation is no longer only for mystics. Western society has discovered that the old gurus really had something, that the ancient eastern wisdom works, and that meditation is not only applicable to our modern society but may be its savior. Meditation is a way to quiet your mind, relax, find inner peace, help you sleep, increase your energy and concentration, and lower your blood pressure—*all without drugs.*

With all that, you may think meditation must be very complicated and takes years of study. Actually, meditation is a very simple process you can learn in five minutes. Then, you may think it must cost a lot to learn. No, although there are companies that will take your money to teach you to meditate if you want to pay. There is no catch because meditation is a natural process and *anyone* can learn it. (Not all of those gurus could have been geniuses.) *I* can teach you how to meditate because the process is hundreds of years old and I doubt that even Buddha has a copyright which lasts that long.

There are many types of meditation, or at least they have different names. But the methods and goals are very similar. The basic principle is to quiet your mind, to assume a passive attitude to allow your mind to take a break from its ceaseless stream of thoughts. By emptying your mind of thoughts and distractions, you can achieve a state that may be

240

even more restful than sleep. Meditation has been found to lower your oxygen consumption, blood pressure and heart rate as does sleep, but it also produces alpha waves, slower brain waves that indicate peace and contentment and are not usually present in a sleep state.

When you meditate, you are totally relaxed—not just in your body but in your mind. Yet you are not asleep and you never lose control. Although you empty your mind of thoughts, you remain aware of your surroundings and can answer a phone or respond coherently to someone who enters the room. But a word of warning: it is best to meditate where you will not be interrupted. You should try to find a quiet place to meditate because if something does disturb you during meditation, it is like being jerked awake from a nap and you are left with a jangled feeling rather than one of peace. You should come out of meditation gently, taking two or three minutes to become alert before you start moving.

To begin meditating, follow these simple steps.

1. Find a quiet place where you will not be interrupted for twenty minutes. (Once you are used to it, you can meditate anywhere, in buses, jets, or at dull parties.)

2. Get into a comfortable position, but do not lie down because you may fall asleep and that is not the state you are seeking. Sit comfortably in a chair or, if you have the flexibility, assume the "lotus position" used in Yoga. This position involves crossing your ankles over your thighs. If you are uncomfortable, forget it. Your goal is to be totally relaxed. You should however keep your spine straight whatever position you choose.

3. Choose something to focus on. It can be an object if you want to keep your eyes open or even a sound. The Japanese focus on a "tokonoma," a simple but beautiful painting or floral arrangement that is often the only ornament in the room. But most people find it easier to ignore distractions if their eyes are closed, so they focus on a mantra, a word, line from a prayer or some other spiritual statement that is meaningful to them.

Dr. Herbert Benson, a professor at the Harvard Medical School, conducted studies on the physiological effects of meditation and concluded that whether you use a mantra, a prayer, or the word "One"—Dr. Benson's suggestion—the results are the same, both physically and mentally.[51] Dr. Benson's book, *The Relaxation Response*, teaches you to meditate in two pages and contains fascinating research on the positive physiological changes meditation produces, as well as a history of the use of meditation throughout the ages—and it's very readable.

His most recent book, *Your Maximum Mind*, goes beyond *The Relaxation Response* and delves into the effects spiritual experiences have on the mind. Benson concludes that meditation is more effective in achieving attitude and behavior changes when combined with spiritual beliefs, and he recommends that you choose a word or phrase that is part of your personal belief system. If you are Jewish, you might choose "Shalom" or, if you are Christian, "The Lord is my shepherd," from the Twenty-third Psalm. If you are not religious, you might select a neutral word like "One," "Love" or "Peace."

The purpose of these words is to give you a focus so you will not be distracted by outside disturbances or by your own thoughts. If the words are inspiring, they act somewhat like an affirmation, programming you with positive thoughts. They may also create a spiritual state in your mind which will have a profound effect on your feelings and your health.

4. Sit comfortably, close your eyes, and use whatever method will start the relaxation process for you. Some people use a deep breathing technique, others use progressive muscle relaxation. Both are described later in this book. I like to start by taking a few deep breaths and then focusing on my breathing. After you have been meditating for a while, you will be able to abbreviate or omit this step and just go directly into meditation.

When you feel somewhat relaxed, focus on breathing through your nose and each time you exhale, think in your mind the word or phrase you have chosen. For example, inhale and then as you exhale, think the word "Peace," inhale and then while exhaling, think "Peace," and continue to repeat this pattern throughout the period of meditation. Just breathe naturally and slowly.

If thoughts intrude, and they will, first acknowledge the thought, let it simply drift away, and return your focus to your word or phrase. Do not fight the thoughts or try to force them out of your mind; you will only create anxiety. It is normal to have thoughts, you have had them for a long time. Just notice them and let them float through your mind, always returning to the word or phrase you are saying to yourself. Sometimes if I am really nervous and my thoughts are racing, I say my word to myself both as I inhale and as I exhale until I am more relaxed. When I am deeply relaxed, I say the word less frequently or sometimes not at all. As with all of these methods, you will use what is right for you. In any event, you will find your thoughts decreasing the longer you practice meditation.

Nothing specific is *supposed* to happen when you meditate, except that you become more relaxed. Everyone has his or her particular experience. So don't worry if you don't think you are achieving the "proper" state or changes in your mental attitude or anxiety level. Just continue to practice meditation for a month or so and you will begin to notice an increasing sense of peace.

242

5. The optimal time for meditating is 10 to 20 minutes once or twice a day. It is better to wait for a couple of hours after meals before meditating because meditation may interfere with digestion.

When you start meditating, the 10 or 20 minutes may seem endless and you will be constantly checking your watch. But after you have practiced for a few weeks, you will find that you no longer have to check the time. Time may seem to pass quickly and your eyes will open automatically after 10 or 20 minutes when your body is sufficiently relaxed.

6. Do not get up abruptly when you have finished meditating. If you stand up quickly you may get dizzy, just as if you stood up abruptly from a nap. Sit quietly for a few minutes and then get up slowly, inhaling as you stand. Savor the peace you have attained for yourself.

7. Dr. Benson suggests an additional step for going beyond relaxation into greater personal growth. After you stop meditating, focus your mind for another five or ten minutes on something positive, a prayer, a passage from a self-help book or even a happy picture. By concentrating on a positive concept, you are imprinting the concept on your brain while it is in its most relaxed and receptive state. Dr. Benson has found the combination of total relaxation during meditation combined with concentration after mediation to be a powerful tool for personal change.

Happiness is a butterfly, which, when pursued is always just beyond your grasp, but which, if you will sit quietly, may alight upon you.
Nathaniel Hawthorne

5. Mindfulness –
How to focus on the present

Survivors of sexual abuse frequently find their thoughts fixated on their past abuse. This fixation on past pain makes it difficult to enjoy present moments, especially during the months of therapy when they are digging up all of the gory details of their abuse. Most survivors feel that they are trapped in a never-ending nightmare. Their silent prayer is, "If I only could forget about it for a day, even an hour."

With therapy and time, the ugly thoughts will begin to subside. But what do you do in the meantime?

There is an answer: mindfulness meditation, a recently revived technique developed from the Buddhist practice of Vipassana meditation. Despite its exotic origins, mindfulness is a simple technique that teaches full awareness of the present moment and present action. Most of us spend our lives ruminating on the past or worrying about the future. Mindfulness is a way of focusing on the here-and-now, of truly living in the present. It is a way of learning to live each moment as if it were our first and as if it were our last.

We spend so much time racing around, trying to get things done, that we fail to enjoy our lives, our friends, our families and the beauty around us. We are always trying to get something done, not realizing that the joy is in *doing* it. We become anxious because we are always doing; we never just are. Our motion sickness makes us "mindless," rather than "mindful." Kirkegaard observed: "Most men and women pursue pleasure with such a breathless pace that they hurry past it."

Mindfulness helps us become aware of what is happening in the present moment by releasing us from our obsessive thoughts, our worries and our fears. This technique teaches us to become a "detached observer" of our thoughts and feelings, by acknowledging them for what they are and then letting them go. It is when we become attached to our thoughts that we upset ourselves.

Mindfulness involves a dual process: awareness of our inner thoughts and feelings coupled with all of our external perceptions and actions. This duality is reflected in the steps for achieving mindfulness.

1. The first step of mindfulness meditation is to sit comfortably, as in meditation, and relax. Close your eyes and notice your breathing. Breathing is extremely important for meditation and for reducing stress in general. If you are breathing from the upper part of your chest and your shoulders are rising and falling when you breathe, your breathing is too shallow and you will find it difficult to relax. Proper breathing comes from the diaphragm, the area in your abdomen below your ribs. You can see how your diaphragm works by lying on the floor and watching it as you breathe. You should always breathe from your diaphragm, as deeply, slowly and rhythmically as possible. As you start your mindfulness meditation, notice your breath and, each time you exhale, notice how you let go, of your breath and of your tension.

2. Focus your attention on the tip of your nose and feel your breath entering and leaving your nostrils. Feel your breath going in and out of your nostrils. And after a moment, just let yourself be aware of your breath as it leaves your nostrils. Throughout this meditation, keep your

attention focused on your nostrils as you exhale each breath.

3. Observe your thoughts and feelings as they enter your mind; do not try to suppress them. One of the purposes of this exercise is to become aware of your thoughts and feelings. So as they come up, just notice what type of thought or feeling you have and label it. For example: "My stomach is growling and it's almost time for dinner," you might label "hunger;" and "I'll never get all my work done," you could label "worry" or "job;" and "My foot hurts," would be "pain." After you have labeled the thought, return your attention back to your breath. Do not resist your thoughts because *what you resist persists*.

You also want to avoid judging your thoughts; remember you are only a detached observer. It may help to just say in your mind, "Ah, that's a sex thought," or "Oh, that's another worry thought." Be merciful with yourself as you watch your thoughts. Notice your lack of mercy.

Watching your thoughts and feelings can give you great insight into your abuse and the emotional reactions it created. You will start to see behavior patterns and notice stimuli which trigger fear, anxiety and anger. Once you become aware of these patterns, they will be within your control.

4. Mindfulness meditation should be performed for 15 or 20 minutes once or twice a day depending on your schedule and what feels comfortable to you. But it can also be practiced during your daily activities in a variety of ways.

Jerry Braza, Ph.D., an expert on health and stress reduction at the University of Utah, introduced me to the concept of mindfulness. He proposed to our class that we try to take a walk or do any simple task such as washing dishes, mindfully every day for a week, focusing on all of the sensations of the present moment. When thoughts came into our heads, we were to label them and let them float by.

I chose to practice mindfulness during my daily walk in my garden and I thought it would be a cinch because I had learned to still my thoughts through meditation. But this was different. I had a great deal of difficulty shutting off thoughts of past and future while I was actively doing something, as opposed to sitting cross-legged with my eyes closed. I became aware of how much time I spend thinking about what was and what might be, and how little time on what is. I thought I had always been mindful when I took walks, that I had noticed and appreciated the beauty and the flow of nature. I prided myself on being someone who stopped to smell the proverbial roses. But I found that I am aware of only the tiniest fraction of what is. Yes, I watch the flight of a bird or the antics of a squirrel, if I happen to see them. I stop to gaze at a few of the prettiest flowers and some of the most impressive views. But I miss the whole, the continuum, the details, the beauty in between my moments of awareness—all that exists while I am lost in thought and worry.

As the week passed, I found myself becoming more and more aware of how unmindful I am in all facets of my life. I ignore my husband too frequently; I drift away sometimes when I am reading; I am always trying to finish something quickly to get to something else.

So mindfulness had a great deal to teach me. Mindfulness was a way of coming back to myself instead of running away from myself.

Dr. Braza recommends a number of simple exercises to make yourself more mindful, more aware of this moment. One is eating mindfully. Eat an almond or an orange slowly, biting off small pieces and chewing slowly, enjoying the taste. Touch it, smell it, feel its texture.

One of my favorite exercises is "bracketing moments." I rush from task to task all day without pausing to change pace. This exercise requires me to take mini-breaks during the day, each time I complete a task or activity. By pausing between activities, I have a chance to focus my thoughts and energy so that I can become aware of what I accomplished and what I have to do next. I am more relaxed and better able to concentrate on my next activity.

Another exercise is to scan your body for any tension during the day or while you are meditating. You can use breathing exercises or progressive relaxation to release the tension.

Dr. Braza also suggests planning a "day of mindfulness," where you have no schedule or "shoulds." It is better to do this alone. Whatever you do, plan to spend twice as much time doing the task. Remember the lyrics in Paul Simon's *The 59th Street Bridge Song (Feelin' Groovy)*? "Slow down. You move too fast. 'Got to make the morning last."

Mindfulness is becoming a very popular new technique and there are many variations on it. Joan Borysenko, Ph.D. and director of the Mind/Body Clinic at Harvard Medical School, recommends mindfulness meditation and includes several illuminating exercises in her popular book, *Minding the Body, Mending the Mind.* Dr. Benson includes a slightly modified version of mindfulness meditation in his bestseller, *The Maximum Mind.* In this book the meditator focuses on the emotional reactions going on within and becomes more aware of the nature of his or her thoughts and feelings. This type of meditation can be a useful adjunct to psychotherapy.

The technique of mindfulness is a godsend for victims of abuse because it gives us a way of focusing on what we have in the present instead of dwelling on the faults and lacks of the past. Mindfulness teaches us to let go of our breath and our thoughts. We need to learn from children, dogs and dying people—they are mindful, they live for the moment. But dying people are no different from us. It is just that they have accepted the truth. We are all dying and we are all terminal. Each moment is all any of us has for certain.

> *It is a flaw in happiness to see beyond our bourn,*
> *It forces us in summer skies to mourn,*
> *It spoils the singing of the nightengale.*
> John Keats, *Epistle to J.H. Reynolds*

6. Quick fixes –
Brief and useful relaxation techniques

Sometimes you may want to reduce tension or release emotions but you may not have the time to exercise or meditate. That's when you can turn to "quick fixes"—techniques you can use in meetings, at parties or in other public situations, and no one will ever notice what you are doing.

Although these quick fixes are effective in removing the immediate symptoms of anxiety and stress, they are not as beneficial to your physical and mental health overall as exercise or meditation and should not be used as a substitute. They are intended for use in emergencies as a booster to the more sustained relaxation techniques. These quickies also provide an excellent way to put you in the proper frame of mind and state of relaxation to begin all kinds of meditation and mindfulness.

Progressive muscle relaxation

Progressive muscle relaxation is one of the most commonly used quick techniques for reducing physical and emotional tension because it is easy, fast and can be used surreptitiously in social settings. You can do it with your eyes open, lying down or sitting, even during a conversation—as long as you are not expected to be a master of wit and repartee. You can do progressive relaxation in a couple of minutes and feel marked relief from tension. There are several variations of this technique and I have selected the two which most people prefer.

247

1. The first is a type of tension awareness that helps you relax bit by bit.

Start by taking a deep breath—and letting it go. Be aware of how your body relaxes as you exhale. Take another couple of deep breaths and notice how your body feels as it lets go of the tension when you exhale. Your exhalations should give you the release you obtain from a good sigh of relief, your muscles slackening as your body softens its rigid posture of fear and anxiety.

Now begin to focus on your feet. Become aware of how they feel and if they feel tense. Breathe in, and, as you breathe out, let go of all of the tension in your feet. You may wish to repeat this process a couple of times until you are satisfied that the tension has been reduced. You may wish to imagine that you are inhaling peace or calm or healing into yourself and that your breath is traveling to the part you are relaxing.

When you have let go of the tension in your feet, notice how your calves and knees feel and release of any tension in your calves and knees when you exhale. Feel the tension flowing out with your breath. Then be aware of any tension in your thighs and allow it to flow out with your breath. Continue up your body, becoming aware of any tension in each part: your pelvis, abdomen, chest, back, hands, arms, shoulders, neck, face and head. You can combine body parts or separate them if you store your tension in a particular area I have not mentioned, such as your fingers. Put the sequence together in a way that is comfortable for you.

Then do a quick scan of your whole body for any remaining areas of tension. Breath peace and calm into those areas and permit yourself to let go of the tension as you exhale. Scan your body again and enjoy the increased feeling of ease and relaxation you have produced in yourself. You are now prepared to meditate or try one of the mindfulness exercises, or simply to cope more effectively with your daily tasks.

2. The second progressive relaxation exercise will make you slightly more conspicuous because you may appear to be a bit jumpy or to squirm in your chair unless you are very subtle. This technique involves tensing and relaxing your muscles and, in addition to meditation and imagery, is one of the best preparations for self-hypnosis. You can also do this technique with your eyes open but some people prefer to do it with their eyes closed so that they can really focus on the sensations.

Again, it is advisable to start with a few deep breaths, noticing how the tension flows out of your body as your breath flows out of you. Then focus on your feet—only this time tense your feet, really tighten them, curl your toes, and hold them that way for a moment. Now relax your feet all at once, letting go of all tension. Feel the relaxation in your feet, the comfort and warmth, tingling in them.

Let this feeling of relaxation move up into your calves and knees, and now tighten the muscles in your calves and knees as tight as you can, feeling the tension you have created without ever being uncomfortable or hurting yourself. Now let go and feel your muscles relax. Notice the wonderful tingling sensation of comfort and warmth. Follow this sensation up into your thighs and repeat the process, tensing and releasing every part of your body just as we did with the first exercise. Be sure to pay particular attention to your back, neck, shoulders, face and especially your jaw, since many people carry a lot of tension in these spots.

When you have finished from toes to head, scan your body for any remaining areas of tension and tense and release those places. Notice how your body feels, and thank yourself for the feeling of comfort and relaxation you have given to yourself. You can now begin hypnosis or the other exercises or return to your daily activities more relaxed and in control.

Breathing exercises

It probably seems superfluous to study breathing techniques; after all, you have been breathing successfully all of your life. But about half of the population does not breathe correctly. Improper breathing significantly affects your ability to handle stress. When people are upset or experience stress, they usually hold their breath or inhale. If they do not bring themselves back to deep regular breathing, they become short of breath, which increases their anxiety reaction.

Stop for a moment and notice how you breathe. If you are breathing in your upper chest and your shoulders are rising up and down, you are part of the half that needs to practice more effective breathing. Your breathing should start in your diaphragm, the area just under your rib cage, where your ribs make a pyramid. This area usually contains a bit of pudginess for those of us who can pinch more than an inch. If you lie on the floor, relax and breathe a few times, you will be able to see where your diaphragm is because you will see it rise and fall. It may help to place a small pillow under the small of your back while you are lying on the floor. With your abdominal muscles slightly stretched, it is almost impossible to maintain upper chest breathing. Don't push, just let your breath do the work. You will be able to feel how diaphragmatic breathing feels.

When you are sitting down or standing, close your eyes and focus on the exhalation phase of your breathing. Do not prolong your exhalation,

249

just be aware of how it feels. As you exhale, feel the heaviness as you are breathing out. As you inhale, just allow your mind to go blank. Feel the heaviness as you exhale. You may even feel this heaviness in the rest of your body as you exhale. After you have experienced the heaviness for a several complete breaths, take a deep breath and open your eyes. You may want to flex and stretch briefly before resuming your activities.

Once you get the feeling of breathing deeply and rhythmically, use deep breathing whenever you feel yourself becoming tense. Remember that shallow breathing or holding your breath will only increase your distress. Keep your mind on your breathing and see how taking deep breaths and letting the tension go when you exhale can decrease your stress. Make a habit of breathing deeply and slowly whenever you feel anxious or tense. Soon it will become an automatic reaction.

This is a simple technique for learning to do what your body was designed to do naturally. You need only breathe a half dozen times to experience relief. Although deep breathing can be a "quick fix," it also has some long-term effects. If you practice breathing properly, you will find a significant difference in your level of stress and in the way you feel in your daily life.

> *The way is smooth.*
> *Why do you throw rocks in front of you?*
> An ancient Zen saying

7. How to control your emotions when you feel out of control

My therapists taught me a seemingly magical technique for quickly controlling intense emotional states. I have found this technique miraculous for regaining my composure during periods of overwhelming fear, rage and depression. I tried it one day after I had been sobbing hysterically for at least a half hour over a particularly brutal memory of my abuse. I reached a state of calm in less than five minutes. This technique usually takes even less time to work.

The technique, Cook's Hook-up, is part of an innovative and effective program called Educational Kinesthetics (Edu-K), which is being used successfully in schools throughout the country to help kids with learning disabilities. Edu-K exercises use movement to alter programming in the brain, improve left brain-right brain functioning and increase reading ability. The Cook's Hook-up technique is designed to balance the energy in your body. Scientists have now established that our bodies contain an energy flow, and we do not function as well if the energy flow is obstructed or unbalanced. Strong emotions adversely affect the balance by increasing the energy above normal levels, and Cook's Hook-up is designed to stabilize the energy and bring it back to normal. Some people also find that they can use this technique to increase their energy level when it is low, but I use it mainly for reducing the excess energy from emotional states.

I know, it sounds like voodoo, but it *works!* Test it out before you reject it. I thought it was ridiculous and was astonished by the results.

Sit comfortably in a chair or on a sofa with your feet on the floor in front of you. Place your left leg on top of your right leg so that your left ankle is on top of your right knee. Wrap your right hand around the top of your left ankle. Then grasp the toes of your left foot with your left hand. Yes, it's a bit of a contortion, but it's designed to make a complete circle of energy with your body.

Now place the tip of your tongue on the roof of your mouth, just behind your teeth. That is the position your tongue should be in when you breathe in. When you breathe out, your tongue should drop back into the bottom of your mouth and your mouth should be slightly open as you exhale through your mouth. So, you breathe in through your nose with the tip of your tongue at the roof of your mouth. Then drop your tongue to the bottom of your mouth and breathe out with your tongue relaxed and flat at the bottom of your mouth. Do this for 30 breaths.

Then let go of your ankle and foot and put both feet flat on the floor. Your legs should be uncrossed for this part. Spread the fingers of your hands and touch the tips of each of your fingers together (thumb to thumb and pinkie to pinkie, etc.). Rest your hands in your lap with the fingers touching. Again breathe as you did before, inhaling with your mouth closed and the tip of your tongue at the top of your mouth, and exhaling with your mouth open and your tongue flat. Do this for another 30 breaths.

If you are really upset, you may need to do the two steps for a slightly longer time. As the energy balances, you may notice a slight tingling in your hands or feet.

This is an extremely useful technique when you recover painful memories. I used it to help me calm down sooner so that I could analyze what I had learned and get some perspective on it. (I also did not waste as much of my therapy time in hysterics at $65 to $90 per hour.) The therapist who taught it to me used this process herself during our sessions to keep from getting too emotionally involved in my pain. I never knew she was doing it until she taught it to me, so it can probably be done in public.

Brain Gym, a booklet used by schoolchildren, is an easy source for learning other useful Edu-K techniques.

> *It is for us to pray not for tasks equal to our powers, but for powers equal to our tasks, to go forward with a great desire forever beating at the door of our hearts as we travel towards our distant goal.*
> Helen Keller

8. Affirmations –
Reprogramming negative thoughts

Victims of abuse are constantly besieged by a flood of negative thoughts. Every day their minds tell them they are bad, they are dirty, they are worthless, they deserve to be punished, awful things will happen to them. Other typical thoughts are: "No one could ever love me," "I don't deserve to live," "I am powerless over my fate," "I am cursed," "What happened was my fault," "My needs will never be fulfilled," and "People will hurt me." These are the thoughts most commonly experienced by abuse victims, and their relentless repetition leads victims into acute depression, paralyzing fear and self-defeating feelings of low self-esteem.

Sometimes victims are not even aware of these destructive thoughts because they have been part of the victim's mind for so many years that the victim's whole personality and behavior patterns are based on them. When I was in junior high school, I was aware of how painfully self-conscious I was; I was sure that no one would ever like me. By the time I graduated from college and lived in Paris for a couple of years, I thought I had outgrown those "adolescent" insecurities. And when I reached my early forties and discovered my childhood abuse, I told my therapist I felt pretty good about myself, despite what I was learning about my past.

But when she asked me under hypnosis how I felt about myself, the most incredible picture of guilt and self-hate emerged. I believed I was evil, a child of the devil, and that even God had rejected me. I believed that I was totally unlovable and that horrible things would happen to me if I were happy. I found out that many of my perverted beliefs had been programmed into me by my parents—my father told me that I was a child of the devil, my mother said I had destroyed the family.

Regaining memories that showed me the origins of my pessimistic philosophy released me from some of my negative feelings about myself. But understanding the cause of my feelings was not always enough to change them. I had also drawn many erroneous conclusions about myself based on my abuse and I had to correct them. Then I learned about affirmations and my life changed radically.

Affirmations are positive thoughts which are intended to replace negative ones. They are positive statements which we say or write to ourselves as a way of consciously challenging the old, destructive ideas that are clogging our minds. By merely saying a positive thought to yourself, you are invoking all of the power of your subconscious mind to make that thought come true.

Your subconscious mind is like a giant computer, accepting what you tell it without analyzing or judging it. Only your conscious mind analyzes and judges what you think. Your conscious mind programs your subconscious mind by feeding it information, by telling it what to think. You can program your subconscious mind to think negatively or positively.

When you were abused, you programmed your subconscious mind to think negatively about yourself and the world. Since your conscious mind could find no rational explanation for the terrible things that were happening to you, it concluded that you had to be bad, that God had to be punishing you or this horror would not be happening. Your conscious mind drew false conclusions about the reasons for your abuse, your subconscious mind accepted and stored those reasons as the truth and you have acted on them all this time. Your mind believes all those negative thoughts. But now you can start reprogramming your mind with the truth you have learned as an adult.

Humankind is just relearning one of the miracles of life—the miracle that we have the absolute power to control our lives by controlling what we think and what we feel. William James, the renowned 19th century philosopher and psychologist, recognized the potential of mind power when he said, "The greatest discovery of my generation is that human beings can alter their lives by altering their attitudes of mind."

What makes people happy? Some millionaires are happy, some are not. Some married people are happy, some are not. Why is one person sad and another happy under the same circumstances? Napoleon had everything men usually want—glory, power, riches, and even Josephine. Yet he said at St. Helena, "I have never known six happy days in my life."

Helen Keller, on the other hand, had none of these things. She was blind, deaf and dumb. Most people would say that she had the worst in life. Yet she declared, "I have found life so beautiful."

We have all heard about Judy Garland, Freddy Prinz, Marilyn Monroe and Elvis Presley. They seemingly "had it all," but relied on drugs and alcohol to mask their unhappiness. But there are others who seem to "have it all" and are happy too. Why are they different? What is their secret?

The secret is positive thinking, a positive mental attitude which sees the good in life *and makes it happen*. Dr. Norman Vincent Peale stumbled upon this truth many years ago and his books and philosophy have helped people find happiness for decades. In *The Positive Principle Today*, Dr. Peale explains the positive principle:

> "There is a deep tendency in human nature to become precisely what we imagine or picture ourselves to be. We tend to equate with our own self-appraisal of either depreciation or appreciation. We ourselves determine either self-limitation or unlimited growth potential.
>
> "The negative thinker engages ultimately in a self-destroying process. As he constantly sends out negative thoughts, he activates the world around him negatively. There is a law of attraction, in which like attracts like. Birds of a feather flock together. Thoughts of a kind have a natural affinity. The negative thinker, projecting negative thoughts, tends thereby to draw back to himself negative results. This is a definite and immutable law of mind.
>
> "The positive thinker, on the contrary, constantly sends out positive thoughts, together with vital messages of hope, optimism and creativity. He therefore activates the world around him positively and strongly tends to draw back to himself positive results. This, too, is a basic law of mind in action."

We can all become positive thinkers. Thoughts and emotions don't just happen; we make them happen, and we can make them happen differently. Affirmations are a way of asserting this control—and it's easy.

All you have to do is decide what thoughts or ideas you want to change or add to your life and devise a short sentence that expresses what you want to think or feel. For example, you might want to change "I am a bad person" to "I am a good person." "No one will love me" can become "I am loveable." Try to keep it simple because you have to repeat it to yourself at least three times, two or three times a day. Yes, the magic formula in fairy tales has some proven validity: three is the optimal number for having your brain accept a new idea. Repeating it fewer than three times may not be enough to allow the idea to sink in, although saying it more than three times will make the idea sink in even more effectively. In fact, the more you say your affirmation, the quicker it will be fully accepted by your subconscious mind and will override all of your earlier thoughts to the contrary.

Don't give up on affirmations too soon. You have programmed your negative thought into your mind many times a day for years. To reprogram your mind with a positive substitute will take a few months; some people recommend at least three months of daily repetition. Louise Hay suggests saying, "I approve of myself," three or four hundred times a day for a month to overcome all of our past put-downs. Just keep repeating your positive thoughts until they become a habit.

The best times to say your affirmations are in the morning before you get out of bed and in bed at night before you go to sleep. These are the times when you are the most relaxed and when your mind is the most receptive to reprogramming. Just repeat your affirmations to yourself mentally, with your eyes open or closed. Repeat each one three times or more and then go on to the next one. Don't worry about whether or not you believe them; the more you say them, the more you will believe them.

Some people like to say their affirmations out loud in front of a mirror. This method can be very effective because you will be able to see your reaction to what you are saying reflected in your eyes. As you continue to repeat your affirmations, you will be able to see in your eyes that your mind is beginning to accept your new thoughts.

Writing your affirmations down on paper is another powerful way of instilling them in your subconscious mind. Writing is a right-brained activity and your affirmation is quickly programmed through this technique. Those teachers who had us write over and over, "I will not chew gum in class," were actually reprogramming us. It might have been more helpful if they had made our reprogramming more positive and constructive.

The best way I have found to program affirmations is through a combination of daily repetition and self-hypnosis. Self-hypnosis reaches the deepest areas of our subconscious minds—where our darkest images of ourselves are buried. Survivors of abuse who have forgotten all or part of their experiences used self-hypnosis to bury their pain. Hypnosis can be used both to uncover repressed memories and to reprogram negative thoughts and feelings, especially when the thoughts and feelings have been suppressed. Self-hypnosis is an effective way to replace unconscious negative thoughts with positive ones. (Self-hypnosis techniques are described in Section 12 of this Part V.) While conscious, daily repetitions of affirmations will eventually reach the unconscious level of your mind, the process may not be as fast as repeating the same affirmations under hypnosis.

If you find the time to repeat your affirmations to yourself throughout the day, your affirmations will take effect sooner. In fact, if you become aware of an old negative thought entering your mind during the day, you should immediately replace it with the positive one. Don't worry about having the old thought, just let it go and think the positive one three times.

It works better to use statements in the present tense rather than the future. It is preferable to say, "I am well" or "I am in perfect health" rather than "I am getting well." Using the future tense tells your mind that you are *only on your way* to attaining your goal. You want your mind to put you where you want to be *now*. Your mind will find the best way to get you there.

An important fact to note is that you do not have to believe your affirmation for it to work. This fact is worth repeating because so many people get hung up on this point. YOU DO NOT HAVE TO BELIEVE YOUR AFFIRMATION. Your thoughts *are* your beliefs. Your subconscious mind accepts what you program into it without analysis. As long as you think or say your affirmation over and over, your subconscious mind will accept it as fact. You may have doubts, you may even think that some of your affirmations are so far from what you perceive to be your present reality as to be ridiculous. But as long as you repeat your affirmations, your subconscious mind will begin to believe them and will replace your old negative thoughts with the positive ones.

Occasionally, a positive thought may be so foreign to what you now see as "reality" that you are just not ready to jump in and state the positive thought as a present fact. If that is the case, don't force yourself, just start your affirmation with "I choose," rather than "I will." For example, if you believe that no one loves you and you cannot bring yourself to say, "People love me," just say: "I choose to have people love me." As you repeat this affirmation, you may find yourself becoming more aware of your fears about people who claim to love you, and of your feelings about betrayal and trust. And you will find that in time your mind will help you obtain what you choose to have.

Your mind takes what you say to yourself very literally and accepts it as true. If you repeat over and over that you are well, your body will do its best to make you that way. Voodoo has proven that the opposite is also true. Black magic spells can be effective because the victims *believe* they will become ill, or even die. It is not magic but rather the victims' fearful thoughts which kill them. They are literally frightened to death by their thoughts!

Recently, scientists have proven that we can affect our bodies' immune systems by our thoughts and our mental images. If we think of lovely things, spiritual experiences, love or peace, our immune system increases the production of white blood cells, the cells which combat disease.[52] Our minds have much more power than we acknowledge, especially to cure disease and keep us healthy.

In one of my favorite books, *You Can Heal Your Life*, Louise L. Hay lists the mental causes of most of the major diseases. (She has also created some of the most beautiful affirmations I have ever read and I highly recommend her book for survivors of abuse.) She and many others have seen convincing evidence that our thoughts and the stress they produce cause all of our diseases. When two children are exposed to chicken pox at school, why does one come down with chicken pox while the other does not? Why did so many people die of the plague during the Middle Ages, while others survived? Doctors don't know why; they speculate that the survivors had stronger immune systems—but *why?* If recent studies are correct that positive thoughts stimulate our immune systems, then positive affirmations may be critical not only to our state of mind but to our physical health.

When you create your affirmations, avoid the use of negatives. Do not try to reprogram your thought of being a bad person with "I am *not* a bad person." Since your mind takes everything you say to yourself very literally, it focuses primarily on the operative words. So you may be reinforcing your negative thoughts because your mind may focus on the words "bad person." Sometimes it's hard to find an affirmative statement to describe what you want. I experienced some difficulty when I tried to program myself for an operation so that I would not feel pain. All I could think of was, "I won't feel pain." It took a lot of thought to come up with the positive statement, "I am pain free." I was still hesitant to use the word "pain," so I added, "I am comfortable, before, during and after the operation."

Sometimes you may not be aware of your negative thoughts. You may think you don't have any. If you truly never have a single negative thought, you are unique to Western society and you should immediately donate your brain to science. Many of us have negative thoughts but we

257

are not aware of them because we do not usually single out one thought from the endless stream that runs ceaselessly through our minds. Some of our thoughts are so familiar that we take their presence for granted, like pets or old friends. If you want to become aware of your negative thoughts, pick a time when you are upset—angry, hurt, afraid—and analyze what you are saying to yourself.

Psychologist Albert Ellis developed rational-emotive therapy which emphasizes the role of thought in therapy. Dr. Ellis designed a simple four-step model to help people analyze their feelings and the thoughts that produced them. It is helpful to write out your analysis of these four steps at least at first, until you are familiar with using them.

A = the Activating event, or the event that caused the emotion. In this first step, you should briefly describe what happened or the event that you found stressful.

B = your Beliefs or thoughts about the event. What did you say to yourself or think about A?

C = the Consequent emotion. How did you feel when "A" happened? (Were you mad, sad, glad, scared, or a combination?)

D = Dispute. What could you say to yourself to dispute the negative self-talk or thoughts in "B"? Check your statements in "B" to see if they are rational and constructive. How could you change those statements so that you would feel better? Can you think of an affirmation that would eliminate your negative feelings about the event?

This exercise will probably reveal some negative thoughts you have about yourself and others. You would be abnormal if you did not have such thoughts, especially if you have been abused. The important thing is to become aware of your negative thoughts and to reprogram them each time they emerge. The minute you become aware of a negative thought, turn it around, think the exact opposite. If you think, "I'm so stupid, I messed it up again," think "STOP, that's a negative thought," and turn it around. Replace it with something like, "So I made a mistake. So what. Everyone makes mistakes. Now, how can I learn from it?"

As you begin to see the results of your mental reprogramming, you will realize the true power of affirmations. You will find that you can use them for an infinite variety of goals. I have been repeating, "I write quickly, easily and perfectly," every day while writing this book. I never thought I could possibly fill so many pages. In college, I used to have a severe case of writer's block when I had to do a ten-page term paper. But this book has just flowed and I have often finished ten pages per day.

The most effective affirmations for you are the ones you create for yourself. You know best what your needs are. However, to give you a start, I have listed a few affirmations to cover some of the basic negative thoughts shared by most sex abuse survivors. The first three are pivotal and deal with aspects of negative self-image that affect most people in the Western world. Try these, but use what works for you.

1. *I am a good person.*
2. *I am lovable.*
3. *I trust myself and others.*
4. *I am safe and I protect myself.*
5. *I let go of the past quickly, easily and safely.* This is a good one to prepare you for therapy and to speed your progress.
6. *I control my life. I am in charge of my life, emotions and relationships.*
7. *Good things happen to me.*
8. *I deserve to be happy.*
9. *It's safe to be happy.*
10. *I am calm and peaceful. I let go of stress quickly and easily.*
11. *I am perfect, whole and complete.*
12. *My needs are all fulfilled.*

The next affirmations are used for healing.

13. *Every day in every way I am getting better and better.* (I often add, "healthier and healthier, happier and happier.") This is a slight modification of the famous affirmation created by French psychologist Emile Coué. Dr. Coué's affirmation, "Day by day in every way, I am feeling better and better," which was tested in an old-fashioned insane asylum in the 1930s. The "incurable" patients improved dramatically after repeating his affirmation for a few months, and his words became popular all over the world.

14. *I heal quickly, easily and perfectly.*

Some affirmations can be far more flowery and inspirational. I use the next one for forgiveness, to let go of the past and all of my anger and hatred. I like it because it reminds me that we all hurt each other at times and must all forgive and heal.

15. *I forgive myself for all those I have hurt . . . intentionally and unintentionally. I forgive all those who have hurt me intentionally and unintentionally. And I accept the forgiveness of all those who have hurt me intentionally and unintentionally.*

16. One of my adolescent abuse clients asked me to include his favorite affirmation, *I am a child of God.* Some of you may want to substitute the line *I am a child of the universe* from the *Desiderata*. Lines from the *Bible*, prayers, poems and other writings of your choice make particularly effective affirmations.

This is an affirmation I use for confidence:

17. *I am divinely guided. The path I take is always the right path. I find a way where there is no way.* You can substitute this last line, *God will always find a way where there is no way.*

Some of the most beautiful affirmations I have seen are from books by Louise Hay. You can benefit from these affirmations just by reading them over and over to yourself, or you can memorize them. This is the one I found most applicable to survivors of abuse.

18. *In the infinity of life where I am,*
    all is perfect, whole and complete.
I no longer choose to believe in old limitations and lacks,
I now choose to begin to see myself as the Universe sees me,
    perfect, whole and complete.
The truth of my Being is that I was created,
    perfect, whole and complete.
I will always be perfect, whole and complete.
I now choose to live my life from this understanding.
I am in the right place at the right time, doing the right thing.
    All is well in my world.

There are as many possible affirmations as there are people. Try some of these and then create or choose your own. You will find that as they become familiar to you, they will become a part of you and you will be on your way to changing your view of yourself and your view of the world.

> *Life consists in what a man is thinking all day.*
> Ralph Waldo Emerson

9. Healing and getting what you want through visualization. Accessing your inner guides

Visualization, or mental imagery, is one of the most powerful techniques for changing your self-image and your behavior. You can discard your shyness and become confident and friendly. You can cure your diseases. You can contact your inner guides who have all the answers you will ever need. You can even learn to play tennis and ski. But what is even more remarkable, you can get whatever you want through visualization. This is not a wild statement; it is not even exaggerated. The only limitation is that your visualization probably will not work if it is harmful to others. I have a strong belief that such a negative visualization would backfire, although I'm not sure because I have never tried it. But otherwise, whatever you want—love, fame, wealth—is yours for the visualizing.

Do you remember Mark Spitz, the American Olympic swimmer who won an unprecedented *five* gold medals? He announced before the events that he would win five gold medals, and the press and his competitors ridiculed his predictions. After winning the five Olympic events, Spitz told a television commentator he had pictured himself receiving the five medals many times before he even reached the Olympics. Brian Boitano, the 1988 Olympic figure skating champion, announced in a television interview that he had visualized himself receiving the gold medal many times before his actual victory. And, during the same winter Olympics, we saw the Swiss slalom champion, sitting on the snow at the top of the ski run, with her eyes closed and her hands moving as she *mentally* rehearsed her run down the course.

But the power of visualization is not limited to athletics. Comedienne Carol Burnett described her childhood in Los Angeles with her alcoholic parents in her autobiography, *One More Time*. Burnett wanted desperately to be an actress and to go to New York, but her family was poor and she could not find the money to move across the country. Then Burnett began to visualize herself moving to New York and acting in a play directed by George Abbott. She saw her vision clearly and was amazed because it was so far from the reality of her life in Los Angeles. A few months later, a stranger offered to finance her trip to New York; the only string attached to the free ticket he offered was that Burnett had to agree to help other people in need when she could.

When Burnett arrived in New York, she had a difficult time finding work as an actress. She finally landed a small part, but not in a George Abbott show. Things did not go well, and the show never opened. Just when she was running out of money and hope, she received a telephone call from the producer of a new Broadway musical. Would she play one of the leading characters? The director was George Abbott.

I scoffed at the claims made by people about visualization until I began to hear them from people close to me. One of my best and oldest friends, Marsha, was a would-be songwriter in Los Angeles. She was determined to make her living through her songs, but she had chosen a difficult and highly competitive field. For almost fifteen years, she lived like a pauper, writing all kinds of wonderful songs that never sold.

Then someone told her about visualization, and, although she did not believe it would help, her desperation led her to try it. She imagined herself receiving royalty checks for songs she had sold. In fact, she imagined opening an envelope and pulling out a royalty check for $4,000.00. She had visualized this event for several months when she received a call from Disney Productions to write songs for their new Winnie the Pooh series. And when Marsha received her first royalty check for her Pooh songs, the amount was $4,000.00! (Her royalties have been much larger since then.)

After Marsha's success and at the urging of several other friends, I decided to try visualization. I had been single for eleven years despite innumerable blind dates and agonizing conventional ones, suffering at singles events and Club Med, and even placing a "personal" ad in *Washingtonian Magazine*. Visualization began to look appealing; at least it was less demeaning. Since I obviously could not visualize a particular man, I was advised to visualize the qualities I wanted.

So I pictured a man who was kind, gentle, loving and intelligent with a good sense of humor. After three months of visualizing, I gave up and decided to console myself with a week of skiing in Park City, Utah. Park City had been my favorite place to ski for several years. My ski instructor, a red haired social worker who had started law school fixed me up with a lawyer she had worked for. To make a long story short, we were married two-and-a-half months later. And he had all of the qualities I visualized.

What was more amazing was the fact that I had also visualized living in Park City but had little hope of finding an eligible single man in a city with a population of less than 5,000. But that is where my husband lived and that is where I live now.

I cannot guarantee that you will find your perfect mate through visualization, but I do know that you have a better chance of getting what you want if you know what you want and if you can picture it in your mind. I have long since given up trying to figure out how visualization works; I only know that it does.

Some people believe that if you can picture yourself doing something and focus on it, you are developing a mind set which can help you bring it about. For example, if a shy person visualizes approaching and talking to new people, he is mentally teaching himself new skills and desensitizing his fears at the same time. And if you clearly picture what you want, your mind can then help you to make decisions and become more sensitive to opportunities which will lead you to your goal. Other people believe that by programming your subconscious mind, you send out signals to the universe that draw to you what you visualize. I do not know which explanation is correct, but common sense teaches that you cannot reach a goal if you don't know what it is. If you can see your vision in your mind, you can find a way to make it come true.

I have only one warning about visualization, one which also applies to prayer. I believe, as many people do, the the universe is benevolent and will provide what is best for me. So although there may be things I really want, I realize that I may not always know what is best for me. Therefore I always protect myself when I visualize or pray by adding, "If it's in my best interest and the best interest of the universe." Some people say, "This or something better," acknowledging that the universe may have planned something even better which they cannot even imagine, and add, "for the highest good of all concerned."

Jack Buckley, an ex-priest turned federal government executive who was my crisis advisor during my White House appointment, gave me this description of visualization:

> *Whatever you*
> *Vividly imagine,*
> *Ardently desire,*
> *Firmly believe, and*
> *Enthusiastically act upon*
> *Must inevitably come to pass.*

Those lines describe the basic steps of visualization. The first step is to "vividly" picture in your mind what you want. If you want to change your personality or behavior, you must picture yourself acting in your ideal way. Watch yourself interacting with people, hear yourself talking to them. Notice your expression and how your body moves, and how people react to the new you. The details are important—that is what "vividly" means. You should see the colors, hear the sounds, smell the smells, feel your movements and your emotions. How does it *feel* to be the new you? The more realistic you can make the scene in your mind, the closer you will be to making it reality.

The same principles apply for obtaining physical things. For example, if you want a new Mercedes, it is not enough to just think that you want a Mercedes. You should mentally picture the model and the color, and you should see yourself as the owner of the car. Say to yourself, "This is my car." Visualize yourself opening the door and sitting behind the wheel. Smell the new upholstery, run your fingers over it and feel how smooth it is. Perhaps you will look at yourself in the rear view mirror. You may want to drive the car. Add any details you like. Remember, the more real you can make it in your mind, the more real it will become. One woman who tried this technique received the Mercedes she pictured about five months after she started visualizing. An uncle she did not even know very well died and left his car to her under his will.

The second step is to "ardently desire" or really want what you visualize. Obviously you will focus your energy only on attaining something that is extremely important to you. Sometimes when people start to visualize something they think they want, they realize that they don't really want it after all. Remember the old Chinese saying: "Be careful what you wish for, because you may get it." Make sure you want everything that may go with what you visualize. For example, if you obtain the $1 million you visualize, will you be happy with the new life style, including tax consequences, investment responsibilities, and other headaches with which you will be saddled?

Sometimes you may fervently desire a new life style and more money but a part of you holds you back. You may believe you don't deserve abundance or feel that if you receive it you will be taking it away from someone else. If that is the case, you need to do some reprogramming (See Section 8, *Affirmations—reprogramming negative thoughts*.) You may also want to do some reading on the concept of abundance. You need to fully accept the fact that the universe is abundant and that there is enough for all of us to have what we want. Just look around you in a meadow, a forest, a field or even in the desert. There is so much life, so many kinds of plants, animals and insects. Each has its own niche, plenty of sun, an ample supply of food. If you really look, you will see that there is so much of everything everywhere.

But you may say as I did, what about all the starving people all over the world? We have all been made to feel guilty over world poverty. But when my parents forced me to eat by telling me about the starving children in China, those children were not affected by my eating or not eating—or even by my guilt.

It is unfortunately true that poverty exists throughout the world. For several years I worked for the United States Agency for International Development, the agency of the government which helps underdeveloped countries. I learned that 80 percent of the world lives in poverty, while 20 percent—including the United States—enjoys wealth and luxury. I assumed that there was not enough food in the world to feed everyone until I saw the statistics. The fact is that there is more than enough food in the world right this minute to amply feed every single man, woman and child on earth. The problem is one of distribution and helping some countries become self-sufficient. Aiding in the effort to rectify these conditions is a worthy goal, but it should not make you deny yourself what you want now.

There is more than enough of everything you want, and the fact that you have luxuries does not mean that someone else goes without. If you use what you want for your own good and in a way that does not hurt anyone else, you are merely taking advantage of the universal abundance available to us all. It is only when you use things to injure others or hoard them so that they are out of the universal energy flow that you are acting in a negative manner. Only human beings produce scarcity; the universe produces abundance.

Jack Buckley's third step is that you "firmly believe" what you visualize. I interpret this to mean that you believe in what you are seeking and that you believe obtaining it will be good for you. While it may hasten the results if you believe you will obtain what you want, belief in the outcome does not appear to be necessary. Although the Olympic gold medalists seem to have believed that they would achieve their goals, neither Marsha nor I held such a belief. We acted out of desperation. We were ready to try anything because nothing had worked so far. But we were dedicated; we were willing to do anything to reach our goals.

I think that dedication and the willingness to do anything necessary to reach one's goal is a major part of the secret of visualization. Jack's fourth step says that you must "enthusiastically act upon" your desires. Visualization alone is not a magic potion. If you only see your goal in your mind, you may never accomplish it. Your mind will provide opportunities and open doors for you, but you have to take advantage of those opportunities and walk through the doors. You may have to take risks, relying on your subconscious mind to make them work out for you. And you will certainly have to work—Marsha could not have received her royalty check if she had not continued to compose first-rate songs. And although I did not have to do much to find my husband, I assure you I have had to work hard to make the marriage work!

Since you are programming your subconscious mind, you should put yourself into a relaxed state before you start your visualization. You might use the progressive relaxation exercise or a breathing exercise in the "quick fixes" section to help you relax. Practice until you can clearly see what you want; the colors should be bright and all of the details visible. Stay with your vision for a few minutes; relax and enjoy it. And be sure to view your vision as though it has already come true. Rejoice and give thanks that you have received what you desired. Your mind will absorb your vision and find the means to make it come true.

Visualization has many beneficial functions. You can use it to improve aspects of your personality, such as getting rid of a bad temper. You can use it to obtain what you want, such as a spouse, money, cars, selling your home, etc. But you can also use it for learning sports, even if you are unable to actually practice. Visualization is a wonderful way to improve your performance while you are ill or injured.

The value of visualization in improving sports performance was first discovered when scientists experimented with basketball players. The players were tested and then divided into three groups of equal ability. The first group practiced throwing baskets for several hours a day every day for a month. The second group did not pick up a basketball, but visualized throwing baskets every day for the month. The last group did nothing. At the end of the month, the three groups were tested. The third group had not improved at all. The first group showed an 84 percent improvement. The second group which had only visualized demonstrated more than an 80 percent improvement, almost equal to the improvement of the group that actually threw the ball.

Recognizing the incredible power of the mind to improve sports performance, companies are now earning millions of dollars from tape and video cassette visualization programs for learning tennis, skiing, golf and other sports. And Olympic coaches have adopted visualization techniques to give their athletes an edge.

The most remarkable results of visualization are in the area of healing. Carl and Stephanie Simonton established a center in California for treating children with terminal cancer. The children are taught to picture their healthy cells overcoming the cancerous ones. Some children picture their healthy cells as the video game "pac men," eating up the cancerous cells. Other children, usually boys, visualize their healthy cells as combat pilots shooting down their cancer cells. Although the mental imagery differs, the results have been impressive. A far larger percentage of these children have had their cancer go into remission than would have occurred through pure chance. These results have prompted the use of visualization by other hospitals and clinics around the country.

The results obtained by the Simontons are consistent with the results of research experiments demonstrating that mental imagery produces endorphins which in turn stimulate the production of white blood cells that combat disease. Many different kinds of imagery appear to be effective from visualizing healthy cells overcoming unhealthy ones, to mentally surrounding the injured area or person with white light, to picturing a medically accepted treatment working effectively for the specific disease. As with all of the self-help techniques, you have to choose the image that makes the most sense to you. The recommended reading part of this book includes a number of references on self-healing.

One of the best visualizations I have encountered specifically for sexual abuse victims is one devised by Stephen Levine in his latest bestseller, *Healing into Life and Death*. (His "Opening the Heart of the Womb Meditation" follows this section.)

Mental imagery can also be used to obtain advice from your inner guides. You have all of the information you need to answer every question you will ever ask inside you right now. You only have to learn how to tap into that knowledge. Therapists are using an imagination technique to help their clients solve their own problems. If clients say that they don't know what to do about a problem, the therapist suggests that they pretend or imagine that they *do* know what to do. Amazingly when clients merely imagine that they may have answers to their problems, they come up with appropriate solutions.

Somewhere inside us we have the answers. Some people believe we have a "higher self" that we can contact for advice. I believe we have an incredibly powerful brain, far more powerful than we acknowledge, and that we all have access to the infinite information we have stored in our minds. I call this all-knowing part of our minds our "total intelligence" which encompasses our conscious and subconscious minds, our health sense, and perhaps even our link to what psychiatrist Carl Jung called the collective unconscious—our connection to all the wisdom of human-kind.

You can access this information in several ways. Some people just sit quietly, ask their questions and wait for the answers to rise to conscious-ness. Others find that answers filter through to their conscious minds during meditation. Still others feel the answers in their gut, using their intuition.

One of the most imaginative ways to tap your source of knowledge is to use mental imagery to meet your inner guide. You can do this by starting with one of the relaxation techniques described in this book. Some people find that it helps to use meditation or hypnosis techniques to become deeply relaxed, but this is not necessary. Once you are relaxed, you merely tell yourself mentally that you want to meet the guide or advisor who is most suitable for you. You should repeat this thought several times. Then just relax and wait for your guide to appear. It may take a little while, so be patient. Do not try to guess who or what your guide will be; it may be a person or an animal, a religious figure, a wise man or woman, a figure from history or even yourself. Accept your guide, whatever it is, thank it for coming and ask it to respond to the questions you always wanted to ask. You can ask something practical such as whether you should change jobs or something metaphysical about the nature of the universe. You may have to ask your question several times and wait for the answer without trying to anticipate the response. If you

267

do not get a direct answer from your guide, do not despair. You will receive an answer from a book, a friend, a television program, or some other source within a couple of days after you ask your question.

Instead of choosing one guide, some people set up a mental council of advisors. This council is based on the theory that all the knowledge of the universe is available to each of us. You choose people, living or dead, real or fictional who you would like to advise you. So you might choose Albert Einstein, Golda Meir, Carl Jung, Merlin, Sister Teresa and Jesus to help in their special areas. Then you would mentally bring them to a round table where you can ask them questions and get their advice. These councils can also be used for more materialistic purposes. One businessman became very successful after setting up an imaginary council which included presidents of Fortune 500 corporations.

You can convene your council in your mind any time you have a need. Your advisors are always available to you because you are really drawing on the vast knowledge of your own mind.

Visualization or mental imagery can be used in ways only limited by your imagination. You can take mental trips to anywhere in the universe; you can create your own hideaway where you can escape to relax, think, or work; you can create color patterns or dances to music; and you can mentally talk to people alive or dead to resolve differences and ask forgiveness. Many excellent books can guide you to exciting new worlds. And there are classes and workshops in most cities that teach mental imagery.

For survivors of abuse, visualization is a mini-miracle. You can work with your therapist to change negative behavior patterns by clearly picturing the behavior you would like to have. You can obtain things you want through visualization and gain confidence in your ability to control your world. You can learn a new sport and meet new friends. And you can create a world of peace and beauty for yourself when you need a respite from thoughts about your abuse. It is a technique worth trying because it can help you change your world in many ways.

Images are not pictures in the head, but plans for obtaining information from potential environments.
Ulric Neisser

10. Stephen Levine's "Opening the Heart of the Womb Meditation"

This is one of the most powerful meditations for sexual abuse survivors I have ever found. Steven Levine's *Healing into Life and Death* contains a number of meditations—such as those on forgiveness, loving kindness and grief—which would be helpful for survivors, but the Womb Meditation had such a potent and immediate healing effect on me that I asked Stephen's permission to include it in this book.

This meditation can be read slowly by a friend or silently to yourself, or you can record it and play it back to yourself.

The following words are those of Stephen Levine:

Some years ago, during a workshop, after a particularly intense letting-go meditation, a few people were gleefully sharing out-of-body experiences which had spontaneously occurred in the course of the exercise. They had, as they put it, "floated free, and watched it all from above," the body of awareness momentarily let loose from the earthen body of flesh and bone. Their excitement filled the room with new possibilities and something of a lust for "mystical experiences."

Then one woman raised her hand and said, "You know, I think all of these out-of-body experiences are real nice, very flashy, but they are not of much interest to me. I'd like an in-the-body experience for a change. I'd like to trust life enough to be able to stay in my body, to not always be on guard, to not always tense as if someone were going to jump out of a dark hallway and do me great injury." Several women in the room nodded in agreement. Each had been sexually abused as a child. Each had found that the body was an unsafe place to be. To be in the body was to be a target. For these women out-of-body experiences were somewhat beside the point. They were not so much interested in what it might be like to die as in what it might be like to be fully born.

Later that afternoon, a woman in her midtwenties took me aside and said, "I have no more room in my heart now than I had in my body when I was two years old and my father raped me!" And instantly the connection became clear between a woman's spiritual heart, her "upper" heart if you will, and the heart of the womb, her "lower" heart. Clearly many women's upper hearts had become inaccessible when their lower hearts had closed due to abuse and frightful mishandling.

At the time, this closing down had been the only way out of an impossible situation. This woman had no choice. But now she was finding that what had been functional in the past made her nearly dysfunctional in the present. She spoke of how many times her heart had been closed in unsuccessful relationships over the past several years. She felt she had been "closed down" and couldn't open to others for longer than she could remember.

In the course of our work together that afternoon, it became abundantly clear that women have two hearts, two sets of smooth muscles in the body—the heart and the womb. Many years ago, when women used ergot as a means of aborting a pregnancy, they would occasionally experience heart palpitations as well. This is because ergotrate is a spasmodic for the smooth muscles of the body. In the case of a woman, these are the womb and the heart. This connection between the womb and the heart was never so clear as with our friend's sharing about the early enormity of her injury.

For many women I suspect the upper heart has been closed by rough handling in the lower heart, in the area of the womb. Having been treated unconsciously, unkindly, maliciously, coldly, in the lower heart, a thick armoring of distrust and fear has barred entrance to the spacious heart of being.

It seems that all women have been touched roughly in the lower heart by one means or another. Some by sexual abuse as children or adults, others by rape, others by insensitive lovers or the uncaring touch of medical personnel. All are abused by the soft pornography of the advertising industry and the hard-core smut which does such violence to us all. Each at one time or another has been seen as an object. If a person sees you only as a body, they can't see your heart, your mind, or your spirit. The greatest abuse is to be treated as an object, to be put out of one's heart. Without seeing someone as an object, as "another," intentional abuse cannot occur. For some women it has been the forcible roughening of the sensitive heart which has caused a callus over the trust and openness that allows hearts to meet and merge in love. For others it has been a cold speculum. It seems that most women have been subject to some level of abuse that has touched their lower heart and left their upper heart that much less accessible.

From these understandings arose the following meditation. It is preceded by a slow and gentle coming into the body with a long softening and opening to sensations beginning at the top of the head and moving ever so slowly and mercifully through the various parts of the body.

In this slow sweeping through the body, the awareness reestablishes contact with being in a body. Then slowly the awareness is brought, with a tenderness beyond imagination, perhaps beyond all previous history, that moves gently and mercifully with profound awareness and not the least increment of time or rushing, up into the vagina. Gently, through the folds of flesh and the muscular ripples into the womb stopping at any point to dwell in love and awareness on the sensations received. Examining the tree of life there, the fallopian tubes spreading out like branches to bear their ovarian fruit. And within each ovary at birth, all the eggs, all the possibilities of birth and rebirth, as seed potential there. All life discovered at the center of the sparkling moment. Healing, touching with mercy and care, that which may so often have been approached with hardness and thoughtlessness. A profound forgiveness entering the body in the womb. A forgiveness that allows us to reenter our lives. A forgiveness that is for ourselves, though it may touch and heal others. A forgiveness that is primarily for our own healing and therefore tends to heal all we come into contact with.

The men who enter this practice will find it as exquisitely useful as the women. To discover the vagina, the womb, the ovaries and eggs that exist within us all brings us into our humanness and allows us to more fully occupy our incarnation. After such meditations, we have had men come up to us and say, "I'll never touch a woman roughly again," tears pouring from their eyes, filled with remorse. Not rapists, not abusers, but husbands and boyfriends acknowledging the pain we all carry. Men have the potential for getting as much healing out of this as women.

For those who have been sexually abused, this meditation can be extremely difficult at times. One woman told me of doing it twice a day for about twenty minutes at a time and finding it to be quite a grind in the beginning, often the least pleasant part of her day. "But I know there is nothing else I can do right now that will do me as much good." The difficulty in doing this meditation defines the condition we find ourselves in. There is so much fear to be approached before we can see beyond fear. After about two and a half months of working with this meditation, she told us, "A miracle happened the other day. I walked into the kitchen, sat down at the table, and looked up and saw the wall. I just saw the wall! I was just here in my body, in the world, in my heart. I saw the wall as if for the first time. I was just there. It was the most wonderful experience of my life!" As her lower heart opened, her upper heart became visible to so many that she was drawn by other women to counsel and share herself. She a now a much sought-after therapist for abused women.

Certainly the meditation doesn't work for everyone, and it may not even be right for everyone's temperament. But for those who find their heart drawn to it, who feel some resonance inside that this may be a way in and through at last, it is worth experimenting with for at least a month. To test, explore, to allow the possibility of healing. To discover

271

that healing may even be possible, even in the aftermath of great injury. To experience the tears of joy our friend wept when that which seemed so unworkable sank into the heart of healing. It is remarkable to find a tool that works in this world of half-truths and superficial approaches to deep pain. If it works, use it, make it your own, share it with your brothers and sisters in similar pain.

Opening the Heart of the Womb Meditation

Find a comfortable place to sit in a quiet room and begin to bring a soft awareness into the body.

Beginning at the top of the head, allow a merciful awareness to gently receive the sensations arising—the softness of the scalp against the skullcap, the roundness of the brow. Releasing any tension around the eyes, allow this gentle awareness to move slowly through the face. Receive the soft flesh of the cheeks, the tingling at the tip of the nose, the warmth of the ears at the side of the head. Feel the muscles of the jaw begin to soften as they let life in, in mercy and loving kindness. The tongue lying gently within the mouth. The weight of the head perfectly balanced on the willing muscles of the neck.

Allow awareness to receive the multiple sensations that arise in various parts of the head and face before it proceeds downward into the neck.

Feel the long muscles that extend from the base of the skull soften as they spread out into the shoulders, gently cradling the head on the neck.

Sensations floating in a gentle comforting awareness which receives the body as living suchness, pulsing, vibrating with aliveness.

Feel how the shoulders support the arms that cradle the sides of the body. Feel the strength in the shoulders, the musculature, the bones, the tendons that so easily allow their remarkable capacity for movement.

Feel how this miracle of life extends, down each arm filling the palm, vibrating to the tip of each finger.

Feel how life animates the muscles, the tissue, the flesh that comprises the shoulders, extending down the arms into the hands.

Feel the capacity for movement, for service, within the hands' ability to reach out and to touch, to bandage and to caress. Feel the aliveness of the hands scintillating in each palm.

Notice how the arms embrace the body.

Feel the chest rising and falling naturally with each breath. How the breath breathes itself in trust, each breath following the last effortlessly. Feel the heart beating within, the lungs gently opening with each breath.

Notice any sensations around the grief point, at the touch point of the heart. Soften any holding there. Let sensations float in a new mercy, in a deeper kindness to oneself.

Notice that wherever awareness enters, life is to be found. Feel the varying densities of different areas of the body. Feel its warmth or coolness. Feel the pressure and release that awareness allows as it opens the body. Wherever awareness is directed, healing arises.

Now allow this gentle awareness to move toward the back. Beginning at the top of the spine where the neck spreads out to form the back of the shoulders, allow this healing awareness to gradually receive one vertebra after another in loving kindness moving from the first to the last vertebra one at a time gently descending the back.

The miracle of the spine supported so perfectly by the flat muscles of the upper back extending down to the long lateral muscles of the lower back. Feel the tissue, the flesh, the remarkable support of the back.

Let your attention move gently to the base of the spine, approaching the lower torso.

Just notice in mercy and awareness whatever sensations, thoughts or emotions arise as you approach the lower torso.

Now let the attention return to the chest area and proceed gently down the front of the body receiving the ribs as they spread out like a protective canopy above the open softness of the stomach and belly.

Allow the belly to soften, to receive healing there. In soft belly there is room for it all. In soft belly is the possibility of completion.

Feel the breath breathing itself in soft belly. Feel the muscles rising and falling all by themselves with each breath. Just breath breathing itself in soft belly. Just life continuing to heal itself.

Continuing gently across the pelvic area notice whatever tension or thoughts arise. Feel this whole area in softness and mercy. No force, just a gentle allowing of sensations to present themselves as they will. Softening lower belly, softening the hips, softening the buttocks.

Allowing awareness to gently move through, let the sensations in the upper legs, knees and feet, be received in whole body. Letting awareness pass tenderly through the genitals continue through the upper legs, thighs, and calves as it slowly moves to the soles of the feet.

Feel the strength and durability of the legs and knees, and ankles and feet. Feel their capacity for movement.

Feel the preciousness of each step they are able to provide.

273

Feel the quality of tingling and vibration in the lower body. Feel both legs, feet, knees, hips, as an aliveness, a presence in the body.

Feel the rootedness with the earth at the bottom of each foot. Its trust.

Begin gradually to allow awareness to fill the legs, gradually moving up from the soles of the feet to the upper legs.

Allow awareness to gradually gather toward the inside of the upper legs. Feel the area between the knees, the sensation of space, the tingling of the skin and muscle. Feel the space between the upper thighs at the very top of the legs.

Let your attention move up to that space at the very top of the legs, where the left leg meets the right leg. Feel the space between the upper thighs at the very top of the legs, where they connect with the lower torso.

Gently.

Gently moving toward the area between the legs.

Just receiving very tenderly whatever sensations are generated there.

Allow this soft awareness to receive the sensations there at the labia with great mercy and tenderness.

Allowing the awareness to gather as it will without the least sense of rushing or urgency, allow a merciful exploration of the entrance into the body.

Feel the ruffled fringe of flesh that protects the tender entrance of the body.

Just allowing awareness to gather there at the opening into the body.

With mercy.

Tenderly moving through the shadows and light into the area of the vulva.

Feel the muscles there, their capacity to receive.

Their capacity to feel.

Their willingness to be this holy body we all share.

Gently allowing the light, the mercy to enter into the vagina.

This moist, merciful entrance.

Touching so tenderly with the mercy the subtle wrinkles, the subtle muscles of the vagina.

Allowing awareness to soften and receive life as it enters the body.

Allowing mercy to receive the sensations in the vagina.

Moving so tenderly into the cervix and muscles. The tissues softening to receive this sweet heart expanding into the dome of the womb.

The cave of life.

Feel its spaciousness, its openness. Its homeness.

Let awareness start to receive the womb with mercy and loving kindness. For yourself. For this tender heart.

Let your womb fill gradually with the light of your mercy for yourself.

Let the heart of the womb open to receive its own nature once again, to come home to itself, to make room for you.

Let the soft light of that heart shine there in the womb.

Opening the womb of mercy, of forgiveness, of compassion for yourself.

Letting the womb soften, letting it open.

Letting it just be at last. In loving kindness, in gentle healing mercy.

Sense the fallopian tubes are extending like branches from this tree of life, the strong trunk of the vagina opening through the cervix into the great dome of the womb, its branches extending like arms embracing itself.

Feel the loving kindness slowly expanding in the womb, filling it with a healing mercy and gentleness, slowly extending life into the branches of the tree through which the essence of all life has always passed.

Allow the light of the womb to move gradually into each of the fallopian channels.

Feel the feathery subtlety there like leaves flowering at the end of the fallopians and feel the ovaries like fruit filled with seeds shimmering at the end of each branch.

Allow the light of this heart to bring mercy to itself.

To heal itself in loving kindness, to allow itself its own embrace, its own fulfillment, its own completion.

Feel the light, warm golden light filling the womb, filling the branches of the tree, shimmering in the ovaries, sparkling in the seeds within.

Feel the whole womb, the whole tree of life filled with light. Filled with mercy. Filled at last with tender mercy.

With tender care.

Let the womb fill with love for itself, for all sentient beings.

And let the heart meet the womb, let the heart gradually sink into the womb, the upper heart and lower heart forming one shimmering star of being, of kindness, of completion.

Let it be. Allow.

Allow your hearts to meet.

Let the heart sink into the womb, let it receive its wholeness, in mercy, in joy.

275

Allow the light to be.

May we be free of a past of pain and confusion.

May we let our wombs, our hearts, be filled with their own natural light.

May we be whole unto ourselves.

May we be at peace.

May all beings be free from suffering.

May all beings know the joy, the healing of their true luminescent nature.

May we all meet in mercy, in noninjury, in compassion.

May we all be healed. May we be at peace.

May all beings be free.

May we all be free.

11. The power of prayer

Although this is not a religious book, I would be doing you a disservice if I did not include prayer among the techniques for self-help. It may be the most powerful technique ever discovered for changing your life and obtaining your wishes, and it has worked consistently throughout human history. Prayer has changed millions of lives and wrought miracles for people all over the world. Prayer is especially powerful for survivors of abuse who have felt the terror of abandonment, causing many of us to cut ourselves off from close relationships with people because we do not trust them or believe anyone will ever help us. If we can begin to believe that someone cares and will help us, we can begin to break down our barriers, start to trust and allow ourselves to enjoy relationships and accept help from others. Praying to God can accomplish all of this.

I started praying in my thirties, not because I believed in God or even that it would work, but out of desperation and a vow I had made to myself. I was so miserable that I had promised myself I would read every self-help book and try every technique until I began to feel happier. I had avoided most religious books and so I had avoided Dr. Norman Vincent Peale's books for several years. But people kept telling me how powerful his books were—the "positive principle" was a household word—so I picked up a copy of *The Positive Principle Today*. Although I am Jewish, my family was not religious and I did not believe in God or prayer. When I discovered my abuse under hypnosis, I also learned that I had rejected God during my abuse because I blamed Him/Her for not protecting me. I also felt that I was bad and concluded that God certainly did not like me.

So when I first tried prayer it was with reluctance and a healthy dose of skepticism. It was a real test for me and I tried to pick something specific where I could easily determine if there were any immediate concrete results. God was only going to get one try!

At the time, I was a director at a federal agency in Washington D.C., having been appointed by President Carter's administration. All directors were required to attend monthly policy meetings which were always long, antagonistic and unproductive. I dreaded those meetings because they were so contentious, and also because I felt I did not handle them well and was not often able to get my positions adopted.

For my test, I chose a meeting where I wanted the support of the other directors on a policy matter which was very important to me. Just before the meeting, I said my first, somewhat awkward, prayer. It was something like, "Please God, help me handle this meeting well, and convince the group of my position. Please help them agree with me."

That meeting was astounding. All of the directors were pleasant and cooperative and voted in favor of everything I wanted! The meeting adjourned in half the usual time and I walked out in a daze. I could not understand it; these were the same people I had battled for months in the same room over the same issues, and yet it was totally different. Some people might toss it off as coincidence, but "coincidence" merely describes two things that happen at the same time, it does not explain *why* they happened. I am beginning to believe Bernie Siegel, the author of the wonderful book, *Love, Medicine and Miracles*, who says: "Coincidence is God's way of remaining anonymous."

It may be that praying works like affirmations and visualization, creating a mind set that directs our behavior and enables us to achieve our goal. It may be that through prayer we tap into our connection with the universe and with all consciousness so that we access the power of all creative intelligence. And that may be how we communicate with God. I cannot explain what happens. I only know that it worked, and that it has worked repeatedly for me since that time.

Being a pragmatist, I use prayer because it works. And because it works, I have come to have faith in God, in people and in the benevolence of the universe. It has been a positive influence in my life and has, I believe, made me a better person. It has certainly helped me face the painful and difficult issues of my abuse. But most important, praying has made me understand that I am not alone, that I am connected to everything, and that somewhere there is a loving power that cares about me.

I have become a little more sophisticated about praying, but I firmly believe that simple prayers which come from the heart are the best. I do not always get what I want when I want it, but the things I really need seem to come at the right time. I have learned to pray only for things which are in my best interest and the best interest of the universe, and I have had to acknowledge that some of my desires may not meet this condition. This is the only rule I follow in praying because I do not believe God wants to see us complicate prayer with a bunch of rules and regulations. I do not see Him/Her as a government bureaucrat in the sky, nor do I envision Him/Her as a divine accountant keeping a ledger of every little thing we do. The God of my experience is infinitely forgiving and has boundless love and compassion for us all.

You may wonder why, if prayer is so effective, I bothered to include any other self-help techniques in this book. The answer is that God won't do it all for you. You have to find the tools to make a good life for yourself. There is an old Arab saying: "Trust in God, but tie up your camel." God will guide you, but S/He can't live your life for you. Prayer will not take away all of life's struggle; without struggle we would be dead. But it will help erase the pain. And you may start finding, as I did, that life is so much easier when you have someone on your side. For those of you who are skeptical, I urge you to give prayer a try. You have nothing to lose and everything to gain.

The two best books I have found on how to use prayer are Dr. Joseph Murphy's *The Power of Your Subconscious Mind*, and Dr. Norman Vincent Peale's *The Positive Principle Today*. But you don't need a book. Just be honest and say what is in your heart. God will understand.

Whosoever shall say unto this mountain, Be thou removed, and be thou cast into the sea; and shall not doubt in his heart, but shall believe that those things which he saith shall come to pass; he shall have whatsoever he saith.
Mark 11:23, *The Bible*

12. Using self-hypnosis for recovering memories and for reprogramming behavior and feelings

Knowledge of self-hypnosis is an invaluable tool for survivors of sexual abuse. Most people who have been sexually or severely physically abused have protected themselves by repressing all or part of their abuse. Self-hypnosis is the most effective way to retrieve those repressed memories and feelings. Survivors with multiple personality disorder or ego states created their amnesia through self-hypnosis and therefore especially need self-hypnosis to heal themselves. (See the discussion of hypnotherapy in Question 28, *Can you explain multiple personality disorder and other dissociative states?*) Knowing self-hypnosis before you start therapy can save you time and money and will make you more comfortable with the process. It will also speed up your healing outside of therapy.

Self-hypnosis enables you to reprogram yourself deep into your sub-conscious so you can change your behavior and the way you think and feel. Saying affirmations to yourself under hypnosis imprints your instructions and new thoughts at a deeper level than when you say them in your usual waking state. All of the affirmations and visualization techniques described in this book are more effective if used under hypnosis because your mind is more relaxed and receptive in an altered or hypnotic state than in the usual waking state when other thoughts intrude. You can also use hypnosis to increase your powers of concentration, comprehension and memory.

There are many myths and misconceptions about hypnosis. Grade B movies and television have created a Svengali image of hypnotists who control the minds of unwilling subjects through magic and mysticism. This is totally false. Hypnotism is a normal everyday phenomenon. You have been in an hypnotic state many times in your life. Have you ever driven your car down a road and all of a sudden realized that you had gone farther than you thought and that you were not aware of how you got there? You did not remember driving past houses or buildings or other streets, but you still drove safely and managed to keep yourself on the road and in the right direction. You were in a light hypnotic trance. Or did you ever read a book or concentrate on a project so intently that you did not hear someone enter the room and call your name several times? Your intense state of concentration was an hypnotic or altered state.

Contrary to popular myth, hypnosis does not mean sleep. In the movies you see people close their eyes when they are hypnotized, but they are not asleep—they are in a state of intense concentration. In fact, hypnosis is a state of extreme awareness. If you are in an hypnotic state, you are acutely focused. You can be hypnotized and have your eyes wide open. And no matter how deep your state of hypnosis, you can always come out of it quickly and easily whenever you want. You are aware of what is going on around you at all times. If the telephone rings, you can snap out of hypnosis and answer it. You may feel slightly drowsy for a few minutes or a bit jangled if you come out of hypnosis abruptly, but that is all.

The most ridiculous tale about hypnosis is that someone can control your mind and make you do things against your will. Hypnotists do not possess any special powers. In fact all hypnosis is *self*-hypnosis. You actually hypnotize yourself. The hypnotist merely acts as a catalyst to help you induce an hypnotic state. You cannot be hypnotized against your will. When people are hypnotized in night clubs, the hypnotist chooses subjects who he sees are willing to be hypnotized and who are susceptible to hypnosis. Many people want to be the center of attention even if they are made to bark like dogs or say funny things, so they allow the hypnotist to use them as subjects.

When you are under hypnosis, you can always hear and understand what the hypnotist is saying to you, and if you don't like it, you will come out of the hypnotic state. Despite the many thousands of people who have been hypnotized, there is no evidence of anyone ever having been harmed through hypnosis or harming anyone else while under hypnosis. No one can make you do anything against your moral will. Although hypnosis increases your suggestibility, you remain in total control of yourself and can always reject any offensive suggestions.

I was very suspicious when I first started learning self-hypnosis so I programmed myself to never do anything to hurt myself. First I said affirmations that I was in control and would not hurt myself. Then after I hypnotized myself, I again told myself that I would never be able to hurt myself and that no one else could hurt me. I programmed myself so that if I ever started to do anything harmful, or anyone else did, I would immediately come out of hypnosis. Knowing what I do now, I don't think this precaution was necessary because our minds are designed to protect us, but it made me feel better. Anything you can do to allay your fears—reading about hypnosis, talking to a qualified hypnotherapist or programming your own mind—will help you to achieve a state of hypnosis more easily so you can get the most out of this beneficial technique.

Hypnosis is a natural state and has been used safely and success-fully by people throughout history to attain their goals and desires. It has only recently been rediscovered in our culture both as a therapeutic tool and as a way of developing our full potential. Hypnosis is invaluable in therapy for treating people suffering from the effects of traumatic events where they have repressed all or part of their experience. Under hypnosis, people can remember what happened and learn to deal with it.

Most people have experienced something they do not want to remember that adversely affects their lives. Now we can help these people quickly and effectively to unearth the reason for their distress without taking years in therapy. We do this by a process called "regres-sion" which involves making the client move back through all of the stored memories to the particular memory that is causing the problem. While this may sound difficult, it is really quite simple because of "your total intelligence," the part of your mind that knows everything about you. It knows every event that has ever occurred in your life and where every piece of information you have ever received is stored.

If, for example, I want to know why a client has a fear of cats, I would ask the client under hypnosis if the fear of cats was caused by something that happened in the past. If the response is yes, I would then ask the client to go back in time to the day or memory where he first became afraid of cats. Usually the client is immediately able to retrieve the memory. If there is more than one memory, I would ask the client to tell me about the next time something happened that made him afraid of cats and I would continue this process until I was sure I had covered all of the memories that might be the basis for his fear.

Abuse victims can easily regress to the first time they were sexually abused or physically hurt. It is only necessary to ask the person's total intelligence to go back to the first incident of abuse where the person was hurt or something sexual was done to her. The person's total intelligence has all of the adult information as well as knowledge of all of the person's memories. The adult portion of the total intelligence understands the instruction and sifts through all of the memories to find the right one. If the adult has repressed memories, she will speak under hypnosis as if she were the age when the memory took place. If the traumatic event took place at five, she will talk and act like a five-year old. This occurs because each memory is stored just as it was when the event took place.

Most memories are available to your conscious mind and can be recalled by you at any time. If something unpleasant happens and your boss reprimands you, you can recall the incident later and analyze it so that you put it in its proper perspective. Perhaps your boss was in a bad mood and you were not at fault at all. But if the memory is repressed, it is not available to your conscious mind so you cannot analyze it. It continues to act on your subconscious with the same raw, unanalyzed emotions you felt when the event occurred. You feel the way you did when you were a child. These are the events that a therapist can help you make conscious so that you can look at them objectively, as an adult. Once you understand them, the violent emotions will disappear.

At this point, it is important to give a warning. NEVER USE THE REGRESSION TECHNIQUE UNLESS YOU ARE WORKING WITH A HYPNOTHERAPIST WHO TELLS YOU IT IS SAFE FOR YOU TO WORK WITH REGRESSION ON YOUR OWN. Although you cannot damage your mind, you can uncover memories that you may not be equipped to deal with on your own. This is especially true of victims of sexual abuse because repressed emotions may be so overwhelming. I did a lot of my own regression because I was experienced in hypnosis. But when I first started, I ended up in the hospital because I uncovered too many memories at once, was unprepared to deal with them and was totally overwhelmed.

Regression must be used in a very sensitive way. After all, you are peeling scabs off wounds that your mind found sufficiently painful to cover up with amnesia. Both you and your therapist should work very carefully in this area to make sure you are ready to proceed. One way to test your readiness is to ask your total intelligence if you are ready to uncover a memory. If the answer is *no*, go on to something else and wait until the answer changes to yes. You should always use this test before you use hypnotic regression and before asking any questions about traumatic events.

After you and your therapist have used regression to recover some of the most painful memories, the two of you can decide if you are ready to use regression by yourself. I would recommend that you use it only after you are totally familiar with the process of retrieving memories and when you are fully able to cope with the painful emotions they evoke. You should practice using regression and handling the memories and emotions with your therapist before you try it at home. When you do it alone, you should have your therapist's consent and you should be especially careful to check with your total intelligence to determine whether you are ready to deal with a particular memory.

You can talk to your total intelligence by using neuromotor responses. This means that your body will provide the answers. Your body responds based on all of your stored knowledge and experience, and it cannot lie. The answers can be confusing because your total intelligence is very literal, so you should ask questions in several ways to be certain that you understand the response.

While you are hypnotized, you can place your fingers on the arms of your chair. Mentally ask your total intelligence to choose a finger for answering *yes*. Tell yourself that the finger chosen for *yes* is getting lighter and lighter and that it will rise up all by itself, without any effort on your part. You may have to repeat this a few times and wait patiently, without forcing it, until the finger floats up. Once you have established a finger for *yes* answers, ask your total intelligence to choose a different finger for answering *no* and repeat the process. Then have your total intelligence choose a finger for *I don't know* or *I don't want to say*. By using your neuromotor responses—your fingers—you can find out whether you are ready to explore your repressed memories by asking yourself—the only person who knows for certain what is best for you.

You can also use your fingers to ask questions about past memories and events without the trauma of re-experiencing them. I asked hundreds of questions about the five years of my abuse before I was able to retrieve the memories. By that time I had a general idea of what my father had done and was able to work with my therapist to adjust to that knowledge so that the specific memories were less traumatic when I recovered them.

If you are able to formulate questions that can be answered *yes* or *no*, you can find out a lot about yourself. You can discover what you really think about people and events. Your total intelligence forms its opinions on the basis of facts it picked up from *all* of your senses, not just the more limited facts your conscious mind is aware of. You may be surprised to find that some people you think you like, you really don't like at all. You can ask about your physical health and whether one doctor or therapist is better for you than another. I learned through neuromotor responses that my problems with my periods were due to my abuse. I also learned that I got colds when I was depressed or wanted to avoid something.

The only thing that does not work is to try to get your total intelligence to predict the future. I found that all answers to "should" questions—should I quit my job, should I buy a new car—are highly suspect. Your total intelligence can tell you what you *would like* to do, but not whether it is best for you or whether something will happen in the future.

Unfortunately, hypnosis and especially regression are used in therapy almost exclusively to expose traumatic experiences. But hypnosis can be also be used for extremely pleasurable and positive experiences. Some therapists do regress their clients to happy or successful experiences, and they use those experiences to show their clients that they can recreate positive experiences in the present.

Dr. Milton Erickson rediscovered the therapeutic uses of hypnosis in our century. He was an extremely creative man who used hypnosis to cure his own paralysis from polio. He discovered an amazing technique for changing and improving mental states and for solving problems, even when a person has no conscious idea how to handle the situation. You just let your subconscious solve the problem for you.

For example, I learned through hypnosis that I was transferring the anger I felt about what my father had done to me onto people I hardly knew, usually painters, contractors and repair people. For once, understanding the situation did not cure it. So I hypnotized myself again as deeply as I could and told my total intelligence that my conscious mind did not know how to heal this situation. I told my total intelligence that I wanted to stop being angry with people because of my father and asked if it could help me. When my *yes* finger floated up, I asked my total intelligence to let me know when it had finished reprogramming my mind by letting the *yes* finger float up again. Then I just waited, relaxing and mentally drifting, keeping my mind as free as possible and letting the thoughts just float by. When my finger floated up about a half hour later, the anger and defensiveness had vanished.

Sometimes it takes a minute, sometimes fifteen or twenty, but when my *yes* finger floats up, the problem is gone! Once I wanted to reprogram something which took so long that I kept asking if my total intelligence was finished, and my *no* finger kept rising. I finally asked if my total intelligence would continue to program if I got up and went to work and I received a *yes*. When I was falling asleep that night, my *yes* finger floated up and started wagging; the programming was complete. This is powerful technique that can be used in therapy or by yourself to change negative thinking.

I have found another technique that has had equally powerful results for me. One day when I was using hypnosis to relieve unbearable menstrual pain without much success, I thought that there had to have been a time in my life when I didn't feel any pain and I asked my total intelligence to take me to that time. All of a sudden my whole body felt wonderful. Not only was I free of pain, but every part of me felt lighter, bubbly, good in a way I had never felt before. I just lay there, basking in the feeling, amazed at the difference between this feeling and the way I felt even when I was in the best of health. I asked how old I was, and the answer was just under three years old, before the serious abuse began. Clearly the stress of abuse had changed the natural, good feeling I felt as a small child to the heavier, tighter, more anxious feeling I had as an adult.

I have used this technique many times since I discovered it and always with the same result. It is becoming easier and easier to reach this state and I am able to sustain it for longer periods of time. Since I started this regression, my periods seem to be improving. Research has shown that although our bodies and cells are programmed genetically, our immune systems seem to be injured by stress so that we experience disease. Since all the cells in our bodies change every seven years, I have wondered if, by letting my body reexperience the way it felt when I was three, I could reprogram my cells back to their original perfect state. I hope that others will experiment with this regression. If you do, please write to me; I promise to answer.

Hypnosis has many other valuable functions. You can use your fingers to discover whether you have blocks or impediments to your goals. You may find that things your parents did or said to you as a child are keeping you from getting what you want now. Once you know what the blocks are, you can reprogram yourself to eliminate the blocks that limit your life. You can also program yourself for success. You can use hypnosis to control pain and cure diseases caused by your mind. And you can use hypnosis to increase your powers of concentration, comprehension and memory so you can keep up with today's information-based society.

Learning self-hypnosis is easy once you have overcome your fears and misconceptions. You can begin by finding a comfortable chair in a quiet place. Loosen any tight clothing and take off your shoes. Once you have learned the technique, you can lie down, but it is better to sit up at first so you don't go to sleep. Start by closing your eyes and taking three or four deep breaths. Then tell yourself mentally that you are going into a state of complete relaxation and that you will be safe and protected. Tell yourself that you will remain awake during this experience, you will be in total control of your mind and you will be aware of your surroundings at all times. Assure yourself that you will not do anything to hurt yourself and that if you might do anything to hurt yourself, you will immediately come out of the state of hypnosis. Then tell yourself you can come out of hypnosis at any time and that you will come out whenever you count backwards from ten to one. With these commands, you have taken care of any fears you might have about harming yourself or staying hypnotized.

Tell yourself you will concentrate only on your own commands, and if you hear any noises, those noises will not disturb you but will help you go deeper and deeper into hypnosis. By programming yourself to use the noises to help you maintain the state of hypnosis, you will be able to ignore them.

If you are uncomfortable with remembering all the commands, you may want to tape record them in your own voice. If you make a recording, use a gentle tone of voice and speak slowly so that your tape won't disturb your relaxation. You might also try some of the commercial hypnosis tapes, but they should not be a substitute for your own work. The best commercial tape I have found is "Deep Self-Appreciation," a multi-evocation tape created by Carol Erickson, a therapist and the daughter of Dr. Milton Erickson, the man who rediscovered hypnosis in our century, and Thomas Condon, a therapist and professor at the University of California at Berkeley. This tape uses three voices, often talking at the same time, and I defy anyone not to be hypnotized by this technique. I play this tape often, especially if I am upset, because it always makes me feel wonderful.

You can begin the process of self-hypnosis by relaxing your mind and body using one of the two progressive relaxation exercises described in Part V, Section 6, *Quick fixes.* Tell yourself that you allow yourself to let go of all tension. With practice, you can reach this state of total relaxation quickly by programming yourself to relax totally on your own command when you say the word "Relax," "Let Go," or any other word which works for you. You will then be able to relax without going through the whole progressive relaxation process.

Once you are relaxed, there are many ways to attain a state of hypnosis. In fact, the relaxation exercise may be enough by itself to put you in an altered state. You can verify whether you are hypnotized or not by using one of these two tests. Tell yourself your eyelids are getting heavier and heavier and your eyes are becoming more and more relaxed. Tell yourself that glue has been placed across your eyelashes and that your eyes are now sealed shut. Tell yourself you cannot open your eyes, unless you say the word "Release" to yourself. Then feel your eyes being glued more tightly shut. Every time you try to open them, your eyelids become more tightly sealed. If your eyes won't open, you are hypnotized. You may come up with other images that make this test easier for you.

The other test is to rest your hands on the arms of your chair. Then choose one hand and concentrate on it. Tell yourself that this hand is very relaxed and is getting lighter and lighter. Air is being pumped into this hand and it is beginning to lift off of the chair and float on its own. Helium balloons are tied to this hand and are pulling the hand up off of the chair. Your hand is rising on its own, without any help from you. You hand should lift off of the arm of the chair without any conscious effort on your part.

If you are not yet hypnotized, there are many other easy ways reach that state. One way is to count from one to ten. Tell yourself as you say each number that you are becoming more and more relaxed and you are going deeper and deeper into hypnosis. Give yourself permission to let go and become more relaxed. For example, "One. I am becoming more and more relaxed. With each number, I become more and more relaxed and go deeper and deeper into hypnosis. I give myself permission to let go and relax even more. Two. I am becoming more and more relaxed, etc."

I have embellished on the countdown in a way that works quickly for me. I visualize an undiscovered door in the back of my closet and I mentally open the door. There is a long flight of circular stairs going down out of sight. I tell myself that I am safe and that it is safe to go down the stairs. And I notice the details of the stairs as I walk down. My stairs are usually made of stone, but they can be wood, carpeted or anything else you want them to be. I tell myself, as I walk down the spiral stairs, that I am going deeper and deeper into hypnosis. I am becoming more and more relaxed. Sometimes I count from one to ten as I walk down the stairs, but most of the time I just descend, telling myself that with each step I am going deeper and deeper into hypnosis. When I am in a deep enough state to begin my programming, I stop. Some more modern people imagine descending in elevators or escalators.

A third way to achieve an hypnotic state is to visualize writing the word "trance" down sheets of paper. Start by giving yourself permission to become even more relaxed, more at ease, knowing that you are in control of this experience. You can type these words or use your own variation. When you are ready, with your eyes remaining closed now, imagine an endless sheet of paper in front to you and a felt tipped pen which makes very heavy dark lines when you write on the light paper. And mentally taking this pen in your hand, at the left side of this paper, write your first name or whatever you call yourself, and over to the right of that on the same line, write the word "trance."

Next, back over to the left, underneath the place where you've first written your name, write your name again. And over to the right of that, just below where the word "trance" first appears, you will write the word "trance" again.

And over at the left, write your name again, and over to the right, write "trance" again. On the left, name, on the right, "trance," and continue down the page. You have plenty of paper so you won't run out, and you can continue to write your name and "trance" down the page as you do go into trance.

You will write as many times as necessary until you feel that you are going into trance. When you feel that you are in trance, you will stop writing for just a minute. And then you will start writing again but this time over at the left, under the last place where you wrote your name, you will now write the word "deeper." And just over to the right of that, just under where you wrote the word "trance," you again write the word "deeper." Now you are writing "deeper" on both sides of the page.

Over at the left, writing "deeper," and over to the right, writing "deeper" and continuing to write, "deeper" and "deeper." And as you write, tell yourself that you are going deeper and deeper into trance with each word you write, knowing that you are safe and in control. When you are deep enough into an hypnotic state to pass one of the tests, you can stop. (If you have managed to put yourself into trance reading these instructions, you will AWAKEN now.)

Although this seems like a long process, it becomes easier and shorter the more you practice. When I started, it took me from 15 minutes to a half-hour to get into a trance. Now it takes me two or three minutes.

One of the best times to hypnotize yourself is just after you wake up in the morning. Most people are already in an hypnotic state at that time, which is why it is a good time to do affirmations and visualizations. You will not have to do very much to get into an hypnotic state deep enough to program yourself at the subconscious level.

Almost anyone can hypnotize himself. If you are having trouble, it is probably because you are tense or afraid. You are not being graded on your performance. Allow yourself just to relax. You will be able to do it with practice. You may want to consult a practicing hypnotherapist who can teach you techniques that work best for you. In fact, hypnosis may work best if you learn it from a professional.

Once you have mastered the technique and are in an hypnotic state, you can do much to improve your life. You can use affirmations and visualization under hypnosis to program a new self-image for yourself at a deeper level of your subconscious. You can use prayer more effectively through hypnosis. In fact, many people are in a state of hypnosis when they pray for any substantial period of time. You can analyze yourself by asking questions about what your goals are for the future; how you can improve your relationships; what your attitude is toward sex, love and marriage. Since you are in a state of intense concentration, you will be amazed how much you learn about yourself and how informative your answers will be.

With hypnosis, you can tap into the vast wealth of knowledge that is available in the world today. There is pressure on all of us to learn more today than we ever would have had to know a century or even a decade ago. Many people feel that they just can't keep up with it all. But with hypnosis you can. First, you can program yourself with affirmations so that you remember and understand what you read. You can put these affirmations into your own words, but they can be very simple: "I remember everything I read and I understand everything I read easily and totally." Since many people freeze up for exams, you may want to add, "I recall everything I read and study quickly and easily. I am calm, relaxed and confident during examinations. Examinations are easy for me. I remember information easily and I do well on all examinations."

Second, you can use visualization to help you retain what you read. You might picture your mind as a sponge, absorbing the knowledge. You can retrieve the knowledge just by squeezing the sponge. But I prefer the image of a computer. You can visualize your mind as a computer which stores everything you read. You can recover the information just by pushing a button. And the information is always available whenever you need it again. The best thing about this image is that it is true. Once you read or hear something, it is in your mind forever.

One of the greatest benefits of hypnosis is its ability to control pain and cure disease. I learned self-hypnosis in order to control pain during an operation to find out why I had such painful and severe periods. Since I had had a bad experience with general anesthetic after a similar operation, I chose a local anesthetic for the second one. My gynecologist warned me that some areas where he would be cutting would not be anesthetized, but I insisted on a local. I was terrified since I had a low tolerance for pain. I hypnotized myself for 15 to 20 minutes once or twice a day for several weeks before the operation, telling myself that I would not feel any pain during the operation. I did not even believe it would work, but when they put the needle in my arm for the tranquilizer, I felt nothing. After a while, I asked my doctor when the operation would be over. He was astonished that I had not felt him cutting and said he was almost finished. I did not feel anything until they wheeled me out of the operating room. Then the pain hit because I had only programmed myself not to feel pain *in the operating room*. I learned to program myself more carefully after that.

The head nurse of Fairfax Hospital, where I had my operation, had an appendectomy under hypnosis with no anesthesia whatsoever. If you learn hypnosis, you might consider using hypnosis instead of a general anesthetic. Not only is the risk to your life considerably less (more people die from complications with the anesthesia than from most operations), but you heal much faster because anesthesia slows down the healing process. Doctors have also finally recognized what Christian Scientists have known for a long time: painkillers impede healing. So if you substitute hypnosis for painkillers, you will get well faster.

I used hypnosis again when I took a bad fall on the top of a ski run in Park City. My ski bindings did not release and I twisted my knee and ankle so badly that they both began to swell before the ski patrol even arrived. The pain was excruciating. Because I had obviously torn some ligaments, the patrolman put my leg in a splint, placed me in a basket and attached me to his snowmobile. It was a long ride, almost an hour to get down the mountain, because this ski run was one of the most inaccessible. After the first few bumps of the snowmobile, I was ready to scream. Then I remembered hypnosis.

My first thought was that it would never work on an injury like this, but I decided to give it a try. Since I used hypnosis almost daily, I could go into a trance very quickly. I kept repeating to myself, "I am pain free. I feel no pain. There is no pain." And the pain stopped! I could not believe it, but as long as I stayed hypnotized and repeated my affirmations, I felt nothing. The only times I felt pain were when my cautious patrolman, following instructions to keep checking to be sure I was conscious, would stop and interrupt my concentration. Since then I have been able to completely control almost all pain.

You can try pain control affirmations or you might try a visualization that worked for me. You can think white healing light into the area that hurts, and also use your affirmations. Visualizing white light works for healing as well as pain.

Many people who are studying hypnotism, including myself, believe that what we presently know is just the tip of the iceberg. It is said that we only use 10 to 15 percent of our minds. I believe that hypnotism can open up the other 85 to 90 percent for our use. If you learn it now, you will be ahead of the game. You may even discover some wonderful new use that will benefit humanity. And you will certainly improve your own life now.

> *I thank God for my handicaps, for through them,*
> *I have found myself, my work, and my God.*
> Helen Keller

13. How to nurture and reparent yourself

I HATE ALL OF YOU. ALL OF YOU LIKE DIRTY GIRLS. WHY CAN'T ANYBODY SEE ME? Why is it always more important to be dirty. I don't want to be dirty. But if I don't Be dirty then the other girls will win and I will be alone.

But I don't like it It doesn't make me feel happy It makes me Feel like crying. But you get mad if I cry. But I can't help it. It Feels scary and hurts me. why don't you care how I feel. why don't you hold me and talk soft like the girls on TV. Their daddy have whiskers that tickle and their daddy smell like smoke. But their daddy holds them and they are not scared anymore and they feel so happy. I want to feel happy and I don't want to Be scared. I want to be on your lap where it is warm and happy. Why don't you notice how hard I try to be good and try to be quiet and not make a mess. But you can only see me when I am dirty that is not what I WANT. I WANT TO BE HAPPY NOT DIRTY NOT THAT. I HATE THAT. I HATE THAT. I HATE THAT.

Please please don't make me do that anymore. Please just hold me. I can sing a song and fold my arms and be reverent. Please love me for being good, I want to be good. I feel sick about those dark things and those noises and how you push on me. That thing is red and you hold it and do things with it. And your face is all funny. And you push me with it. I feel scared when you do that. I don't know what it means. You show me what to do but I don't know about it. I cant remember. I don't like to touch it and it feels awful then you touch me with it. I don't know what it is. Its not like on TV—on TV it is light and happy and everyone has clothes on the daddy and the girl has clothes on and it is light and they are not secrets.

I HATE THAT red thing that's not on TV. THAT IS NOT what it is suppose to be, like why does it have to always be dark and never tell anybody. Moma likes me to be a good girl like at church. Moma doesn't like this. SHE would say that's not a good girl. She wouldn't take me to church so I can sing a song and fold my arms and be reverent. At church they say to do things and you will be happy. When you say to do things, I am not happy. You said you would love my sister and not me if I am not dirty and don't like that red thing and put it in my mouth but I can't breathe and you act funny and when I cry, then you will hit me but I can't breathe. IT IS SO BIG and I am too little in my mouth. And when I cry then my nose is all stuffed up and I cant breathe with that thing like that. IT IS SO HARD AND BIG AND red. I don't want this part, I don't like it. I want to be like a different girl like a happy girl.

You say "I will fuck you," you say that I like it. But I don't. That is why I cry and whimper like the puppy does, that is what that means, that I don't like it. How come you don't hear me. You only say "I want to fuck you." You push on me with that thing and it hurts. That doesn't fit there. It hurts so much right in the middle and it makes blood and everything is all wet and messy. When you go, I can't sleep cause it hurts my insides and my legs are all pushed out and my pp feels sting on it and everything is messy. I have to get my underpants on the floor and pull down my nightgown. You said it would make US happy, but it doesn't. You said I want to make my old man happy don't I? But you don't act happy, you act scary. Its not like I want it. I want to be like the girl on TV. HOW COME YOU DON'T SEE I DON'T LIKE IT. DON'T KEEP SAYING I LIKE IT. I DON'T. THAT IS NOT HAPPY.

You took my blanket because I didn't like to say "pussy" in your ear but Moma was there and she would be mad at me. Mama will hear. Moma will know and then she will not love me anymore. Moma doesn't like it when you are bad with girls and she hates those girls and screams about them. I can't say "pussy" in your ear with Moma here. So you burned my blanket in the stove. My blanket who sleeps with me and makes me happy. Didn't you know that my blanket makes me happy?"

These words portray the unmet needs of an abuse victim. They are the words of Ellen, a vivacious and articulate executive, who wrote a letter in therapy to her deceased father and truly reached the child in her. She not only was able to release the feelings she had as a child, but she expressed them as a child would. Her poignant words illustrate the isolation, pain and deprivation of needs experienced by victims of sexual abuse. Ellen allowed me to use her letter because she wants to help other abuse victims overcome their pain.

As adults, abuse victims often feel lonely, unloved and unlovable. We seem to have an insatiable need for love and approval, but no matter how many compliments we receive, how many successes we have, we feel empty inside. Deep down, many of us believe our needs will never be met, so we see ourselves as perennially unfulfilled. These feelings are not unrealistic but are based on facts that were once painfully true. We were alone when we were being abused; no one met our needs for safety, love, comfort, security, affection, caring, kindness, dependability and nurturing. The earlier our abuse began, the more deprivation we experienced. And the more deprived we were, the greater is our adult need to make up for what we lacked as children.

Adults who have been deprived of nurturing as children are like cups without a bottom. No matter how much love and approval goes in, it is never enough to fill the cup. The bottom of the cup, the foundation for an adult's sense of love and security, is established early in childhood through consistent love and nurturing bestowed on a child by her parents. But this does *not* mean that if you were deprived of nurturing as a child, it is lost to you forever. You can create your own foundation, repair the bottom of your cup. It is easy and even fun.

The process is known as "nurturing" or "reparenting yourself." You have the ability to give yourself the love and nurturing you did not receive as a child. You can become the loving parent you did not have. You can fulfill your own needs.

The most important step in nurturing yourself is learning to love the child in you. Most abuse victims cannot bear to acknowledge the pain they felt in childhood and so they cannot acknowledge themselves as children. And most victims never really were children. They were forced to cope with events and emotions far beyond their years and never had a chance to experience freedom or fun. People who have been sexually abused are generally joyless; they don't know how to let go and have fun.

I was no exception—as an adult, I was an intense, serious over-achiever. Everything I did had life-or-death repercussions. When I was in therapy, I poured over my childhood photographs for clues as to what I was like as a child, and, since my father was a camera buff, there were hundreds of them. But I could find none of a smiling, happy child, only a sad-looking pig-tailed girl with shell-shocked eyes. I was never a child. I cannot remember ever running and shouting with joy. I rarely played games, unless forced by my teachers. I was too busy just trying to survive.

To many of you, this may sound all too familiar. If you look at your own childhood photographs, you will see how young and vulnerable you were. It may be painful for you to see the hurt child that was you. Many victims deny the child in them because they cannot face the hurt they still carry inside. They believe it is safer to see themselves only as a capable adult. Then they do not have to admit how helpless and terrified they used to be—and still are inside. Victims sometimes hate them-selves as children because they were so weak. But that child is still inside you. And the sad fact is that as long as you hate a part of you, you cannot love yourself and you can never accept love or give love to others.

If you want to heal the child in you, you must get to know that child. Search your memories for information about what you were like before, during and after your abuse. How did you change? Did you lose your innocence, your joy, your affection, your spontaneity? What decisions did you make about yourself, others and your life? If you have no conscious memories, you may have to recover them under hypnosis with the help of a therapist. You can also look at childhood photographs which tell a great deal about how you felt and what your life was like. You need to recognize the pain you suffered as child and to discover the many wonderful ways you protected yourself and enabled yourself to survive.

I have enormous admiration, even awe, for me as a child. During the years that I was being raped and tortured by my father, from age four to almost eight, I got almost no sleep. My father was a writer who worked at night and I would stay awake and listen to the sound of his typewriter. If the sound stopped, I knew he was coming for me. I had to drag myself out of bed in the morning to go to nursery school or kindergarten. I was exhausted all the time. I never understood why one of the few childhood memories I had was of colored pillows at school. I learned under hypnosis it was because I was allowed to lie down on those pillows and sleep for one merciful hour at nap time—one of the few pleasant events in my life. Sometimes I hid in the grass in the empty lot next to my house and slept in the afternoon. Somehow I survived. My intelligence and my anger kept me going. I am grateful for both.

As I learned more about myself and how I coped, I came to realize that I was a very special child. I had to be exceptionally strong to stay sane and alive. How many adults could face what we did as children day after day without cracking? And as I began to understand the pain I felt and how I protected myself, I really started to love and care for myself as a child, and then began loving and caring for myself as an adult.

But starting to *love* the child in me was not enough. I knew I still had to *nurture* that child in order to feel fulfilled as an adult. There are many ways to nurture yourself. One of the most effective is to buy things for the child in you, things you wanted as a child. For example, Ellen, who wrote the letter to her father, bought herself a beautiful, soft baby blanket to replace the one her father burned. She will sleep with it for as long as her child needs it. (As the child in us is nurtured, she begins to grow up and does not need as much attention.)

Another survivor bought herself an expensive teddy bear. When she was shopping for the right toy, she followed her usual pattern and started looking in discount stores. But she suddenly realized that her child deserved something special and she did not have to limit her search to bargains. Her child deserved the best!

Many of us deny ourselves the things we *really* want. We need to stop skimping on ourselves and compounding our childhood deprivation. When we buy the child in us the best, we are saying our child is worth the best. *You* are worth it! The idea is to spoil yourself, lavish yourself with the love you lacked. Allow yourself to give your child the kind of love you would really like to have, deep down. And know that you cannot give a child too much love, especially one as hurt as you.

You can also nurture your child by learning to play and have fun. Take your child to places you always wanted to go, such as Disneyland or the zoo. Swing on the swings at a playground and see how high you can go. Teach your child to swim or ski. Do things for your child that you never had a chance to do. If you feel silly going by yourself, take your own kids or someone else's, but do what they want to do and be one of them, not the controlling parent.

I realized I was a serious kid who never took risks. Although I summoned the courage to learn to ski, I was ludicrously timid and never progressed beyond an intermediate level for *sixteen* years. When I decided to have fun and to give my child a chance to play, I forced myself to follow the children I saw on the mountain. I sailed up embankments, slipped through trees, and even flew over some jumps. (O.K., small ones, but my skis still left the ground!) It was scary but fun and I realized that I do not have to be so stiff and so careful. And I finally ski fairly well.

Many survivors of abuse have achieved startling results by talking to their inner children, saying prayers with them, and visualizing hugging and kissing them goodnight. The objective is to take care of your child in your mind the way you wish someone had taken care of you. Hold your child when she cries, soothe her and show her that she is safe now. One survivor in her fifties said she visualized hugging, kissing and comforting herself as a child at different ages every night and sometimes during the day for a couple of weeks. When it became comfortable for her to give and accept love as a child in her mind, she found that she really liked herself as an adult for the first time in her life.

Visualization and imagery have been found to be effective in a variety of circumstances. If you have difficulty getting in touch with yourself as a child, you might try a visualization exercise we sometimes use in our AMAC groups. First use one of the relaxation techniques in Section 6 of Part V, *Self-help techniques.* When you are relaxed, visualize yourself in your safe place, a place that is beautiful and where you feel comfortable. It might be at the beach, in the mountains, in a forest, or even, as one of my clients chose, Disneyland. Picture yourself walking, perhaps feel the sun warming you or a cool breeze caressing your skin. Smell the sea, the flowers, or the scent of pine trees. Hear the waves or a trickling brook or the sound of a roller coaster. Make it beautiful, make it just the way you want it to be. It is your special place and it is perfect for you. You can come to this place anytime you want.

When you have explored your special place and become familiar with it, you see a figure walking toward you, coming closer. It is a young child. As this child approaches, you see that it is you as a child. The child is happy to see you and runs up and hugs you. Talk to the child and get to know him or her. Then give the child a gift you know she needs, a special gift which will help her, one you know she wants. Your gift makes her very happy. Show the child your special place and let her enjoy it. Play with her or walk hand in hand. Realize what she did for you. How she protected you, adapted so you could survive. You can use this visualization as often as you need to learn more about yourself as a child and as long as you need to give yourself love.

You can also nurture your child by doing kind and nurturing things for yourself. Make time for yourself. Improve your mind, your health and your life. Taking the time and spending the money to go into therapy may be the most nurturing thing you can do for yourself, because you are taking control of your life and helping yourself heal. Exercising and taking care of your body is another way of nurturing yourself. By taking care of yourself, you are telling yourself you care about yourself and are worth the effort. If you find new things you enjoy doing for relaxation, you are giving yourself the message that you like yourself and think it is important for you to have pleasure. You are also telling yourself that *you* can give yourself pleasure; you are not dependent on anyone else.

No one will ever be able to take care of you the way you want. Only you can do it the way you want it done. So learn to pamper yourself and treat yourself as the special person you are. Take a bubble bath, read some poetry, listen to music, go to bed early, take a nap. A favorite of one AMAC group was to send themselves flowers. Charlie said he had sent many women flowers and sending them to himself made him feel marvelous.

If you want to reparent yourself, you have to let go of the parents who failed you. "Letting go" means that you must face the fact that your parents did not give you the love you wanted and needed and that they never will. Then you have to work through your anger and disappointment and grieve over what you lost—or never had. Accepting the reality of your parents' inability to love you is painful and frightening. This is especially true if your abuser was also the nurturing parent—the only one who provided any love or affection. It is difficult for victims to express anger towards their abusers, not only because they are family members, but because the victims would have to give up the only shreds of love they have known. One woman in our AMAC group cried for weeks about the fact that she protected her father by clinging to the "crumbs" of affection he gave her. Without those crumbs, she would have had to admit that she had been totally unloved and totally alone as a child.

The fear of being alone is the most terrifying of human fears. Victims do not want to face the paralyzing fact that they were totally alone and helpless during their abuse. But the truth is we *were* alone. And the feeling of being alone is what haunts us as adults. We will do anything, including staying with abusive partners, rather than face being alone. But until we realize that we have been alone and survived, we cannot be free. Once we realize that we have faced the most terrifying situation a human being can face and survived, we can know deep down inside that we can survive anything. We can take care of ourselves.

But we have to give up clinging to the people who hurt us. We have to really understand we can make it alone because we can now be our own parents. We can now give ourselves the love we did not get. We can give ourselves the pleasure we did not have.

Another way of reparenting ourselves is to find substitute parents. Sometimes we can find a teacher, a scout leader or parents of our friends who are willing to give us some of the love and support we need. In my early childhood, I had a piano teacher who gave me extra affection to make up for what she knew I lacked at home. When I was twenty, I was fortunate enough to meet the parents of my brother's schoolmate when we were all on our way to Paris. Ron and Rosemary took me under their wing, asked me to live with them since I was alone, and treated me like a second daughter.

Over the years, they became more and more like parents to me. We even joked about my being their child. But it became less and less a joke for me. They were there when I needed them. They gave me the unconditional love and approval I craved. Rosemary telephoned me when Ron was dying so I could see him a last time, something my mother failed to do. And I was able to cry when Ron died, although I felt only relief when my birth father died. But most of all, Rosemary and I have been able to share our joy and our grief as I never could with my mother who has always denied my feelings. Rosemary has shared some of the agony of my revelations about my sexual abuse and she believes me, unlike my birth mother who still denies everything. Ron and Rosemary have given me kindness, love and support which have speeded my healing and restored my trust in people. They taught me what love is and provided a model for a loving relationship. I am very grateful to them.

A word of warning: Because our need for parental love and affection is so great, we have tendency to unconsciously look for substitute parents in many people we meet. Often the demands we place on these people, friends, employers, lovers or even our own children are inappropriate; these people cannot make up for the deprivation and hurt we endured as children and they have no responsibility to do so. You can lose relationships if you try to put someone in a parental role who does not want to play that part. I lost friends I really cherished because I kept putting them in the position of having to take care of me.

It is important to choose your substitute parents carefully and to move slowly. Do not expect too much at first. Make sure the person you choose has the desire and the capacity to give you the support and nurturing you want. You certainly do not need to pick another parent who cannot love. And give the relationship time to grow—there is no birth bond with substitute parents. When you know the person fairly well, you might mention that you look upon the person as the parent you wish you had had and test the reaction. Some people, such as Ron and Rosemary, have a lot of love to give and are able to accept it from many sources.

But having substitute parents is not a one-way street. Ron enjoyed being a mentor to me and Rosemary appreciates the love and friendship of an adoring daughter, one who listens to her and accepts her advice. We like and respect each other, and the trust has grown. I have learned not to demand too much and to treat each encounter with my parents as a priceless gift. Such a relationship is precious beyond words and I believe you can find one if you look for it. Many people have the capacity for giving love and if you are open to them, you will find them.

A final but extremely potent way of nurturing yourself is through affirmations. (If you have not read Section 8, *Affirmations—reprogramming negative thoughts*, in Part V, please read it now.) The events you have suffered have programmed your mind to deprivation and lack. Your needs were not fulfilled as a child so you believe they will never be fulfilled. By believing in negatives, you draw to you circumstances that confirm your beliefs. For example, if you believe no one will ever love you, you will constantly test your friends and lovers, watching for any slight or betrayal. And what you look for, you will find.

The truth is your needs cannot be fulfilled by others; you are the only one who can fulfill yourself. So program yourself to have your needs fulfilled. State positively to yourself several times each day, "My needs are all fulfilled." If you are not ready for such a direct statement, you might say, "I choose to fulfill my needs" or "I can fulfill my needs."

Another helpful affirmation for allowing your needs to be fulfilled is "I accept love, support and approval from all those around me." Sometimes if we do not believe our needs will be fulfilled, we do not accept the good that comes to us. Louise Hay opens her arms in a wide embrace as she affirms: "I am open and receptive to all good." The words and gesture declare to the universe that you are ready to accept love, prosperity and abundance. These affirmations confirm that you are renouncing the deprivations of the past and claiming your right to all the good the universe offers. If you can accept the goodness you deserve, you will succeed in nurturing yourself.

If we cannot love ourselves, where will we draw our love for anyone else? People who do not love themselves can adore others, because adoration is making someone else big and ourselves small. They can desire others, because desire comes out of a sense of incompleteness, which demands to be filled. But they cannot love others, because love is an affirmation of the living, growing being in all of us. If you don't have it, you can't give it.
Mildred Newman and Bernard Berkowitz,
How to Be Your Own Best Friend

14. Energy balancing and reprogramming techniques

In my search for methods that would take away my pain and bring me peace, I stumbled upon some unusual and innovative concepts. Being a lawyer, my first reaction was always skepticism, which made me respond with intense investigation and cross-examination. Only if I personally knew and respected people who had success with the technique would I try it. And being a suspicious former victim, I always went in with the idea that I would invest $60, or whatever the cost was, one time; if the technique worked, I would use it again, and if it did not, I would find something else. It was an uncompromising test, but it allowed me to keep an open mind about new discoveries. I recognized that there were many new methods and theories being developed every day and I did not want to overlook one that might work for me.

In my search for healing, I found many unfamiliar and yet effective techniques, but none with the seemingly miraculous effects of Educational Kinesthetics (Edu-K) and the Circles of Life program. Although many of their techniques and purposes differ, I have included them together in this section because some of their methods are similar. Educational kinesiology involves educating and integrating brain functions through movement. Simple physical movements have been designed to affect certain brain functions controlling such abilities as reading and hearing. Edu-K is now being used in schools throughout the country because of its success in eliminating certain learning disabilities.

The Edu-K exercise which is of most benefit to survivors of sexual abuse is called "Dennison laterality repatterning," and involves integrating the whole brain. In recent years, scientists have discovered that the two hemispheres of the brain have different functions. The left half of the brain is logical and handles our thoughts, language, facts, analysis, rationality, and the right side of our body. The right hemisphere is emotional and controls our feelings, creativity, imagination, intuition, and the left side of our body.

If we are to function at an optimal level, the two hemispheres must be integrated; they must work together at the same time. But often they do not, usually because of some trauma in a person's life. In this case, one side of the brain will switch off and the other side will dominate in certain circumstances. Then your brain is "homolateral." When your brain works homolaterally, it does not mean that one side of your brain is dead or injured. It merely means that one side takes over most of the work.

Having only one side of your brain working in an emotional situation can have one of two results. If the emotional right side of your brain shuts down, you will react without feeling to situations, such as a death or your spouse's frustrated pleas for attention. People will find you cold and analytical, and you will wonder why you don't feel anything. If the analytical left half of your brain switches off, only your emotional side will function. But without any analysis of what is happening, your reactions will be exaggerated and out of control. If someone spills coffee on you in a restaurant, your left brain is not there to tell you that it was an accident, not deliberate, and that you can easily have your shirt cleaned. You may overreact and cause a scene because you think people are careless and out to get you.

But more important for survivors, you may overreact to events based on your past abuse. If someone cuts you off on the freeway, you may feel helpless and controlled the way you did when you were abused. If your left brain is not around to tell you that the other driver is just a jerk on the freeway who didn't mean anything, you could become furious for a long time and drive in a dangerous manner.

Your brain can be reintegrated by the Dennison repatterning exercise without your ever having to discuss, analyze or remember the events that made you homolateral. This exercise is deceptively simple and only a little awkward. You stand and lift your left leg so that your foot is off the floor and your thigh is almost parallel with the floor, while you slap your left thigh with your right hand. Then you do the same thing on the other side, lifting your right leg, up parallel with the floor, slapping your right thigh with your left hand. This is why the exercise is called "crossovers." You keep alternating hands and legs as you prance around the room. When you have mastered that part, continue with the steps, but look up to the ceiling on your left, *without turning your head* and hum a note continuously. This should be done for thirty or more steps.

The next part of the exercise is the "homolateral crawl." You raise your left hand and your left leg at the same time, like a puppet, and then repeat with your right hand and right leg. While you are stepping, you should be looking down to the right, without bending your head or shoulders, and counting thirty steps.

Now you are ready for integration. Slowly clasp your two hands together in front of you and feel the two halves of your brain working together.

You should do the entire exercise, with humming, for sixty steps, twice a day for two weeks. If you have difficulty coordinating your hands with your legs during the crossovers, you probably are homolateral and you need this exercise. Continue doing the crossovers until they are really easy for you.

To test whether you have succeeded, sit down and close you eyes. With your fingernail, lightly draw an "X" in the middle of your forehead with each side of the X going down to your eyes. You should be able to feel the X on your skin. Be sure to center the X in the middle of your forehead, just above your nose. Then with your eyes still closed, mentally picture where the X is. If the X stays in the center of your mental vision, your brain is integrated. If the X wanders to one side or the other, you are homolateral. Most people are homolateral, which is why this technique is so important.

Edu-K has a variety of other exercises and techniques which can be very helpful to survivors of abuse. You can be programmed through movement to overcome negative assumptions about life. For example, I tested very negatively about believing the world was safe and whether it was safe to be happy. I had always experienced the world as a dangerous and brutal place. Whenever I started to be happy, my mother hit me or my father raped me. In less than two hours, my Edu-K instructor had reprogrammed my mind to override my experience and to accept the idea that the world was safe and that it was safe to be happy.

The reprogramming is verified by a process called "muscle testing" which is a recently discovered way of using your own body as a lie detector. If you lie, your muscles lose some of their strength and an outstretched arm can be easily pushed down, even though you try hard to resist. If you tell the truth, or, in our example, if your mind accepts the new principle, your arm will resist the same pressure. Accepting the principle that the world is safe decreased my level of fear and improved the way I dealt with people and the world.

The Circles of Life method also focuses on reprogramming and uses muscle testing to verify its effectiveness. Circles of Life is based on the recognition of energy fields in the human body. The ancient Indians, the Chinese (acupuncture is based on these energy fields) and other cultures have known of the existence of these energy fields for hundreds of years. Western civilization has just begun to "discover" them. Psychiatrists have used electric shock treatment to cure extreme depression for decades without understanding how it worked. But now doctors and researchers are beginning to realize that a type of electrical energy flows in our bodies and our brains along with our blood. Neurologists have discovered that our brains discharge some kind of electrical energy when we think and this energy creates patterns in our brains. And a whole area of scientific study called "bioelectromagnetism" has been created to study energy fields in the human body.

Circles of Life is founded on the theory that our bodies operate on a continuous flow of energy, similar to electrical energy, which must be balanced if we are to remain physically healthy and emotionally stable. Any imbalance or blockage results in "dis-ease" or negative emotional states. Intense emotional reactions caused by trauma disrupt our energy balance. Extreme trauma, such as that caused by sexual abuse, can cause victims to repress their emotions and these emotions are stored in the body in the form of negative energy until the emotions are released. Results from Edu-K and Circles of Life seem to indicate that this negative energy can be released by balancing the energy of the body, *without* having to bring the memories and emotions to consciousness. Although in some cases repressed memories and emotions surface through these techniques, in other cases the stored emotions are eliminated without the victim ever becoming aware of their nature or what occurred to cause them.

Although Circles of Life worked wonders for me, I cannot begin to explain how it works. A person sets a goal which may center around self-esteem issues, developing forgiveness, clearing dyslexia or other challenges. Circles of Life identifies and reharmonizes discordant energy patterns related to the goal so that it may be accomplished more easily.

While it sounds complex and mystical, Circles of Life is really quite simple and the results are dramatic. I felt instantaneous changes; not just in my emotions but in the way my body moved. However bizarre the process seemed, the difference between going into the session sobbing hopelessly and coming out all smiles was enough motivation to keep me going back.

However, the Circles of Life training program has a couple of drawbacks. The major one is that it is one of those organizations that insists on swearing its trainees to secrecy. If you want to learn the process to help others, you are forced to sign a document promising not to disclose anything you learn. Most reputable programs, such as Edu-K, do not have such a requirement. Their aim is to help as many people as possible and they are not concerned if some people are healed for free, or if they are subjected to scrutiny. It is a shame that Circles of Life adheres to this policy because many therapists, including myself, refuse to enroll in courses where the information cannot be freely distributed; yet the techniques are certainly worthy of study and wider distribution.

The other possible drawback is the long-term effect of erasing and reprogramming our minds, without having an opportunity to analyze what we are editing. If I had erased all of the memories of my abuse without becoming aware of the problems, I would have deprived myself of all of the lessons my memories contained. As horrible as they were, those memories taught me so much about myself, my behavior, my family and people in general. If I had erased the memories, I would be much less sensitive, understanding and aware than I am today. If I had the choice to make again today, I would choose the pain and the enlightenment over a numbing obliteration of my past.

I should stress that Circles of Life can uncover memories as well as wipe them out, so you do have a choice. But the temptation is there to take the easy way out, without knowing what effect it would have on your future. This question becomes even more pressing because the techniques used by Circles of Life may be able to integrate multiple personalities without bringing them to consciousness. Again, it may be dangerous to wipe out a mental creation which contains so much information and so many memories. On the other hand, it might save victims with multiple personality disorder a great deal of pain. This is certainly an area that should be explored and I hope researchers will investigate it.

These techniques have only been recently rediscovered and appear to be powerful tools in helping survivors of abuse. They deserve more attention from researchers because what we have learned so far is just the tip of the iceberg. Although the concept of electrical energy fields in our bodies may seem strange to us now, electric lights also seemed very strange not so long ago. I hope that more studies will be done in this area because these techniques have the potential for revolutionizing traditional therapy.

For the present, my recommendation is that you approach these techniques with a healthy dose of skepticism. Try them once and if you find the results to be positive, continue. If not, at least you will have passed an interesting hour.

> *Indeed, what is there that does not appear marvelous when it comes to our knowledge for the first time? How many things, too, are looked upon as quite impossible until they have been actually effected?*
> Pliny the Elder, A.D. 23-79
> *Natural History*

15. Support networks

All of us need people. Survivors of abuse have an even greater than average need for help and approval, but they usually have few friends to whom they can turn for support. We often have difficulty sustaining relationships because our abuse made closeness suspect and dangerous; our childhood betrayal programs us to see betrayal everywhere, even before it occurs. And our low self-esteem often prompts us to select friends who dump on us, which makes us more wary of friendship. So many of us become fiercely independent—we don't need anyone—and we find ourselves alone. We justify our lack of relationships, saying we are too busy, we just moved, or we don't need any more friends. Whatever the excuse, the fact is we are alone.

Victims of sexual abuse have an overwhelming fear of being alone, yet they push people away, often without knowing it. Louise Hay says if you don't have what you want, you are not allowing yourself to accept it. If you are lonely, she points out that there are billions of people on this planet. So if we are lonely, it is not because there are not enough people, it's because we put walls up and will not allow the love to come in.

Survivors need to rebuild their trust and accept their human need to rely on others. They need to increase their circle of friends and establish a network of people they can call on in times of need. Joining a therapy group is an excellent way to obtain support and learn social skills at the same time. If you can afford the expense of both individual and group therapy, you should consider joining a therapy group for survivors of sexual abuse. In a therapy group you have the guidance of a trained therapist as well as the benefit of interaction with other survivors which can provide you with a different perspective about your abuse. You have an opportunity to listen to other people who are struggling with the same problem, and all of a sudden you realize, with a clarity you have never experienced before, that you are not alone. You are not the only person who has been abused, and you have not been singled out for some terrible punishment.

You may also be able to make friends with members of the group if your group permits relationships outside of meetings, and most do. And you will learn how your interactions within the group impact on your ability to make friends outside of the group. By analyzing your reactions to group members, you will be able to see how you react to people generally. If you find you have been pushing people away without knowing it, you can modify your behavior.

Another type of group offering similar benefits to survivors of abuse is a support group. Although most of these groups do not have a full-time therapist to lead them, they provide survivors the chance to interact, discuss their experiences and help each other. Support groups may be sponsored by various churches and agencies. Some of the best in Utah are arranged by Parents United. A few groups do provide therapists to lead the discussions, but informal support groups without a therapist or leader can be very effective. Now that people are talking openly about sexual abuse, support groups are mushrooming in both urban and rural areas, so you should not have difficulty finding one in your area.

Most therapists recognize the value of such groups and will do what they can to help you set one up. Unfortunately, a few therapists make it difficult for their clients to form support groups, hiding behind a misconception of their duty of confidentiality. While therapists are constrained by law to keep their clients' identities confidential, they can certainly ask whether or not clients would like to have their names released so that they could be included in a support group. If you would like to set up a support group and your therapist refuses to cooperate, ask people in your local social service agencies, your friends or your rabbi, minister or priest for their help. You will be able to find other survivors who long to talk about their experiences to someone they know really understands.

Of course, there are many other ways to increase the network of people you can count on. You can meet people with similar interests by attending lectures and concerts, enrolling in classes in your local adult education program or at a trade school or university, or joining religious groups, book discussion groups at your public library or bridge clubs.

Sports enthusiasts can find teams for bowling, volleyball, hockey, basketball, etc., or join tennis, golf or athletic clubs. If you ski, there are ski clubs; if you swim, there are neighborhood pools or the YMCA/ YWCA. There is truly something for every interest, and if you are interested, you will meet people you like. When I was living in Washington, D.C., I signed up on a whim for a Smithsonian Institution trip to see the wild horses on Chincoteague Island and met a woman who became a very special friend. It was inevitable; we were the only two people on the bus under sixty!

An important part of the healing process is to learn to relate to people. You have seen the hurtful side of people, now you need to give yourself a chance to see and accept the other side. It may take you a few tries, so be gentle with yourself. The energy it takes to establish warm, supportive relationships is worth the effort. If you use your imagination, you can find some fascinating things to do and meet people at the same time.

You can assess your own social support network by doing the following exercise:

• Write down the names of ten people with whom you relate on a regular basis. (The first ten who come to mind. They can be friends, relatives, acquaintances, repair people, business associates, etc.)

1. _____   6. _____

2. _____   7. _____

3. _____   8. _____

4. _____   9. _____

5. _____   10. _____

• Now fill in the left side of your chart with eight names from your list. Rank them from one to eight according to their importance to you. Your MOST necessary person is "Number One" in your life.

	E	G	U	T	I	W	B	J	0	+	-	R
1. _____												
2. _____												
3. _____												
4. _____												
5. _____												
6. _____												
7. _____												
8. _____												

Then rate each person as to what role they play in your life. Explanations for the letters are provided below. Each person can be rated with more than one letter.

E = Someone to whom you can go in an **E**mergency.

G = Someone with whom you can share **G**ood news.

U = Someone who really **U**nderstands you.

T = Someone you **T**rust totally and implicitly.

I = Someone you **I**dentify with.

W = Someone who brings out the **W**orst in you.

B = Someone who brings out the **B**est in you, makes you feel attractive and scintillating.

J = Someone who makes you feel **J**oy, who is fun to be with, and who is ready to share your fun.

0 = Someone who is a **0** (Zero), who does not add to or subtract from your life.

+ = Someone who is nurturing.

— = Someone who is an absolute drain on you.

R = Someone with whom you can be **R**eciprocal; you both accept each other for who you are, without judgment.

• After you fill in the boxes, complete the following sentence:

This is what I have learned about my social support system:

When you complete this assessment, you will have an idea of where you need to improve your support network. Consider making relationships a priority in your life. Spend a little extra time talking to your neighbors, your colleagues at work, people on the bus. Invite people to your home or to attend a meeting or concert with you. Write down goals for how you plan to meet people and give yourself deadlines for meeting those goals. Your efforts will pay off because you will be breaking the patterns of abuse that are causing you to be isolated. And you will find there are people you can trust and enjoy.

> *A friend is a present you can give yourself.*
> Robert Louis Stevenson

✽ ✽ ✽ ✽ ✽

These techniques for stress reduction and good physical and mental health may seem awkward, even strange, at first. You may also wonder where you will find the time to fit them into your already crowded day. But if you promise yourself to do whatever you choose for one month, you will see the benefits. By then, it will also have become a habit, like brushing your teeth. You won't even have to think about it, you will do it because it feels so good.

I have selected only a few of a world full of wonderful techniques, philosophies and theories for helping people heal and find happiness. To me all of these methods are like a giant smorgasbord; I want to sample all of them and then come back and gorge myself on the ones I like best. But what has worked for me may not work for you. There are certainly hundreds of useful books, tapes, techniques and theories of which I am unaware, but which might be exactly what you need. So, try these and any others that attract your fancy—because one or more of them will work for you.

Most of us have been taught that learning is hard and requires much effort. I worked hard reprogramming myself to accept that learning and healing are *quick, easy* and *fun*. That reprogramming made a tremendous difference in the progress of my healing and the quality of my life. If only we could all remember what Mary Poppins showed us: If we change our attitude, even taking medicine can be a joyous experience, and foul-tasting syrup can become rainbow-colored ambrosia.

Healing is in the mind and the heart.

You have suffered enough. I hope you will choose to make your healing easy and fun. The rainbow is right there before you and friends are everywhere to share it with you.

Reach for the Rainbow

Recommended Reading

Exercise

McCluggage, Denise. *The Centered Skier*. New York: Bantam Books, 1983.

Morehouse, Laurence E. and Gross, Leonard. *Total Fitness in 30 Minutes a Week*. New York: Pocket Books, 1976.

Families and raising children

Dodson, Fitzhugh. *How to Single-Parent*. New York: Harper & Rowe, 1987.

Dyer, Wayne. *What Do You Really Want for Your Children?* New York: Avon Books, 1985.

Gordon, Thomas. *PET—Parent Effectiveness Training*. New York: Peter H. Whyden, 1970. (See also the PET Book for adolescents and check into the courses for parents offered by this organization.)

Nelson, Jane. *Positive Discipline*. New York: Ballantine Books, 1987.

Radl, Shirley. *Mother's Survival Guide*. Racine, Wisconsin.: Western Publishing Company, 1984.

Satir, Virginia. *People Making*. Palo Alto, California.: Science and Behavior Books, 1972.

Silverman, Marvin, et al. *Parent Survival Training*. North Hollywood, California.: Wilshire Book Company, 1987.

Healing

Cousins, Norman. *Anatomy of an Illness*. New York: Bantam, 1981.

Levine, Stephen. *Healing into Life and Death*. New York: Anchor Press/ Doubleday, 1987.

Siegel, Bernie. *Love, Medicine and Miracles*. New York: Harper & Row, 1974.

Simonton, Carl and Stephanie Simonton. *Getting Well Again*. New York: Bantam, 1980.

Hypnosis

Adams, Paul. *The New Self-Hypnosis*. California, Wilshire Book Company, 1967.

Arnette, J. L. et al. "Use of Hypnosis and Self-hypnosis for Assisting Students with Academic Problems." *Journal of College Student Personnel*, 16 (No. 1975), 522.

Arons, Harry. *Hypnosis for Speeding Up the Learning Process*. Irvington, New Jersey: Power Publishers, Inc., 1974.

Philosophy and meaning

Bach, Richard. *Illusions*. New York: Delacourte Press, 1977.

Bach, Richard. *Jonathan Livingston Seagull*. New York: Macmillan, 1970.

Campbell, Joseph. *Myths to Live By*. New York: Bantam Books, 1988.

Frankl, Viktor. *Man's Search for Meaning*. Boston, Massachusetts: Beacon, 1963.

Kushner, Harold. *When Bad Things Happen to Good People*. New York: Schocken Books, 1981.

Levine, Stephen. *A Gradual Awakening*. New York: Doubleday, 1989.

Levine, Stephen. *Who Dies*. New York: Anchor Books/Doubleday, 1982.

Suzuki, Shunryu. *Zen Mind, Beginner's Mind*. New York: John Weatherhill, Inc., 1977.

Self therapy

Beattie, Melody. *Codependent No More*. New York: Harper & Row, Publishers, Inc., 1987.

Burns, David. *Feeling Good: The New Mood Therapy*. New York: Signet, 1981.

Buscaglia, Leo. *Living, Loving and Learning*. Holt, Rinehart & Winston, 1982.

Butler, P. *Self-assertion for Women*. San Francisco, California: Harper and Rowe, 1981.

Dyer, Wayne W. *Your Erroneous Zones*. New York: Avon Books, 1977.

Dyer, Wayne W. *The Sky's the Limit*. New York: Pocket Books, 1980.

Fadiman, James. *Be All That You Are*. Seattle, Washington: Westlake Press, 1986.

Glasser, William. *Taking Effective Control of Your Life*. Cambridge, Massachusetts: Harper & Rowe, 1984.

Hay, Louise L. *You Can Heal Your Life*. California: Hay House, 1987.

Helfner, Ray. *Childhood Comes First: A Crash Course on Childhood for Adults*. East Lansing, Michigan. Ray E. Helfner, 1978.

Hendricks, Gay and Wills, Russell. *The Centering Book, Awareness Activities for Children, Parents, and Teachers*. New Jersey: Prentice Hall, Inc., 1975.

Hendricks, Gay and Kathlyn. *Centering and the Art of Intimacy*. New York: Prentice-Hall, Inc., 1976.

Jampolsky, Gerald G. *Love Is Letting Go of Fear*. New York: Bantam, 1981.

Jampolsky, Gerald G. *Teach Only Love*. New York: Bantam Books, 1983.

Kopp, Sheldon. *Even a Stone Can Be a Teacher*. Los Angeles: Jeremy P. Tarcher, Inc., 1974.

Maltz, Maxwell. *Psycho-Cybernetics*. New York: Pocket Books, 1969.

Maltz, Maxwell. *The Magic Power of Self-Image Psychology*. New York: Pocket Books, 1970.

Murphy, Joseph. *The Power of Your Subconscious Mind*. New York: Bantam Books, 1982.

Newman, Mildred and Berkowitz, Bernard. *How to Take Charge of Your Life*. New York: Bantam Books, 1981.

Newman, Mildred and Berkowitz, Bernard, with Owen, Jean. *How to Be Your Own Best Friend*. New York: Ballantine Books, 1974.

Patent, Arnold M. *You Can Have It All*. New York: Money Mastery Publishing, 1985.

Peale, Norman Vincent. *The Positive Principle Today*. New York: Fawcett Crest, 1976.

Sexual abuse

Allen, Charlotte V. *Daddy's Girl*. New York: Berkeley Books, 1981.

Bass, Ellen, et al. *I Never Told Anyone: Writings of Women Survivors of Child Sexual Abuse*. New York: Harper & Rowe, 1983.

Burgess, Ann W., et. al. *Sexual Assault of Children and Adolescents*. Lexington, Massachusetts: Lexington Books, 1978..

Gil, Eliana. *Outgrowing the Pain*. New York: Dell, 1988.

Hunter, Mic. *Abused Boys*. Lexington, Massachusttts: Lexington Books, 1990.

Miller, Alice. *Thou Shalt Not Be Aware*. New York: Farrar.Straus.Giroux, 1985.

Russell, Diana. *Secret Trauma: Incest in the Lives of Girls and Women*. New York: Basic Books, 1986.

Sanford, Linda. *Silent Children: A Parent's Guide to the Prevention of Sexual Abuse*. New York: Doubleday, 1980.

Sgroi, Suzanne M. *Handbook of Clinical Intervention in Child Sexual Abuse*. Lexington, Massachusetts: Lexington Books, 1982.
Sgroi, Suzanne M. *Vulnerable Populations*. Lexington, Massachusetts: Lexington Books, 1988.
Tower, Cynthia C. *Secret Scars: A Guide for Survivors of Child Sexual Abuse*. New York: Viking, 1988.

Sexuality

Boston Women's Health Collective. *Our Bodies, Ourselves*. New York: Simon and Schuster, 1973.
Comfort, Alex. *The Joy of Sex*. New York: Crown Books, 1972.
Heiman, J., et al. *Becoming Orgasmic: A Sexual Growth Program for Women*. New Jersey: Prentice-Hall. 1976.
Masters, W.H., Johnson, V.E., and Lolodny, R.C. *On Sex and Loving*. Boston, Massachusetts: Little, Brown. 1986.
Raley, Patricia E. *Making Love, How to Be Your Own Sex Therapist*. New York: Avon, 1980.

Stress reduction, meditation and mindfulness

Benson, Herbert. *The Relaxation Response*. New York: Avon Books, 1976.
Benson, Herbert. *Your Maximum Mind*. New York: Times Books, 1987.
Borysenko, Joan. *Minding the Body, Mending the Mind*. Reading, Massachusetts: Addison-Wesley Publishing Company, Inc., 1987.
Dass, Ram. *Be Here Now*. New York: Brown Publishing Co., 1971.
Feng, G. and Wilkerson, H. *Tai-Chi: A Way of Centering and I Ching*. New York: Macmillan, Collier Books, 1969.
Masters, Robert and Houston, Jean. *Mind Games*. New York: Viking, 1972.
Selye, Hans. *The Stress of Life*. New York: McGraw Hill Book Co., 1976.

Visualization

Gawain, Shatki. *Creative Visualization. New York: Bantam Books*, 1985.
Gawain, Shatki. *Living in the Light*. Mill Valley, California: Whatever Publishing, 1986.

Note—An excellent mail order source for hard-to-find abuse-related books is Full Circle Books, 2205 Silver SE, Albuquerque, NM 87106. Write for an extensive, annotated catalog on abuse, addiction recovery and eating disorders.

Endnotes

[1] Daugherty, Lynn B. (1984) *Why Me? Help for victims of child sexual abuse (even if they are adults now.)* Racine, Wisconsin: Mother Courage Press, 11.

[2] Finkelhor, David. (1986) *A Sourcebook on Child Sexual Abuse.* Beverly Hills, California: Sage Publications, 22-27.

[3] Byerly, Carolyn M. (1985) *The Mother's Book, How to Survive the Incest of Your child.* Iowa: Kendall/Hunt Publishing Co., 41.

[4] Finkelhor, David. (1986) *A Sourcebook on Child Sexual Abuse.* Beverly Hills, California: Sage Publications, 19.

[5] Corey, Gerald. (1985) *Theory and Practice of Group Counseling, Second Edition.* Monterey, California: Brooks/Cole Publishing Company, 315.

[6] Beattie, Melody. (1987) *Codependent No More.* New York, New York: Harper & Row, Publishers, Inc., 31.

[7] Summit, Roland and Kryso, JoAnn. (1978) "Sexual Abuse of Children: A Clinical Spectrum." *American Journal of Orthopsychiatry.* 48(2), 237, 248.

[8] Kaufman, Irving; Peck, Alice; and Tagiuri, Consuelo. (1954) "The Family Constellation and Overt Incestuous Relations Between Father and Daughter." *American Journal of Orthopsychiatry.* 24:, 266-79.

[9] Zuelzer, Margot; and Reposa, Richard. (1983) "Mothers in Incestuous Families." *International Journal of Family Therapy.* 5(2), 98-109.

[10] Byerly, Carolyn. (1985) *The Mother's Book, How to Survive the Incest of Your Child.* Iowa: Kendall/Hunt Publishing Company, 43-44.

[11] Burgess, Ann W. et al. (1978) *Sexual Assault of Children and Adolescents,* Lexington, Massachusetts: Lexington Books, 133.

[10] Finkelhor, David. (1986) *A Sourcebook on Child Sexual Abuse.* Beverly Hills, California: Sage Publications, 126-130.

[13] Sgroi, Suzanne M. (1982) *Handbook of Clinical Intervention on Child Sexual Abuse,* Lexington, Massachusetts.: Lexington Books, 230-1.

[14] Kuleshnyk, Irka. (1984) "The Stockholm Syndrome: Toward an understanding." *Social Action and the Law.* 10:2, 37-42.

[15] Pittman, Frank. (1987) *Turning Points.* New York: Norton, 308.

[16] Goulding, M. and Goulding, R. *Changing Lives Through Redecision Therapy.* 118.

[17] Hay, Louise (1984) *You Can Heal Your Life.* California: Hay House, 14.

[18] Zastrow, Charles and Kirst-Ashman, Karen K. (1987) *Understanding Behavior and the Social Environment.* Chicago, Ill: Nelson-Hall Publishers, 134-138.

[19] Pittman, Frank. (1987) *Turning Points.* New York: Norton, 308.

[20] Successful rehabilitation in over 90% of incestuous families treated at the Child Sexual Abuse Treatment Program in San Jose. Summit, Roland and Kryso, JoAnn. (1978) "Sexual Abuse of Children: A Clinical Spectrum." *American Journal of Orthopsychiatry.* 48(2), 237, 249.

[21] DiNitto, Diana M.; and Dye, Thomas R. (1987) *Social Welfare, Politics and Public Policy.* New Jersey: Prentice-Hall, Inc., 152.

[22] Corey, Gerald. (1986) *Theory and Practice of Counseling and Psychotherapy.* Monterey, California: Brooks/Cole Publishing Company, 11-16.

[23] Miller, Alice. (1985) *Thou Shalt Not Be Aware, Society's Betrayal of the Child.* New York: Farrar. Straus. Giroux, 136. See also, Pittman, Frank. (1987) *Turning Points.* New York: Norton, 302 and references cited therein. [Some researchers have found evidence that Freud himself may have been a victim of sexual abuse. See Hunter, Mic. (1990) *Abused Boys.* Lexington, Mass.: Lexington Books, 295.

[24] *Diagnostic and Statistical Manual of Mental Disorders (Third Edition - Revised)* (1987) Washington, D.C.: American Psychiatric Association, 247-272.

[25] *Ibid* 269 - 272.

[26] Beahrs, J.D. (1983). "Co-consciousness: A Common Denominator in Hypnosis, Multiple Personality, and Normalcy." *American Journal of Clinical Hypnosis.* 26 (2), 100-113; Bliss, E. L. (1980) "Multiple Personalities: A Report of 14 Cases with Implications for Schizophrenia and Hysteria." *Archives of General Psychiatry.* 37 (12) 1388-1397; Braun, B. G. (1984) "Hypnosis Creates Multiple Personality: Myth or Reality?" *International Journal of Clinical & Experimental Hypnosis.* 32 (2) 191-197; Kluft, R. P. (1986) "Preliminary Observations on Age Regression in Multiple Personality Disorder Patients Before and After Integration." *American Journal of Clinical Hypnosis.* 28 (3) 147-156; Kluft, R. P. (1987) "An Update on Multiple Personality Disorder." *Hospital and Community Psychiatry.* 38(4) 363-373. Wilbur, C. B. (1984) Treatment of multiple personality. *Psychiatric Annals.* 14 (1) 27 - 31.

[27] Schwartz, Richard. (1987) "Our Multiple Selves." *Networker.* March-April, 25, 27.

[28] *Diagnostic and Statistical Manual of Mental Disorders (Third Edition - Revised.)* (1987) Washington, D.C.: American Psychiatric Association, 269 - 272.

[29] *Ibid*; Kluft, P.P. (1987) "First-Rank Symptoms as a Diagnostic Clue to Multiple Personality Disorder." *American Journal of Psychiatry.* 144 (3) 293-298.

[30] *Diagnostic and Statistical Manual of Mental Disorders (Third Edition - Revised)* (1987) Washington, D.C.: American Psychiatric Association, 269-277.

[31] Moody, Raymond. (1986) *Life After Life*. New York: Bantam Books; (1988) *The Light Beyond*. New York: Bantam Books; and Ring, K. (1984); *Heading Toward Omega*. New York: William Morrow.

[32] *Diagnostic and Statistical Manual of Mental Disorders (Third Edition - Revised)* (1987) Washington, D.C.: American Psychiatric Association, 271-2.

[33] Walker, Edward, et al. (1988) "Relationship of Chronic Pelvic Pain to Psychiatric Diagnosis and Childhood Sexual Abuse." *American Journal of Psychiatry*. 145:1, 75 - 80.

[34] *Coy v. Iowa*, 108 S.Ct. 2798, 101 L.Ed.2d 857 (1988).

[35] *Assault and battery*. 6 Am. Jur. 2d. Sec. 47.

[36] *Ingraham v. Wright*, 97 S. Ct. 1401, 51 L. Ed. 2d 711 (1977).

[37] *State v. England*, 220 Or. 395, 349 P.2d 668, 89 A.L.R.2d 392 (1960)

[38] *Chastain v. Chastain*, 50 Ga. App. 241, 177 S.E. 828; *Small v. Morrison*, 185 N.C. 577, 118 S.E. 12, 31 A.L.R. 1135.

[39] New York eliminated the doctrine in *Gelbman v. Gelbman*, 23 N.R. 2d 434, 439, 245 N.E.2d 192, 194 (1969); *Dunlap v. Dunlap*, 84 N.H. 352, 150 Atl. 905, 71 A.L.R. 1055; Restatement, Torts 2d, Sec. 895G; 19 A.L.R.2d 423, 427, Sec. 1.

[40] *St. Michelle v. Robinson*, 759 P.2d 467 (Wash. App. 1988).

[41] Donaldson and Gardner, (1985) "Diagnosis & Treatment of Traumatic Stress among Women after Childhood Incest," in *Trauma and Its Wake: The Study and Treatment of Post-Traumatic Stress Disorder*, 356. (C. Figley ed.).

[42] *Diagnostic and Statistical Manual of Mental Disorders (Third Edition - Revised.)* (1987) Washington, D.C.: American Psychiatric Association, 269 - 272; Bowman, Blix & Coons, (1985) "Multiple Personality in Adolescence: Relationship to Incestual Experiences," *Journal of the American Academy of Child Psychiatry*, 109.

[43] Putnam, "Dissociation as a Response to Extreme Trauma," in Kluft. R. ed. (1985) *Childhood Antecedants of Multiple Personality*, 80.

[44] *Tyson v. Tyson*, 727 P.2d 226, 229 (Wash. 1986).

[45] *Hammer v. Hammer*, 418 N.W.2d 23 (Wisc.App., 1987). (As this book went to press, the California Court of Appeal followed the *Hammer* Case in *Mary Doe v. John Doe* (Cal. Dist. Ct. of Appeal, 6th Cir. Nov. 30, 1989). Contact Attorney Shari Karney, Encino, California.)

[46] Larselere, R. E. (1986) "Moderate Spanking: Model or Deterrent of Children's Aggression in the Family?" *Journal of Family Violence*, 1(1): 27- 36; Welsh, R. S. (1985) "Spanking: A Grand Old American Tradition?" *Children Today*, 25 - 29, January-February.

[47] Beahrs, J. D. (1983) "Co-consciousness: A Common Denominator in Hypnosis, Multiple Personality, and Normalcy," *American Journal of Clinical Hypnosis.* 27 (2), 100 - 113; Bliss E. L. (1980) "Multiple Personalities: A report of 14 cases with implications for schizophrenia and hysteria,"*Archives of General Psychiatry.* 37 (12) 1388-1397; Kampman, R. (1974) "Hypnotically Induced Multiple Personality." *Psychiatria Fennica.* 201 - 209.

[48] Wilbur, C. B. (1984) "Treatment of Multiple Personality," *Psychiatric Annals.* 14 (1) 27 - 31.

[49] Corey, Gerald. (1986) *Theory and Practice of Counseling and Psychotherapy*, 3rd Ed. Monterey, California: Brooks/Cole Publishing Company, 31 - 32.

[50] Sgori, Suzanne M. (1982) *Handbook of Clinical Intervention in Child Sexual Abuse.* Lexington, Massachusetts: Lexington Books, 147-9.

[51] Benson, Herbert, M.D. (1976) *The Relaxation Response.* New York: Avon, 161.

[52] Achterberg, Jeanne. (1984) "Imagery and Medicine: Psychophysiological Speculations," *Journal of Mental Imagery.* 8 (4), 1 - 14.

Order Form

Tear out and mail this form with your check to:

Changes Publishing
P.O. Box 681539
Park City, UT 84068–1539

Please send me:

_____copies of *Reach for the Rainbow* @ $12.95 (U.S.) each
                                              $14.95 (Can.) $_____

If you live in Utah, please add $.90 per book sales tax $_____

Shipping and handling:
$2.00 for first book, $1.00 for each additional book
(Canada – $2.50 first book, $1.25 each additional book) $_____

Total Amount Enclosed $_____

Allow 2 to 4 weeks for delivery.

I understand that I may return my order for a full refund of the book price if not satisfied.

(Please Print)

Name_____

Address_____

City, State_____ZIP_____

❏ I would like information on workshops and lectures by Lynne D. Finney